From Object to Concept

Praise for *From Object to Concept: Global Consumption and the Transformation of Ming Porcelain*

"The book has an impressive historical scope, from the14th to the 21st century. Secondly, it ranges over a variety of interesting topics relevant to the history of a famous commodity—in addition to discussing the economic production, social use, and reception of Ming porcelain throughout the world, it has a novel and often amusing account on the treatment of Ming porcelain in modern popular UK and US culture. It presents an extensive coverage of recent English-language work on Chinese porcelain, and attempts to put the study of Ming, and by extension Chinese, porcelain in a wider conceptual framework, that of transcultural shifts in the use and meaning of art objects."

—**Joseph P. McDermott**, University of Cambridge

From Object to Concept

Global Consumption and the Transformation of Ming Porcelain

Stacey Pierson

HKU PRESS
香港大學出版社

This publication has been generously supported by the Sir Y. K. Pao Publication Fund for publications in Chinese art and architecture.

Hong Kong University Press
The University of Hong Kong
Pok Fu Lam Road
Hong Kong
https://hkupress.hku.hk

ISBN 978-988-8139-83-5 (*Hardback*)

British Library Cataloguing-in-Publication Data
A catalogue record for this book is available from the British Library.

Digitally printed

Contents

Acknowledgements

The idea for a study of the effects of consumption on Ming porcelain first came about during preparations for an exhibition at the former Percival David Foundation of Chinese Art in London (*The Ming Vase: Deconstructing an Icon*). The exhibition was small and there was no catalogue for it, but the interest generated by it suggested that a book-length study of the wider subject would be worth pursuing. In so doing, a number of people assisted with research, sometimes unknowingly, but thanks are due especially to Elizabeth Lin, Patricia Pierson, Peter Gunthorp, Chi Fan Tsang and members of the Oriental Ceramic Societies in London and Hong Kong. The School of Oriental and African Studies gave me a period of leave in which to pursue this research, and the Polytechnic University of Hong Kong provided a desk and access to the rich resources of Hong Kong. The work was completed while I was a visiting assistant professor at the University of Hong Kong, and I was grateful for the opportunity to return to Hong Kong. The comments on the manuscript by anonymous readers for the press were very useful; their efforts and attention are much appreciated. At Hong Kong University Press, I would like to thank Jessica Wang, Christy Leung, and especially Michael Duckworth for commissioning and guiding the production of this work.

Illustrations

Abbreviations

BM	The British Museum (*in their accession numbers*)
OCS	Oriental Ceramic Society, London
PDF	Percival David Foundation of Chinese Art
SOAS	School of Oriental and African Studies, University of London
TGKW	*Tiangong kaiwu*
TKS	Topkapi Saray (*in accession numbers for objects in the Topkapi Palace Museum, Istanbul*)
TOCS	*Transactions of the Oriental Ceramic Society*
V&A	The Victoria and Albert Museum
VOC	Verenigde Oost-Indische Compagnie (the Dutch East India Company)
WSXRJ	*Weishuixuan riji*

Notes on Romanisation

The Chinese used in this text is based on the *Hanyu pinyin* system of romanisation. Exceptions include some proper names and titles for which standard, published or commonly used alternatives exist, such as 'Ch'ing-te-chen' in older book titles or *T'ao shuo*.

Introduction

Ming ceramics are among the most widely admired ceramics in the world. From the first blue and white porcelains and celadon stonewares seen in Europe, to the technologically advanced monochromes of the early 15th century and the sophisticated polychromes of the Chenghua period (1465–87), this category of ceramics is extensive and diverse. As everyday objects and 'works of art', Ming ceramics have also been collected and consumed continuously since the Ming period (1368–1644) itself, both within China and elsewhere. In consequence, Ming porcelains and stonewares can be seen in most museum and public collections of Chinese art worldwide. They also appear regularly in the literature of 'Chinese art', in commercial sales of Chinese ceramics and other objects, and in visual representations of things Chinese.

Ming ceramics are therefore a well-established category of Chinese ceramics, and one which now has a relatively long history in both connoisseurship and scholarly studies of ceramics, both in China and elsewhere.[1] In Chinese history, certain Ming-period ceramics have been praised and singled out by collectors from the Ming period onwards and ceramic archaeology has been dominated by sites dating from the Ming period, such as the imperial kilns at Jingdezhen and the multiple sites for Longquan ware in Zhejiang province.[2] As a result, there are numerous studies of most aspects of Ming ceramics and Ming ceramics appear in the canonical historiographies of both Chinese ceramics and Chinese art in general, in Chinese and other languages. More recently, Chinese ceramics of the Ming period have begun to be used as data for studies of worldwide commodity exchanges, which position Ming ceramics, especially porcelain, as a significant factor in the development of global economic activity in what is known as the early modern world.[3] In these studies, Ming porcelain, and that of the succeeding Qing period (1644–1911), is seen to have had a significant impact on world cultures as a consequence of global consumption.

Most of the existing literature in various languages on Ming ceramics consists of surveys of individual objects, such as in museum or exhibition catalogues focusing on Ming ceramics, or selected studies of the remains of Ming pieces from archaeological sites. In conjunction with the use of Chinese porcelain as an exemplar in world history texts, the English-and European-language literature further presents a view of Ming ceramics which is object-or material-focused and is essentially outward-looking, such that we can identify a wide range of Ming characteristics in ceramics of that period and we can describe the impact of Ming ceramics on other cultures. However, as a result of this outward focus, we have very little information about the impact of consumption, in all forms and locations, on Ming ceramics themselves. This is not surprising, because the standard methodologies for ceramic studies, Chinese or otherwise, are those of art history or archaeology, and now perhaps 'world history', which all assume a fixed identity for the objects concerned. Ming ceramics are defined simply as Chinese ceramics of the Ming period, wherever and whenever they were or are encountered. While this approach is satisfactory in many ways, it does leave us with a problem when we encounter unusual phenomena. To take one particular case, how do we explain the transformation of Ming porcelain objects into the literary and colloquial concept of 'the Ming vase'? Today it is not unusual to have any object of antiquity or high market value (or even a person) described as 'precious as a Ming vase', but the origins of this concept have so far remained unexplored.

This conceptual transformation is not the only one that resulted from global consumption of Ming ceramics. Certain Ming porcelains were physically transformed into different objects or even visual imagery, sometimes to such an extent that the original forms or designs were completely obscured. The most familiar example of this can be seen in the 'mounting' of Ming ceramics, that is the application of metal supports or appendages to reshape or revalue sometimes relatively ordinary (by Chinese standards) pieces. This physical transformation, destructive in its methods, also often resulted in a new identity for the Chinese pieces—a bottle could become a ewer, for example, or a bowl become a *tazza*. Either way, whether intellectually or physically, there are well-known instances of the transformation of Ming ceramics that at present are simply fitted into general object surveys but that—with a little creative thinking—can be seen as part of a wider process of identity change which has yet to be recognized as such, not just in Chinese ceramics but in collected objects in general. This also requires us to think about objects from a different perspective, using methodologies from anthropology and sociology, for example, rather than art history and archaeology.

The notion of object identity and the possibility of change over time and place is one which emerged with studies of object biographies, such as in *The Social Life of Things*,[4] and some cultural historians have worked on the development and conceptions of 'art' as an object category, particularly with reference to what used to be called 'ethnographic' material.[5] But few have looked at the impact of such transformation on the actual object. It is a fact that identity transformations often involve manipulation, whether physical or conceptual, and 'Ming vases' are just one example. Another is the process of becoming an 'antique', which Baudrillard characterized as a mythological transformation and a form of marginalisation.[6] However, with Ming porcelain, such a transformation is but one aspect of what might better be characterized as a transculturative process where a new 'culture' is created through encounters between two others.[7]

The idea of transculturation is normally associated with human cultures, not objects, but its tenets might provide a way of understanding the impact of other cultures, and human agency, on Ming ceramics, and thereby their different identities across time and place. The 'Ming vase' is part of the history of Ming ceramics, but until now, there has been no way to characterize this. As this book will demonstrate, the concepts and identities associated with Ming ceramics evolved from the consumption and reception of actual objects and is a process which is closely associated with location, both geographical and cultural. Rather than a survey of selected individual objects, therefore, of which there are many excellent ones in print, this book looks at the meaning of Ming ceramics, particularly porcelain, in the various locations in which they were consumed and how this movement across cultures has an impact on their reception, appropriation, and most importantly, interpretation, thus transforming their identity. It is not a global history of Ming porcelain, though this topic is addressed generally, nor is it a catalogue of a particular collection. The individual porcelains discussed here are referenced as part of a wider narrative about the construction of object identities, and the role of humans within this.

As the history presented here is neither linear nor comprehensive, a broadly chronological but categorical structure has been chosen to give the narrative some direction. In chapter one, the origins and nature of Ming porcelains as ceramics of Ming China are explored, in order to establish what these objects meant in their culture of origin and some of the ways in which they were appreciated in Ming-dynasty China. The next chapter examines what happened to these ceramics when they left China during and shortly after the Ming period. Without giving a history of the export trade, which has already been presented elsewhere,[8] this chapter instead examines examples of the impact of local appropriative practices on the reception of these objects and how this changes their identity from Chinese to local material culture. In chapter three, the most radical transformation of Ming ceramics is explored, from actual object to invented concept, suggesting a chronology for the development of the literary and colloquial motif of 'the Ming vase'. This transformation is the most extreme because it involves a complete rejection of the materiality of the original object, in order to invent a new concept which reflected (and still reflects) the values and prejudices of early 20th century Anglo-American society. In spite of this transformation, the original object nonetheless still exists in parallel with its linguistic alter ego in what Becker defined as the art world,[9] part of a social system that is now, for Chinese objects at least, 'global' in its widest sense. It is this last, but perhaps not final, identity for Ming ceramics which is considered in chapter four.

Ultimately, the basic thesis of this book is that objects, in particular Ming porcelains, have more than just 'social lives'. They also have what might be called 'cultural lives' in the sense that objects can change their identities as often as humans do, and the ways in which this is effected can reveal much about the societies in which the changes take place. Objects have agency but so do humans in their treatment of objects. As this book will demonstrate, an object can be transformed physically as well as conceptually, consequently having an impact on many aspects of human cultural life. At the same time, a category of object can be treated in different ways within the same society and time period, as we will see.

The conceptual landscape for this book is grounded therefore in several different disciplines, including the author's own, art history. In order to reveal the processes of object identity transformation in the case of Ming porcelain, it was necessary to delve into literary history and theory, world history and its issues, as well as cultural anthropology and sociology. The focus nonetheless is on a type of object, whether actual or imagined, so that object studies form the foundations of the arguments presented. It is entirely possible that some key tenets of other scholarly disciplines have been mis-or re-interpreted in ways which might seem cavalier; but the intention is to suggest a new way of looking at a group of very familiar but not well-understood objects from China, and, by extension, a new, more comprehensive approach to object study.

is also very much characterized by location. In Ming China, porcelain was made at a number of different locations, but its production was centred at Jingdezhen in Jiangxi province, southeast China. By the Ming period, this location already had been producing ceramics for one thousand years and specifically porcelain wares since at least the 10th century.[3] The earliest porcelains from Jingdezhen were of a different chemical structure[4] but by the early Ming period, the body material consisted of locally-sourced kaolin (china clay) plus china stone, with a glaze based on glaze stone and glaze ash in varying proportions.[5] This combination produced a hard, strong and translucent porcelain that would set the standard for porcelain production and connoisseurship worldwide.

Jingdezhen was chosen (and was successful) as a production site because it was well-located for raw materials, fuel and transportation. It became, in fact, the 'porcelain city', which it is still designated today. The study of Jingdezhen, its history, economy, and society has proved to be of interest in multiple fields of scholarship,[6] not just art history, because a significant amount of relevant data survives from the Ming period and later which can tell us much about this area's economic and social development.[7] The study of Jingdezhen also illuminates important innovations in China's technology. For example, it was here that certain new kiln designs were pioneered and implemented, mineral technologies developed, and mechanized production methods introduced into a large-scale workshop or factory system that pre-dated similar such developments in Europe.[8] The volume of production at Jingdezhen in the Ming period is notable, especially at certain periods in the 16th century, surpassing all other contemporary ceramic production sites in China. For example, in 1547 (Jiajing 嘉靖26年), over 120,000 porcelains were ordered for the court.[9]

Because Jingdezhen is so well documented and excavated, the traditional historiography of Ming porcelain focuses on what was produced at Jingdezhen rather than other locations; this is reinforced by the high proportion of Jingdezhen porcelain in the export trade and overseas markets. Nonetheless, much of the Chinese porcelain from the Ming period which survives today, within China or elsewhere, was indeed made at Jingdezhen and this apparent dominance is based on evidence from surviving pieces as well as from archaeology. The other production sites for porcelain in the Ming period include, for example, a number of locations in Fujian province, which produced Dehua or 'blanc de chine' ware and 'Swatow' or Zhangzhou ware at Pinghe and other sites.[10] However, these are rarely classified as 'Ming porcelain' in a collective sense because Jingdezhen porcelain occupies such a central position.

Domestic Markets, Distribution and Classification

The position of ceramics in Ming China is also defined by their role in the Ming economy and commerce. Thus it is important to remember that one reason southern porcelain became such a successful product in Ming China and beyond is the geographical location of Jingdezhen and its proximity to excellent raw materials and transport links. It was also situated in a region which was characterized by active merchants and a highly developed trade network. As a result, Jingdezhen has been described as 'one of the first great industrial centres in China, and probably one of the earliest in the world', hence its popularity as a model for

1

Porcelain in Ming China (14th–17th centuries)

Introduction

In Ming China, porcelain was an important domestic product that was consumed at all levels of society. It was also exported and given as foreign tribute, collected and written about by Chinese consumers; its manufacture created and supported a vast industry employing thousands. Large quantities of Ming-period porcelain survive today, and its production sites have been extensively excavated. Much therefore is known about the mechanics of Ming porcelain but rarely is it considered as a manufactured product that can illuminate aspects of Ming daily life and economics. Instead, Ming porcelain objects are traditionally studied as works of art and thus subjected to the hierarchies and methodologies associated with the history of art.[1] Certainly, it was long assumed that this was a primary way in which Ming porcelains were appreciated in Ming China, but that raises several other problems, not least the necessity to define the term 'art' in a Ming Chinese context, and the position of ceramics within this. Such definition has been undertaken elsewhere,[2] and it is in fact but a minor aspect of the consumption of porcelain in Ming China.

With a view to situating porcelain in the wider context of Ming culture, here we will focus, instead, on porcelain in general, rather than exclusively on individual porcelain objects, an approach to history-making which is inherently problematic. Where individual porcelains are significant for our discussion, they will of course be given due consideration. What follows is a study of the major themes associated with porcelain in the culture of Ming China. This provides a starting point and background for the primary focus of this book: how and why Ming porcelain was transformed outside of China.

Porcelain Manufacture and Technology in Ming China

Location: Jingdezhen and Its Porcelain

As a ceramic, the fundamental factors concerning and underpinning Ming porcelain are its materials, production and manufacture. Generally speaking, ceramic objects are the product of the transformation of one material, clay, into another, ceramic. Technology is a key factor in the visual appearance of porcelain objects and, therefore, their appreciation and analysis. It studies of global exchange and economics.[11] Ming Jingdezhen became an industrial centre when both the quantity and quality of production increased dramatically.[12] While many have ascribed this to practical factors such as raw materials, labour supply, management, etc., Michael Dillon has demonstrated that the local transportation system and access to a nationwide marketing network, especially Jingdezhen's position within the well-studied and successful Huizhou merchant community, were equally if not more important.[13] Crucially, Jingdezhen was located on the river Chang which connected it to main arteries of river transport.[14] Through this, Jingdezhen ceramics were transported all over China and the world, as we will see in the next chapter.

It is significant that Jingdezhen had been a market town (*zhen* 镇) before becoming an industrial centre; it had also been a distribution centre for ceramics produced in other local regions. Even before the Ming period, it was a location for ceramic production as well as commerce.[15] The marketing network thus established revolved around the guilds, and these in turn were managed by brokers overseeing warehousemen and wholesalers.[16] Much of this activity was private and separate from the section of Jingdezhen that was given over to state-controlled production, that of the official or 'imperial' kilns.

The state could and did impose taxes on Jingdezhen production, products and producers which is why much helpful data survives in the form of local gazetteers or *difangzhi* 地方志 compiled by local magistrates.[17] One of the most detailed with respect to Jingdezhen is the *Jiangxi sheng dazhi* 江西省大志.[18] In another example, written just after the end of the Ming period, the commerce of Jingdezhen was described in the 1682 gazetteer *Fuliang xianzhi* 浮梁县志 as follows:

> … There is one town, Jingde, a large urban area in the south of the county [Fuliang county].
>
> As for its line of business, this is where the potters and the ceramics traders are … Boats and carts crowd together here, merchants and traders rush about, people from the five directions mingle, all spreading out their wares, so numerous it is truly magnificent![19]

A gazetteer for Hejian states: 'The salt merchants come from Cangzhou and Tianjin, the wood merchants from Zhending. Those who sell porcelain and lacquerware come from Raozhou and Huizhou', [20] thus confirming the Huizhou connection and demonstrating how, for the Ming government at least, porcelain was commodified. There is even textual evidence from the merchants themselves, in the form of merchants' manuals, as Anne Gerritsen has pointed out.[21] In one of these the route from Huizhou to Jingdezhen is clearly described.[22]

Thus as part of the successful Huizhou network and as a sprawling market town, Jingdezhen exploited the locally available raw materials to make a product that could be widely and easily distributed and, crucially, was desirable both at home and abroad. Consumers of this porcelain included members of the court and the scholarly classes. It is through the writings of the latter that we find information (albeit limited) about how much some porcelains and ceramics cost once they got to market. As Clunas has noted, relatively speaking, porcelain was cheap for wealthy people in the Ming period. It was also for the most part used in quantity rather than as individual items for upper class daily life activities. In the 1562 inventory of a Ming official whose belongings were confiscated after he was found to be corrupt, porcelains are listed as large groups of items such as incense burners, bowls, flower pots, etc.[23] These represent huge amounts of tablewares which were probably therefore used for entertaining and events such as feasts. What is very interesting, but to this author's knowledge not mentioned elsewhere, is that, according to a Ming text cited by Clunas, ceramics for such uses were available for rental much as they are today in the West.[24]

While this indicates that much Jingdezhen porcelain was unremarkable, even within the Ming period certain taxonomical conventions existed (and are still used) which are related to the standards established for writing about Chinese objects, both in Chinese and other languages. One of the most prominent of these conventions is the use of imperial reign periods to periodise the ceramics.[25] Thus the porcelain traditionally is named after, or classified by, the reign period in which it was made, such as 'Ming dynasty, Chenghua period (1465–87)' 明成化. [Fig.1.1] Official porcelain was made at Jingdezhen from the very first Ming reign period, that of the Hongwu emperor 洪武 (1368–98), during which time commissions were sent from the court on a regular basis to kilns and workshops set aside for what is traditionally called 'imperial production'.[26] As a result, most surviving Ming porcelain objects today are classified in Chinese using a binary system such as 'imperial' 官 (*guan*)/'non-imperial' 民窑 (*minyao*; 'folk ware' or 'commercial'), 'domestic' 国内 (*guonei*)/'export' 国外 (*guowai*), demonstrating that production is defined by consumer type in the literature. This was not necessarily the case during the Ming, however, when the broad classification 'imperial' was used differently.[27] Instead, specific reign periods were mentioned in the cultural literature, such as 'Xuande' 宣德 (1426–35) or 'Yongle' 永乐 (1403–24), with reference to some ceramics and other objects.[28]

Certainly, those porcelains made at what today are often misleadingly called 'the imperial kilns' 御器厂 (*yuqichang*) were, in the early 15th century, given a trademark which designated (in theory at least) separate production and raw materials. This trademark, or 'reign mark', also appears on other official products of the period, including metalwork and lacquer ware.[29] But whether it was used exclusively at only those designated kilns at Jingdezhen is not known, especially because records attest that in some periods demand from the court was such that 'imperial' production had to be contracted out to non-official kilns which may have been able to apply the reign mark.[30] In any case, we can only guess at the purpose of the reign mark. Instead of being an indicator of quality and exclusiveness, as it is interpreted today, could it have been a way of identifying commissioned pieces? Similar inscriptions on earlier ceramics suggest that this might be the case. For example, the inscription on some 10th-century Ding wares reads *guan* 官 ('official') or *xin guan* 新官 ('new official'); we might point also to the functional inscriptions on the ceramic figures in what is known as the 'terracotta army'.[31]

The reign mark also may have been a way of designating or separating those porcelains that were made using separate raw materials, as there are references in Ming and later texts to the ring-fencing of certain raw materials for exclusive use at 'imperial' kilns, the clays being called *guan tu* 官土 or 'official clay' in Ming texts.[32] A precedent for this can been seen in the production of Ru ware during the Northern Song period (960–1127) when imperial orders were supplied from pre-existing kilns and these orders specified the use of particular raw materials.[33] For the most part the raw materials for Ming porcelain made at Jingdezhen were sourced locally, but at times they were brought in from further afield as good-quality supplies diminished.[34] This occurred at various times during the Ming period, most notably during the reign of the Jiajing emperor (1522–66) when extravagant court orders were difficult to fill without contracting out production and searching more widely for the best raw materials. This system of contracting out production was known as *guanda minshao* 官搭民烧 ('official partnership with private kilns') and was introduced in the 16th century.[35]

Another interpretation of reign marks is that they designated time:

> The reign titles of emperors, and the written characters of the Chinese language that embody them, may well be the most widely understood pieces of Ming Chinese outside the Chinese-speaking world, through their presence on the base of the ceramic vessels that are one of the period's most enduring and widely dispersed physical legacies.[36]

Such marks thus situate the object within a specific time period which in fact would also be useful for separating these objects from more general productions of the same factory or workshop, which usually are not dated or inscribed. Unlike signatures on individually-produced works of art, however, reign marks do not singularise a piece, even though today the implication is that a ceramic with a reign mark was 'used by the emperor'. There is no avoiding the fact that even marked porcelains from Jingdezhen were essentially mass-produced, using a range of related materials and manufacturing methods which had the opposite effect of standardizing the objects.

Workshops, Makers and Regulation

This standardization began with the raw materials, which, for the imperial kilns at least, were controlled. For Jingdezhen porcelain these were kaolin, a white-firing clay, and porcelain stone, a low-clay acidic rock which was also used as a glaze material. To these were added mineral pigments for decoration, including techniques discussed in the next section such as underglaze painting (using cobalt and copper) and overglaze enamels (with iron, copper and manganese). Similar pigments were used for producing monochrome or single-colour glazes. During the Ming period, monochrome-glazed porcelains were a popular style and were also considered necessary for several types of court commissions, including ceramics in dedicated colours for imperial ceremonial altars.[37] The colours for certain porcelain products were thus highly regulated, in keeping with imperial practice at the time.[38] This regulation of the appearance and production of imperial luxury products and commodities extended in ceramic terms to decoration, the types of motifs and the colours used to paint them. For example, there is a uniformity of designs and colours on products found in imperial tombs and other locations which suggests that design patterns were used, and it is likely that these would have been provided by a drawings office administered by the court.[39] Evidence of how this itself was regulated can be found in the *Da Ming huidian* 大明会典 (Collected Statutes of the Ming Dynasty), chapter 194, which quotes an order for porcelains sent to Jingdezhen in 1433 from the Bureau for Imperial Use requesting the manufacture of 433,500 pieces of porcelain 'in accordance with patterns to be brought there by an official of the Board of Works (*Gong bu* 工部)'.[40] It is through these regulations and their surviving records that imperial commissions can be identified, and they are one of the reasons why much is known about the design of 'imperial' Ming porcelain.[41]

Along with regulation, production methods were also highly systematized as these ceramic products were made in factory or workshop settings, some larger than others, but nonetheless, not, as is often (and wishfully) assumed, as individual products of independent potters. Apart from the use of the potter's wheel (human-powered) the factories were not mechanized in the same way as European industrial revolution-era factories were. But the production process consisted of multiple, consecutive stages manned by different workers who performed the same actions all day long—a form of assembly line. That is why we can say that the products were standardised and mass-produced. A partly idealized series of images of this process and production method was created in the 19th century [Fig. 1.2].[42] However, it was also described in detail (but with later illustrations) in the 1637 text *Tiangong kaiwu* 天工开物 or 'The Exploitation of the Works of Nature',[43] which is arranged as a manual or encyclopaedia of various technologies. For example, in Part II there is a chapter on 'Ceramics' which describes, minutely but not necessarily accurately, the manufacturing processes for tiles, bricks, water jars and white porcelain.[44]

The nature of factory production is crucial for understanding the status and economics of porcelain (and other ceramics) in Ming China. But in Western connoisseurship today, the description of Ming porcelain as factory ware is deemed to be a pejorative interpretation of an exceptionalised type of object, one that is instead a 'work of art'.[45] This relates to the disdain accorded to 'factory-made' ceramics in early 20th-century Britain by critics and studio potters such as Bernard Leach (1887–1979), who were themselves informed by the ideals of the Arts and Crafts Movement of the 19th century.[46] The present-day attitude towards mass-produced ceramics thus presupposes that factory-made products were deemed inferior in Ming China as well, but there is, as yet, no evidence of this. In fact, as we will see in the next chapter, factory-made objects were often presented as evidence of China's achievements to foreign rulers, with reign-marked pieces given as imperial gifts.[47] This is partly because the production process was extensive but only partly mechanized and much of the power was provided by humans, apart from the firing in the kilns. Thus many, many human workers were required to support this industry, as well as vast quantities of raw materials, a clear indication of productivity. For example, during the Jiajing reign period, more than 10,000 people in Jingdezhen were involved in ceramic production.[48]

Rather unexpectedly, however, there are references in surviving Ming and Qing texts to named potters of the Ming period, not associated with the imperial factory, such as 'Hao nineteen' 昊十九 and Zhou Danquan 周丹泉.[49] The first of these potters is mentioned quite specifically in the diary of Li Rihua 李日华 (1565–1635) whose *Weishui xuan riji* 味水轩日记 (Diary from the Water Tasting Studio) was compiled in the early 17th century. The diary entries for the years 1609 to 1616 give a glimpse of the lifestyle of a member of the educated civil service elite in the later prosperous years of the Ming dynasty.[50] Fortunately for us, Li was also an artist and collector, so his diary contains much useful information about contemporary collecting activities and practices. Porcelain was part of his collection, and he discusses deals made and conversations held with a potter from Jingdezhen referred to as 'Hao nineteen' (昊十九), although we should be careful with this designation, as it is not clear what his actual role in the creation process was. It is unlikely that Hao nineteen was one of the lowly staffers who prepared the clay or trimmed the pieces after throwing.

In April 1610 Li noted: 'Nineteen is a skilled ceramicist. Everything he makes in the style of the Yongle, Xuande and Chenghua kilns is near-true. As a person he is elegant, enjoys chanting poetry, and likes painting.'[51] In the same entry, Li then states that he met Hao in the spring of 1598 while buying imperial wares [御用各色窑器] from several kilns at Jingdezhen (an interesting admission in itself). 'Even then his hair was white. I gave him an order to make shallow bowls in a flowing mist style [流霞盏], glazed in a secret colour that combines cinnabar and lead, and paid him thirty taels in cash. Then I had to leave and he promptly forgot all about the bowls with the flowing mist.' He goes on to say that he had received a letter from Hao: 'Today the letter arrived telling me that Nineteen completed fifty items, then gave them to Shen Biehe [沈别贺] to bring to me, but they have disappeared.'[52] According to Timothy Brook, 'Shen was a notorious hustler from Hangzhou who kept tax accounts for one of the princely establishments'.[53] As Li notes, 'None of the gentry will have anything to do with him. No surprise that my bowls have flown.'[54] Clearly, at least for some later Ming consumers of porcelains, contemporary styles were less desirable than those of the earlier Ming and it was relatively straightforward to order copies of earlier wares, presumably with reign marks. This might help to explain, or at least provide a different explanation for, the numerous later Ming porcelains with reign marks of earlier periods, such as Xuande or Chenghua, rather than assuming an archaizing trend in design.

Apart from this diary, there is further physical evidence of the existence of Hao who, like most 'potters' at Jingdezhen, came from a family involved in that industry. His brother, Hao the Tenth, also a potter, left behind an intriguing piece of Ming porcelain which hitherto has not been noted in any English-language texts, probably because it is not a vessel. In the Jiangxi Museum, the province where Jingdezhen is located, is a round blue and white porcelain epitaph tablet dedicated to Wu Bangzhen 吴邦振 (aka Hao the Tenth 昊十) which, in addition to featuring a long inscription detailing his family tree and the *feng shui* of the burial, is also (as is necessary with such objects) dated to the twenty-fourth year of Wanli 万历 (1596).[55] The existence of such an epitaph tells us that the Wu family was, or professed to be, of some importance in Jingdezhen, but this should not be read as the naming of an 'artist' in the sense of the European notion of the authored 'masterpiece'. With a few exceptions, ceramics at Jingdezhen were not 'signed' in the Ming period, unlike some sculptural ceramics from workshops in Fujian and Jiangsu. This includes imperial or official Jingdezhen ceramics.

Official ceramic production at Jingdezhen was also discussed in another text which has received very little attention in ceramic scholarship but includes an interesting anecdotal description of production at Jingdezhen during the Hongzhi 弘治 period (1487–1504). The text is an essay called *Guan tao shuo* 观陶说 (Talks on Looking at Ceramics) by Shao Bao 邵宝 (1460–1527), who was Minister of the Nanjing Board of Rites (a very prominent position) and stationed in Nanchang, Jiangxi province during the late 15th century.[56] The essay is informal in nature, like the main text in which it appears. Here he recorded his observations of production at the official kiln workshops in Jingdezhen during his tenure, listing and describing some of the processes involved in production. For example, he says: 'To make vessels from clay is difficult! The clay after quarrying in the mountain is just stone. [It is then] pounded to become powder, washed with water, levigated through channels, thickened [by soaking up the excess water] with bricks, and mixed well into wet clay. Only then can one knead and shape it.'[57]

At the end of the description of manufacture, Shao compares this process to that of 'a gentleman pursuing moral cultivation in order to become something useful':

> [His] qualities are equivalent to clay; [his] diligent study is equivalent to the pounding; [his] cautious attitude is the washing; [his] frugality is the levigation; [his] following righteousness is the drying; [his] practice of earnestness is the kneading; [his] observing rituals is the shaping; [his] investigating the essence is the trimming; taking of friends as teachers is the grinding; [his] writings of poetry are glazing; manifesting proper deportment is the decorating; [his] self-testing and verifying is the removing of the flaws. [This process takes a gentleman] 10 years for the faster ones, [or] 30 to 40 years for the slower ones. Even then [he] might not [have the chance] to look up at the emperor's gate and enter his service. [He] might even end his life in the rustic mountains. So, how do [you] feel about ceramics? I, Bao, have just compared ceramics with men, and only then found that [becoming useful] is harder [for men].[58]

As has been noted by its translator, this text is possibly unique for the analogy it makes between Jingdezhen ceramics and the moral self-cultivation of a Confucian gentleman.[59] Along with the comments from Li's diary, this suggests that the common assumption held by connoisseurs today of a general negative opinion of Jingdezhen ceramics among members of the Ming scholarly class (in contrast to 'elegant' Song stonewares) was perhaps not universal; Jingdezhen could be viewed as a location for morally improving craft production, and its objects, particularly the finer court products and copies thereof, could be appropriate for collecting.

While not noted in the literature, except with reference to two potters, there were also in the Ming and Qing periods numerous private kilns and potteries operating in Jingdezhen, and this may be where the Wu family name attained its prominence.[60] Nonetheless, under the Ming administrative system, private artisans were required for a period to also dedicate some of their time to working in the imperial factory to fulfil corvée labour requirements.[61] The imperial factory was of course extensive; according to 19th century texts, there were fifty-six kilns operating in 1430 and twenty-three specialized workshops. In the 16th century, there were 300 to 500 craftsmen (including potters) employed in this manufacturing complex, all with corvée obligations.[62] The private sector consisted of family enterprises, like that presumably of Wu Bangzhen.[63]

The other 'potter' associated with Jingdezhen whose name comes down to us from the Ming is most often noted for his ability to make copies of earlier wares, particularly Song ceramics such as Ding ware. Zhou Danquan (fl. late 16th–early 17th centuries) is mentioned in the *Jingdezhen taolu* 景德镇陶录 (Records of Jingdezhen Ceramics), which was first published in 1815 and translated into French and English in the mid-19th and 20th centuries respectively.[64] This text will be quoted at length because, although written in the Qing period, it may reveal much about Ming attitudes towards both ceramics and the art market and illuminate aspects of contemporary Ming culture.

> At the end of the Ming period there were Chen Zhongmei and Zhou Danquan; both were skilled in copying antique ware vessels. [Since the wares] were taken to distant places [for sale], the people of [Jingde] zhen rarely acquired them. Zhou's ware is well-known.[65]

> During the Long[qing] and Wan[li] eras, there was a man named Danquan; originally registered in Wu [Suzhou], he came to Changnan [Jingdezhen]. In making vessels, his was a famous hand of the times and he was especially good at copying antique vessels. Every time a famous vessel-type was produced, everyone wrangled to buy them. Zhou, however, would reserve the best pieces for his own pleasure; the others he took to Su[zhou], Song[jiang], Zhang[zhou] and Chen[jiang?] to sell to collectors. Even experts were fooled. His copies of Ding-ware tripods, and Ding-ware vessels, of 'King Wen caldron' incense burners and libation jars ornamented with animal faces and halberd ears, all were so close to the originals as to be without parallel. People spent a thousand gold-pieces [to buy his wares] in the competitive market. Even today this is still talked about.[66]

Unlike (so far as we know) Hao Nineteen or Ten, Zhou Danquan specialized in making fakes and was recorded as such for posterity. The culture of fakes and collectors will be discussed later in this chapter, but it is clear from the mentions of both these 'potters' that production of porcelain in the Ming was much more complex than is commonly assumed or reflected in the official literature. Neither Hao nor Zhou would likely be considered 'artist-craftsmen' in the modern sense, except perhaps in their obvious production skills. Apart from one interesting fact: in the National Palace Museum in Taiwan is a yellow-glazed 'archaistic' porcelain *ding* which is signed 'Made by Zhou Danquan' 周丹泉制.[67] [Fig. 1.3] This form of signature is unusual in Ming ceramics, as we have seen, because very few 'signed' Ming-period ceramics survive. Most of those with what are assumed to be 'names' actually have imperial reign marks, which are of course anonymous in their identification. Other Ming signed ceramics tend to come from the Dehua kilns in Fujian mentioned earlier, where in the late Ming certain sculptors of figurines signed their work (e.g. He Chaozong 何朝宗, fl. 1522–1612), or the Yixing kilns in Jiangsu province, which were famous for their teapots, many of which were sculptural. It is this quality which perhaps lends itself to the stated authorship of these ceramics because sculpture is a singular skill much admired in other materials (e.g. rhino horn, ivory or silver); it contrasts with the dozens of processes often involved in making a standardized ceramic vessel.

Zhou Danquan appears to have signed his work for a different reason—commercial desirability or 'branding', if you will. There must therefore have been a market for his particular wares, as is attested by the textual references noted above, although this phenomenon is not usually noted in traditional historical surveys of 'Ming ceramics'.[68] In Taiwan, the signed piece by (presumably) Zhou Danquan is singled out as an important piece in the collection of Ming porcelains, but, as we will see in chapter four, that does not mean it was or is admired in China as a piece by a master faker. Its prominent position in the National Palace Museum collection is also somewhat ironic because this collection was founded with a large supply of objects from the former imperial palace in Beijing. Presumably, then, most of the pieces on display were formerly in the imperial collection. The Zhou piece is displayed with other later Ming porcelains, including a number with reign marks, thus confirming its relative value today. This type of display of singular 'masterpieces' of Ming ceramics reinforces the modern assumption that ceramics (especially those designated 'imperial') were highly valued in Ming China, because such ceramics are valued today. However, it is clear that only some ceramics were so valued, when they could become individualized objects through transformation into collectible antiques, desirable fakes, or containers for gifts—even then they were perhaps less valuable than the gift itself.[69] For the most part, ceramics in Ming China were functional objects made from a readily available, not inherently valuable, material.

Visual Appearance and Reception: Techniques, Decoration and Forms

One might therefore consider the value of ceramics in the Ming period from a different perspective, that of aesthetics and associated techniques, especially form and decoration. The most visible manifestation of the highly developed technology applied at Jingdezhen, and the visual characteristic that made its porcelain so appealing, was its hard white surface and the colours and painting which could be and were applied to it. One of the most common decorative techniques used in the Ming period was that of underglaze cobalt blue painting. [Fig. 1.4] This technique was not technically difficult, but it produced a strong visual result which had worldwide appeal. 'Blue and white', as such wares are popularly known, was not a style created in the Ming period (we would have to look back to the Tang dynasty (618–907) to trace its origins),[70] but it is Ming 'blue and white' which was encountered in the greatest numbers around the world. It is this material which further stimulated the taste for Chinese porcelain (and for China itself, as some have suggested)[71] globally.

As it happens, underglaze blue painting is an ideal decorative technique for a mass-produced product which was transported long distances domestically and worldwide. The technique consists of painting pigment directly on to the clay body before firing. It is therefore slightly absorbed by the clay and later protected by a fired glaze layer. As a result, the decoration is essentially permanent and extremely durable—like the porcelain material itself. However, 'blue and white' was not necessarily the only type of porcelain common in Ming China, nor was it the most popular with consumers in China. Based on the large proportion of polychrome wares recovered in excavations of the Ming levels at Jingdezhen,[72] a decorative technique that appears to have appealed to the Ming Chinese consumer was that of overglaze enamel decoration. This technique is more colourful than underglaze blue painting; it involved the use of up to five colours during the Ming period. It was also a more complicated technique because it was a two-step process involving painting underglaze blue first, either as outlines in the *doucai* 斗彩 technique [Fig. 1.5] or as highlights in the *wucai* 五彩 technique [Fig. 1.6], and then the colours in a separate, additional application on top of the glaze. This necessitated two firings because the first firing was at a high temperature for the initial glaze and the second firing was at a much lower temperature for the overglaze enamels. Both *doucai* and *wucai* decoration are mentioned in Ming texts, especially the highly prized *doucai* wares of the Chenghua reign period; Chenghua *doucai* wares are also highly valued in today's market for Chinese porcelain.[73] Overglaze enamel decoration is significantly less durable than underglaze blue because much of it lies on the surface of the glazed porcelain body. It was not, therefore, an ideal porcelain type for export in the Ming period, although some examples found their way as far as Europe (see chapter two).

As noted previously with reference to design regulations in court porcelain, another type of porcelain popular in Ming China was one covered with monochrome coloured glazes. [Fig. 1.7] Monochrome colours were popular in a wide range of Ming ceramics (including architectural) but, again, in vessels the colours were sometimes prescribed by their usage. For example, the primary monochrome glaze colours used on porcelains for official ceremonies in the Ming period were red (copper), yellow (iron), white (colourless) and dark blue (cobalt).[74] Other monochrome colours, not evidently associated with any particular rituals or religion, were also used, such as turquoise, brown, iron red and copper green. The monochrome glazes were made using mineral pigments, including the cobalt that was also used for underglaze painting, in a variety of base glazes, both high firing and lower firing. For example, cobalt blue monochromes were made with a standard high firing porcelain glaze, whereas iron red (a more orange colour than copper red) and copper green monochromes were made using lower firing lead-fluxed base glazes.[75] Interestingly, these latter two colours appear on a Ming porcelain type that was exported in the 16th century. It was and is popular in Japan, hence its common classificatory name of '*kinrande*' 金襴手 or 'gold brocade' ware. These wares are normally simple porcelains decorated in blue and white inside and monochrome glazes outside, that are in turn embellished with gold-leaf patterns (see Fig. 2.7 in the next chapter). Several examples of these have been found in European and American collections with further embellishments of silver gilt mounts of the 16th to 19th centuries which transform the Ming porcelains into recognizably European forms, such as the *tazza*, as will be discussed in the next chapter.

Like so many other techniques used in the creation of Ming porcelain, both overglaze enamels and monochrome glaze colours had been used and developed before the Ming period. With the former, the earliest examples demonstrating this technique were not porcelain at all but rather stonewares made at what are today known collectively as the Cizhou kilns. These kilns were spread widely throughout North China, but the main excavation site (but not the only production site) is located at Guantai, Cixian, Henan province.[76] Here, enamels, as they are popularly known today, were first used at the end of the 12th century. The range of colours was quite limited, consisting of black, red and yellow, but the effect was striking. Until that time, most 'Cizhou' wares were black-and-white or brown-and-white, so the addition of new colours was notable. At Jingdezhen, where most Ming porcelain was made, enamel decoration had been used experimentally during the Yuan period (1279–1368),[77] but it was not until the early 15th century that single-colour enamels were introduced and then, in the second quarter of the century, multiple colours.[78]

What is interesting is how this decorative technique evolved during the Ming period, from a complex process with full underglaze blue outlines for all the design elements (*doucai*) to a simpler version with most of the outlining carried out in on-glaze enamels (*wucai*). This transition took place in the early years of the 16th century so that by the Jiajing reign period the latter technique was standard. It appears to have been much less admired in later periods, however, as the Qing copies of Ming enamelled wares usually utilize the *doucai* technique. With this technological shift, we see yet another example of the non-linear development of ceramic technology in China. The classic progressive model of technological history does not allow for such movement from complex methods to the more simple, but in China, at least with ceramics, that was often the case. As has been noted elsewhere, a most striking example of this is found in glaze technology which saw the introduction of high-fired glazes before low-fired glazes, thus a less sophisticated technology followed the advanced version.[79] What is at issue here therefore is our model of technological development.[80] Certainly there is no reference in Ming ceramic-related literature to the notion of low-fired Han lead glazes being less sophisticated than high-fired Shang celadons (nor the use of such technical descriptive terms).

A similar parallel can be seen in the development of monochrome glaze colours in the Ming period. One of the earliest to be developed, for example, was a monochrome copper red, which is one of the most difficult colours to achieve.[81] One sees versions of this in earlier Song-period porcelains from Guangxi,[82] but in the Ming period, what is notable is that, according to the archaeological record, this glaze appears before monochrome yellow, which is technically simpler. However this is analysed, what is now evident is just how important colour was in ceramics for certain Ming consumers (something also notable in other Ming arts), in contrast to the ware with a relative lack of colour (just one) which was more popular overseas: blue and white.

But even within this limited category of single-colour decoration, technology continually advanced, as can be seen in the refinement of the cobalt mineral pigment. Throughout the Ming period, there were numerous empirical experiments with cobalt from various different sources and in various concentrations; true refined cobalt, free of impurities, was developed in the Wanli reign period (1573–1619).[83] At the same time, experiments continued with body materials, with glaze chemistries and viscosities, with kiln designs and fuels, as well as with forming methods. If judged from surviving finished pieces, Ming ceramics, particularly 'imperial' examples, can seem conservative; but if looked at from a technological perspective, this was clearly a time of experimentation and technological advances, particularly in terms of decoration.

Designs and Form

The whiteness of Ming porcelain, or really porcelain in general, makes it an ideal surface for decoration, but the fine-grained texture of Ming Jingdezhen porcelain also enabled the production of designs and forms of many types. While the common manufacturing process for underglaze-decorated Ming porcelain required much of the decoration to be painted on to a dry but not fired surface (thus porous and slightly absorbent), the texture of this surface was very fine, so skilled painters could create almost any design imaginable. What this means for Ming-period porcelain is that the decoration was not limited by inferior materials or a lack of skill, so the designs reflected Ming taste and approaches across the media, in terms of style, technique, colour and aesthetic. What might be called the Ming aesthetic (in the Baxandall sense of 'the period eye'), reflected in surviving Ming porcelains, can also tell us something about how such objects were appreciated in Ming China, in addition to any contemporary texts.

The blank slate of porcelain was, at that time, decorated with designs and motifs that were universally popular, using a wide range of painting techniques; these even included text as part of or the whole design. Text can be, and is often, seen as a foundation of Chinese culture, and in the Ming period, its importance was as strong as ever. The text used on Ming porcelains was often simple, consisting of such meaningful characters such as 'long life' 寿, 'good fortune' 福, 'happiness' 喜, as well as everyday terms such as 'tea' 茶 or 'meal room' 食房. Text could also take the form of poems written on porcelains [Fig. 1.8] in standard forms of calligraphy or, as will be discussed below, dedicatory inscriptions. Thus the medium of porcelain fitted into a pre-existing taste for decorative text and writing, writing as art, without having to be specially treated, unlike metalwork, which necessitated the engraving process for applying text, or textile embroidery or weaving, which also required complex processes to add text. With porcelain, text could be applied much as with ink on paper or silk.

This easy adaptability was also suited to figurative painting, and most Ming porcelain was decorated with pictorial designs, narrative scenes or collections of motifs. Geometric designs were rare as the main decoration and usually only appeared as borders, in the form of key frets for example. In fact, many designs on Ming porcelains are framed by borders, or in later examples, cartouches, which suggests that porcelains in any form were seen as a pictorial surface.[84] This aesthetic, combined with the taste for text or calligraphy, is part of what defines the visual characteristics of Ming porcelain. In terms of the inspiration for the designs most often seen on Ming porcelains, this also reveals a particular taste in Ming China for designs (as well as inscriptions) with standardized, recognizable or 'auspicious' meanings, such as 'long life' or 'good fortune', in lieu of text. Motifs could also be purely decorative but within a relatively restricted range of patterns, and, significantly, they are standardized patterns rather than freehand drawings. This is related to several aspects of Ming society. Firstly, with the few exceptions noted previously, the decorators of porcelains were not individually recognized artists. The painting on porcelain therefore was not meant to represent an identifiable individual style, unlike, say, that of a famous painter or calligrapher. Even the named 'potters' are not described in Ming (and later) texts in the same way as painters or calligraphers, who are simply named. Hao Nineteen, for example, was not called by his surname 'Wu' 吴 but rather as no. 19, a *taoshi* 陶事 or 'maker of pottery', and unlike the work of painters, his pieces do not have individual titles.[85]

A second aspect of Ming society which defined the appearance of its porcelain was the conception of porcelain as a material. It was not (and still is not) inherently a valuable material, being made from clay, and thus individual ceramics were not of great monetary value until or unless they had been exceptionalised in some way. This could be done by commissioning, for example, so that a piece became valuable for its purpose and uniqueness. A porcelain could also become an antique, and therefore valuable within that category of object, but in the Ming period it was usually other types of ceramics that were collected as antiques, not porcelains, with just a few exceptions. According to middle and later Ming connoisseurship texts, most of the antique ceramics collected were Song stonewares (including

Ding ware, which is not a true porcelain), and the most acceptable porcelains were those made in two reign periods—Xuande and Chenghua in the fifteenth century.[86] Thus, for the most part, porcelain was a contemporary ceramic material that suited a lot of purposes but not that of 'art', and it therefore was decorated in a style that was expected of an object in regular and common use. Interestingly, it was considered acceptable for this mainly quotidian purpose at different levels of society. Everyone, including the emperor, came to need ceramics, and porcelain was the most widely used of the ceramic body materials available at that time. For example, in Ming China, porcelain was not only used as a surface for decoration in the contemporary style but also for making a wide range of contemporary forms and shapes. Because it was a fairly plastic ceramic, almost any shape could be made in porcelain, and thus these shapes can tell us much about Ming taste in objects. Generally speaking, one sees the expected dishes, bowls and drinking vessels which, to the present-day connoisseur, can be and are said to reflect Ming approaches to such ordinary forms. However, porcelain could also be used to replace more monetarily valuable materials (silver, gold or bronze, for example) when cheaper alternatives were needed, and it could also reflect the Ming interest in the potential of technology to imitate other materials in a skeuomorphic manner. For example, porcelain was used to make fake lacquer, wood or metalwork; the only reason for this would be to demonstrate technical mastery which clearly then had some aesthetic and commercial value in Ming China.[87]

Since porcelain could be decorated and shaped in most of the ways desired, it could also contribute to the Ming aesthetic of archaism. This was reflected in the taste for things of the past, whether the actual things, or copies of them, or simply decorative references to them.[88] In Ming porcelains (and other decorative arts), 'archaism' or 'copying the ancient' (*fang gu* 仿古)[89] was adopted in several ways, through forms of the past (often from other materials such as bronze), designs from the past from a wide range of materials, texts of the past, in the form of Tang or Song poems painted on vessels, or even reign names from the past, such as a 'Xuande' reign mark painted on a Chenghua-period vessel, for example.[90] This practice has a long history in the arts of China and was well developed as an identifiable style by the Ming period. Most scholars do not think of archaism in terms of design, but a recent study of decorative arts of the Ming and Qing discusses it as a notable approach to decoration.[91] In ceramics, however, it was certainly part of the decorative and formative repertoire without being prescriptive; if surviving objects are anything to judge by, there was no single definable 'archaistic' look or design, except in the case of porcelains made for official rituals or ceremonies.[92] An examination of such objects with archaistic designs and/or forms reveals a range of motifs and patterns which are recognizably archaistic, as well as certain forms which fall into this category and which are to some degree standardized. For example, beyond those made for specific court uses, there is a range of forms both loosely or more closely based on ancient bronzes which were fashionable in the Ming period. These include incense burners of *gui* 簋 form, the *jue* 爵 cup in blue and white, the *hu* 壶 form which evolved into the 'temple vase', the *gu* 觚 and even drums. These also indicate that certain aspects of 'the past' were popular in the Ming, and thus archaism itself was subject to fashion.

This was also true of designs or motifs which could represent the archaic but in ways which were complex to decode, at least from the perspective of today's observer. Some of these designs appear to have been decorative, for example those with imitation 'hanging blade' designs (from Shang bronzes). Narrative scenes from ancient stories (such as *San guo yan yi* 三国演义 or Story of the Three Kingdoms) might also fall into this category, but they are often interpreted as didactic in purpose. However, other designs which were inspired by the past were also functional in the sense that they determined how the ceramic would be used. A very good example of this, which has been the subject of an extensive study by Maggie Wan, is the 'Eight Trigrams' (*ba gua* 八卦) design on porcelains for the Jiajing court.[93] That the use of this motif was functional as well as decorative is proved by its application in traditional as well as reverse order: 'the configuration of the Eight Trigrams on Jiajing official porcelain is closely connected to popular Daoist concepts of internal alchemy and ritual, which pervaded the court during that period.'[94]

We should also consider that the subjects of some designs could themselves be archaistic in their references to the past, and that archaism rather than instruction might have been their purpose. For example, on a porcelain tile in the British Museum, we can see a civil official holding a tally, standing on a bridge which leads to what appear to be imperial palace structures enveloped in clouds. One of these structures is identified by inscription as the Fengtian men 奉天门 or 'Service to Heaven Gateway'.[95] This would have been the gateway to the Service to Heaven Hall, which was a real place located in the early Ming imperial palace at Nanjing. This tile is dated by an inscription at the top to 1551, thus during the Jiajing reign period, and the subject matter references a palace location from the Hongwu period in the early Ming (1368–98), where the emperor would have received congratulatory memorials from officials.[96] In both subject and inscription the Jiajing emperor is visually associated with the founder of the Ming, Hongwu, because he had essentially to start his own lineage upon the death of his predecessor.[97] The text appearing above the main image on this tile is that of an imperial edict concerning moral behaviour, rare enough on porcelain, but what is interesting for our purposes is the shorter inscription (Fengtian men) relating to a location from the past. It is this location, and the reference to it, which would have made this tile most meaningful at the time it was made, and knowledge of this helps to date the piece.[98]

Archaism could also be filtered through earlier period styles. One might find, for example, a Ming Chenghua mark and period porcelain with a form and glaze style based on a purportedly Song original [Fig. 1.9], which has been related to a trend for Southern Song (1127–1279) academy painting styles in the 1440s.[99] This type of archaism could be extended to a bronze form with a Song-style glaze which may have been inspired by a Song interpretation of that same form, rather than an ancient bronze original. These examples demonstrate that 'the past' could be very distant or somewhat more recent in terms of decorative inspiration and that its transmission as a style may not have been direct. This can sometimes take quite sophisticated forms in Ming ceramics; a famous example is the Chenghua-period blue and white porcelain with a Xuande reign mark mentioned previously which was excavated from the Chenghua levels at Jingdezhen.[100] There must have been consumers who would have understood the meaning of such a subtle reference, just as there may have been consumers who were misled, whether intentionally or not.[101] Broadly speaking, Ming ceramics, therefore, were a form of visual communication, just as paintings with inscriptions on them were at the same time.

Another social trend reflected visually in Ming porcelain is the taste for foreign things, or at least things that looked foreign to the Ming consumer. As early as the beginning of the 15th century, porcelains were being made in foreign shapes, some which are now widely believed to be Chinese, such as the 'moon flask' or *baoyueping/bianhu* 宝月瓶/扁壶, which had been adopted from Middle Eastern glass forms. This is usually said to be a reflection of the Yongle emperor's imperial programme, involving the travels of Zhenghe, etc., but foreign shapes were also taken from other cultures closer to home, such as Tibet, where a textile form was borrowed for porcelain vessels in China, the so-called 'monk's cap ewer' or *sengmaohu* 僧帽壶.[102] Interestingly, 'foreign' inspiration for designs on Ming porcelains could also take the form of text. One sees, for example, Tibetan script on several surviving early 15th-century Ming vessels; in the later Ming, during the Zhengde 正德 reign (1506–21), one also sees Arabic and Persian script on porcelains. Some of the best known of these porcelains take the form of functional vessels for use in calligraphy, such as brush rests, or associated forms such as table screens [Fig. 1.10]. The foreign text on these vessels ranges from the truly mundane ('brush rest') to the somewhat more meaningful, such as a passage from the Koran, but in both cases the foreign text is presented as decorative and part of the design. It functions in much the same way as the Chinese text discussed previously, which often similarly describes what is seen on a porcelain vessel or what it is to be used for ('tea', 'long life', etc.).

A final issue which should be considered is the relationship between the visual appearance and function of porcelain in Ming China. Porcelain clearly was considered to be an acceptable material for the production of a wide range of objects, much wider than those made in stoneware or wood, for example. This is partly to do with its adaptability—almost any form or decoration could be made from it or on it. But it is also because the material itself was abundant and did not have any intrinsic value. In contrast to precious metals, for example, or lacquer, which was incredibly labour-intensive to produce, there seemingly was no object for which porcelain was deemed unsuitable. Both everyday and religious vessels, burial goods and trade items were made of porcelain, and porcelain objects were used at all levels of society. Owning gold plate was an obvious visual sign of wealth, so its use always made a statement about its owner. In contrast, using porcelain in certain situations might suggest straitened financial circumstances, simple efficiency or simply a desire for good performance. You could cook, pickle, chill, serve, sit on, etc. a porcelain object but not gold, silver or lacquer ones.

Thus in terms of use value porcelain in some ways had greater value than more precious materials in the Ming. It was used not only as a building material but also to make furniture in the form of garden seats, which are still being manufactured and enjoyed today. Bird feeders were also made of porcelain, as well as cricket jars for cricket games,[103] land deeds for burial sites, ritual vessels for imperial ceremonies, and so on. It was a material that defined, reflected and supported multiple aspects of life and death in Ming China.

Consumption and Functionality

Dining and Burial at Court

Some of what we know about the use of porcelain in Ming China is related to specific consumption patterns, and in these cases, it is often only the ceramic remains that can indicate and illuminate such forms of consumption. One of the most notable experiments carried out at Jingdezhen, for example, was the production of porcelain roof, wall and floor tiles for religious and imperial architecture.[104] These were not widely manufactured or utilized but their production demonstrates the perceived versatility of porcelain as a raw material. The tiles were made for such disparate institutions as the first Ming palace in Nanjing;[105] the early Ming imperially-sponsored pagoda, the Da Baoensi 大报恩寺, also in the same area; and speculatively for an as yet unidentified location which is represented by the blue and white floor tiles excavated from the Xuande levels at Zhushan.[106]

The production of porcelain tiles for the first Ming palace demonstrates the disparate usage of porcelain products by one primary consumer group: the Ming court. We have seen, for example, how porcelain, usually in vessel form, was a significant craft material employed mainly for dining purposes but also for functional storage of liquids,[107] for altar vessels and other ritual purposes such as imperial and princely burial objects, as imperial tribute goods (see chapter two), and even for calligraphy accessories such as brush rests, pen handles and brush pots. A lot of this 'imperial' porcelain was decorated, which suggests that plain, unadorned porcelain vessels were undesirable. It was not, therefore, the essential material itself that appealed, but rather the visual appearance of things made from it. Apart from monochrome porcelains used for specific ceremonies (but still essentially as table ware), most if not all court-consumed porcelains were decorated; this is true of most objects used at court in general. Surface decoration (and colour) was extremely important, as can be seen on textiles (also necessary for denoting rank), lacquerwares, metalwork and of course paintings. That this was not a period of decorative austerity in China is evidenced by the Ming goods that survive today, which have been described as a form of 'cultural capital that was visible to all those who could similarly identify themselves with the luxury of decoration'.[108]

Interestingly, in the palace precincts, porcelain vessels were sometimes marked for use (rather than or in addition to reign marks). Such marks denote either location or function, and provide evidence of how some forms were used at court. One surviving example which demonstrates this clearly is a small bowl from the second half of the 15th century which is inscribed *shifang* 食房 or 'meal room' [Fig. 1.11], a name which has been traced to a specific location in the palace.[109] Other examples with the inscriptions *chafang* 茶房 (tea room), *Dianshan suoyong* 典膳所用 (for use in the Foods Office), etc. have also been found, thus providing more evidence for the practice.[110] These complicate the discussion of the broad but enduringly popular category of Ming 'imperial' porcelain. Does this rather quotidian object for a dining space deserve classification as 'imperial'? In some respects it could be seen as a representative and confirmed example of an 'imperial' object as it was clearly made for use in the palace precincts and it is decorated with a dragon. However it is not known whether such a vessel would actually have been used by the emperor, an assumption which is often made about Ming (and Qing) porcelains designated as 'imperial'. In those terms, Ming porcelains with reign marks would also be seen as confirmed 'imperial' objects, but as noted above, some scholars suggest that this marking merely situates them in time rather than denoting a particular consumer, or declares separated production (for a time at least).

Much more interesting are those Ming porcelains found in imperial tombs. Not only are they not very plentiful in such locations but they appear with other more intrinsically valuable goods such as gold or weapons.[111] Porcelains have been found in the tombs of princes as well as emperors. The Wanli emperor's tomb contained, among other porcelains, eight blue and white 'plum vases' or *meiping* 梅瓶 jars.[112] In a prince's tomb, a single blue and white stem cup was found with a specially-made gold lid and a lacquer stand.[113] In another tomb of a regional prince [or king, as some would translate it], a single blue and white 'pear-shaped' bottle or *yuhuchun ping* 玉壶春瓶 was excavated in 1961.[114] This piece is quite distinctive because its decoration features none of the minor bands which are typical of early Ming ceramics, especially a Hongwu-period piece like this, and consists of a single design of a five-clawed dragon amid clouds. That said, some quite ordinary ceramics have been found in the tombs of regional princes, for example the Jiajing mark and period blue and white dish with a dragon design that was found in the tomb of Prince Yizhuang and his wife in Nancheng county, Jiangxi province.[115] This suggests that some, and possibly all, the porcelains and ceramics found in Ming upper class tombs may have been pretty functional and should not be viewed as prized objects, unless perhaps those that have been embellished, such as the stem cup from the tomb of Prince Zhuang of Liang, mentioned above, which was given a gold lid.[116] Some of the other, non-mounted porcelains from this same tomb are of great interest in ceramic typological histories, but it is not clear how important they were in the context of this tomb, as all of them are functional forms that would have been used widely in the early Ming court: stem cups, wine storage jars and dishes. The only really unusual porcelains found in this tomb—unusual because no others like them appear to survive—are a pair of stem cups with gold decoration of dragons on a white ground.[117] The decorative technique used on these cups may be an example of fired-on gold leaf, with which Jingdezhen kilns seem to have experimented in the Yongle period. The process was not very successful, a fact which can be seen on several excavated pieces from the Yongle strata at Jingdezhen where the gold has run, thus blurring the decoration.[118] A similar problem has occurred with the stem cups. As they clearly were technologically flawed, it is surprising that they were buried in an imperial tomb, unless they were highly prized for their experimental technology or their connection to precious metalwork which, it has been demonstrated, was usually more highly valued than porcelain in the Ming period, a fact that is notable in elite burials.[119]

If we examine further the only excavated imperial tomb of the late Ming period, that of the Wanli emperor at the Dingling Mausoleum, we can see that very little had changed in the burial of ceramics by this period. This suggests that their perceived function in official burials was, like much imperial activity, very traditional and highly regulated.[120] In this tomb, several blue and white wares were interred, including the requisite wine-storage jars (called *meiping*—noted above) but with their lids, which usually do not survive, and a bowl which had been given a gold saucer and domed lid.[121] The lid and saucer for this blue and white bowl have an inscription which is longer than what is normally seen in these types of ceramics, but typical for metalwork: '*Wanli nian zao liu cheng wu se jin zhong si liang ba qian*' 万历年造六成五色金重四两八钱 and similarly '*Wanli nian zao liu cheng wu se jin zhong ba liang qi qian wu fen*' 万历年造六成五色金重八两七钱五分, thus giving the time of manufacture, the weight and value. In addition, several of the wine jars have Wanli reign marks on them.[122] Another example, however, has a Jiajing reign mark[123] as does a covered *meiping*,[124] suggesting that such pieces had been in continuous use at court.

The most surprising ceramics in this tomb, in light of our usual assumptions about 'imperial' wares, are the polychrome pieces, including an archaistic incense burner with what is known as a *sancai* 三彩 glaze, unusually featuring its metalwork inner fittings intact; and a pair of archaistic *gu* vessels with yellow and brown glazes on the biscuit.[125] All three vessels are of types generally ignored in discussions of 'imperial taste'. Clearly, however, they were valued enough that firstly, they have Wanli reign marks, and secondly, they were buried in the imperial tomb. This fact alone should force us to reconsider what we believe to be 'imperial taste' in ceramics of the Ming period. Looked at from the perspective of official tombs in general, these seemingly unusual forms actually represent the kind of ceramics that are often found in elite burials, which frequently include altar vessels.[126]

Interestingly, monochrome porcelains are less often found in these contexts, but numerous examples have been excavated from the imperial kiln sites at Jingdezhen.[127] One buried example is the bluish white or *qingbai* 青白 bowl found in the tomb of prince Zhao of Chu (d. 1424), Hubei province, in 1991[128] which dates to the Yongle reign. As we have seen, in Ming official literature, monochrome ceramics are associated with specific court rituals, such as ancestral ceremonies[129] but not with interment, so monochromes may not have been deemed appropriate for this purpose. The example noted further is not of a form associated with court ceremonies (nor of a relevant colour; however some 'white' ceramics were actually pale blue). In addition, rarely, apart from the Wanli tomb, are polychrome porcelains found in royal tombs (i.e. those of princes, as the tombs of the other emperors have not been opened), which suggests that polychrome wares might have been subject to hierarchical restrictions. This is interesting because, again, in the traditional historiography of Ming ceramics, particularly of 'imperial' porcelains from Jingdezhen, certain polychrome wares, like *doucai*, are placed high in the hierarchy because of an assumption of value based on their greater technological difficulty (as compared with simple blue and white wares). As noted, relatively few ceramics in fact are found in royal tombs, compared with other materials, so it is difficult to make wider assumptions about their significance in this context.

Beyond the Court

With reference to *doucai* wares, the usual assumption is that the style was established in imperial porcelain for the Chenghua court. However, an earlier example that is more fully developed than the experimental pieces known from the Xuande period has been found in a non-royal tomb dated to 1464.[130] In fact, a much wider range of Ming ceramics have been found in tombs of members of the sub-imperial classes (some more prominent than others), and these give an insight into two things: how certain ceramics may have been valued, and their possible function in a tomb (they may simply have held other things, as in royal tombs). One interesting tomb which dates to the early Qing but contains porcelains from a range of time periods, including Ming, features examples in both blue and white and polychrome (as well as very high quality jades and other materials).[131] There are several Chenghua mark and period porcelains, including a pair of *doucai* wine cups with grapes decoration,[132] a Jiajing mark and period *doucai* archaistic incense burner with the Eight Trigrams or *ba gua* motif, and a Wanli mark and period *wucai* dish decorated with Daoist immortals.[133] The tomb's occupant, buried at Xiaoxitian, Xinjiekouwai and identified by an epitaph simply as the clan name Heŝeri 赫舍里, the young daughter of court official Suoetu 索额图 (and sister-in-law of the Kangxi 康熙 emperor), was from a prominent family, and the antique ceramics were part of a prized group of objects selected by her father for the tomb (which also included a jade vessel created by the celebrated Lu Zigang). The objects selected for this tomb are significant because they were used in the girl's domestic circumstances, which happened to be the court but not the inner household. They are also objects from earlier periods, which was partly necessitated by the early Qing date of the burial. Furthermore, as we will see, the literature of collecting from the Ming period onward is written about collections (i.e. a group of specially selected objects, not necessarily 'art collections'), or about specific objects, collected by their owners; it is not about collections formed on behalf of someone. This tomb (and others like it) can be seen to represent the latter sort of collection, and may force us to reconsider certain ceramic (and other object) consumption practices.

Another surprising tomb find, this time of the Ming period, is that of two porcelain figurines in blue and white, a type of Ming porcelain that is usually ignored in typologies and historiographies, where the vessel reigns supreme. In a tomb in Xi'an City, Shaanxi Province, a blue and white figure of Shoulao, dated to around the 16th century, was found,[134] as well as a figure of a lady, of around the same date.[135] Finding ceramic figurines in a tomb is not in itself unusual—quite a few Ming tombs have some form of ceramic figurines (including that of a Ming prince, King Zhuang of Yi, d. 1556)[136] in a continuation of very early object burial practices in China—but porcelain examples are more rare. As objects, they are not usually mentioned, positively or negatively, in the Ming collecting literature unless in reference to Dehua ware, nor are they considered 'important' amongst collectors today.

Jingdezhen ceramics of the mid-15th century are also dismissed by present-day collectors and scholars for a host of reasons, including the political turmoil of the period, which affected court porcelain production, and the lack of good quality finds at Jingdezhen. Yet in fact, quite a few have been found in dated tombs.[137] In one tomb dated 1451, what appears to be a complete set of blue and white vessels was found in 1989.[138] In this group were two vases of simple temple vase form and a coordinating tripod incense burner of archaistic form. This set of three thus predates the general expansion of ceramic temple set pieces from three to five in number which occurred in the 16th century.[139] A more surprising vessel was found in a tomb dated 1463, just before the beginning of the Chenghua period, at Zhonghuamenwai in Nanjing City. This tomb of Huai Zhong contained a Xuande-period white *meiping* with the inscription *neifu* 内府 or 'inner palace' on its shoulder in underglaze iron brown.[140] Other examples of such vessels with this inscription survive, but this is one of the few to have been excavated from a dated site and from a non-imperial tomb. One can only guess at how this piece was acquired by the deceased,[141] but it certainly helps to support the more widespread distribution and consumption of 'imperial' ceramics which has been posited here.

If their tombs are anything to go by, we also need to consider upper-class women as consumers of ceramics in the Ming period. As with many forms of Chinese 'art' or material culture, women are often ignored or marginalised as consumers of ceramics. The evidence from tombs and from a few surviving later pieces which appear to have been commissioned,[142] however, suggests that in fact they were independent users of this material and objects made from it. The tombs of consorts of Ming princes have revealed a number of ceramics that are very similar in style and quantity to those found in the princes' tombs.[143] For example, the tomb of the consort of Prince Liao at Balingshan, Hubei Province, yielded a white lidded *guan* 罐 jar which is very clearly from Jingdezhen and of the Yongle period.[144] In Hubei, the tomb of the consort of an as yet unidentified prince revealed three very high quality, but unmarked, Xuande to Zhengtong (1436–49)-period blue and white wares, including a dragon stem cup and a censer with a design of men playing a board game.[145]

A final notable characteristic of ceramics in non-elite tombs of either gender in the Ming is their regional character. Certain combinations of ceramics, for example, are only found in tombs in the South, such as the burial of small covered porcelain jars, in sets of five or four, containing in some cases Buddhist relics or grains.[146] In the latter case, they might be seen as a continuation of an earlier Southern practice of burying ceramic jars with grain offerings.[147]

A form of consumption that is related to burial but somewhat less personal is that revealed by hoards of goods which were often hastily thrown together in times of strife. Hoards have proved to be an important source for a wide range of valued goods, from gold and silver in the Tang period (for example, at Hejiacun 何家村, near Xi'an),[148] to celadons and porcelains in the Song (Suining 遂宁, Sichuan)[149] and ceramics from all over China in Yuan-period Inner Mongolia (Jininglu 集宁路 site).[150] Ming hoards have also been found; their ceramics are for the most part somewhat ordinary.[151] However one very fine piece was found in a Ming hoard in Hubei province. This is a Chenghua mark and period stem cup painted in blue and white with a design that is not well known in the Chenghua repertoire as it consists of a combination of birds on flowering branches, phoenixes and chickens.[152] Due to their nature, hoards generally cannot be precisely dated; but whether this stem cup is contemporary with the hoard or an antique, it is certainly an 'imperial' marked piece that was not buried in a court situation.

Special Commissions

Unlike the small number of these pre-made or ready-made porcelains selected for burial or hoarding, a number of Ming porcelains were specially-commissioned for specific purposes such as for use in named temples, as gifts to friends, for recording of posthumous land deeds or re-interments, and also as wedding gifts. In many cases, such porcelains feature informative inscriptions, but in others it is the decoration which suggests or denotes function, such as families of chickens on wine cups for weddings, or fish on new year vessels [see fig. 1.6 above]. Often the pieces specially-commissioned for burial or temple use tell us the most because their inscriptions are necessary for making the objects functionally effective and appropriate. In one surviving example, the re-interment of a father by his children was recorded on an appropriately rectangular-shaped porcelain tablet, and in this inscription we learn the name of the deceased, his family, the dates of death and reburial and the reasons for reburial (better *feng shui*).[153] [Fig. 1.12] In this example, we also can read the standardized language used for such burial tablets, such as references to filial piety. In this case, porcelain was the ideal medium for such an object because it was very durable and it could be painted permanently with an inscription and/or design. It is notable that this object is blue and white, and not polychrome which is rarely seen in surviving porcelains used for this purpose.

In the temple, some porcelains were specially commissioned as gifts from devotees, with dated inscriptions appearing on the more expensive examples; these represent the continuation of an earlier tradition which began in the Yuan dynasty. At this time, sets of objects were displayed in the temple and donated for specific purposes, such as the death of a member of the family, a wish for the birth of sons[154] or as a gift to curry favour with the temple itself. In the Yuan, ceramic examples were usually made and presented in sets of three, including several surviving today with dated descriptive inscriptions, for example a Longquan ware temple vase dated 1327, and the so-called 'David vases' dated 1351.[155] As noted previously, in about the middle Ming period, the sets of three ceramic pieces expanded to sets of five, with the addition of candlesticks to the set, and porcelain became the most common ceramic material for these.[156] An important surviving Ming example of one type of vessel from these sets, commonly described as a 'temple vase', is the blue and white one dated 1496, in the Percival David Collection. [Fig. 1.13] Its inscription is typical of those found on such vessels, referencing as it does the family name of the donors, their hometown, the name and location of the temple being gifted, the reason for the gift (wishing for success in business, in this case) and the date.[157] Interestingly, these porcelains made for altars [aka 'altar vessels'] also became popular as export items because of their shapes, rather than their functions. Thus a number of the so-called 'Ming vases' in foreign collections are random pieces from altar sets with forms that have been readapted for use in other locations, such as chimney pieces in Georgian England.[158]

Surviving Ming porcelains also indicate that religious institutions in China commissioned their own porcelains, possibly for everyday use. Several dishes in collections around the world feature the inscription 'Jin Shan si' 金山寺 or 'Jinshan temple', a Buddhist monastery located on an island off the south coast of China that was visited, and depicted in a painting, by the famous Ming painter Wen Zhengming (1470–1559).[159] Other surviving specially-commissioned pieces commemorate gifts for people or non-religious places, and it is interesting that porcelains should have been the vehicle for such gifts. Stoneware was equally a possibility but for some reason not as desirable. This might be because Jingdezhen made it easy to commission such wares or because fine-textured porcelain provided the ideal canvas for decoration or inscriptions. Coloured decoration was also much more pleasing on a white background, and in China, unlike in other ceramic-producing cultures, white glazes usually were not used on stoneware bodies to make them white. (Those that appear white usually have a colourless glaze over a white background such as slip.) Among the more interesting surviving Ming porcelains with inscriptions recording their function as gifts is a white dish in the Percival David Collection which dates to the Ming (Hongzhi period) but was painted later in the Qing dynasty with the image of a scholar in a landscape in *famille verte* enamels.[160] [Fig. 1.14] Along with the figure scene, the title of the image is given on the back of the dish (*Xichun tu* 惜春图 'Picture of Cherishing Spring'), along with a dedication (*Wuzhai yawan* 务斋雅玩 'for the amusement of Wuzhai') and the signature of the artist who was the famous 'Yangzhou eccentric' Jin Nong 金农 (1687–1763). The artist was a passionate antique collector and had taken an old white dish and decorated it as gift for the nobleman, Li Shimin 李時敏, whose studio name was Wuzhai. This bowl thus represents quite a rare example of an artist presenting his work on an old piece of porcelain, in this case Ming, rather than on more conventional painting media such as silk or paper, and of the re-use of Ming porcelain in the Qing period.[161]

Taste and Hierarchies; Containers and Prices

The Ming dish (presumably) decorated by Jin Nong became much more valuable after its transformation into a painting. As a special commission, however, it is difficult to put a monetary value on it. The diary of Li Rihua, cited above in our discussion of the potter Hao Nineteen, tells us how much he paid Hao for a set of fifty cups—three ounces of silver, which was still pretty cheap.[162] Statements of price, however, are fairly unusual. The Ming dynasty literature of connoisseurship, as it is traditionally categorized in English, contains much information about ceramics, but most of it concerns their function, and in some cases, appropriateness for certain specific functions. For example, a primary function for ceramics in the Ming period was as containers for, among other things, liquids, beads, food or flowers. This last function is one which is not normally discussed in ceramic studies, but there are two surviving texts that discuss ceramics strictly from the perspective of containers for flowers. This reminds us, too, that flowers, their cultivation and arranging, were a popular pastime in the Ming period. The fashion for flower arranging is associated with both decorative interiors[163] and gardens, by extension. The earliest surviving 'systematic' gardens manual in fact is from the Ming period, Ji Cheng's 计成 *Yuan ye* 园冶 (The Craft of Gardens) of 1631.[164] In the Ming, flowers were both displayed in vases and potted, as part of a tradition of 'basin landscapes' or *penjing* 盆景 which can be seen as landscapes in miniature form, with compositions modelled on painting.[165] Not surprisingly, as with other types of objects associated with elite pastimes, flower containers were subject to ranking and prescriptive use in terms of location in the home, size of vessel, etc. There are several late Ming connoisseurship texts which address this, including Wen Zhenheng's *Zhangwu zhi* 长物志 (Treatise on Superfluous Things) of 1621–27[166] and Li Yu's *Xianqing ouji* 闲情偶寄 (Random Repository of Idle Thoughts, 1671),[167] as well as specialist texts focusing on flowers themselves.

One such specialist text which survives and is often quoted is the *Pinghua pu* 瓶花谱 (Treatise of Vase Flowers) of 1595. The author, Zhang Chou 张丑 (1577–1643), tells us in great detail that:

> To make (a) flower arrangement, it is necessary to select first the vessel. In spring and winter, the choice is bronze, while in summer and autumn, it is porcelain. In halls, the vessel should be large; in the study, small. This is in accordance with the location.
>
> Porcelain and bronze wares are preferred ... The vessels should not have rings on the side and they should not be in pairs, looking like temple decorations.
>
> ... To cherish things, ancient bronze wares are of course the best. Among the ceramics, the most valuable ones are Chai and Ru wares, but these are now scarcely preserved. The most precious ones at present are Guan, Ge, Xuan(de) and Ding wares. And vases of Longquan, Junzhou, Zhangsheng, Wuni and Chenghua are also gradually becoming treasured.[168]

We also learn from this author which vases and styles of porcelain are deemed suitable for 'elegant decoration' and which ones were not, a significant concern among so-called 'literati' of the later Ming period.[169] In the text of two letters from 1599, the author Yuan Hongdao 袁宏道 (1568–1610) enclosed his *Pingshi* 瓶史 or 'History of the Vase' for a friend's consideration.[170] Yuan describes the text as 'a record of flower nomenclature and the traditions associated with the various flowers'.[171] It too is a discussion of flowers and their arrangement, in which porcelain features as a material for vessels/containers. He echoes the sentiments of the previous author when he states:

> In general terms, it is appropriate for the vases placed in one's studio to be small and squat, and both the copperware...and the porcelain vessels ... should all be diminutive in size of manufacture before they are fit playthings for the man of elegance. If not, how would they differ from the vessels used during Ancestral Rites in one's Clan Hall? Even were they to be ancient, they would nonetheless seem vulgar.
>
> ... precious antique vases are not mere baubles. Impecunious and unimportant scholars, however, have not the wherewithal to possess such things, and even to get hold of a porcelain vase or two from such kilns as those of the Xuande and Chenghua reign periods makes one feel like a beggar who has suddenly come into a fortune.[172]

Yuan Hongdao thus echoes the sentiments expressed by his peers in the late Ming period who also commented on the porcelains of the Xuande and Chenghua period with reference to their rarity and expense. Such wares would of course have been antiques by this time, and this is an important category of 'Ming ceramics', that is, the wider definition of ceramics used or consumed in the Ming period. As we have seen, the types of antique ceramics that were valued by several arbiters of Ming taste were initially stonewares of the Song dynasty, as is evidenced by their prominent position in Cao Zhao's *Gegu yaolun* 格古要论 (Essential Criteria of Antiques) of 1388.[173] In later Ming texts, as was traditional in Chinese historiography, Cao's lists were repeated and referenced as an authority on the subject but to this were added porcelains of the 15th century. In the *Zhangwu zhi*, Xuande, Yongle and Chenghua porcelains are mentioned and noted to be 'expensive'.[174] Another Ming writer, Shen Defu (1578–1642) confirmed this when he noted:

> In ceramics, the dearest is Chenghua, then comes Xuande. A cup used to cost only several *jin*, and when I was a child I did not think of them as valuable treasures. A pair of Chenghua wine cups now reaches 100 *jin*, and a Xuande incense burner almost as much.[175]

Interestingly, Shen blames the high prices on those who wish to imitate the 'leaders of fashion in Suzhou' who made them the subject of their 'elegant discussions'.[176] The role of objects in social hierarchies and associated anxieties of the Ming period has been discussed extensively by Craig Clunas[177] and thanks to his work, we now have more information about how antiques and contemporary objects circulated through pawn shops, as well as monasteries and 'elegant' shops,[178] in the later Ming period with references to specific prices paid or offered. As a result, Clunas has concluded that in the late 16th century, antique ceramics were becoming very expensive indeed. One very telling example is a white Ding incense burner that was purchased in the 1580s for 350 ounces of silver. A similar incense burner belonged to a friend of the potter (and clearly also dealer) discussed earlier, Zhou Danquan, who promptly copied it and sold the copy to the friend for 40 ounces. This copy was later sold to an unaware collector as an antique for 1,000 ounces of silver.[179]

Fakes and Faking

Faking is thus also a consideration in the story of ceramics in Ming China. But this is to be expected in what was by the late Ming period a highly developed social system of collecting and an associated art market. Nor was it unique to the Ming, but Ming writers had much to say about it. A ceramic faked in the Ming is therefore as much a representation of Ming culture as an 'authentic' one made at the same time. It can also perhaps be even more informative about the values of the consuming classes in Ming society. As early as the late 14th century, Cao Zhao gave advice about the market, listing terms used by antique dealers, and later commentators even went so far as to give connoisseurship advice for those buying in Beijing markets.[180] Liu Tong 刘侗 (d. 1637) stated in a guidebook that recent imitations of Yongle porcelain cups give themselves away by their thickness and that the reign marks on porcelains can be faked.[181]

Another perspective on the faking of ceramics in the Ming is given in additional records of the activity of Zhou Danquan:

> Zhou Danquan of Wumen surpassed others in his talents; … whenever [he] went to Jingdezhen in Jiangxi, he would copy the old shapes, making vessels in order to deceive the credulous; in decoration and markings, in colour and luster [they] were astoundingly close to the real thing.[182]

Zhou was therefore not just a very skilful craftsman but also clearly a master forger. It is possible, therefore, that the vessel by Zhou on display in the National Palace Museum may have been collected as a genuine Song piece in the Ming period, even though its appearance today is very obviously not characteristic of actual Song-period ceramics. He could well have been exploiting a lack of connoisseurship ability among quite a few of his buyers. Nonetheless, the issue of fakes in Ming ceramics is complicated by the decorative fashion for objects made in imitation of styles or forms from the past, to which Zhou may also have contributed.

As this overview of the production, economics and cultures of porcelain in Ming China demonstrates, the aesthetics for ceramics (if not connoisseurship of antique ones) clearly were well developed in the Ming period and their consumption was spread across the social classes. In terms of reception, however, porcelains were not widely admired (or even considered) but were desired and used for multiple functions, including ceremonial ones. Today, these domestic porcelains are categorized as works of art but, in contrast to export wares, their distribution beyond China did not occur during the Ming period itself. Nor did their conceptual transformation into works of art occur at that time, the only equivalent being the transformation of some Ming ceramics into antiques. In order to understand the transformative process, and the consequent development of awareness of China in general and Ming China in particular, we need to examine another category of Ming porcelain, that is, Ming ceramics made or designated for trade and distribution. Such ceramics represent an aspect of Ming culture—but one that was not experienced by many Ming-period Chinese. This in itself demonstrates how highly developed the ceramic industry was in Ming China, such that a whole separate area could be devoted to production of goods for non-domestic consumption. The image of Ming that was sent around the world was therefore not the sophisticated and culturally complex one possessed by Ming Chinese but rather a standardized and simplified version that is nonetheless, part of Ming culture, and should be acknowledged as such. This process of worldwide transfer of Ming culture through ceramics will be discussed in the next chapter.

2

Ming Porcelain in the World (15th–17th centuries)

Transformative Consumption

Introduction: Distribution Mechanisms

In addition to the large-scale domestic production discussed in the previous chapter, during the Ming period Chinese porcelain was exported around the world, to as far east as Japan and as far west as the Americas. The export trade in the first century of the Ming, from 1368–1400, was very much a continuation of the extensive trade that was established during the Yuan period (1279–1368).[1] In fact, some early Ming exported porcelains are indistinguishable from those of the late Yuan, but this situation changed as new, more distinctive styles were developed at the factories and workshops at Jingdezhen and at other kilns located primarily in the southeast. These products, which are classified as 'Chinese export porcelain', have been studied extensively, and there is a large body of information about export ceramics of the Ming period—their destinations and individual characteristics, for example—but much of it focuses on surviving objects or shipwreck finds, which are notoriously unreliable. As the focus of these studies is on surviving examples, which in many (but not as many as is widely assumed) cases are what might further be described as 'luxury goods',[2] there is in addition some information about how these so-called 'export wares' were consumed overseas in seemingly distinct foreign markets, and some consideration of what impact they had on foreign consumer habits, such as in Britain.[3] But these texts rarely if ever consider the impact these foreign consumers might have had on the Ming porcelain itself. As we will see, this impact is often transformative, both physically and conceptually. Yet the impact of consumption on objects (as opposed to reception) has not been widely explored for any cultural objects, including those of Ming China.

When objects are considered from this perspective, however, we can see not only that the patterns of consumption of Ming ceramics overseas were sometimes vastly different within the many cultures that consumed them, but also that their reception and interpretation could also be widely different, either in different geographical locations, as might be expected, or sometimes even within the same location. Contrary to the usual assumption of constancy, Ming Chinese ceramics were both Chinese material culture and objects of foreign cultures at the same time, as a consequence of global consumption. In the next chapter, we will see how this activity further transcended materiality during the post-Ming period, where, in the literature and language of Anglo-American society, Ming ceramics (particularly blue and white porcelain) began to have a presence beyond daily life, thus furthering their transformative development into the realm of the iconic concept.

In order to understand the mechanisms by which consumers were able to transform Ming ceramics, however, it is important to consider briefly the various patterns of its trade during and after the Ming period. We are fortunate to have recent studies of how the trade in ceramics was organised and managed so that we can see this activity from the Chinese perspective, as well as that of the foreign-consumed object, which has dominated scholarship. In a volume of the monumental *Science and Civilisation in China*, Rose Kerr gives a brief summary of the main issues and events associated with the export of ceramics from China, including a section on the Ming period. According to Kerr, during the Yuan period, ship-building was aided by official capital and trade managed as a profit-sharing scheme with the government.[4] This system continued in the early Ming period with the addition of tribute 'trade' or exchange, a form of foreign relations which dates back to the Han period (202 BC–AD 220).[5] As Brook explains, 'The tribute system required foreign rulers to send embassies to China bearing tribute in the form of local exotica. The emperor in turn presented these emissaries with gifts of equal or greater value, which they took back to their rulers. The emperor also bestowed titles on tributary rulers ... It was a device for mutual recognition and mutual legitimation that propped up China's claim to world hegemony.'[6] In the early Ming period, numerous overseas states participated in this system, with envoys arriving from as far afield as Champa (in modern-day Vietnam), Coromandel (India) and Tibet. Through this system, in 1383 alone 57,000 pieces of porcelain were sent to Thailand, Java and other locations in Southeast Asia as an imperial gift.[7]

Beyond the tribute system, which was sometimes fraught with difficulty, restrictions were often placed on non-governmental foreign trade in the Ming period. This was heavily regulated, particularly when special supervisorates were established along the coast in 1370 charged with collecting customs duties and preventing smuggling of contraband.[8] Smuggling was a major problem, as was the arrival in China of foreign ships, over which the government had little control if this activity was not reported.[9] The coast was thus an important border and a major source of revenue. Restrictions placed on overseas trade meant that kilns in China had difficulty supplying orders, even though some products did travel through the illegal private trade network. This unofficial trade could be fairly substantial, as indicated by the excavations near Ming warehouses in Yangzhou which revealed over 30,000 ceramics dating from the Hongwu to Hongzhi periods.[10] A lack of competition from official Chinese suppliers thus enabled other producers to enter the market, such as Vietnam, which produced blue and white (stoneware, not porcelain) in the period sometimes known as the 'Ming gap'.[11]

Private trade continued after official bans were lifted in the 16th century, and this is the period in which Europeans began to participate in the trade (discussed below). But it should be borne in mind that usually ceramics were not the primary trade item as other goods were much more highly valued. Thus we should not assume that Ming ceramics were necessarily highly desired overseas. In fact, in the fifteenth century, silk and silk products were

China's most important exports,[12] and the story of Ming trade is very different if one views it from this perspective.[13] In some cases, however, individual Ming ceramics were desired by foreign consumers and considered suitable for a wide variety of functions. Their consumption therefore reflected the interests and practices of the cultures that consumed them, not those of China. With this in mind, we will examine the mechanics and consequences of this practice in a selection of foreign consumer cultures during the Ming period, with a view to considering these Ming ceramics from a more localized, less universalist perspective. This is not a comprehensive history, but rather a consideration of key case studies from a variety of geographical locations which demonstrate the range of consumption practices for Ming porcelain outside China.

East Asia: Japan and Korea

As a geographical and cultural neighbour of China, Japan has a long history of encounters with and consumption of Chinese ceramics. From the earliest imports of Chinese goods during the Han to larger scale imports of ceramics during the Tang to Yuan periods, Chinese objects of many different types became part of Japanese material culture.[14] Like those for Chinese objects in general, the patterns of consumption of Chinese ceramics in Japan were complex and varied, and in some cases even transformative. During the equivalent of the Ming period (later Kamakura and Muromachi periods in Japan), an important catalyst for new consumption practices was the development of tea drinking culture and rituals. Older Chinese ceramics, particularly Song and Yuan stonewares, were part of this, but some Ming ceramics also came to be included. Ming porcelain, however, was not generally accorded the same status as stoneware or earthenware vessels, whose relative value in Japan was higher than their equivalent status in China. Some were even named and designated as important objects, a particularly Japanese approach to reception.[15] Ming porcelains, however, were simply used as functional vessels in this context, in contrast to the somewhat crude large earthenware jars from China.[16] More generally, Ming porcelain from Jingdezhen later came to be appreciated not as individual objects but rather as things to be used and presented in large quantities. From the later 15th century, larger quantities of Chinese ceramics were used in Japan and recorded as sets rather than individual pieces, especially blue and white porcelain.[17] The two methods of consuming Chinese ceramics in Japan coexisted, however, and are exemplified by the finds at Ichijodani in Fukui Prefecture.[18] This was a residence of the Asakura *daimyo* who ruled Echizen from 1472 to 1573.[19] Quite a few of the Chinese ceramics excavated here date to the 13th and 14th centuries and were therefore antiques, but another group consists of large quantities of Ming blue and white, used in sets for entertaining.[20] Judging by the relatively low quality of these finds, which appear to be standard export ware types, their quality was not a hindrance to their appropriation as tableware for the Japanese elite. The location of this find, Fukui, is considered a regional site in Japanese archaeology, away from the court centres of Kyoto and Tokyo, for example, but some of this regional archaeology has proved to be of much interest for the study of Ming ceramics in Japan. For example, Okinawa has yielded quantities of excavated porcelain, unsurprisingly considering its location in the Ryukyu Islands, which played an important role in the Pacific-Asia trade route. Among the more significant finds in the history of Chinese ceramics in Japan are the 250 Yuan blue and white pieces recovered from a castle site at Katsuren.[21] Another trade centre, but associated more usually with the Ming period, was Sakai in Osaka Prefecture, where a large number of Ming ceramics have been found (including typical *Kraak* wares; see below for discussion). Further examples exist in Hokkaido and western Japan.[22] What these and other finds demonstrate is that the pattern of consumption of Ming ceramics in Japan changed in practical terms during the Ming period and also expanded to include trade items rather than just singular pieces. The greater consumption of Chinese ceramics at this time was of course made possible by the concurrent development of maritime trade.[23]

Several scholars have noted how ideas and approaches to Chinese objects in general, not just to ceramics, changed in this period developing from a broad *karamono suki* 唐物数奇 ('taste for Chinese goods') into a real passion for lavish display or *basara* 婆娑羅 which included Chinese objects, and Ming porcelain was part of this.[24] The fashion for Chinese things and their display at this time was governed by strictly defined cultural and official rules, such that Chinese ceramics were given new identities in Japan which were quite different from those in contemporary China.[25] For example, earlier individual Chinese ceramics became Japanese treasures associated with persons, such as the Song Jian ware (天目 *temmoku*) tea bowls [Fig. 2.1] which were owned by, and identified with, Japanese tea masters such as Rikyū (1522–91).[26] Similarly, Chinese ceramics produced in the Ming, especially blue and white, became part of the visual display involved in lavish entertaining practices in military-elite Japan associated with specific *daimyo* families, even though they were not of the same high quality or status as antique Song ceramics. In the death inventories of the military elite vast sets of Chinese ceramics have been noted.[27] Their appeal, therefore, was in their quantity (and probably their Chineseness), rather than their individual characteristics or associations. This reflects differences in consumer groups for the two types of Chinese ceramics, as well as different social practices.

The catalyst for greater consumption of Chinese ceramics in Japan was therefore new social customs. These latter in practice were not that different from those in China; ceramics were tablewares after all. In Japan, however, these customs needed Chinese goods to be put into effect, either because local versions were not available or perhaps because their Chinese/foreign origins were still part of their appeal. A demonstrative example is recorded in the death inventory of Shogun Ieyasu (1543–1616). Its section 10, on 'utensils for entertaining', lists a large number of Chinese porcelains as sets: 'blue and white teabowls, 1,000 in ten boxes or small blue and white dishes, 200 in two boxes'.[28] In some of the listings, the designs of the porcelains are noted, such as 'grass', 'tortoise shell', or *fuyo* 芙蓉 (Kraak style—see Fig. 2.16).[29] Interestingly, by the late Ming, it appears that Chinese porcelains were used in sets for dining and entertaining even at other levels of society. This can be seen in the sets of porcelains excavated at the site of a barracks for low-ranking samurai in Tokyo.[30] Most of these date to the late Ming period, when, interestingly, porcelain was being made in Japan at the same time. This suggests that Chinese porcelains still retained some value as imported or foreign goods. Ordinary tablewares have also been excavated from temple sites, such as the Hongoku-ji in Kyoto,[31] a further location of consumption of Chinese ceramics in Japan where both singular pieces and quantities of celadons and porcelains were acquired from the Song period onward.[32]

In addition to the mass quantities of generic export porcelains, it appears that some table wares were made specifically for Japanese dining practices. Confirmation of this can be seen in the late Ming porcelains decorated in styles which are interpreted as reflecting Japanese taste, as well as some forms which were not popular in China at that time but which were used in the meals which accompanied the tea ceremony practices of the time.[33] For example, a triangular mountain-shaped shallow dish can be seen in the Asian Art Museum San Francisco collection. It has blue and white decoration in a common late Ming style but its shape references both lacquer trays and ceramic versions made by Oribe (1544–1615).[34] It has been suggested that such pieces were specially commissioned by Japanese tea masters and thus embody Japanese, rather than Chinese, aesthetic preferences.[35] This gives another example of the ability of Jingdezhen factories to supply both special orders, either externally or internally, and to mass produce more standard wares for both markets as well.

It should be noted, however, that much of the Ming porcelain consumed in Japan in the late Ming period (and other Asian markets) did not come from Jingdezhen, but rather from kilns in Fujian which produced what is popularly known as 'Swatow' ware or Zhangzhou ware in China. This type of porcelain is noticeably different from that made at Jingdezhen, in both style and raw materials, representing a very different aesthetic. It too was primarily tableware but in relatively limited forms. Nonetheless, it appears to have been exported to Japan and markets in Southeast Asia in significant quantities.[36] This is further confirmation that the currently popular universalist interpretation of the consumption and impact of 'Chinese porcelain' outside of China is insufficient to explain the complex character of this phenomenon.

Korea

The consumption of Ming ceramics in Korea is less well documented than the consumption of earlier Chinese ceramics, and there is less evidence of it in Korea than in Japan at the same time. Nonetheless, a slightly different pattern of consumption of Ming ceramics can be seen in Korea, where the Choson court was much more closely allied to that of the Ming than was the Japanese equivalent, as Japan was merely a tributary trading partner (and later an adversary), rather than a vassal state.[37] The Choson court established relations with the Ming court officially in 1401, through investiture, which gave Korea a measure of autonomy and enabled trade through two-way tribute.[38] Culturally, as Heekyung Lee has noted, 'since these two states based their diplomatic relations on Confucian rites, they made much of the balance of etiquette between them', and this is reflected in the Ming ceramics used there.[39] This milieu for consumption was limited to the court, but there are official records of ceramic encounters as a result. For example, in 1428 and 1430, the Ming emperor Xuande (1426–35) presented blue and white ceramics to the Choson king.[40] These Ming porcelains were diplomatic gifts, a means of cultural contact between the courts of China and Korea. It is likely that they were retained as part of the Choson court collection, becoming from then on, examples of Korean court material culture, rather than Chinese.

At the same time however, there was not an extensive commercial trade system in place which would enable substantial supplies of Ming porcelain to enter Korea. In fact, very little evidence exists for the few pieces that did make their way over. It is stated that there was an unofficial trade between the two countries and that Korean ambassadors to China brought back Ming porcelains[41] but apparently China outlawed the sale of porcelains to foreign envoys in 1448.[42] The same source notes that Chinese blue and white nonetheless continued to circulate in Korea, among both aristocrats and 'commoners'.[43] It is entirely possible that after the Xuande period, porcelain was not considered to have an exchange value within the tributary system between the two countries. China wanted horses, ginseng and paper from Korea (as well as people and gold and silver), and Korea wanted dragon robes, silks, jade and books in return.[44] In either case, the situation is complicated by the fact that porcelain was being produced on a wider scale in Korea from the early 15th century onwards; thus the consumption of Ming ceramics is perhaps less significant in this country than in others. But this also parallels Korea's earlier consumption patterns of Chinese ceramics, particularly during the Song/Goryeo period.[45] From an early date, Korea was able to produce very high quality celadons and porcelains, with similar raw materials to those used in southern China, which likely prompted less extensive consumption of Chinese wares.[46] Japan, in contrast, was much more dependent on Chinese originals.

There is however evidence of design transfer from Ming ceramics to Korean ceramics. The blue and white style in general was made here from the 15th century onwards and not before but, somewhat contrary to the usual expectation, these early examples do not closely imitate actual Ming styles. Instead, an identifiable early Ming style of blue and white porcelain featuring rampant dragons and several border patterns typical of that period was adopted in Korean porcelain with underglaze blue decoration much later, in the 18th century. [Fig. 2.2] Not only does this indicate that early Ming porcelains were still extant in 18th-century Korea but also that the Ming style (or a particular Ming style) was deliberately recreated long after the Ming period ended, perhaps for referential or revivalist purposes.

West and South Asia: Iran, Ottoman Turkey and the Mughals

The pattern of design transfer seen in Korean blue and white, where earlier styles from a distant past came to be applied in later years, is interestingly enough, also seen in West Asia, particularly in Iran and Ottoman Turkey, where there is also evidence of the continued use of older, even antique, Chinese ceramics from the Ming period. Generally speaking, in West Asia, the consumption of Ming porcelain and its trade before the 17th century was more extensive than in East Asia, even though it was geographically and culturally more distant. Building on a long history of the consumption of Chinese ceramics, and blue and white in particular,[47] by the early Ming period, the trade routes and consumption patterns in this region were well established. Not unlike Japan, a tradition of the continued use of older Chinese ceramics existed; it appears that antique ceramics were used almost as often as contemporary ones. This is notable in two mostly extant official court collections or assemblages from Ottoman Turkey and Safavid Iran. In Turkey, particularly the Ottoman capital of Istanbul, Chinese porcelains were consumed in such quantity at the court that they formed a substantial assemblage in the kitchens of the Ottoman palace.[48] In Iran, if the evidence from visual images can be trusted, it is clear that Chinese ceramics were also used at court from at least the time of the Timurids (1409–47) onwards.[49] Chinese ceramics, therefore, were a notable part of both Ottoman and Iranian court material culture, a pattern of consumption which reached its peak in the first half of the 17th century.

The 17th century encompasses the later part of what is known as the Safavid dynasty (1501–1736) in Iranian history, a time when Ming porcelains formed a substantial part of what has become a famous 'collection' of Chinese ceramics, which was displayed in the treasury at the Shrine at Ardebil.[50] In this location, religious buildings associated with a Safavid ancestral shrine were refurbished in the early 17th century by Shah 'Abbas (r.1587–1629) to help establish his sovereignty. Among these was a room formerly called the 'Dome of the Princes', a domed building which was redesigned and converted into what was specifically called a *chinikhaneh* or 'china house' in the plans, for the purpose of housing some of the royal treasures belonging to the Safavid royal family.[51] This type of structure has a long history in Safavid and perhaps earlier Persian architecture, and it likely began as a room faced with ceramic tiles, rather than one which held actual vessels.[52] In the version created for Shah 'Abbas, the *chinikhaneh* at Ardebil features niches in the upper walls which held ceramics, while the lower walls would have been faced with ceramic tiles, thus reflecting both the long tradition of ceramic-decorated architecture and vessel display in Iran.[53] The structures at Ardebil were originally built as a tomb for Shaykh Safi (d. 1334), a Sunni saint, and thus the space was transformed from one which commemorated martyrs to one which venerated and presented objects, with the intention of publicly demonstrating the power and prestige of Shah 'Abbas, Shaykh Safi's Shiite descendant.[54] The renovations were completed in 1608 and the ceramics (mostly foreign) were installed with books in the same space. Both types of object represented 'expensive collections associated with royalty'[55] which were in turn presented as a gift to the shrine complex. As such, these objects were from previously formed collections and were a certain type of gift, that of an endowment or *waaf*.[56] They had previously been housed in the imperial treasury at the Isfahan palace where the ceramics had also been displayed in similarly designed niches built into an arch.[57] Like the shrine at Ardebil, the Isfahan palace had been rebuilt in the 1590s (a refurbishment of a pre-existing palace)[58] and this included the gatehouse where the ceramics were housed.

The ceramics that were later placed in the shrine at Ardebil sometime before 1607 were movable treasures associated with the court and probably had been shifted from yet other royal locations in earlier periods as they are, for the most part, not contemporary with the reign of Shah 'Abbas. Thus it is not possible to determine where they all came from or when they were acquired.[59] Most of the Chinese ceramics in the Ardebil Shrine[60] which survive today (about 800 out of an original 1100 or so in the 1607–8 gift) date from the Ming dynasty when there were substantial trade and diplomatic links between the two nations, but a significant number are from the Yuan dynasty, when there were close relations between the

Yuan and Ilkhanid courts (both ruled by relations of Qubilay Khan).[61] A few might be dated to the early 17th century, but in fact most of these Chinese ceramics were antique in 1607 and thus one has to question their significance as they were not newly acquired or recently encountered things. They are said to have influenced local ceramic traditions, and examples of Chinese-style blue and white wares were indeed made in 17th-century Iran[62] (see Fig. 2.13) but these same types of Chinese ceramics (or feasibly even some of the same exact ones) had clearly influenced local production during the earlier Timurid period.[63]

In Iran, therefore, as in the Ottoman Topkapi Palace, as we will see, Chinese ceramics were seen as important court objects, even though, and perhaps because, they were foreign. There are therefore a number of Ming (and Yuan)-period Chinese porcelains which are not associated culturally with China in general ceramic historiography today. They are studied as part of a wider tradition of 'Chinese' ceramics but their identity has become 'not Chinese', even though they were made in China. [Fig. 2.3] In these cases, Ming Chinese ceramics have become part of foreign material culture history for this region in a way which has not been considered before.[64] For example, the standard approach to material culture histories is to focus on the origins of the objects and to situate them within a continuous typology of the objects of that culture or nation. However, using methodologies from anthropology, we can also consider the 'life history' of these same objects and how their consumption/reception/appropriation in different cultures and time periods changes their identity.[65] In fact, such objects and the consequences of encounters with them can become part of the debate surrounding the notion of 'cultural hybridity'. For example, as the Ming ceramics in the collection of the Safavid Iranian court become part of that nation's material history, they can be viewed as having an impact on that culture (and its history) which is not that of a dominant culture on a passive one.[66] Traditionally, when examined through the lens of ceramic history alone, the Chinese ceramics in West Asia, specifically Iran and Turkey, have been presented as having a profound and lasting impact on local production, such that the impression given is that Chinese porcelain and the designs thereon, once seen, cannot be resisted.[67] However, there was clearly a desire, in these cultures, and in others, for actual Chinese-made ceramics as well as what might best be called 'imitations' made locally. That said, this is a model for understanding the position of Ming ceramics in some foreign cultures but not all, or at least not all the Chinese ceramics consumed by these cultures.

Where the above argument becomes more complex is in the area of intercultural diplomatic gifts or exchange. The significance of these Ming Chinese porcelains lies primarily with their 'Chineseness', but they obtain further value by being exceptionalised objects within a non-Chinese culture so that their presence in imperial holdings, whether as collected objects or table wares for daily or ceremonial use, increases their value by association with the highest social class in that society. Thus another little-studied area which is of interest in a global history of Ming ceramics is the exchange of these ceramics between royal courts, such as we have seen in principal form with Korea, for example. In some cases, however, it is not known whether such exchanges represent compulsory tribute (as likely happened with the porcelains bearing Qarachaghay's inscription in the Ardebil Shrine)[68] or a social transaction. But either way they constitute a specific form of exchange which is conceptually and practically separate from market transactions.[69] Another Safavid example is the large early 15th-century blue and white dish now in the Brooklyn Museum which features two significant inscriptions added later in its history: the *waaf* seal of Shah 'Abbas which can be seen on a number of the porcelains in the Ardebil Shrine and the engraved inscription 'Shah Jahan son of Jahangir Shah, 1053 (1643–44)'.[70] This is therefore an antique Chinese ceramic which had been possessed by Shah 'Abbas in Iran and then in some way given to the Mughal court in India around the same time, where presumably it was inscribed with a local identifier, a good example of what might be called secondary exchange.

The Mughals and their predecessors were significant consumers of Chinese porcelains from the Yuan and Ming periods, as is attested by literary references such as Ibn Battuta's observations and the archaeological finds in the remains of the Tughlaq Palace in Delhi, which was destroyed in 1398.[71] There were primary diplomatic exchanges between early Ming China and various parts of India which included porcelains,[72] and the literature of the early Mughals, such as the *Baburnama*, mentions Chinese porcelain in different contexts.[73] Indian miniature paintings depicting official events such as Akbar (1542–1605) receiving the Iranian ambassador also show what must be early Ming blue and white dishes being used at banquet tables.[74] [Fig. 2.4] These visual images are similar to those produced in Iran which also show Ming blue and white (or possibly even earlier examples) being used for official occasions during the 16th century—usually as table wares but also on display in niches, as noted above. As in Japan, banquets were a form of display for entertaining (and in that case demonstrations of power), and certain types of Ming porcelain were considered to be an important part of this practice in West Asia as well.[75] It is also interesting that the Ming porcelains depicted in these ceremonies are not contemporary, that is, of the mid-16th century to mid-17th century. Beyond the visual images, there is material evidence that early Ming ceramics were being re-identified in later periods in Mughal India, much as we have seen in Iran at the Ardebil Shrine. An early 15th century ewer with underglaze blue decoration has been published; this has an inscription assigning it to the household property of Shah Jahangir dated 1038 [1628].[76] This ewer could well have just entered that household in the early 17th century as a gift or purchase, but the inscription does not tell us whether this piece was destined for the kitchens or for a treasury, which is where the more valuable court objects were usually kept in Muslim courts at that time. Nonetheless, the inscription tells us that the piece had been given a new identity as a catalogued object in 17th-century India and further as an object possessed by that court. It is no longer a 'Chinese' object in the possessive sense but rather an Indian object of Chinese origin.

A similar re-identification of Chinese porcelains suggests that in Ottoman Turkey, as in other locations, the ceramics used here were presented and generally consumed in different ways at the same time. For example, thousands of Chinese ceramics, both porcelains and celadons, have been catalogued in the collections of the Topkapi Palace in Istanbul, which was built in the mid-15th century for the Ottoman sultans. Here Chinese ceramics of the Yuan to Qing periods were stored and used for a wide variety of purposes. These ceramics first appear in a register of 1495 in which five pieces were recorded.[77] The 'collection' (it is a museum collection today but was part of the palace holdings and not an 'art' collection during the Ottoman period) was continuously added to over a long period of time and was in use for dining, ritual and gift purposes. The method of acquisition is not precisely known, but it is assumed that many of the ceramics were acquired through normal trade channels and as booty, such as was recorded in a document dating from 1514 which gave an inventory of the booty taken by Selim I (r. 1512–20) in his campaign against the Safavid Shah Ismail of Persia. This lists sixty-two or sixty-four porcelains which are thought to have come from the Palace of Hesht Behesht in Tabriz.[78] This process was part of a system of confiscation known as *muhallefat* or 'inheritance'.[79] Locally, Chinese porcelains were also acquired through sequestration rules which required that property of statesmen who died or were removed from office would be given to the palace.[80] The names of previous owners whose objects were acquired in this way have been recorded in sequestration records along with the quantities of objects. According to a recent report, over 395 Chinese ceramics (porcelains and celadons) came into the palace in this way in the 16th century and over 3100 in the 17th century.[81]

Among the over ten thousand Chinese porcelains eventually amassed by the Ottomans, a number were from the Ming period. One would assume that these were acquired in the Ming but there are also Ming-dated pieces that have been reused later, as we will see in our discussion of some key individual pieces. Within the Ottoman court, the ceramics were also exchanged intra-culturally for both ceremonial and diplomatic purposes. For example, it is known that some Chinese porcelains were given as wedding gifts for the daughters of sultans and to state functionaries, in which case, interestingly, they were expected to be returned to the palace upon the death of the new owner.[82] The ceramics were also used in quantity at court festivities, such as the ritual circumcision of the son of Sultan Murad III in 1582.[83] Some of the Ming-period porcelains in this 'collection' have Arabic or Persian inscriptions and thus may represent special commissions or gifts. According to one source, the ambassador to the court of Selim I visited China, where he was given two porcelain bowls with Arabic inscriptions as an official gift from the Zhengde emperor (1506–21) to the Sultan.[84] There are in fact two bowls with Zhengde reign marks and Arabic inscriptions in the remaining collection in the Topkapi Palace,[85] but it is not possible to determine if these are the same ones. As we have seen in chapter one, porcelains with Arabic and Persian inscriptions were made for use at the Zhengde court and much has been said about this emperor's affinity for the Muslim religion.[86] But the possibility has now been raised of the use of these porcelains beyond the Zhengde court, for political diplomacy in West Asia, where such porcelains (or at least the inscriptions on them) would possibly have been better appreciated than in China.

Originally, most of the Chinese ceramics in the Topkapi Palace were stored in treasuries with precious metal objects, as was customary at courts across West Asia at this time. Some were removed and taken to the kitchens where, during the reign of Suleyman the Magnificent (1520–66), a special storeroom for porcelain used as tableware was built. Unfortunately much of this was destroyed by a kitchen fire in 1574.[87] For our purposes, it is further interesting to note that the individual ceramics were often treated differently, with some being left as is or repaired when broken, while others, about 273 of them, were altered physically and materially with the addition of metal mounts and jewelling.[88] The altering or material transformation of Chinese ceramics is something we will see in a number of foreign cultures, but it is the Ottomans who did this using the most precious materials, such as gold and gemstones. To give but one example, in the Topkapi collection is an early Ming white ewer which has been given an ornate domed lid, ornamented with rubies.[89] The mounts have been identified as the work of Serzergeran Mehmed (active 1588–1606), who was the chief court jeweller during the reign of Murad III (r. 1574–95).[90] Thus the ewer is early 15th century; the mounts are late 16th century and have been identified as an elaborate form of repair.[91] In this case, we have what constitutes further evidence of a wider practice at the Ottoman courts, particularly in the 16th century, of embellishing objects that were considered precious, such as those made of jade, rock crystal, and Chinese porcelain, as well as of the transformation of Chinese porcelain into an Ottoman object. We can see this more clearly on examples which have been more radically altered in style, and sometimes completely in form. For instance, among the most common jewelled Chinese porcelains in the Topkapi collection are small bowls, generally of the *kinrande* type or plain monochromes, whose sides have been completely embellished with inlaid precious and semi-precious stones. [Fig. 2.5][92] In these, the jewels have been set in mounts which are inlaid into shallow grooves in the surface of the porcelain, grooves which have been added by the jewellers. Thus not only is the visual impression of the object completely changed, from ordinary Ming style to Ottoman style, but also the actual material has been manipulated permanently. The objects have thus been damaged in one respect and then literally made more valuable, by the addition of gold and precious stones, in another.

The fact that these bowls and other mounted vessels were Chinese was clearly important for there are very few, if any, examples surviving of local ceramics with such mounts.[93] The appearance of these foreign objects clearly had to be altered for a particular purpose, which may have been an event or ritual that is no longer known. It may also have been for display purposes in conjunction with other similarly embellished objects in a manner analogous to the transformation of *naturalia* into *artificialia* in the European *Kunstkammer*.[94] While the form of these particular bowls has not been altered, in other examples this is indeed the case. One surviving piece which now functions as an incense burner was constructed of two such jewelled bowls placed mouth to mouth, a metalwork stem, and another Chinese porcelain dish to create an egg-shaped vessel joined to a base with a high foot.[95] In this example, the Chinese vessels have been used as construction materials for the creation of an entirely new object, a form of transformation that is seen with Qing porcelain in Europe. The style of the object is however consistent with other Ottoman jewelled objects of the late 16th–early 17th century so in this way it fits neatly within an established stylistic repertoire. The consistency is provided by the embellishments and by the form that has been created, which is similar to others made deliberately in metalwork. What is unusual is the construction of this object using Chinese porcelains. The bowls and dish which make up the new objects are of two types: *kinrande* and simple blue and white, of probably the mid-16th century. Other similar bowls have been left in their original form, so it seems with the incense burner that the porcelain was desirable as a material, and the original vessels themselves were not of interest on this occasion.

This incense burner is not unique in its transformative shape. Another 16th-century vessel, this time a blue and white squared vase or jar with a dragon design, has been turned upside down and given two spouts, transforming it into a type of water vessel known as a *matara* which was of the type carried by Ottoman sultans as a symbol of power.[96] What we have, therefore, is a varied attitude towards Chinese ceramics that reveals, on the one hand, a comfort with a type of object that was clearly readily available but also, crucially, imported, and on the other hand, a way of thinking about the value of these imported ceramics that is often ignored. This notion of transforming the visual and sometimes formative aspects of the objects, as well as their surfaces, suggests that the traditional approach to the study of the Topkapi Chinese ceramics is somewhat one-sided. Those multiple large dishes that are seen as having been so influential in design and indicative of the wide-reach of 'global exchange' in fact were probably not very important for the Ottoman court. They were just another type of goods—whether purchased or seized, acquired along with a wide range of expensive things. In this way, the Ottoman reception of Chinese ceramics, at least some of them, is quite different to that of the Safavids in Iran, in around the same time period. Yet both usually are lumped together as representing 'Islamic' collections.

Even more interestingly, the way these two different cultures appropriated Chinese ceramics (in every sense) is linked to the approach practiced in Europe but this connection has yet to be made, except to be noticed as a way in which individual objects moved around the world. The great model for this is the gift of Chinese porcelains presented to Lorenzo de' Medici (1449–92) by the sultan Qaitbay of Egypt in 1487.[97] This had been preceded by a gift of another exotic item, a giraffe, in 1486.[98] This previous gift had a specific purpose, and so did the porcelains because the Mamluks were attempting to persuade the Florentines to side with them against the Turks in an inter-Muslim conflict that had begun in 1467.[99] As rulers of the Florentine republic, the relationship between the Medicis and other princely courts was such that gifts of that nature were relatively common and constituted a form of power politics and diplomatic relations.[100] Chinese porcelain had a long history in Egypt, and this location was an important entrepôt for the trading of goods between East and West. The Mamluk sultans have been recorded as giving gifts to not only the Medicis in Florence but also a Doge of Venice in 1461.[101] As early as the 15th century, therefore, Chinese porcelain, if that is indeed what these references are to, was used as a diplomatic tool, one transferred inter-culturally from Egypt to Italian states, but was not an object made in Egypt. It is therefore a foreign product that represented Egypt in a particular way, in this case its wealth and ability to trade.

Europe: Princely Collections and Mounted Wares

What the Mamluk example represents is a further way of consuming and conceptualizing Ming ceramics which involves exchange but not in the sense which is usually discussed. We saw this form of intercultural exchange of foreign objects and goods in Safavid Iran and Mughal India, but it also occurred more widely in Europe and also often included Ming ceramics. Most examples are associated with the activities of various European courts so that, in addition to the evidence from mounted Chinese pieces, there are textual records of Chinese porcelains in European collections in the 15th and 16th century, including the inventories of Charles V of France which listed ten pieces of porcelain tableware.[102] One of the best known of these princely collections is that of the Medicis, including ten pieces acquired by Grand Duke Piero de' Medici (1416–69) and another fifty acquired by Lorenzo il Magnifico.[103] Beyond this family, as we have seen, it is known that porcelains were given as gifts to the Doges of Venice in 1461 and 1490.[104] In the 16th century, the 1553 inventories of the collections of Cosimo I (1519–74) recorded over 400 pieces of *porcellana*.[105] Apparently, in the year of 1547 alone Cosimo acquired over 120 pieces, mostly blue and white.[106] Cosimo's son, Francesco I (1541–87), was the family member associated with the 'invention' of so-called Medici porcelain, a form of technology transfer from China that is seen as a landmark in the history of European porcelain production. [Fig. 2.6] Medici porcelain, as it is called today, was the result of a project initiated by Cosimo I to manufacture porcelain (and fritware) in palace workshops which was completed during the tenure of Francesco I (r. 1574–87).[107] Visually, these experimental pieces resemble the material of Ming Chinese porcelain, but usually they were made with European shapes and designs. Technologically, they are also different and classified as 'soft paste' porcelains as they are made with lower-firing, non clay-based raw materials, unlike true Chinese porcelain. Incidentally, some of these Medici porcelains themselves were given as gifts to fellow European rulers; one example was made with the coat of arms of Philip II of Spain and given to the Bourbon King in 1582.[108] This suggests that the appreciation of Ming porcelain in Italy at least was primarily for its material, not its cultural origins.

For the purposes of the present study, it is another Medici whose role in the appropriation of Ming Chinese ceramics in Europe deserves further attention. Cardinale Ferdinando (1549–1609) has been described as 'the greatest collector of his time'.[109] In 1590, he gave fourteen pieces of Ming ceramics to Christian I of Saxony (1560–91).[110] His reign as elector was short, but he and his predecessors had established good relations with Italian princes and this was manifested by the exchange of luxury goods, artists and horses. The gift of fourteen ceramics was recorded in the register of gifts kept by the Medici court.[111] What is unusual is the nature of some of the ceramics included in the gift. It is typically assumed that the Ming porcelains (excluding celadons from this category) consumed at this time in Europe were all either blue and white or white porcelain with enamels, such as the *kinrande* types mentioned earlier. In the Medici gift, however, were porcelains with what is known as 'enamel on biscuit' decoration, in a colour palette known as *su sancai* 素三彩 in Chinese, with yellow, green and aubergine being the dominant colours. Their forms are also unusual in that one vessel is in the form of a phoenix and the other a crayfish.[112] There are apparently traces of old gilding on these vessels which would be consistent with 16th-century Chinese ceramics of this type. The crayfish-shaped vessel is a water dropper but it was apparently used as a pepper pot by the Medici, as it is listed as such in their inventory. At Dresden, it, along with the other Chinese vessels, was displayed in a *kunstkammer* and thus was not for daily use.[113] While these Ming porcelains may not be considered the finest examples today, in Italy, according to one source, during the late 15th century porcelain was considered a desirable gift, not because it was inherently valuable but because it was considered beautiful: 'There are some that prefer the tiniest little vase of that material which they call porcelain to vases of silver and of gold even though the latter are of higher cost. It does happen occasionally that the excellence of the gift is not judged so much by its cost, as by its beauty, its rarity and its elegance.'[114] This might explain why imitation porcelain would also have been considered appropriate for gifts in the following century.

Nonetheless, in addition to these zoomorphic vessels, the Medici gift to Saxony also included *kinrande* wares and blue and white. Among the blue and white pieces is a cup with a scene featuring a sailing ship.[115] This, like the *kinrande* bowls, appears to be Jiajing period (1522–66), which would be within the appropriate date range for the gift. What we do not have in this gift, or indeed in the collections formed at this time in Italy and Saxony, is any evidence of specially-commissioned Chinese ceramics. This is likely a direct result of the trade conditions of that time and the limited access these provided to China itself. Up to now, we have only seen the results of second-hand trade or exchange of Chinese ceramics. But other Europeans would later develop a direct relationship with China that would have an impact on the consumption of Chinese ceramics outside China in the Ming period. The pioneers of this were of course the Portuguese who reached Asia in the early 16th century.[116] The history of their trade activities in Asia is well recorded and studied, but their role in the appropriation of Ming ceramics has drawn less attention, except from the perspective of the identification of individual pieces. Generally speaking, once a Portuguese base was established in Macao in 1557, they were primary agents in the movement of Ming ceramics westward, to Europe, the Middle East and the Americas, a situation that will be discussed in the following section.

Apart from Italy, the pattern of consumption of Ming ceramics in Europe and England is somewhat less well defined than the quite precise methods of consumption which can be viewed in selected areas of West Asia. Europeans, for example, had several different attitudes towards Chinese ceramics and consequently a number of different methods of consumption and encounters.[117] However, the later Ming period was the time in which direct trade between Europe and China was established, and ceramics then became a very useful product which could be both ballast and a trade item. In terms of classification, the Ming porcelains that reached Europe during the Ming period itself were of three general types: singular pieces that were displayed (e.g. mounted porcelains), specially commissioned wares (e.g. with Portuguese arms) and large quantities of standardised mass-produced wares (such as what is known as 'Kraak', which will be discussed below). The trajectory of the first type is difficult to trace but a number of pieces survive which have European mounts that are dated. The example with the earliest mounts is that which is known as the Katzenelnbogen bowl, which is in the Landesmuseum, Kassel, Germany. This bowl is, by domestic Chinese standards, a rather ordinary Longquan celadon bowl with local silver-gilt mounts featuring the arms of Count Philip of Katzenelnbogen, which were in use until 1453.[118] The mounts have transformed the simple bowl shape into a lidded, high-footed chalice, a form which was much more understandable in 15th-century Europe. Among surviving mounted Chinese

Ming ceramics, this one is unusual because it appears to have arrived much earlier than other examples and it is also a celadon (stoneware, not porcelain).

Much more common are the examples from the 16th century which are usually of Jingdezhen porcelain and either blue and white or decorated with enamels and gold in the *kinrande* style. *Kinrande* wares are given this Japanese name meaning 'gold brocade' because their decoration resembles textiles, and they were in fact quite popular in Japan. In Europe, six have been recorded as being in the collections of Schloss Ambras, Austria in 1596[119] and these too would have had a place in the fashionable *kunstkammern* or 'cabinets of curiosity'.[120] In the Victoria and Albert (V&A) Museum is another example with German mounts, this time dating to c. 1583, which is known as the 'Manderscheidt cup' because according to the inscription on the base of the mount of its pair, it was previously owned by Count Eberhart von Manderscheidt, who bought it in Turkey in 1583 and had it mounted in honour of his brother.[121] This piece has also been reshaped through its mounts, transforming it into a European object, similarly to the porcelains physically modified by the Ottoman jewellers. [Fig. 2.7] The bowl that was mounted would have been made in China during the Jiajing period when the *kinrande* style was first developed.

A plainer bowl with an earlier-dated mount is in the Percival David Collection and is known, once again after its collector, as 'the Lennard cup'. [Fig. 2.8] The Lennard cup has English mounts of 1569–70; it is a white bowl with incised and some blue and white decoration inside, rather than an enamelled and gilt bowl like the previous examples discussed. It belonged to Samuel Lennard who was Lord of the Manor at Wickham Court in Kent during the mid-16th century.[122] That someone who was not a member of the court was in possession of a mounted Chinese bowl demonstrates that by this time, mounted Chinese porcelain was still rare but available for those who could afford it. The porcelain itself was a material not then available in Europe so its materiality was exotic; it was also associated geographically with Asia; and it was literally made more valuable by adding precious metal to it. This transformed its shape but also crucially, like the jewelled Ottoman vessels, its material nature. It could be argued that this type of Ming porcelain is therefore yet another example of the disputed notion of 'hybrid culture', which will be discussed in detail below. The mounting and refashioning of Chinese porcelains continued in Europe after the end of the Ming period and became especially sophisticated in 18th-century France through the intercession of dealers in luxury objects and furniture, the *marchands mercier*.[123]

Armorials and Special Commissions

Portugal

In the collection of the V&A there is an additional mounted 16th century ewer which represents the second type of Ming porcelain consumed in Europe before the 18th century. In addition to the mounts, it features a Portuguese armorial, perhaps that of the Peixoto family.[124] [Fig. 2.9] This piece has Persian silver mounts rather than European, which demonstrates that mounted wares also circulated secondarily. The mounts used here have not changed the overall shape of the vessel apart from extending the spout and providing a lid in a shape that would not have been used in China. However, the ewer is very interesting in several respects because with its painted armorial, it was obviously a specially-commissioned object for a consumer in Portugal (or a Portuguese overseas). It also features a Jiajing reign mark and is of the period. It therefore belies the conventional view that such porcelains were always 'imperial' and not 'export'. It further has foreign-sourced mounts which were added during its journey to Europe.

This combination of attributes has led the V&A to include it in a catalogue of 'Masterpieces of World Ceramics'.[125] According to Maria Antonia Pinto de Matos, Peixoto was a navigator and merchant who reached Canton in 1542 where he was refused entry. He then went on to be one of the first Portuguese to reach Japan.[126] He thus had the appropriate background for acquiring, and clearly commissioning, such an unusual 'Chinese' object. This background also raises questions about the object's primary identity as it was made in China but for a foreign consumer. Should we perhaps consider the role that the destination for an object or its intended consumer plays in determining its identity? In traditional object study methodologies, it is normally an object's origins which for the most part determine its primary identity, particularly in the art market. The few exceptions are those objects which are associated with a named owner (whether a person, nation or institution), such as the Lennard cup mentioned earlier. However, the object biography approach[127] allows for changing identities over time, with identities determined by a number of factors, not just origins: changing ownership over time; different locations in its 'life history'; and changes in the value systems in which the object circulated as posited by Clifford.[128] The Peixoto ewer could be as much 'Portuguese' or 'Persian' as it is 'Chinese'. To further complicate the discussion of the Peixoto vessel, its shape is also interesting because it is not one that would have been known in Europe, being much more of a standard Middle Eastern form. So is this really a 'Chinese' porcelain object or something else altogether?

A closely related piece in the Metropolitan Museum of Art, New York, may help to clarify this issue. It also features Portuguese arms, as yet unidentified, but they have been applied upside down, presumably unintentionally. [Fig. 2.10][129] The form is unusual and described as 'Islamic',[130] as is the ewer above. More interesting is the reign mark on the base, which is an apocryphal one of the Xuande period, as the vessel seems to date to a century later. As we have seen in chapter one, such apocryphal reign marks appeared occasionally on ceramics with an archaistic style in the Ming, but one would not expect to see them on specially-commissioned porcelain for a European consumer. In this case, therefore, and perhaps in others, the reign mark can be seen as both a dating and a trademark tool in the sense that it was essentially a standard brand that was available to some of the potters or workshops at the time of manufacture, and clearly not as restricted as is normally assumed. Perhaps the broker for this transaction felt that the mark would make the piece appear more valuable, as it would likely have to a Chinese consumer in the Ming, or more 'Chinese', which may also have enhanced its value to foreign consumers.

In addition to these commissioned pieces, it was in the 16th and 17th centuries that large quantities of Ming porcelain began to arrive in Europe and to be used as tableware,[131] as well as for display and diplomatic gifts. These represent the third type of Ming porcelain consumed in Europe before the 18th century, and they began to be traded to Europe from the mid-16th century onward. But as standardized, high-volume products, much less is known about their consumption, as opposed to their transportation, as most have been found in shipwreck sites. At this time in Europe, therefore, Ming porcelain could be encountered and experienced both as singular objects and things used in quantity.

But quantity and wider availability did not result in fewer commissions. These singular pieces can also be much more informative than those consumed *en masse*, which are more difficult to associate with individual consumers. Among the singular examples, the most important pieces are perhaps those with armorials as these are direct evidence that Europeans (and probably Ottomans) were specially commissioning porcelains in China during the Ming period.[132] As we have seen, in Europe, the Portuguese were the first to engage in this activity, and were the first to make direct contact with China and Chinese merchants, so their role is not surprising. Textual references attest to this, however, as well as surviving pieces. Examples of these include those mentioned above, which were both mounted and unmounted and made for merchant families (e.g. Peixoto).

Two more surviving commissioned pieces are worth mentioning as one has a date written in European numbers and the other is decorated with Renaissance 'grotesque' mask motifs.[133] The first is now in the Walters Art Museum collection in Baltimore, thus attesting to the continuous history of Ming ceramics in the USA (discussed in chapter four) and was acquired in 1911 [Fig. 2.11].[134] It is a simple bottle of *yuhuchun* form (pear-shaped) with blue and white decoration of Buddhist lions with brocade balls, plantain leaves and hanging jewels, all very typical of the mid-16th century in China. However, further to this is an inscription written upside down which reads: 'Jorge Alvrz n egeo nam dou—a era de 1552 reina' (Jorge Alvares ordered this to be made in the year 1552 of the reign [of King Joao III]).[135] On the base of this vessel is an inscription in Chinese, a typical blessing that appears on such wares in this period: *wan fu you tong* 万福优同 ('May infinite good fortune surround you').[136] This inscription, like some reign marks in the 16th century, may have been a stock pattern that could be applied by potters to any vessel not made specifically for the court, and probably therefore should not be considered a distinguishing 'mark', unless it can be associated with a single workshop, for example.

The piece in the Walters collection is primarily of interest because unusually it is dated by inscription. Its presumed first owner was a Portuguese ship captain like Peixoto. In addition, its style is, apart from the inscription, typical of its period in China. It therefore represents both Chinese style and European taste in one piece. This is also true of another piece of specially-commissioned porcelain that survives, the bowl mentioned above that is decorated with Renaissance 'grotesques' and is now in Stuttgart.[137] This motif was fashionable in 16th-century Italian art and was ultimately derived from Roman wall painting.[138] Its use on this Chinese-made bowl provides unexpected evidence for the spread of this motif in Europe in that century. Here, however, it is further combined with a Jiajing reign mark and is thus what might be considered a hybrid piece like the others. In each of these we can see a precursor of the 'oriental' style that developed in 18th-century Europe with *chinoiserie*, where a European idea of Chinese style was invented and imposed, sometimes on items made in China (for example, the 'willow pattern' invented by Spode).

However, there are other similarly 'hybrid' pieces which combine design elements from two cultures but which are specific to a particular consumer, for example, a *kraak*-style dish in the British Museum with typical *kraak*-style decoration around the sides but with the arms of Don Joao de Almeida in the centre.[139] Almeida was another Portuguese captain who settled in Macao around 1570, and there are only two other surviving dishes with the same coat of arms.[140] Even more unusual but in keeping with the apparent fashion for imposing European motifs on Chinese porcelains is a large bowl with a hydra and a Latin motto, also within a *kraak*-style blue and white background.[141] [Fig. 2.12] This piece has been dated c.1600–1620 and is said to have been made for a Portuguese consumer because of its similarity to a piece in the Santos Palace (discussed below). However, an identical bowl appears in a Dutch painting by W. C. Heda dated 1638[142] and there is a Persian fritware copy in the V&A[143] [Fig. 2.13] which suggests that the so-called hybrid pieces may have circulated more widely than is usually assumed. The copy made in Iran further suggests that the design authenticity of foreign ceramics was not always a consideration for consumption or copying. This piece was copied from a Chinese-made object but not one with a purely Chinese design, which reminds us that it was for the most part a separate tradition of 'Chinese ceramics' that circulated beyond China, a tradition which most Chinese would not have been familiar with in the Ming and Qing periods.

In addition to the porcelains commissioned by Portuguese merchants, there are also several surviving pieces that were made for the court, some of which have the royal Portuguese arms and the personal armillary sphere of King Manuel I (r.1495–1521), for example.[144] One of these pieces, a ewer, also has a reign mark, this time of the Zhengde period. Manuel's engagement with Chinese porcelain is attested to by several surviving textual records, including letters both from him and to him from other royal rulers and his representatives in India and Malacca.[145] Additionally, like other European royals and states, the Portuguese court also used Chinese porcelain as diplomatic gifts, such as a documented gift in 1505 of blue and white from the Queen of Portugal to her counterpart in Spain.[146] Other strategic gifts include three given to the Church by Manuel, which are also documented.[147] This might explain why one surviving piece features the armillary sphere of Manuel I and an Ave Maria inscription, a bowl which has been dated to the Jiajing period.[148] Thus there is also a Christian reference on some of these early armorial pieces which further reflects their alternative origins as 'Portuguese' pieces.

Spain

The Spanish were also consumers of commissioned porcelains from China in the Ming period and were of course instrumental in establishing Manila and the so-called Manila galleon trade in the Pacific at the end of the 16th century.[149] Unlike in Portugal, however, very little Ming porcelain has been found in Spain itself, in spite of evidence for the existence of court collections. In Portugal, for example, we have clear evidence of widespread use of Chinese porcelain both by the court and in society in general. There is the famous 'collection' of 261 16th- to 17th-century blue and white dishes which were mounted on the ceiling of a room in the Santos Palace. Moreover, there are records which attest to the fact that in 1580 there were six shops selling porcelain in Lisbon.[150] The Santos Palace is another location often associated with 'export' porcelain from China because the porcelains date from the mid-16th to the early 17th century, perhaps no later than 1613, when the Lancastre family then resident in the palace moved to Madrid. It has been suggested that the porcelains had been collected by Manuel I and his successors, who resided in the palace from 1501 to 1589, which is possible but not confirmed.[151]

In Spain, a large court collection is noted in the inventory of Philip II's (r. 1554–98) goods after his death in 1598 which is said to record over 3,000 Chinese porcelains.[152] He was of course also King of Portugal (and its overseas territories as well as a number of European countries) after the two countries were 'annexed' in 1581. Unlike the pieces with specific Portuguese armorials, quite a few with a generic Spanish crest survive, including one in the British Museum. [Fig. 2.14] While these have been, for the most part, dismissed as unimportant because of their ubiquity, in fact their style is quite interesting, combining as it does both European and Chinese motifs separately and together in new motif constructions. The Portuguese-identified pieces with combined motifs have designs which kept the motifs separate. In contrast, on one side of these 'Spanish' vessels is a traditional Chinese narrative scene of a scholar in a landscape with a servant and on the other a European coat of arms surrounded by curious tulip-like flowers painted in a Chinese style as well as a strapwork roundel. These vessels, popularly known as 'pilgrim flasks', all date to the Wanli period (1573–1619) and were clearly part of a large batch of vessels commissioned for use in Spain/Portugal or its territories. More ordinary (i.e. not commissioned) Ming porcelains were also in limited use in Spain, as literary references suggest. According to one scholar, three writers of the 16th and 17th centuries made reference to Chinese porcelain and its placement on the sideboard, where normally precious metal vessels were displayed.[153] A small number of individual sherds of late Ming porcelains have been found in several locations in Spain; these relate closely to examples found in Spanish shipwrecks, such as that of the *San Diego* which sank in December 1600.[154] Compared to Portugal, however, it appears that Ming porcelains were not as popular in Spain, perhaps because Chinese silk was so much in favour.

Another interesting group of Chinese porcelains associated with Spanish markets survives and includes a blue and white *guan* jar with the Habsburg emblem of the double eagle.[155] According to several sources, the use of this emblem was granted to the Augustinians of Manila in or after 1575 by Philip II following the supposed discovery in Cébu of what was thought to be a miraculous image. Thus, this piece, which in earlier publications was said to represent Spanish royal consumption or commissioning of Ming porcelain, is now also interpreted as an instance of commissioning by a Spanish religious order in the Philippines.[156] During the Wanli period of Ming China, religious orders in China and abroad were significant consumers of porcelain (see chapter one for domestic examples), and this is why it is possible to see Buddhist, Daoist and Christian imagery on a number of late Ming examples. The Jesuits, of course, were part of this, and several pieces of specially-commissioned ceramics for this order survive, including a blue and white jar in the Gonçalves collection, Museum of Anastácio Gonçalves, Lisbon.[157] This jar features the arms of the Society of Jesus (two guardian angels holding an oval shield with the IHS monogram)[158] as well as the initials of St. Paul in further decorative medallions. This jar and a similar one in London have been associated with St. Paul's college in Macao, which was built in 1594 and the remains of which can be seen in the ornate façade in old Macao.[159] Whether these attributions are correct, these jars are also of interest from a design perspective because of their combination of both Chinese and European patterns beyond the religious emblems. For example, there are stylised floral sprays which have been related to similar examples in European embroideries of the early 17th century.[160]

Once again, we have what appears to be a hybrid style in which both Chinese and European designs have been combined to create an object which to the contemporary eye may yet have looked 'foreign' because the use of motifs from different sources visually emphasized the differences between the two cultures. The commission instructions do not survive, but it is clear that a completely 'European'-style object was not desired. These religious-commissioned objects were for overseas residents in Asia; however, as we have seen, the porcelains which appear to have been commissioned for use in Europe also demonstrate the use of combined Chinese-European stylistic elements. These all could be described as 'hybrid' but the word should be used with caution as this concept is much debated due to its political and pejorative associations. According to Leibsohn and Dean, the notion of hybridity is dependent upon the recognition of difference—a form of discrimination, of us v. them,[161] not a perception that relates to these porcelains. They may not be 'hybrids' as such but rather 'combined styles' that serve to create something new altogether, as in the concept of transculturation.[162]

New Spain and Holland

The Spanish role in the distribution of Chinese porcelain globally is better documented than their own consumption of Ming porcelain. After establishing 'New Spain' in Mexico and trade from Manila across the Pacific in the 1570s, the Spanish became important agents in the triangular Asia trade that was fuelled by silver.[163] Ming porcelain was a by-product of this trade, not a focus of it. Unlike silver, the patterns of consumption for Ming porcelain were those of objects as well as commodities, and therefore revealing of cultural habits as well as the consequences of cultural contact. Europeans were therefore distributors of an aspect of Ming culture throughout the world in the period concerned (sometimes referred to in European terms as 'early modern'), just as they were with silver.[164] The difference, of course, is that porcelain was consumed in vessel form, could be personalized, and was not inherently valuable, as silver was. These personalized items, whether transformed at source, in China, or at 'home' with metal mounts, created a new visual language based on a contemporaneous Chinese visual culture; thus an aspect of Ming China not known in China was being experienced around the world during the Ming period itself. Therefore different but concurrent conceptions of 'Ming' or at least 'Chinese' goods existed at that time because they were consumed and encountered in so many different ways.

As a result of Spain's presence in the Americas, for example, Ming porcelain for that market reflects a combination of several of the consumption and design transfer patterns discussed above but also new, localized ones. Among the earliest records of a so-called Manila galleon, which participated in the Asia-Pacific trade route established by Spain, is that of the *Santiago* registered in 1572 in Manila that listed a range of materials required for the voyage as well as 400 pieces of porcelain which belonged to the merchant Julian de Arbolancha.[165] Not surprisingly, therefore, Chinese porcelains dating from this period have been found in sites in Mexico and Peru, the latter as a result of inter-colonial trade.[166] It appears, that like many Europeans, South Americans (or Spanish consumers resident there) also favoured *kinrande* wares and blue and white. Such porcelains were used at most levels of society, with the wealthy also displaying Ming wares on shelves and sideboards.[167] Chinese porcelain vessels were further used in localised drinking habits; chocolate, which had originally been drunk from coconut shells, could now be drunk from more hygienic porcelain. Ming porcelain has been shown to have impacted life in Mexico through the development of a new style of local ceramics (Puebla pottery), which itself was based on borrowed *majolica* technology from Spain.[168] Chinese porcelain was also used for what may be a unique purpose: as coinage. Shattered porcelain shards which had accumulated on ships were apparently used as money for daily transactions. This coinage even had a name, *chinitas*, a common currency used alongside the Mexican *peso*.[169]

Much of this activity took place during what was the later Ming period. With reference to the consumption of Ming porcelain outside China, especially Europe, it might be argued that the period of greatest encounters and consumption, at least with respect to quantities was the first half of the 17th century. This is certainly apparent if one focuses on the activities of the VOC or Dutch East India Company, which left behind copious records of shipments and trade activities[170] that enable quantification. However such numbers must be treated with caution as they do not reveal the complete picture.[171] The VOC trade is well studied and does not need repeating here. What has been less well treated is the consumption of Chinese porcelain in the Netherlands during this time, particularly before 1650. Chinese porcelains appear to have been used and conceptualised differently in the Netherlands than in other European locations, and this has much to do with the nature of Dutch society at the time.

In discussions of Chinese porcelain and the Dutch, the story usually begins in the early 17th century, when the Netherlands suddenly became a society awash with consumer goods from around the world.[172] Chinese porcelain, particularly blue and white, became very popular in the Netherlands and the Dutch became major importers of this material.[173] However, there are instances of earlier consumption which parallel those of other societies of the 16th century we have already discussed, including outside Europe. For example, the German painter Albrecht Durer (1471–1528) was resident in Antwerp during the 1520s, and he notes in his diaries that during that time he was given four pieces of porcelain from local government officials.[174] These later appear to have entered the collection of Durer's friend Willibald Pirckheimer (1470–1530) as they are listed in an inventory of Pirckheimer's great nephew Willibald Imhoff's art collection of 1573/74, along with a number of other gifts Durer had received.[175] It is further possible that Durer owned Chinese porcelains even before the 1520s as a drawing in the British Museum of 1515–18 attests. [Fig. 2.15] The drawing features fanciful emblematic designs for columns which are made up of various objects including blue and white porcelain (and a peasant man, among other things).[176] A surviving Dutch religious painting of the same date (1517) also appears to feature a Ming blue and white ewer or bottle in which have been placed white lilies in the foreground of an annunciation scene.[177]

By the late 16th century, even before the founding of the VOC, Chinese porcelain appeared in religious Dutch painting, in for example Pieter Isaacsz's (1569–1625) 'The Corporalship of Captain G. Jasz. Valckenier and Lieutenant P. Jacobsz Bas', 1599.[178] This dates to just three years after the first literary reference to Chinese porcelain in Dutch in Jan Huygen van Linschoten's *Itinerario* of 1596. This recounts his visit to India while employed by the Portuguese and mentions that while in Goa he saw Chinese porcelain for sale in the markets.[179] Thus the Netherlands can be seen as entering the field of Ming ceramic collecting and consumption relatively late, but Chinese porcelain was incorporated into local visual culture seemingly very soon after first encounters. By the 1620s, consumption of Chinese porcelain was much greater than might be expected, especially in comparison to other European nations at the time. The evidence for this is firstly the sales of ship plunder acquired by the Dutch sinking of Portuguese ships laden with Asian goods, including porcelain. The contents of two such ships, the *San Iago* and the *Santa Catarina*, were auctioned off in 1603 and 1604 respectively.[180] Also notable are the contents of the Dutch *Witte Leeuw*, which sank off the coast of St Helena in 1613, and the more frequent appearance soon after of Ming blue and white in other genres of painting: interiors and still lifes.

The *Witte Leeuw* or White Lion is considered a benchmark in the study of Chinese export porcelain history primarily because its sinking can be precisely dated and because the ceramic cargo was all of the so-called *kraak* type. *Kraak* was quite popular with overseas consumers in Europe (as well as most of Asia) as the large numbers imported by the Dutch attest.[181] The *Witte Leeuw* was a VOC ship and had picked up much of its cargo, including the ceramics, at Bantam (Java), which within a few years would be a VOC headquarters in Asia.[182] The ceramics were not the most valuable cargo and in fact did not appear in the ship's manifest[183] but spices and diamonds did. Instead, the ceramics were found under the ship's hull and in style are consistent with the early 17th century. While they were not the primary purpose for trade in Asia, for the Dutch, late Ming ceramics were a sufficiently important part of it that from the early 17th century, they began to specially order porcelains in significant quantities, seemingly much more than the Portuguese in the 16th century; these were supplied along with bulk ceramics in generic styles. Orders from 1608 (which may not have been supplied) requested European forms for ceramics[184] and a confirmed order which required provision of models for such ceramics is dated 1635.[185] No models survive but certainly new forms began to appear which can be attributed to such activity. One such example is the '*klapmuts*' or deep bowl with a flattened rim. [Fig. 2.16] This form is not Chinese; it has been given a Dutch name but its origins could also be Portuguese. It is thus a new shape and one that appears extensively in VOC records, as well as occasionally in Dutch paintings, with the earliest example dated to 1601,[186] the same year that the VOC was founded, so commissions must have been supplied before that date. What is interesting is that this approach to commissions, requiring production in European forms, represents a new attitude towards Ming ceramics (which were probably not seen specifically as such). Moreover, some of the new forms requested apparently were not originally ceramic[187] so that we have outside of China the first systematic attempt to shape the large-scale manufacture of a foreign product for commercial purposes. We have seen this type of activity earlier, such as the specially-commissioned pieces for Portuguese consumers, but these were for private customers and do not appear to have been ordered speculatively. The VOC, however, was getting involved in design and production on a large scale, and fortunately the records they kept of this have survived. From these we can see that forms 'in the Chinese manner' were requested in orders from 1635 and 1637,[188] thus in addition to Dutch forms. Depending on which source you credit, a number of examples of these types of Chinese porcelains with Dutch forms survive, including the *klapmuts* (as well as an unusual hybrid Chinese/Dutch shape in the Rijksmuseum),[189] but the use at this time of Western designs on such wares for the Dutch market is not recorded in the VOC records. On surviving pieces, however, there are examples with hybrid designs consisting of tulip motifs and European-style houses combined with Chinese figures in landscapes.[190] Nevertheless, the widespread use of Western motifs on porcelains for the Dutch market did not become common practice until after the 1690s.[191]

What the Dutch managed to do, in a short period of time, was to create a new Chinese product by approaching the appropriation of Chinese ceramics from a commercial perspective. This is very much in keeping with the wider changes in Dutch society during the same time period when national wealth increased dramatically and with it the supply and availability of commercial goods from all over the world.[192] With this, not surprisingly, came conflicted attitudes towards wealth, consumption and luxury goods. As Norman Bryson has noted, we can see the reflection of this in Dutch still life paintings of the period.[193] For our purposes, it is interesting to examine the role of Chinese porcelain within this, as it became associated with the kind of material possessions depicted in the sometimes moralistic themes of paintings. Once again, we can see how ceramics considered ordinary by Ming Chinese standards could be appreciated entirely differently in another country at the same time because of their 'Chineseness' (which may have just been seen as broadly 'oriental'); their material, which as we have seen was not yet being made in Europe; and because of the distance they had travelled to the Dutch consumer, representing physical evidence of global trade and the success of the VOC within this. They are, in this sense, souvenirs which enabled the owner to have physical as well as visual contact with Asia.

In the many extant Dutch still life paintings, Chinese porcelains are depicted with other highly valuable items, from fruits (a luxury),[194] to glassware, carpets and *kunstkammer* items such as mounted nautilus shells. Along with fruits, Chinese bowls and dishes appear relatively early in these paintings, suggesting what might have been considered a proper use for such vessels at the time. This can be seen for example in a painting of 1617 by Floris van Schooten (1590–1655) which shows fruits piled high in seven such dishes on a table.[195] Chinese porcelains also appear in paintings of flowers, shown in abundance. Very often in these paintings of both types, the porcelains appear as tablewares, without mounts. A few of these paintings depict Chinese porcelains with mounts, including one of the most famous which is by Willem Kalf (1619–93) and which shows both a ewer of the 'magic fountain' type[196] and a large dish, both with ornate mounts. [Fig. 2.17] The style of porcelain in these paintings is usually *kraak*, for that is what was widely available (if not cheap). Thus they were for most part contemporary, and not antiques (except the mounted examples), and they include some with western designs, such as the bowl in W. C. Heda's painting of 1638 which is very similar to that with the hydra design, both mentioned earlier. This is an unusually distinctive piece to depict in a Dutch still life, and it is given prominence in the composition. If these paintings, and the earlier religious ones, can be seen as documentary, then it is clear that there was a complex and varied appreciation and consumption of Ming porcelain in the Netherlands, somewhat more varied than in southern Europe at this time, and perhaps linked with trade.

The use of Chinese ceramics as props in paintings is not new in the Netherlands of the early 17th century, but the way they are used is quite different to how they appear in other European paintings of an earlier date. For example, in Italian paintings of the 15th and 16th centuries, Chinese porcelains usually appear as vessels in a religious scene, whether as the singular items seen in Francesco Benaglio's (1432–c.1492) 'Madonna and Child' of 1460–70 (National Gallery, Washington, D.C.) or Mantegna's (c.1431–1506) 'Adoration of the Magi' of the very late 15th century (Getty Museum, Los Angeles), or as multiple vessels in a religious banquet scene, as in Bellini's (c.1430–1516) famous 'Feast of the Gods' of 1514 (National Gallery, Washington, D.C.). In the latter painting, the vessels are blue and white basins which appear to be of early Ming date and so might be antiques. Bellini of course was working in Venice and was responsible for the paintings in the ducal palace, so he might easily have seen or known about the pieces given to the Doges.

Beyond the typically generic contemporary ceramics depicted in still life paintings, there is evidence of some Dutch commissions of more unusual porcelains at around the same time. For example, in the British Museum is a square bottle with underglaze blue decoration of the crucifixion and of *putti* in clouds.[197] These are combined with Chinese border patterns, and the bottle shape is very similar to Dutch glass and stoneware bottles.[198] With its European shape and designs, combined with Chinese motifs and the Christian imagery, this piece is more closely related to those, discussed earlier, which were commissioned by religious orders or institutions; the VOC was perhaps just one avenue for the acquisition of very late Ming porcelain in Holland therefore Accordingly, the function of the Chinese porcelain in the early 17th century also varied. For example, the Dutch were also using Chinese porcelain for diplomatic gifts in the 17th century, including to France (Henry IV) and Russia.[199]

England and Display

Generally speaking, after the 16th century, Chinese porcelains were more abundant in Europe, but they appear less frequently in both southern European and Dutch religious/mythological paintings, although they are prominent in still life paintings. Evidence from visual culture thus suggests that after commercial trade in porcelains became possible and exposure increased, attitudes towards the material changed quite dramatically in Europe and Britain. This especially can be seen with the consumption and conceptualisation of Chinese porcelain in England at that time. The English East India Company had been founded two years before the VOC, and it too began to engage in the shipping of porcelain (as a minor cargo) from China through indirect, then later direct, routes.[200] Initially, however, the commercial porcelains were purchased in Amsterdam from shipwreck sales[201] even though the English had a longer history of using Chinese porcelain than the Dutch. We have seen, for example, that Ming Chinese porcelains were acquired in England by the 1560s when Samuel Lennard owned his eponymous mounted cup (see above and Fig. 2.8). There are earlier recorded references to Chinese ceramics in England, one to a celadon which is known as the 'Wareham bowl' in an inventory of c.1532 for New College Oxford and one to other (possibly celadon) Chinese ceramics in the inventory of Henry VIII's Jewel House of 1550.[202] However in the English language at this time, the terminology for porcelain was fluid so references to 'purslane', as the pieces were described in the Jewel House inventory, could be to another material altogether.[203] By the second half of the 16th century, however, mounted porcelains were gaining in popularity, just as in the rest of Europe. A number of early examples survive in addition to the Lennard cup, such as the blue and white ewer in the V&A with English mounts dated 1585–86[204] and several *kinrande* bowls with silver gilt mounts.[205] These porcelains were destined for collecting and display in much the same way as their counterparts in European *kunstkammern.*

How these Ming porcelains were acquired in England is not well documented for the 16th century, but there is information about several shipwrecks and diplomatic encounters which may have brought Ming porcelain to England during the Elizabethan period. For example, there are references to Francis Drake (c.1540–1596) having left behind a group of blue and white ceramics on a stop off the coast of Northern California (now called 'Drake's Bay') and to having given porcelain to Elizabeth I (1533–1603). However these come from the colourful writings of Richard Hakluyt (c. 1553–1616) which have been shown to have been mostly fictionalised.[206] The English did participate in maritime plunder with their capture of Portuguese ships, one of which apparently included porcelain in its manifest.[207] The porcelains recovered from such ships, and those found at Drake's Bay, were all of the *kraak* type, and thus this style of blue and white was also popular in England as well as the rest of Europe in the late 16th century. Fortunately, the Cecil family, who built Burghley House in Lincolnshire, kept records of its various holdings, and these included Chinese porcelains which were given English mounts as early as 1585–1600.[208] Some of these were still at Burghley House in the late 19th century.[209]

Like the Netherlands, where Chinese porcelain became associated with other luxury goods (and foods), there was a distinct change in the consumption patterns for Chinese porcelain in England in the early 17th century. This was a result, to some extent, of greater supply, as now provided by more extensive long-distance trade, but it was also to do with the development of commerce (and prosperity) domestically and the greater number of shops selling a wide range of goods, including porcelain from China.[210] Concurrent with this was a fashion amongst the wealthy for separate rooms to house luxurious objects, an extension of the *kunstkammern* of the previous century.[211] While the origins of this practice are traditionally attributed to continental Europe, there are several references in inventories of prominent homes in England to 'posslyn' houses or 'cabonetts' furnished with 'chyna'. However, it should be noted that mounted porcelains were listed separately with plate at the same time, thus maintaining their distinctive status.[212] This is not surprising as collections of 'curiosities' were still in fashion in early 17th-century England, for example, those of Walter Cope and John Tradescant the Younger; these were displayed in dedicated rooms.[213] There was further a distinction between what might have been daily-use porcelains and mounted examples at court, as the list of goods from the 'Commonwealth Sale' which took place in 1649 after the execution of Charles I attests.[214] This source also indicates that the monetary value of Chinese porcelain was declining at this time, due to greater supply, and this would continue throughout the 17th century.

The greatest changes in the consumption of Chinese porcelain in England and Europe occurred in the second half of the 17th century, when drinking and dining habits changed quite dramatically. It happened that these changes were facilitated by Chinese porcelain, which proved to be the most useful and desirable material from which to make new vessels. This period is beyond the scope of this book, but it did set in train the circumstances for the extensive consumption of Chinese porcelain in England and other countries around the world, which in turn led to the transformation of Ming porcelain into a popular figure of speech in the English language, a process which will be discussed in the next chapter.

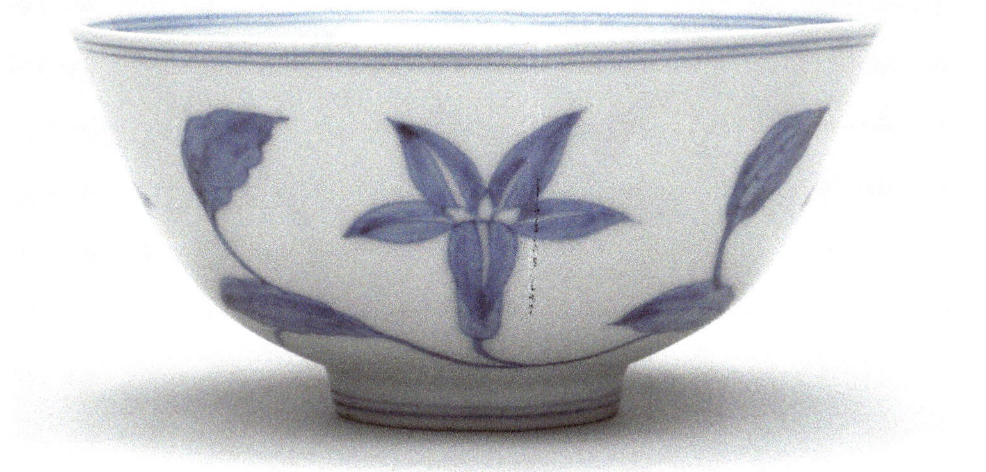

Fig. 1.1

Bowl with underglaze blue decoration, Ming dynasty, Chenghua mark period (1465–87), often described as a 'palace bowl', PDF A650, British museum. ©SOAS and the Trustees of the British Museum.

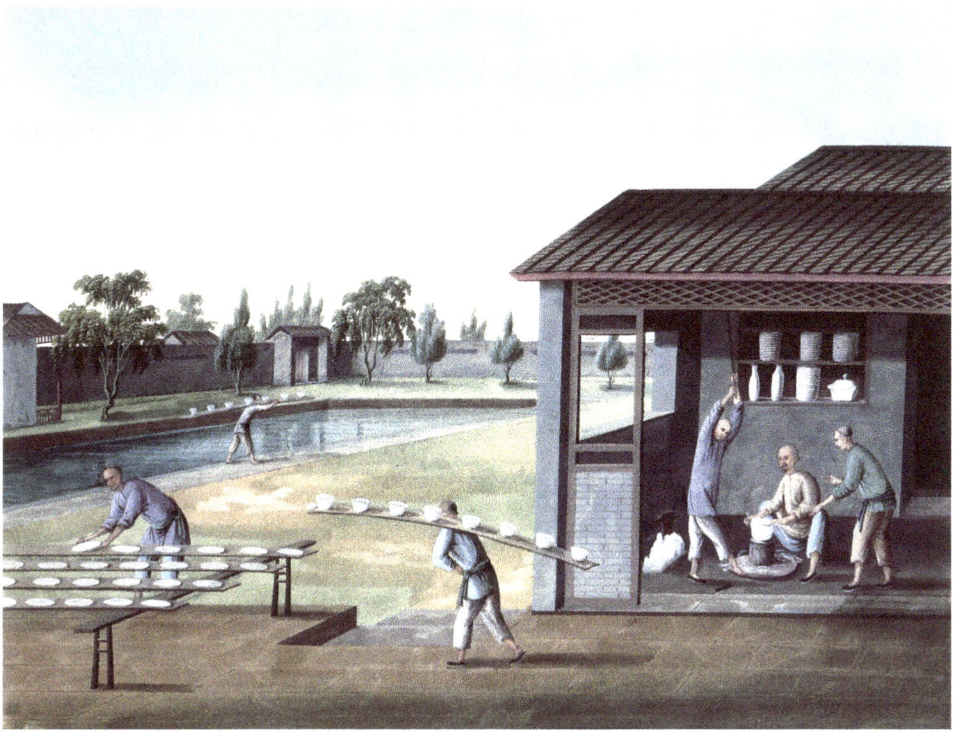

Fig. 1.2

Throwing a bowl at the porcelain factory. Watercolour and ink on paper, China, Guangzhou, 1810–20. Winterthur Museum, Gift of Leo A. and Doris C. Hodroff, 2004.47.14.4. Courtesy, Winterthur Museum.

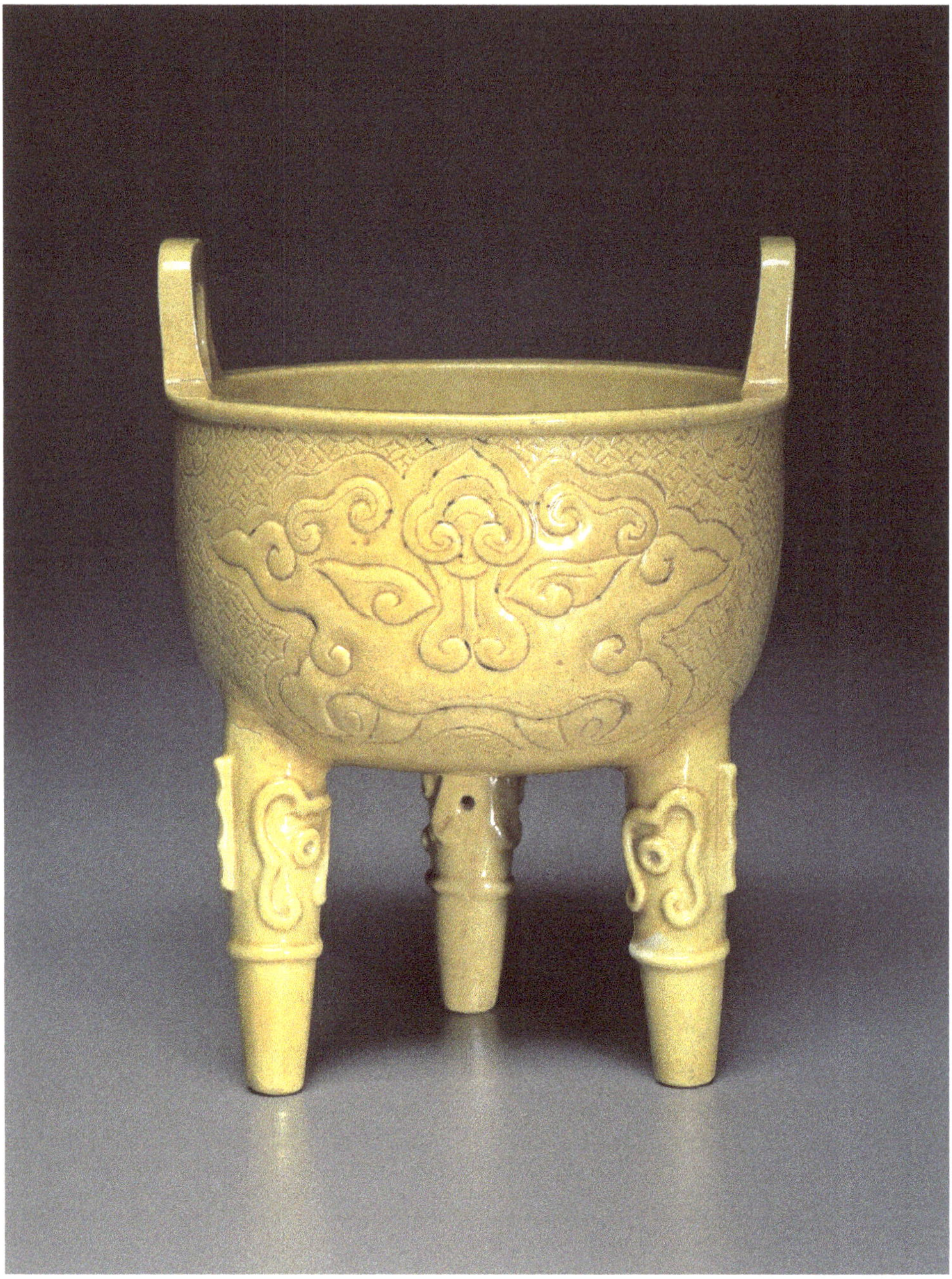

Fig. 1.3

Porcelain *ding* with incised decoration and yellow enamel and the mark of Zhou Danquan, Ming dynasty, early 17th century. National Palace Museum Taipei. ©Collection of the National Palace Museum.

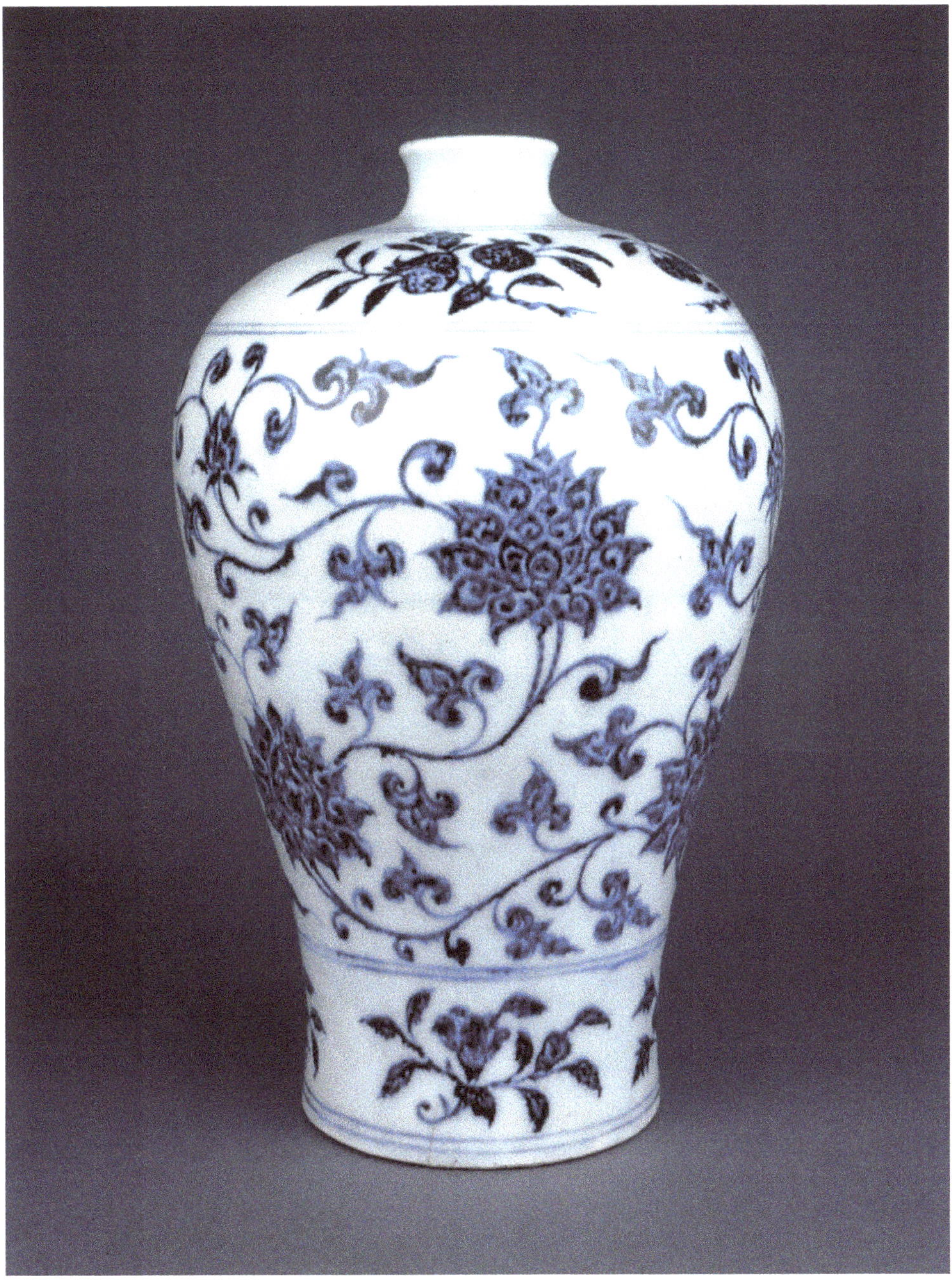

Fig. 1.4

Meiping bottle with underglaze blue decoration, Ming dynasty, early 15th century, PDF A639, British Museum. ©SOAS and the Trustees of the British Museum.

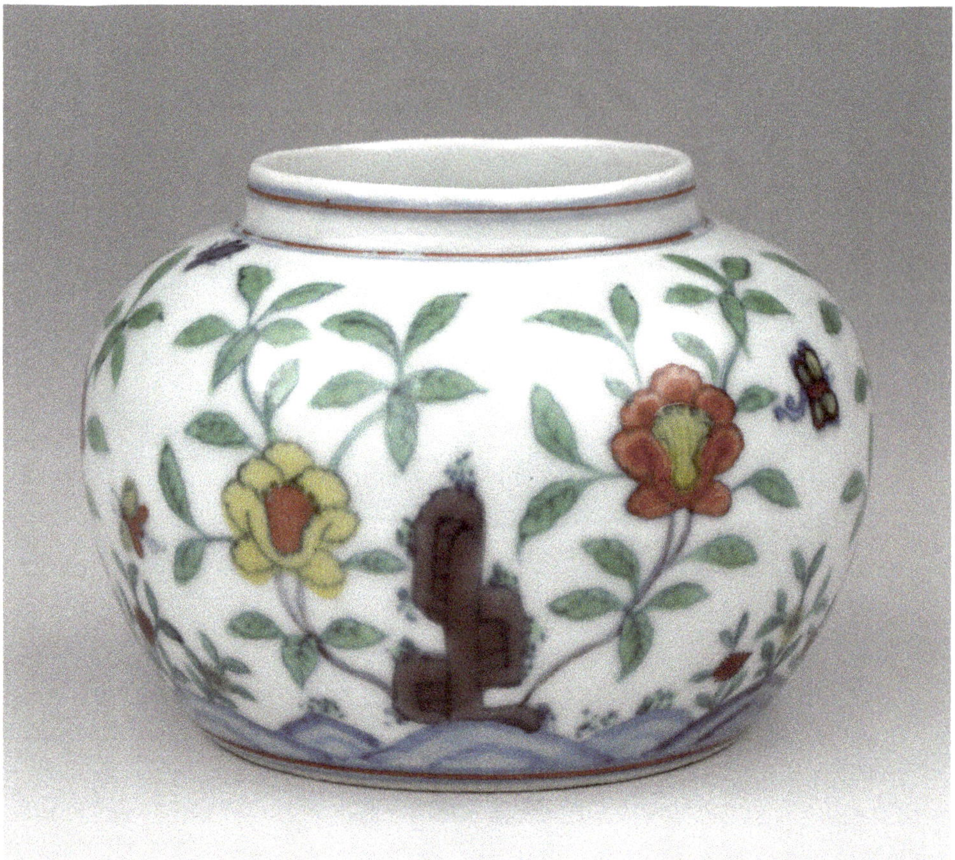

Fig. 1.5

Jar with underglaze blue and overglaze enamel decoration in *doucai* style, Ming dynasty, Chenghua mark and period (1465–87), PDF 797, British Museum. ©SOAS and the Trustees of the British Museum.

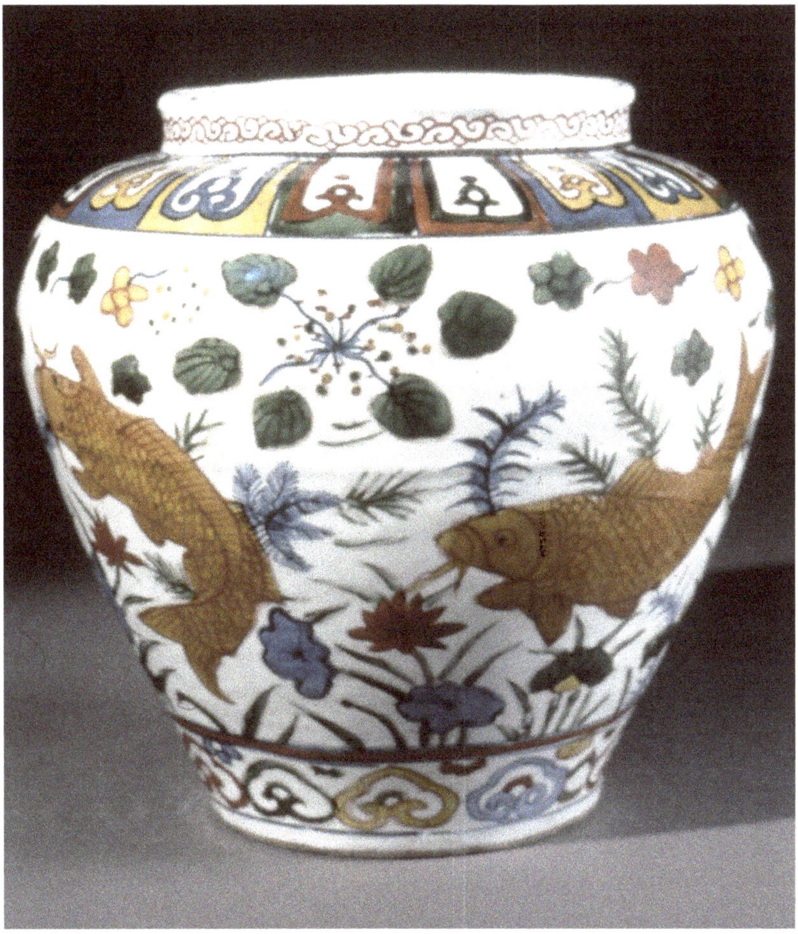

Fig. 1.6

Jar with underglaze blue and overglaze enamel decoration in *wucai* style, Ming dynasty, Jiajing mark and period (1522–66), British Museum, 1947.0712.269.b. ©Trustees of the British Museum.

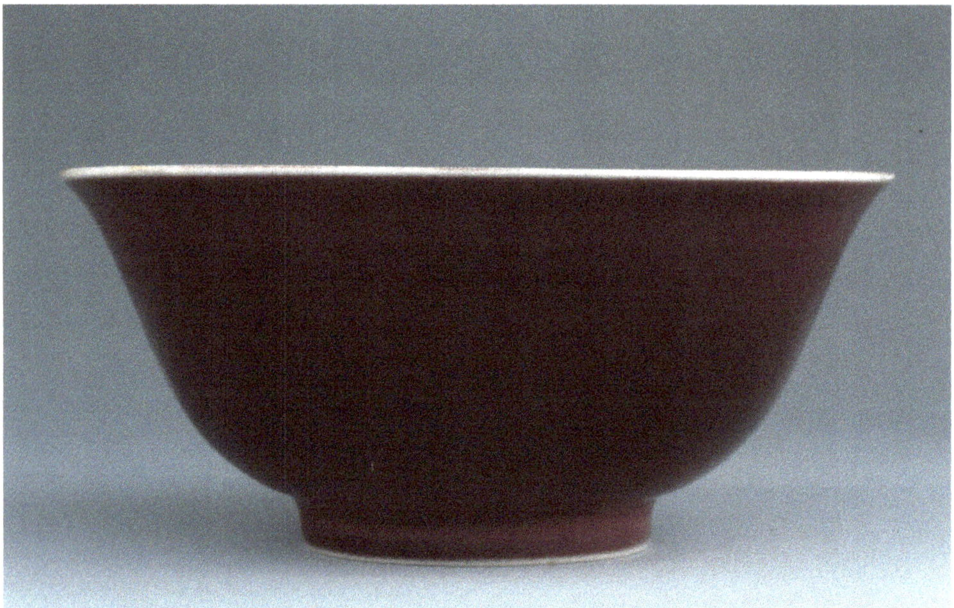

Fig. 1.7

Bowl with copper red glaze, Ming dynasty, Xuande mark and period (1426–35), PDF 520, British Museum. ©SOAS and the Trustees of the British Museum.

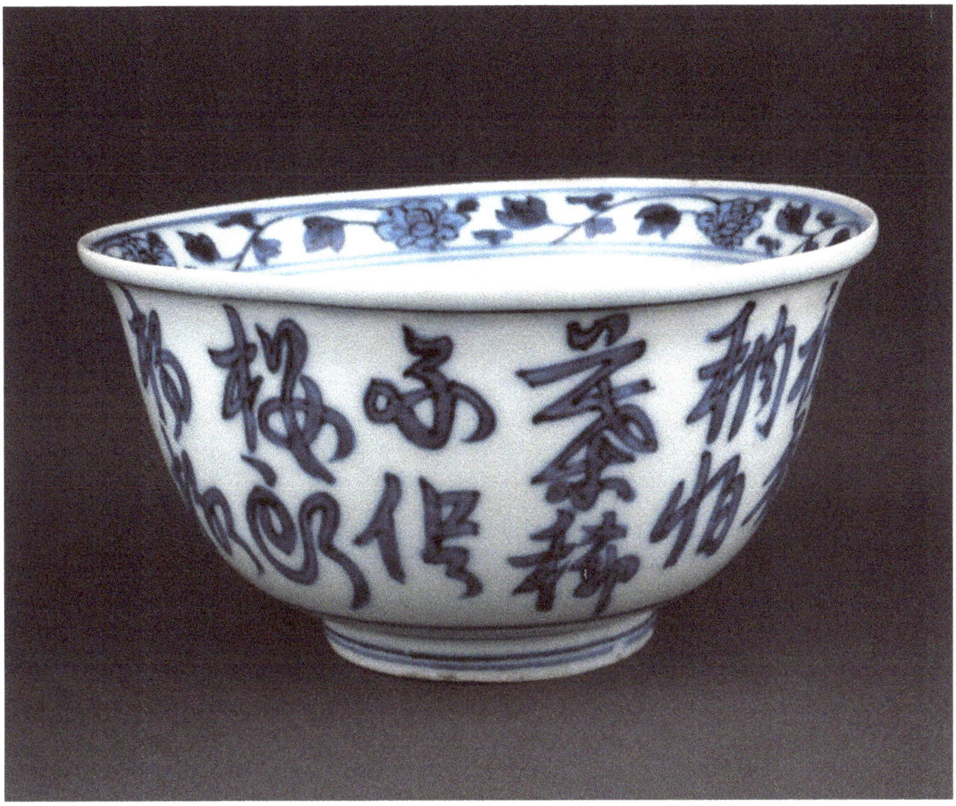

Fig. 1.8

Bowl with underglaze blue decoration and poem by Xie Fangde in cursive script around the exterior, Ming dynasty, Longqing mark and period (1567–72). PDF 622, British Museum. ©SOAS and the Trustees of the British Museum.

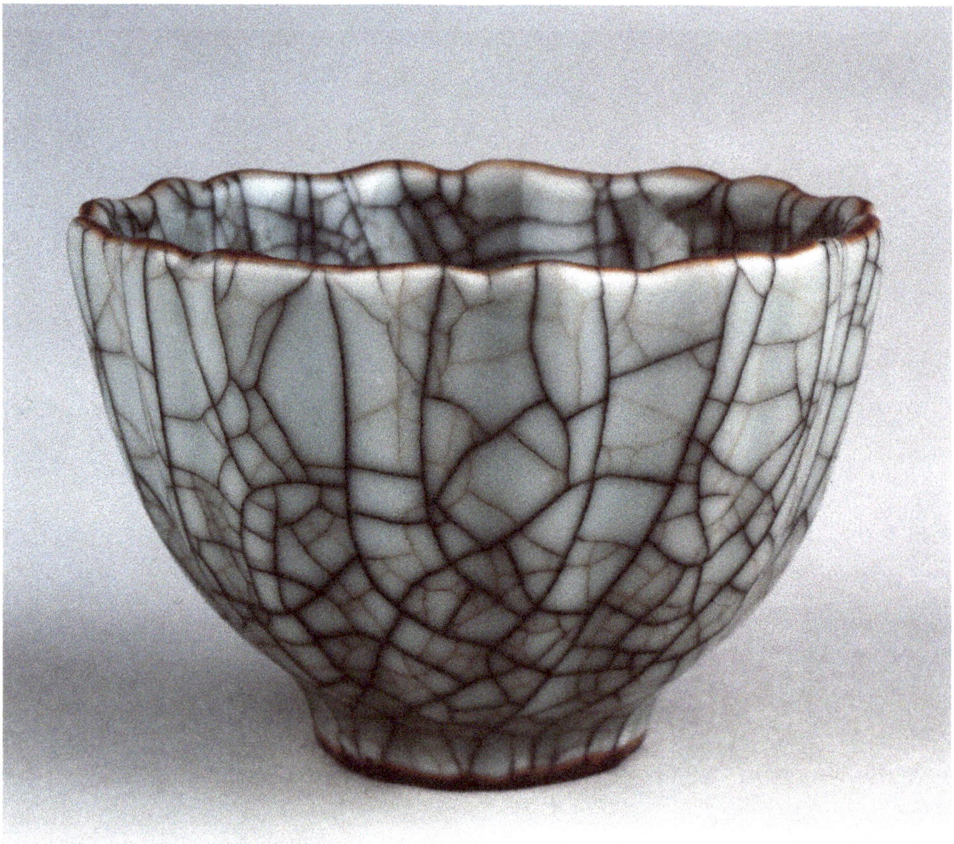

Fig. 1.9

Wine cup with Song-style crackled glaze and mark in underglaze blue, Ming dynasty, Chenghua mark and period (1465–87), PDF A57, British Museum. ©SOAS and the Trustees of the British Museum.

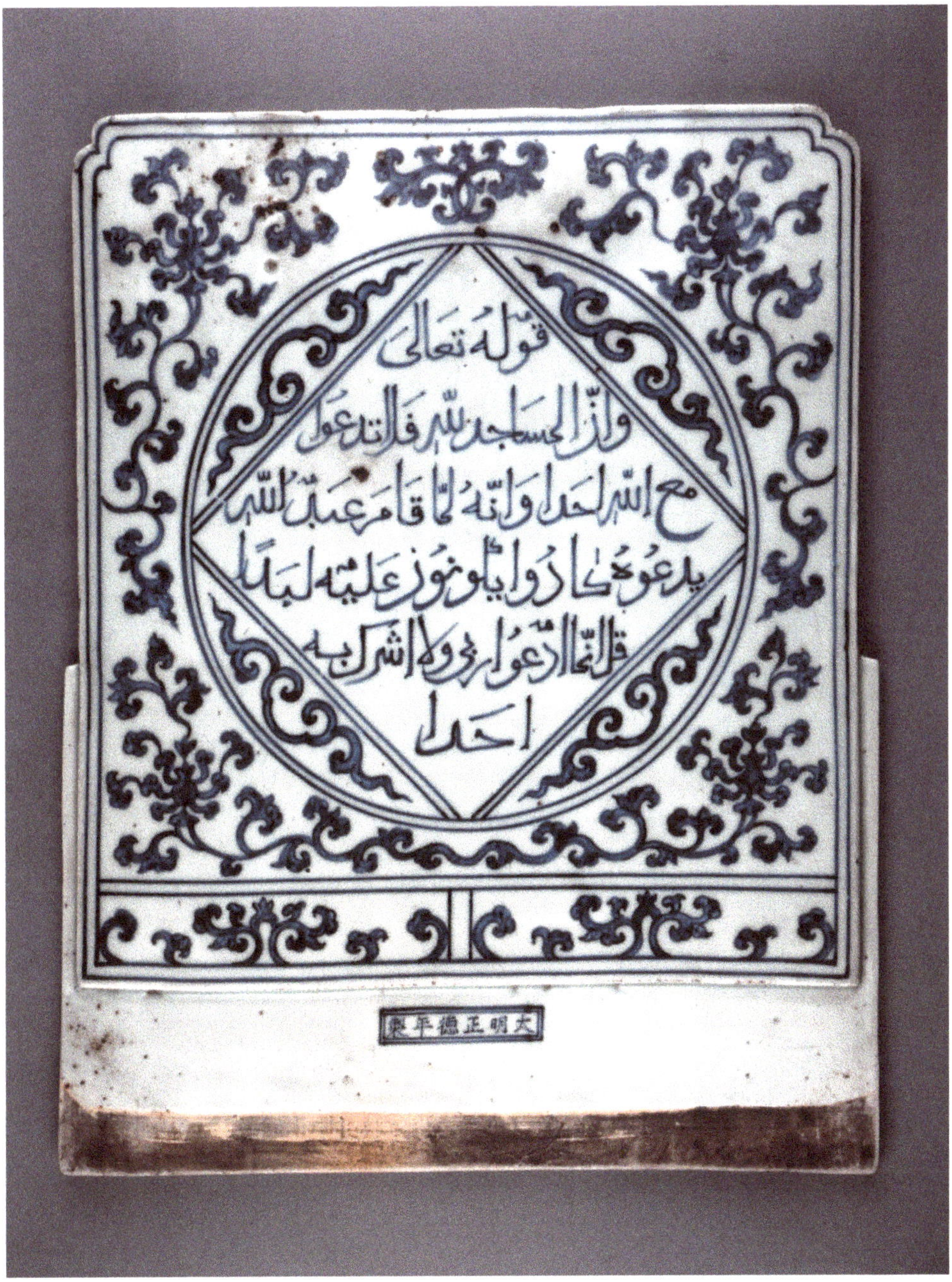

Fig. 1.10

Table screen with underglaze blue decoration and inscription in Arabic (from the Koran), Ming dynasty, Zhengde mark and period (1506–21), PDF B687, British Museum. ©SOAS and the Trustees of the British Museum.

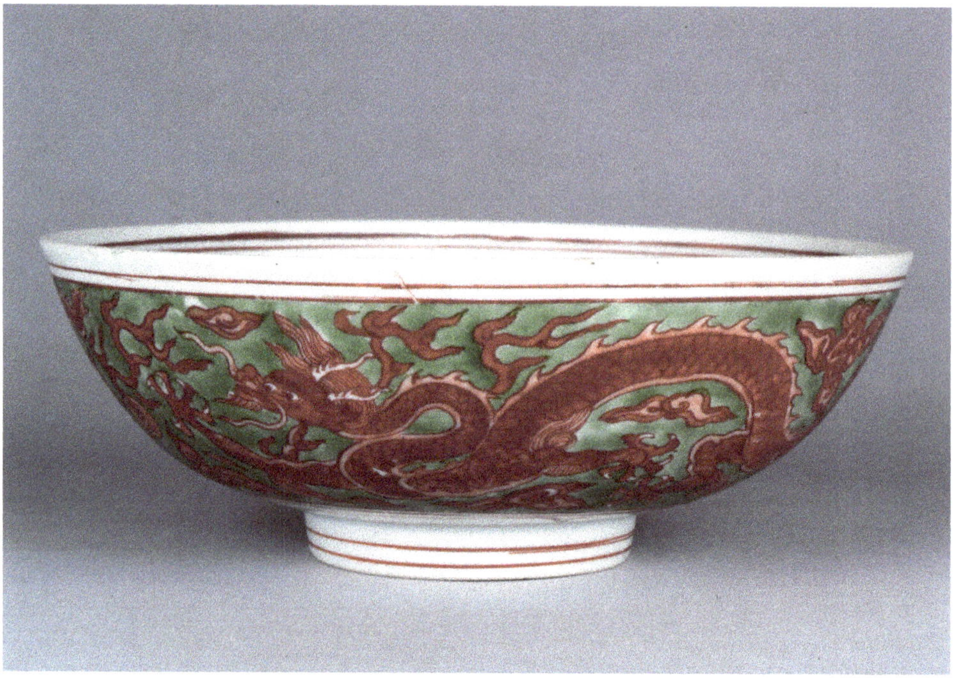

Fig. 1.11

Bowl with overglaze enamel decoration and inscription *shi fang* (‘meal room’), Ming dynasty, mid-15th century, PDF A767, British Museum. ©SOAS and the Trustees of the British Museum.

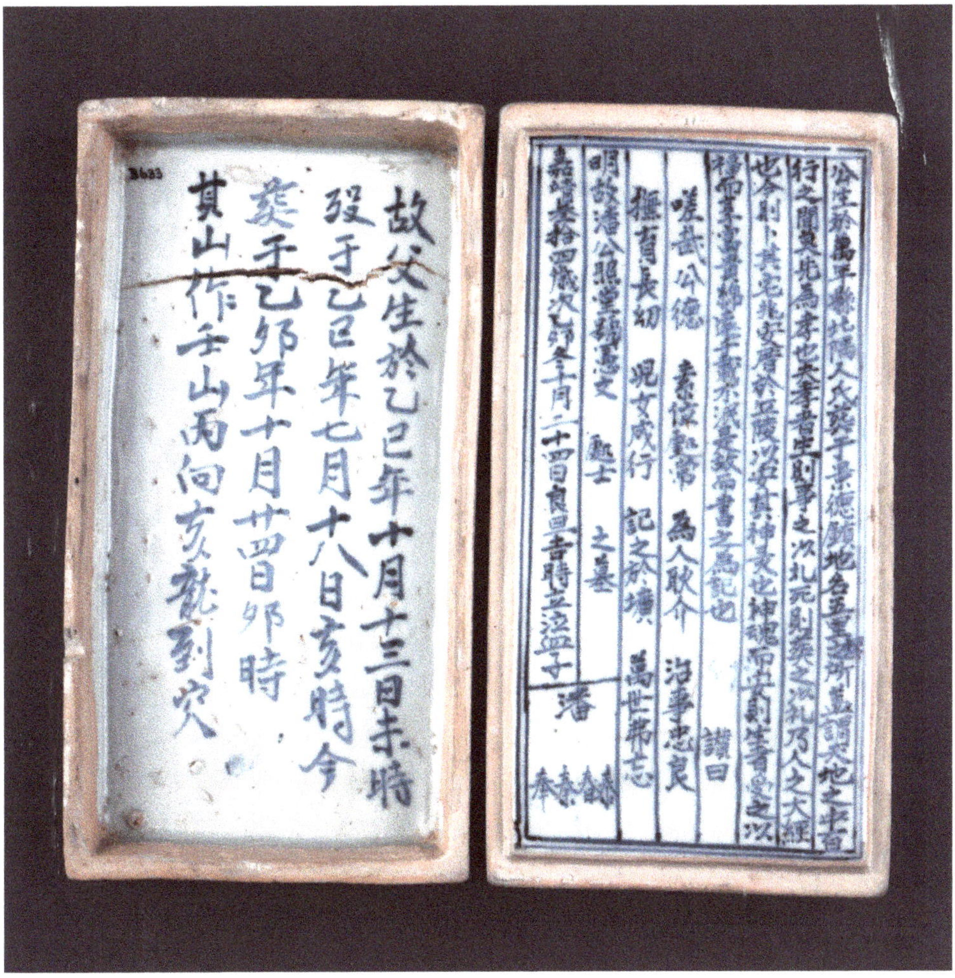

Fig. 1.12

Tomb tablet and cover with underglaze blue decoration, Ming dynasty, Jiajing period, dated 1555, PDF B633, British Museum. ©SOAS and the Trustees of the British Museum.

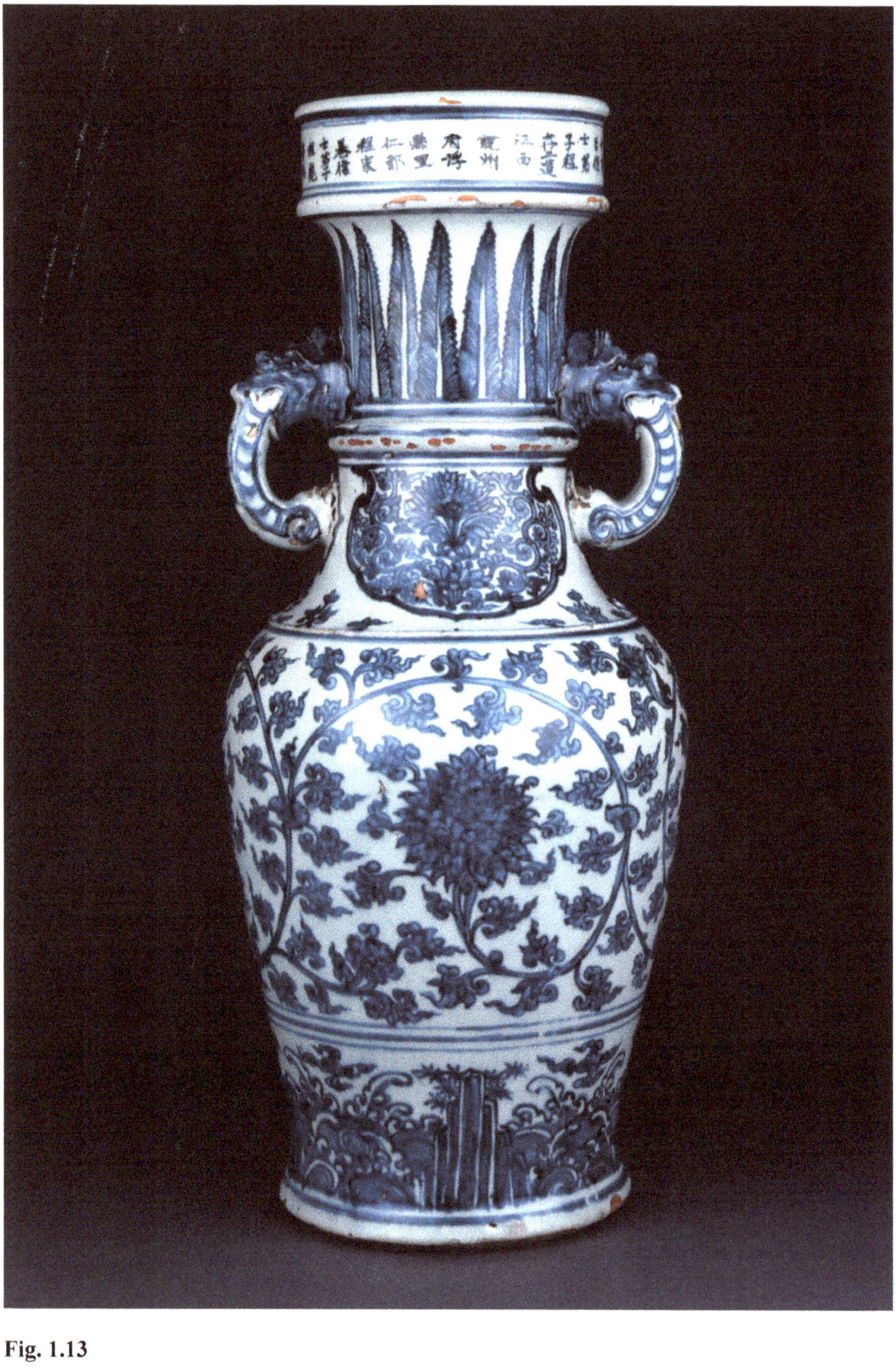

Fig. 1.13

Temple vase with underglaze blue decoration, Ming dynasty, Hongzhi period, dated by inscription to 1496, PDF 680, British Museum. ©SOAS and the Trustees of the British Museum.

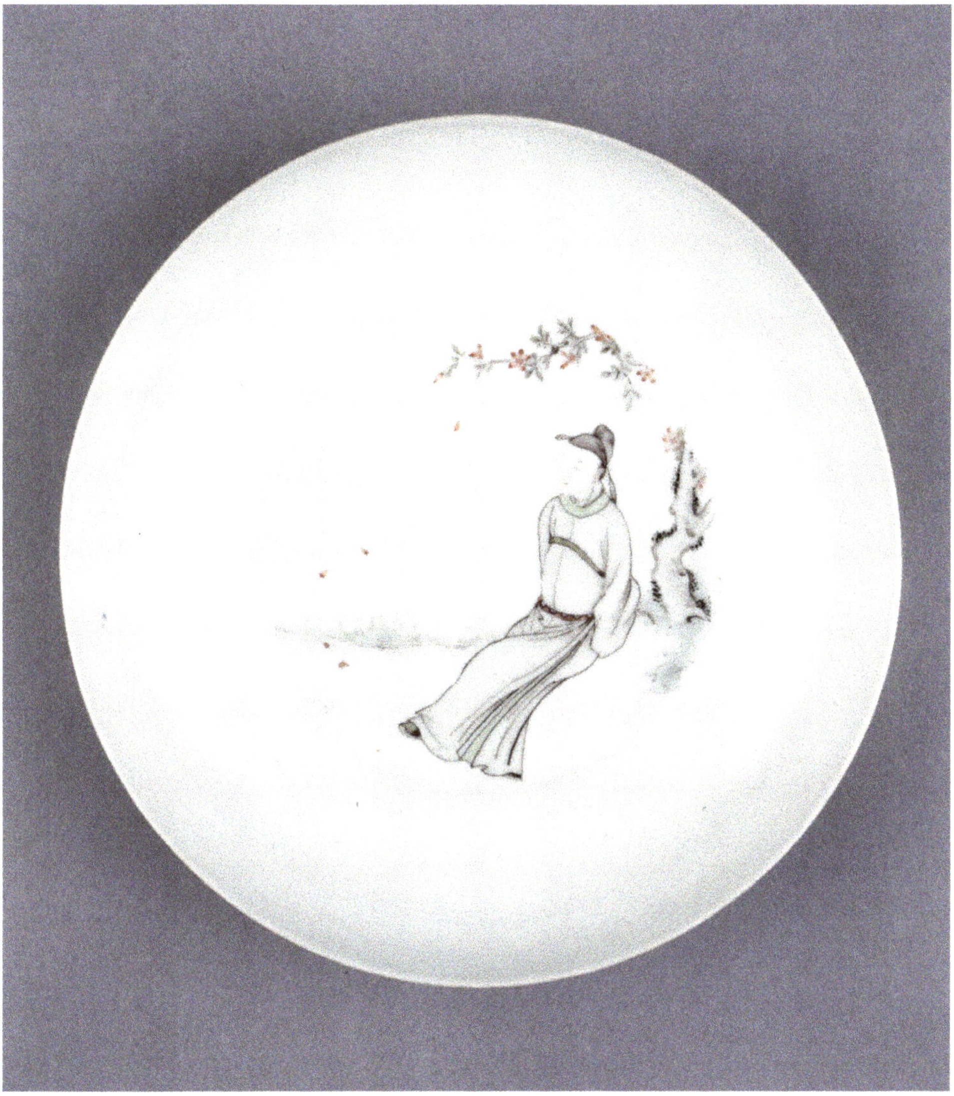

Fig. 1.14

Dish with overglaze enamel decoration over earlier slip decoration and an inscription on the reverse, Ming dynasty, Hongzhi period, late 15th–early 16th century, the overglaze decoration, 18th century, PDF A815, British Museum. ©SOAS and the Trustees of the British Museum.

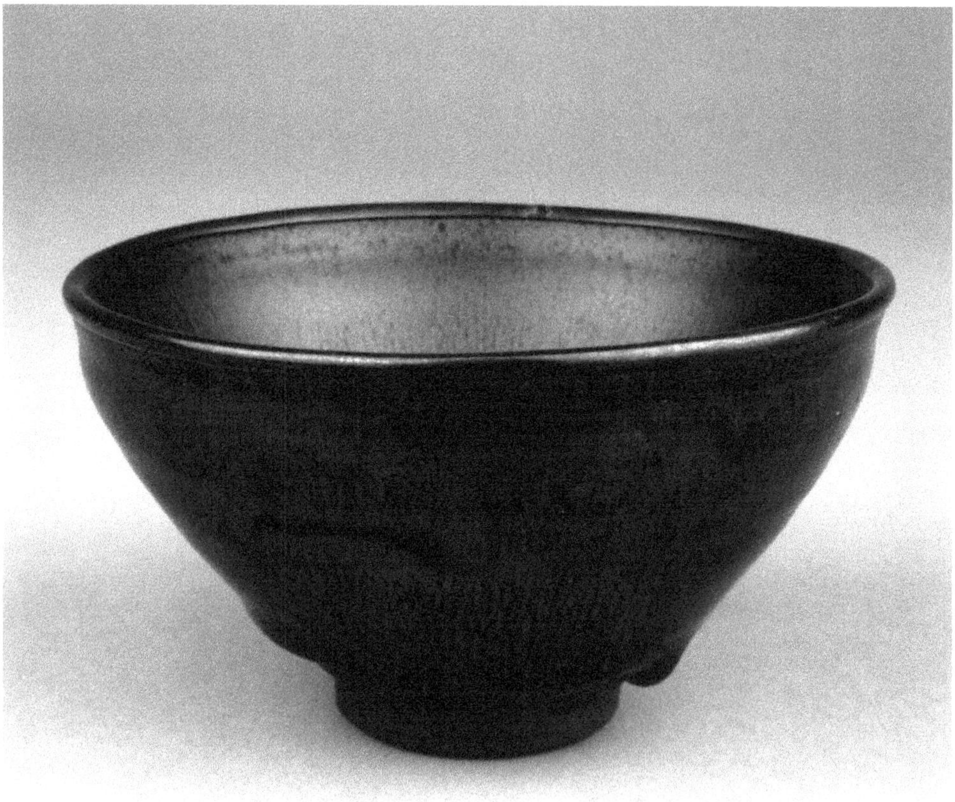

Fig. 2.1

Stoneware tea bowl, Jian ware, Southern Song period (1127–1279). PDF 303, British Museum. ©SOAS and the Trustees of the British Museum.

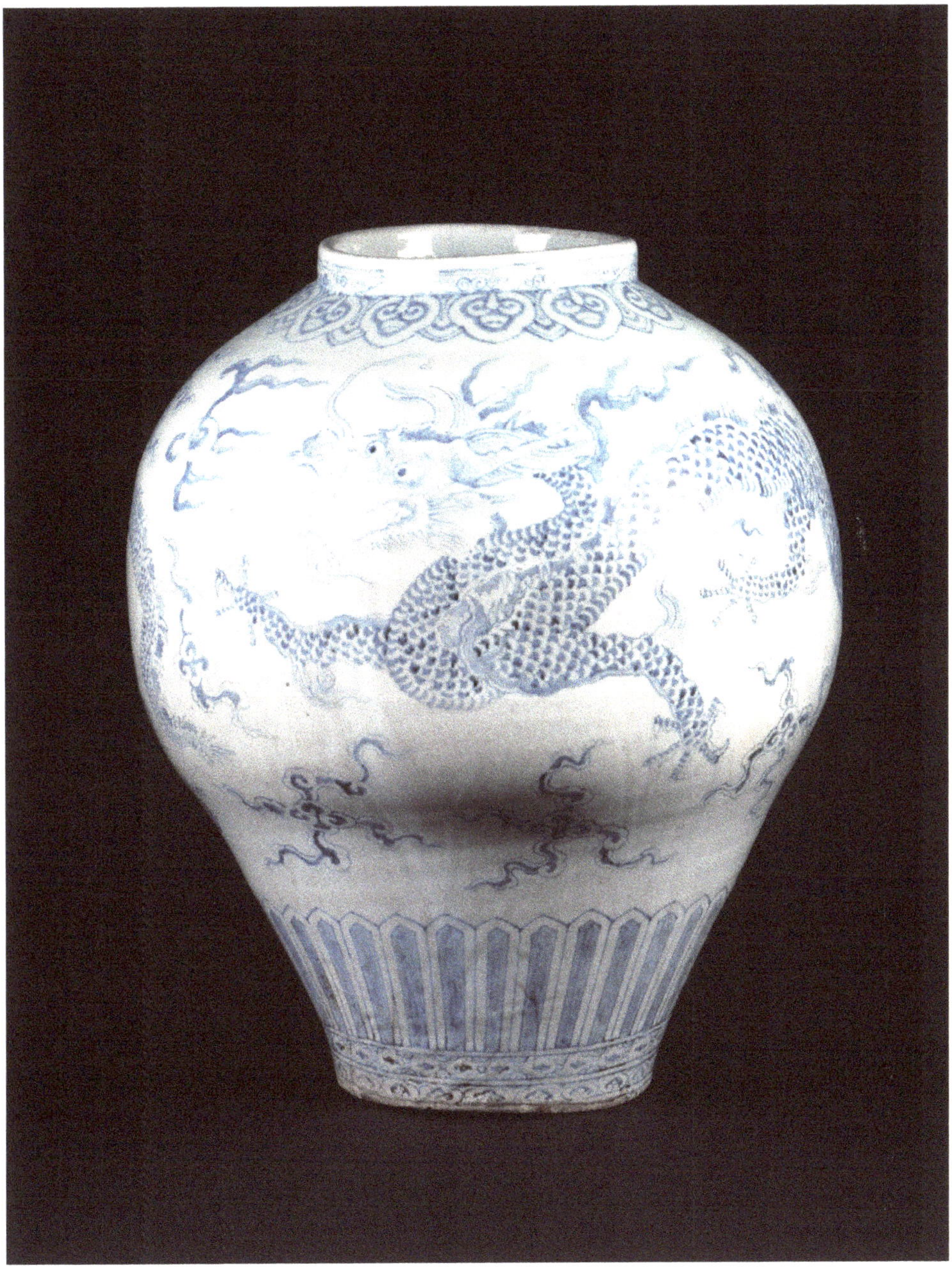

Fig. 2.2

Porcelain jar with underglaze blue decoration, Korea, Choson period, c.1750–1850. V&A C.83–1927. ©Victoria and Albert Museum, London.

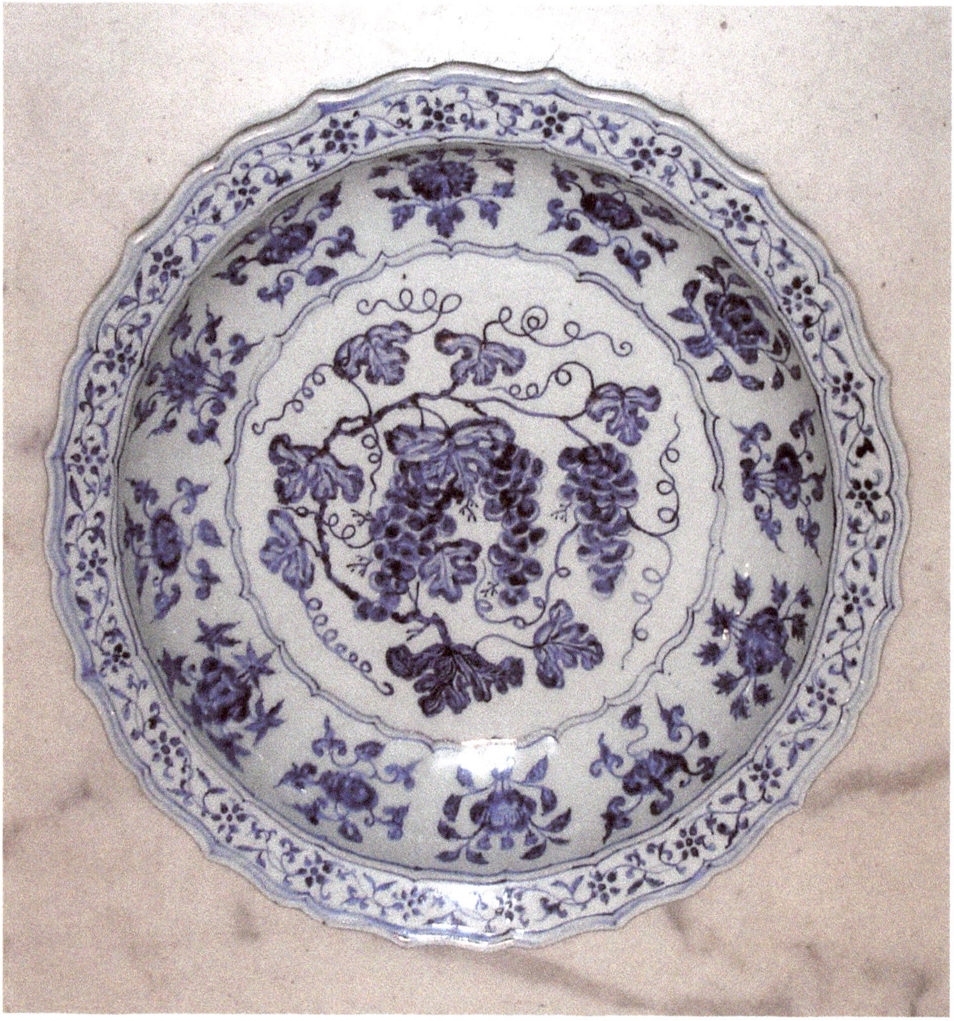

Fig. 2.3

Dish with underglaze blue decoration, very similar to an example in the Ardebil Shrine, Ming dynasty, early 15th century, British Museum. BM 1968.0422.27. ©Trustees of the British Museum.

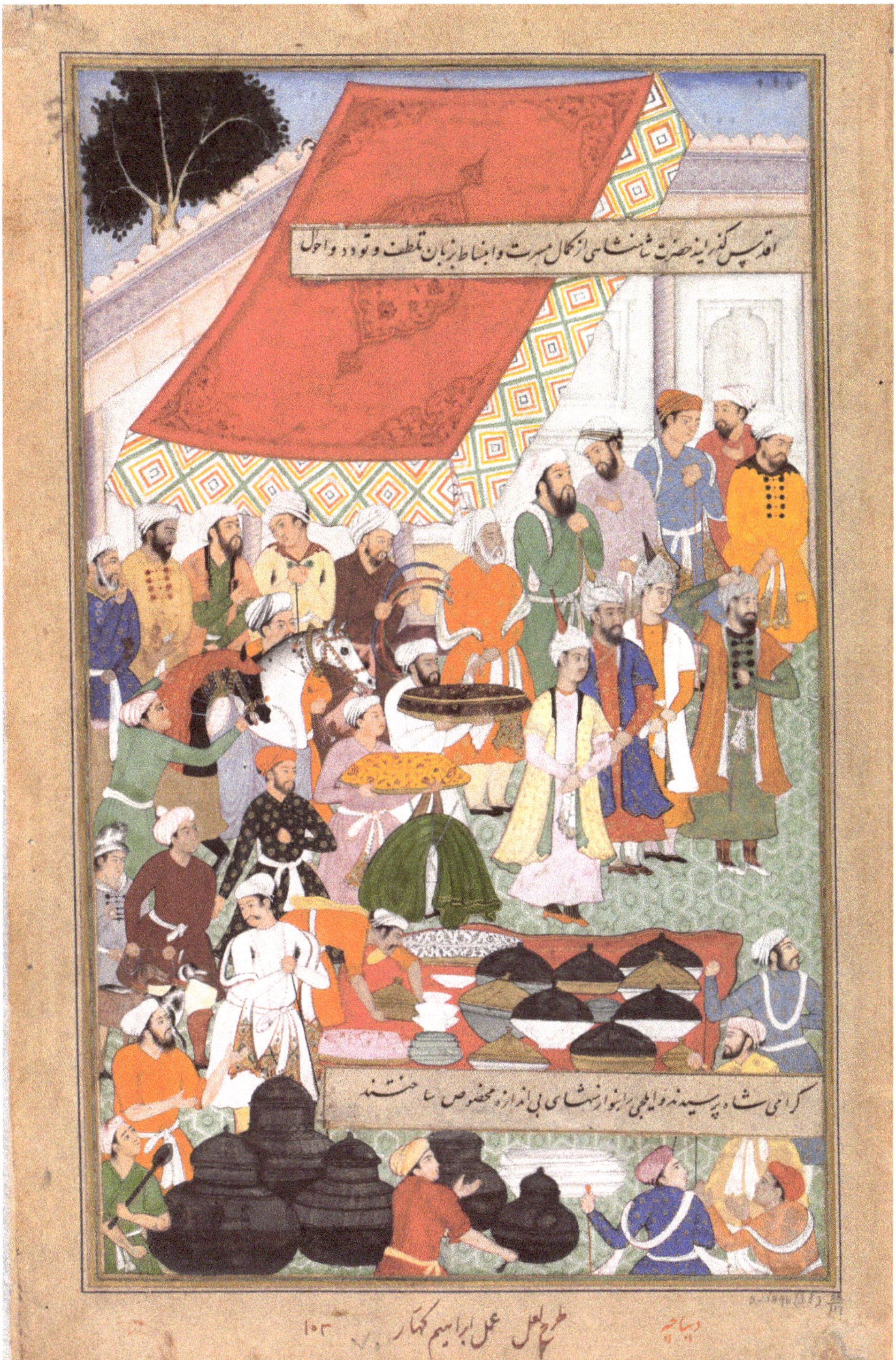

Fig. 2.4

La'l and Ibrahim Khahar, *Akbar Receives the Iranian Ambassador Sayyid Beg in 1562*, scene from the Akbarnama, opaque watercolour and gold on paper, India, 1590–95, V&A IS.2-28 1896. ©Victoria and Albert Museum, London.

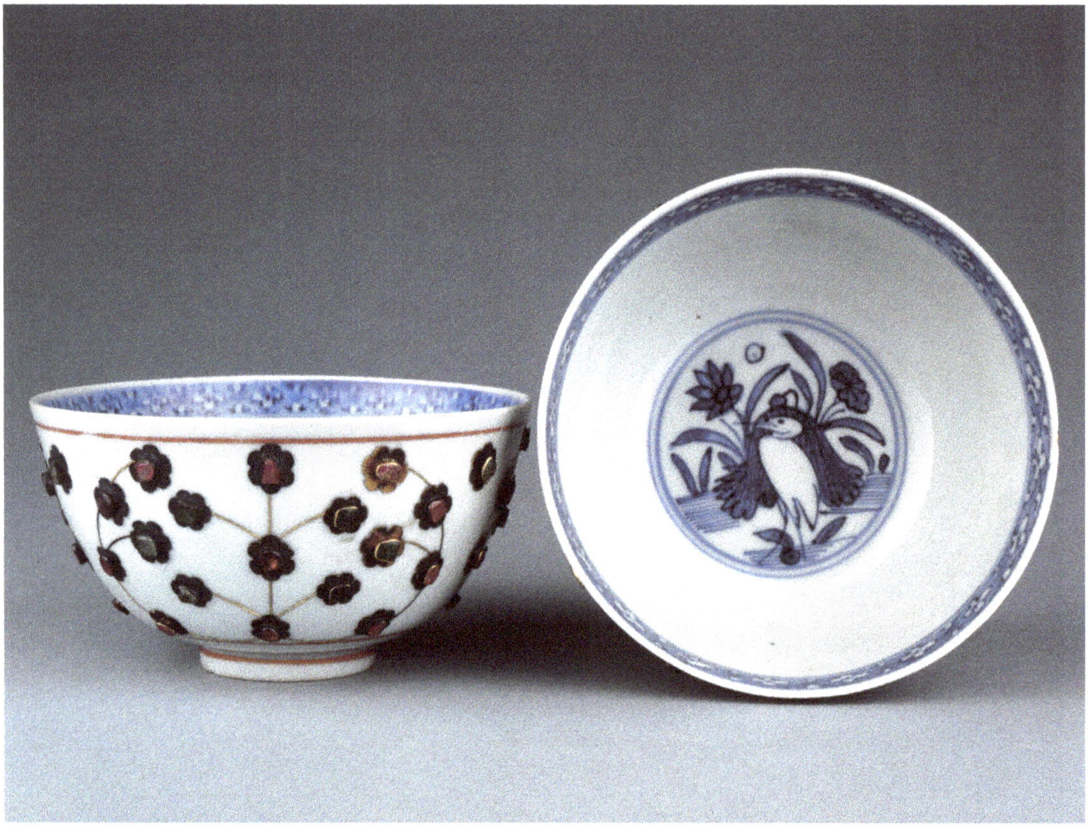

Fig. 2.5

Bowls with underglaze blue and overglaze enamel decoration, with semi-precious stones in gold and silver settings on the exterior. Ming dynasty, Wanli period, late 16th century. PDF A794, British Museum. ©SOAS and the Trustees of the British Museum.

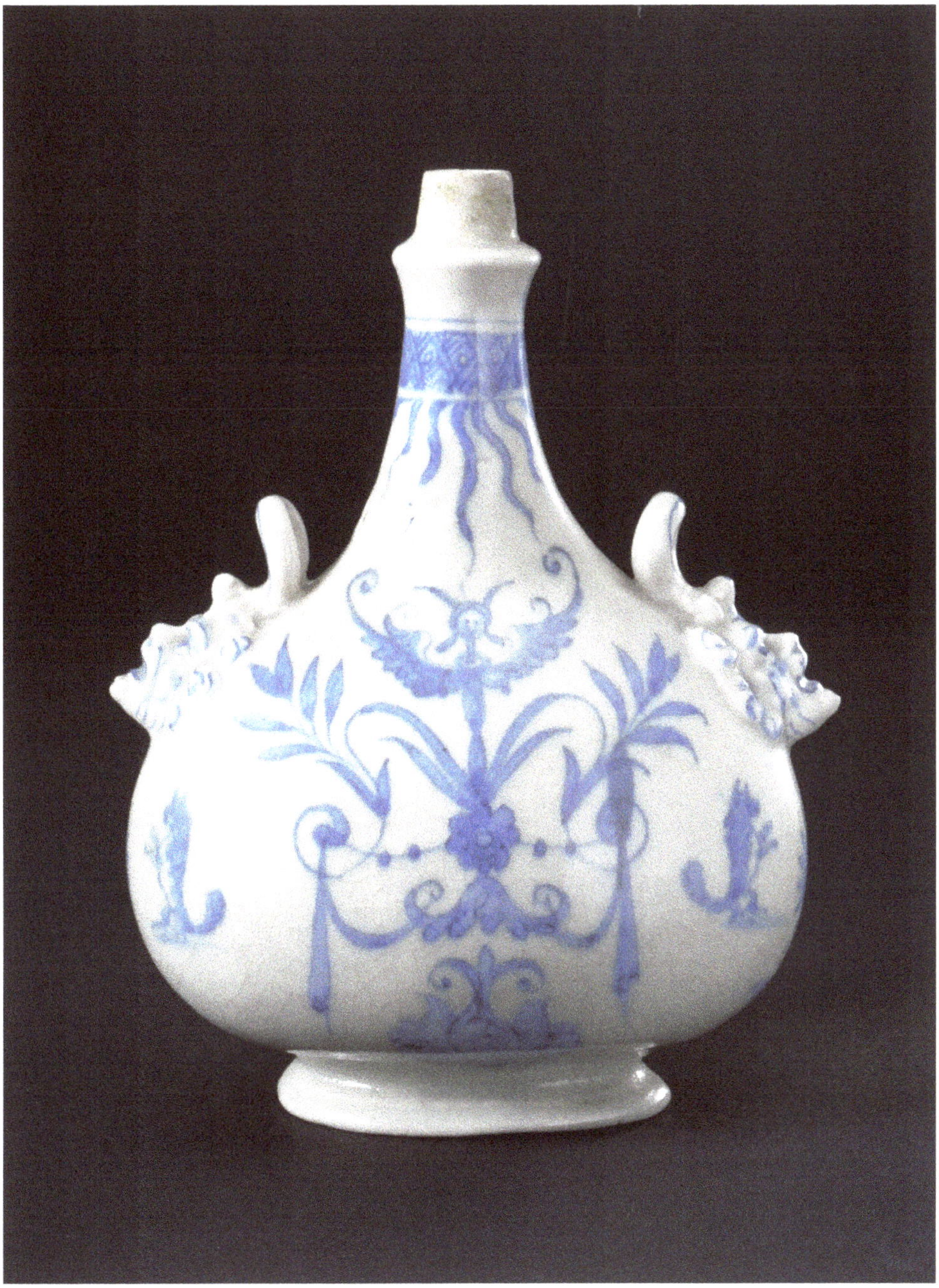

Fig. 2.6

Pilgrim bottle with underglaze blue decoration, soft-paste Medici porcelain, Florence, Italy, c.1575–87, V&A C.2301–1910. ©Victoria and Albert Museum, London.

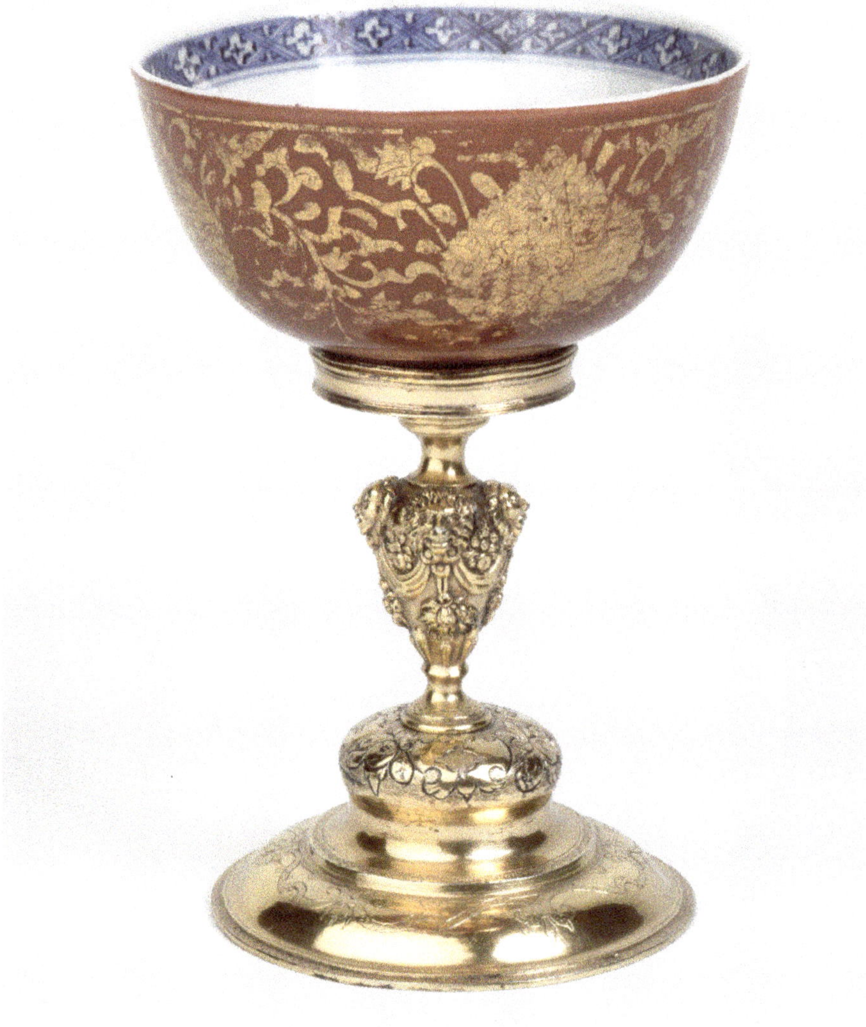

Fig. 2.7

Bowl with underglaze blue and overglaze enamel decoration with gold in *kinrande* style, and silver gilt mounts, known as the Manderscheidt cup. Bowl Chinese, Ming dynasty, Jiajing period (1522–66), mounts Germany c.1583. V&A M.16–1970. ©Victoria and Albert Museum, London.

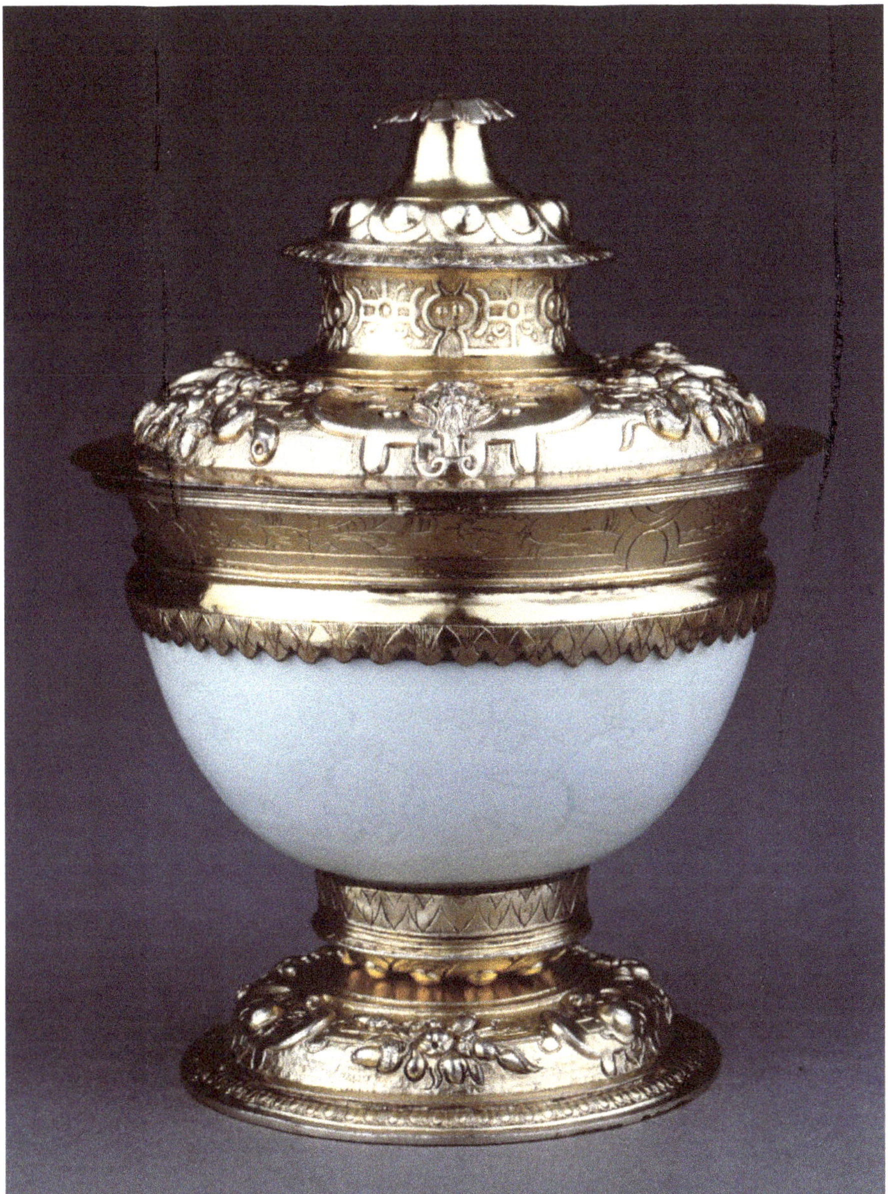

Fig. 2.8

Bowl with silver gilt mounts, incised and underglaze cobalt blue decoration, Ming dynasty, Jiajing period (1522–66), the mounts with London goldsmith mark for 1569–70. Known as the Lennard cup. PDF 695, British Museum. ©SOAS and Trustees of the British Museum.

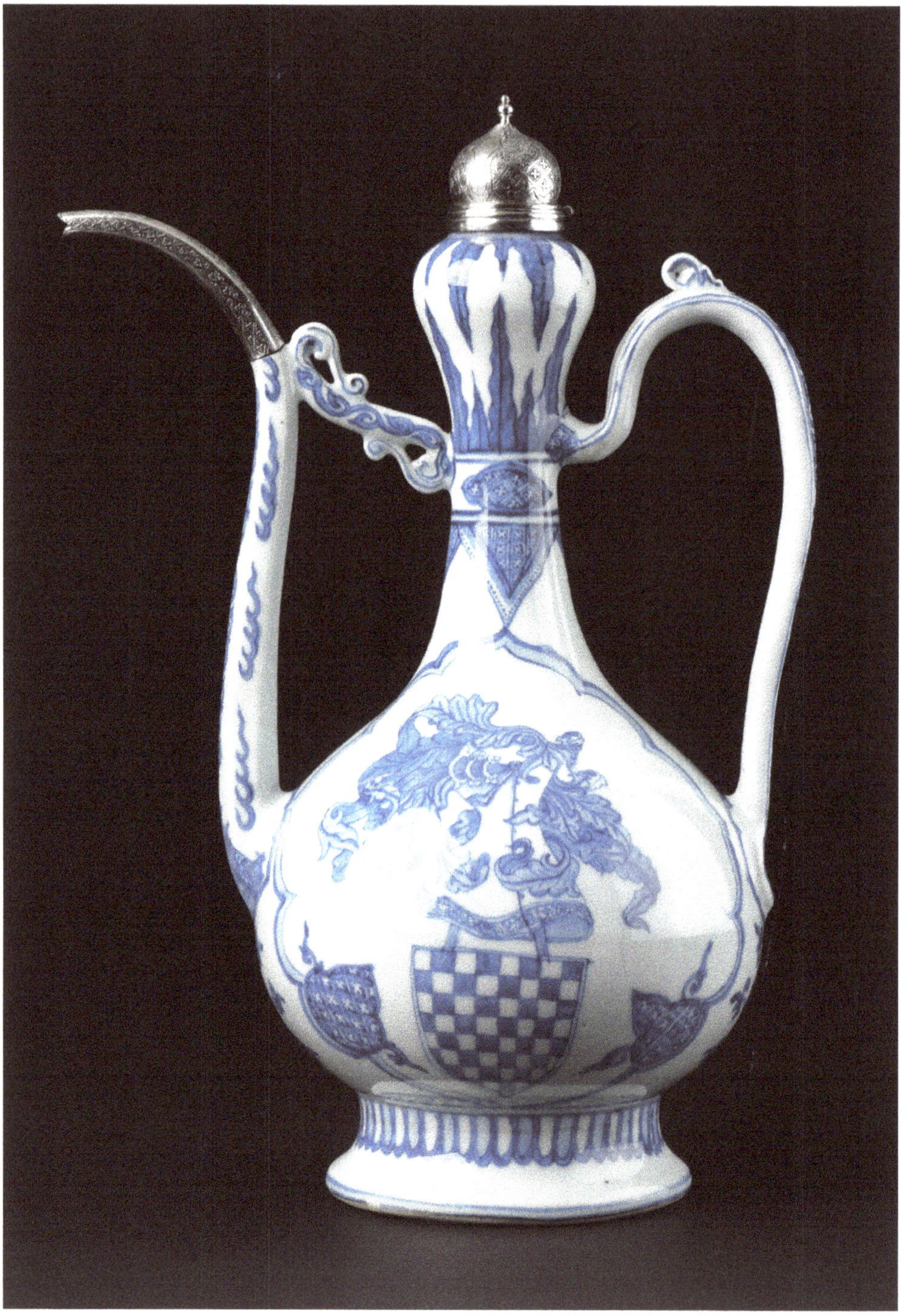

Fig. 2.9

Ewer with underglaze blue decoration and engraved Iranian silver cover and spout, Ming dynasty, Jiajing mark and period (1522–66), with the arms of Peixoto. V&A C.222–1931. ©Victoria and Albert Museum, London.

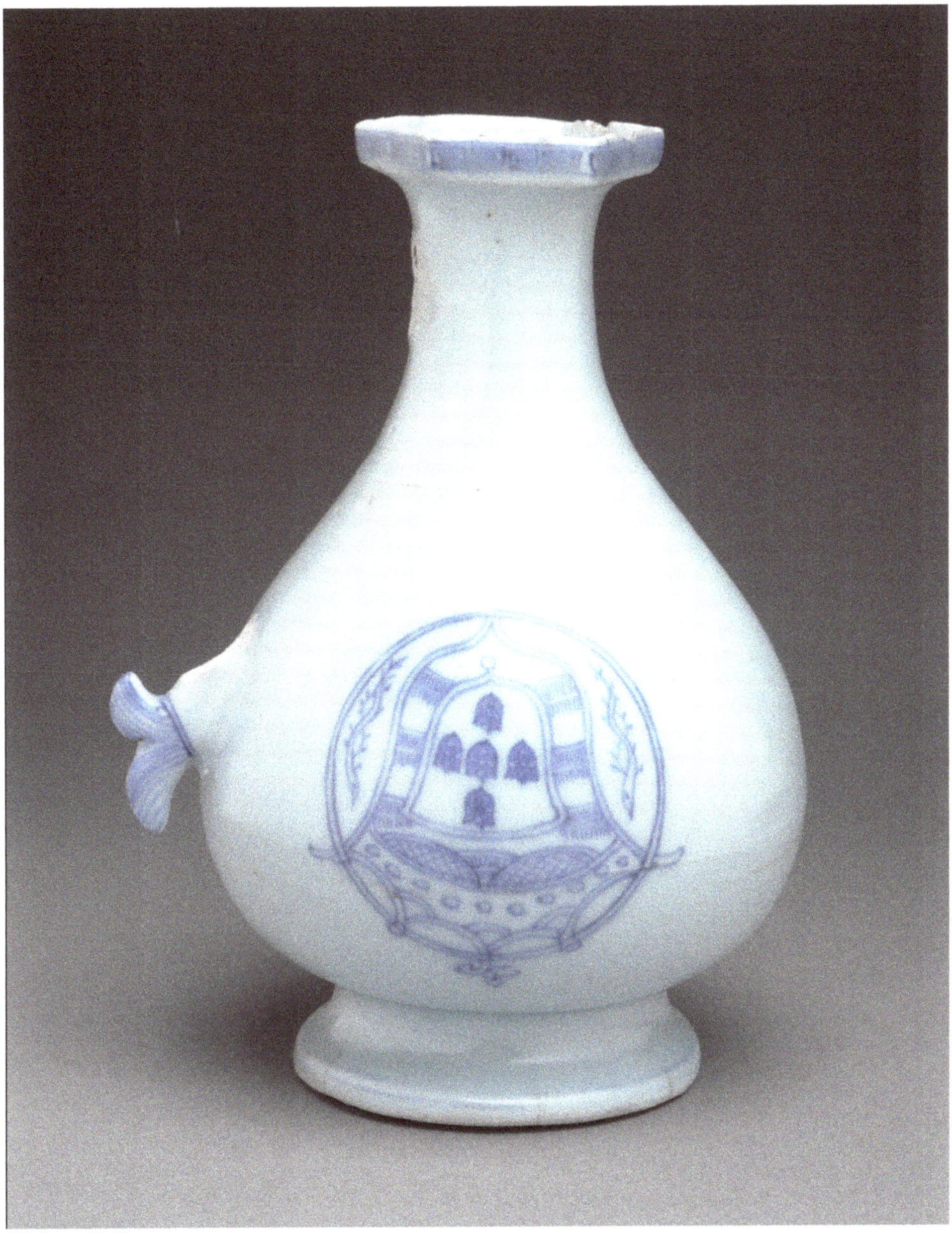

Fig. 2.10

Porcelain jug with underglaze blue decoration, upside down armorial and Xuande mark, Ming dynasty, c.1540–45, Metropolitan Museum of Art, New York, acc. no. 61.196. ©The Metropolitan Museum of Art.

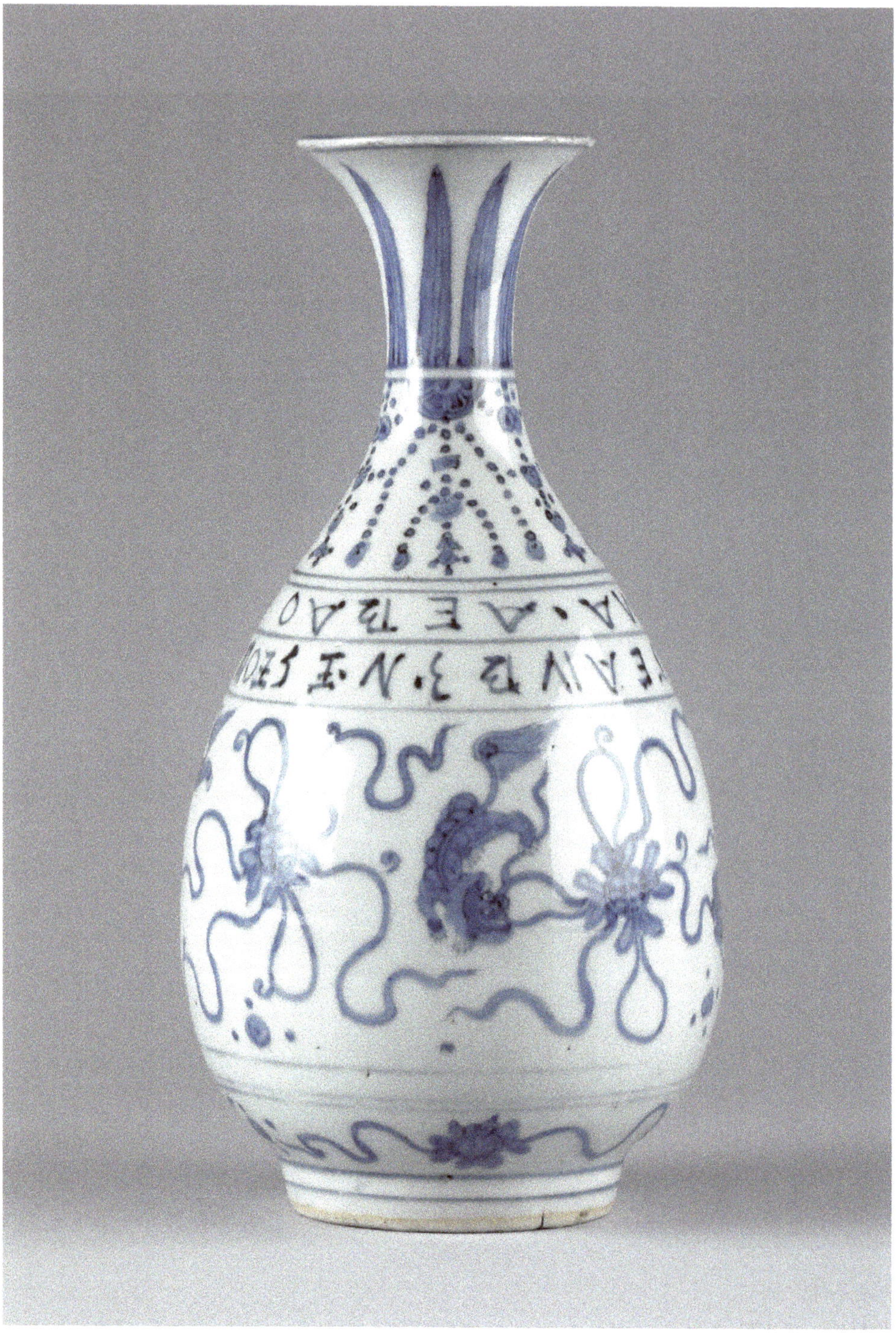

Fig. 2.11

Pear-shaped bottle with underglaze blue decoration and upside down inscription, Ming dynasty, dated 1552. Walters Art Museum, Baltimore, acc. no. 49.1616. © The Walters Art Museum.

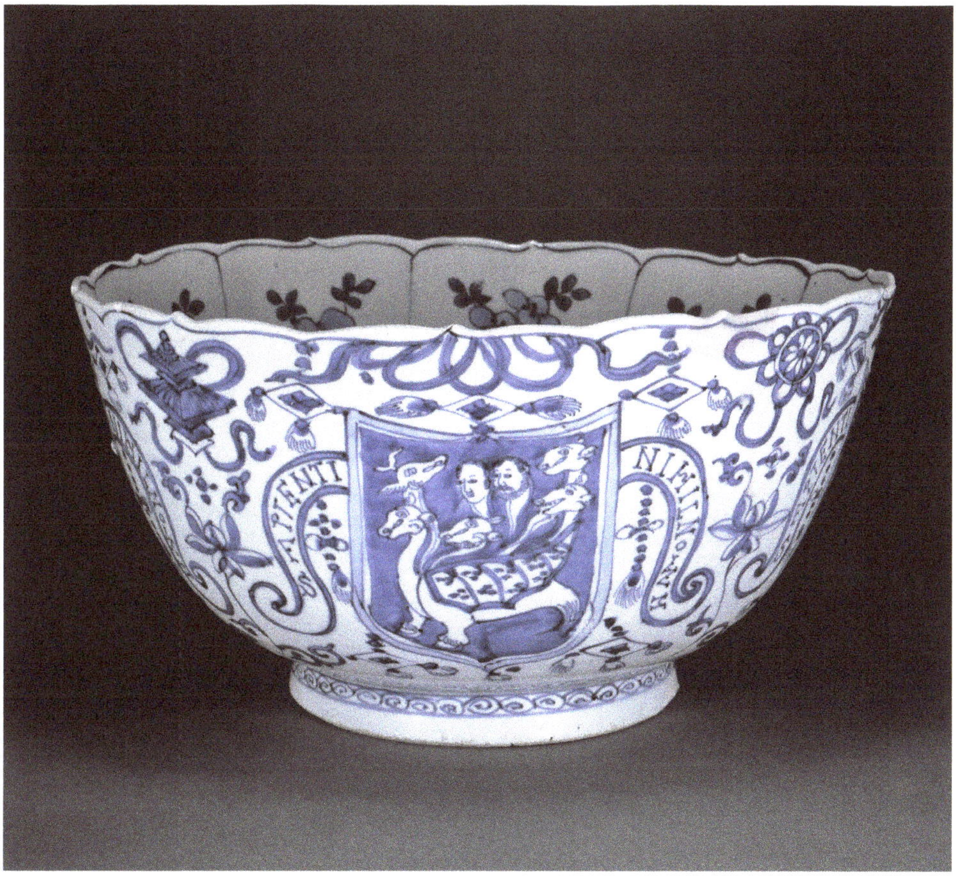

Fig. 2.12

Bowl with underglaze blue decoration in *Kraak* style, with hydra shield, Ming dynasty, Wanli period, 1600–20, British Museum. BM 1957.1216.19. ©Trustees of the British Museum.

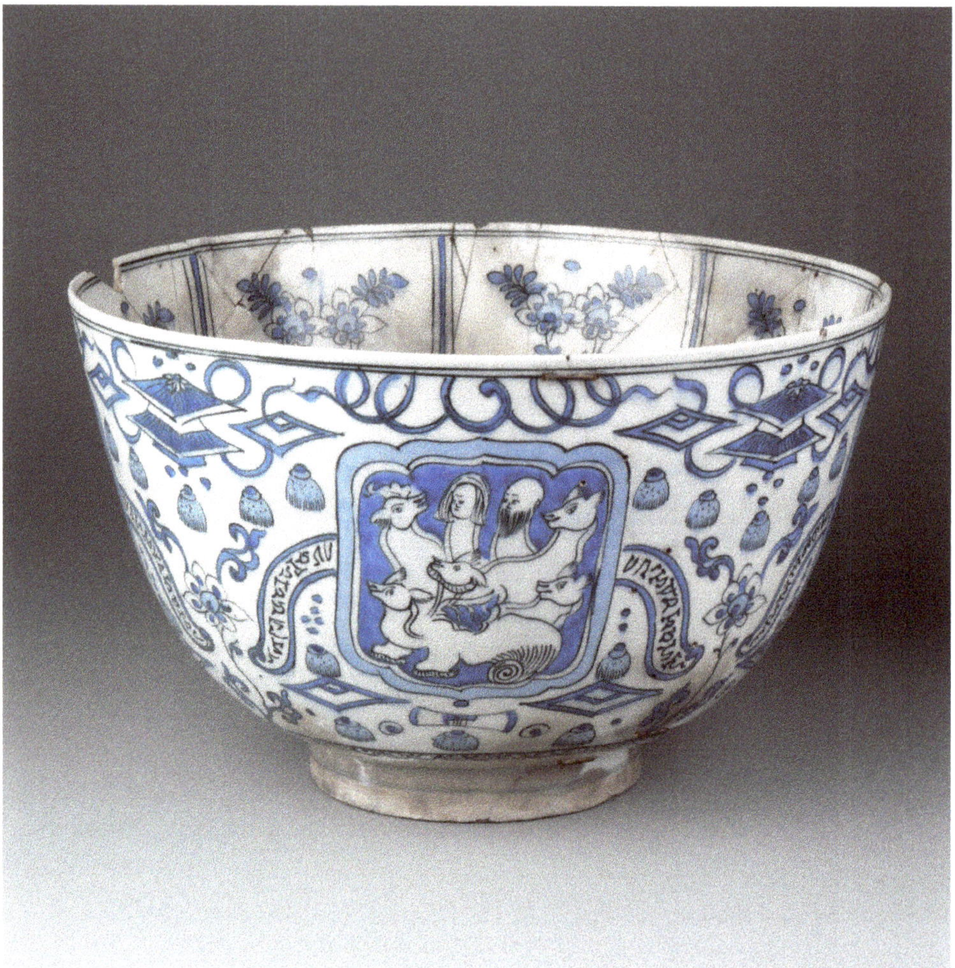

Fig. 2.13

Fritware bowl with underglaze painting in blue and black, Iran, 1639–60, V&A 2904–1876. ©Victoria and Albert Museum, London.

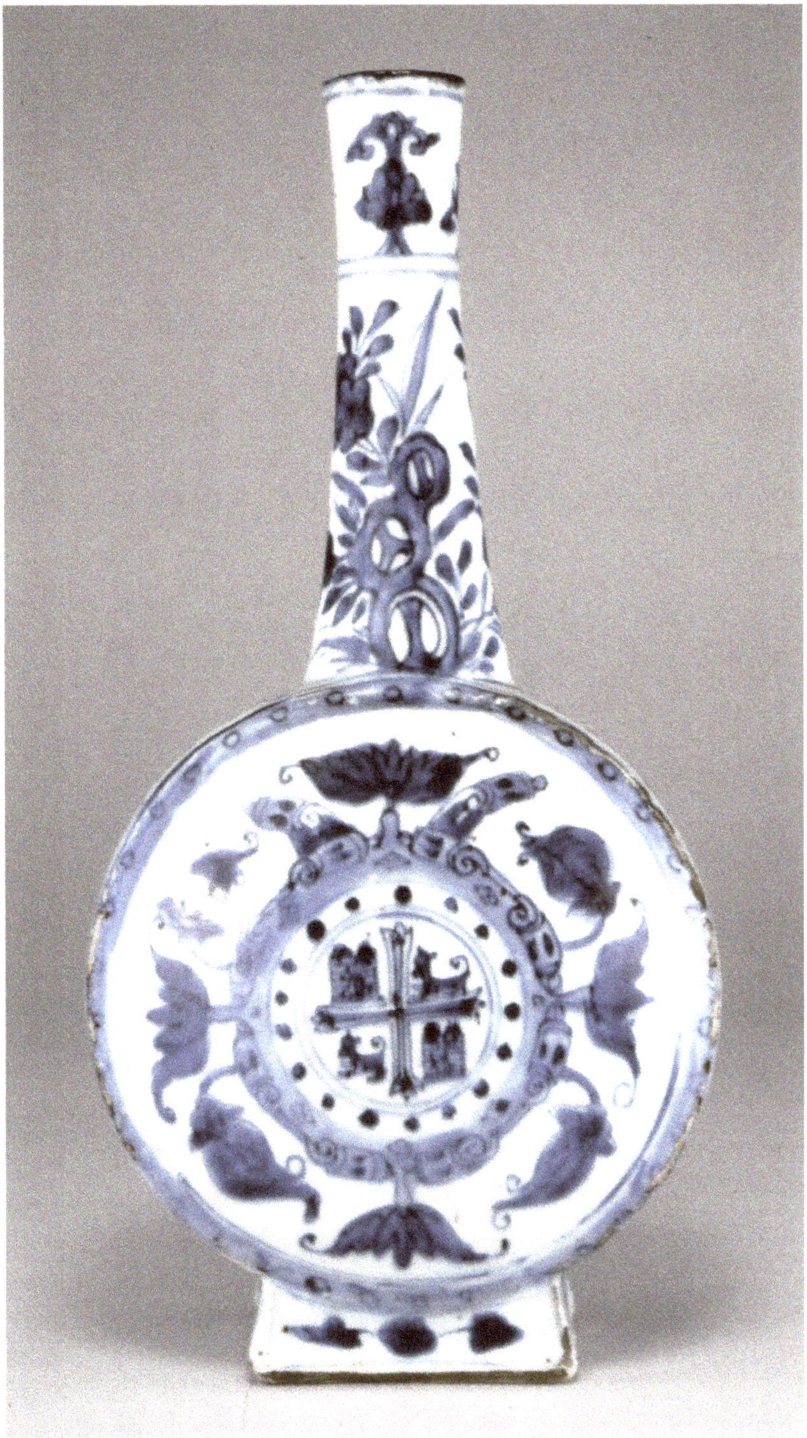

Fig. 2.14

Porcelain flask with underglaze blue decoration and Spanish crest, Ming dynasty, Wanli period, 1590–1620. British Museum, Franks 778+. ©Trustees of the British Museum.

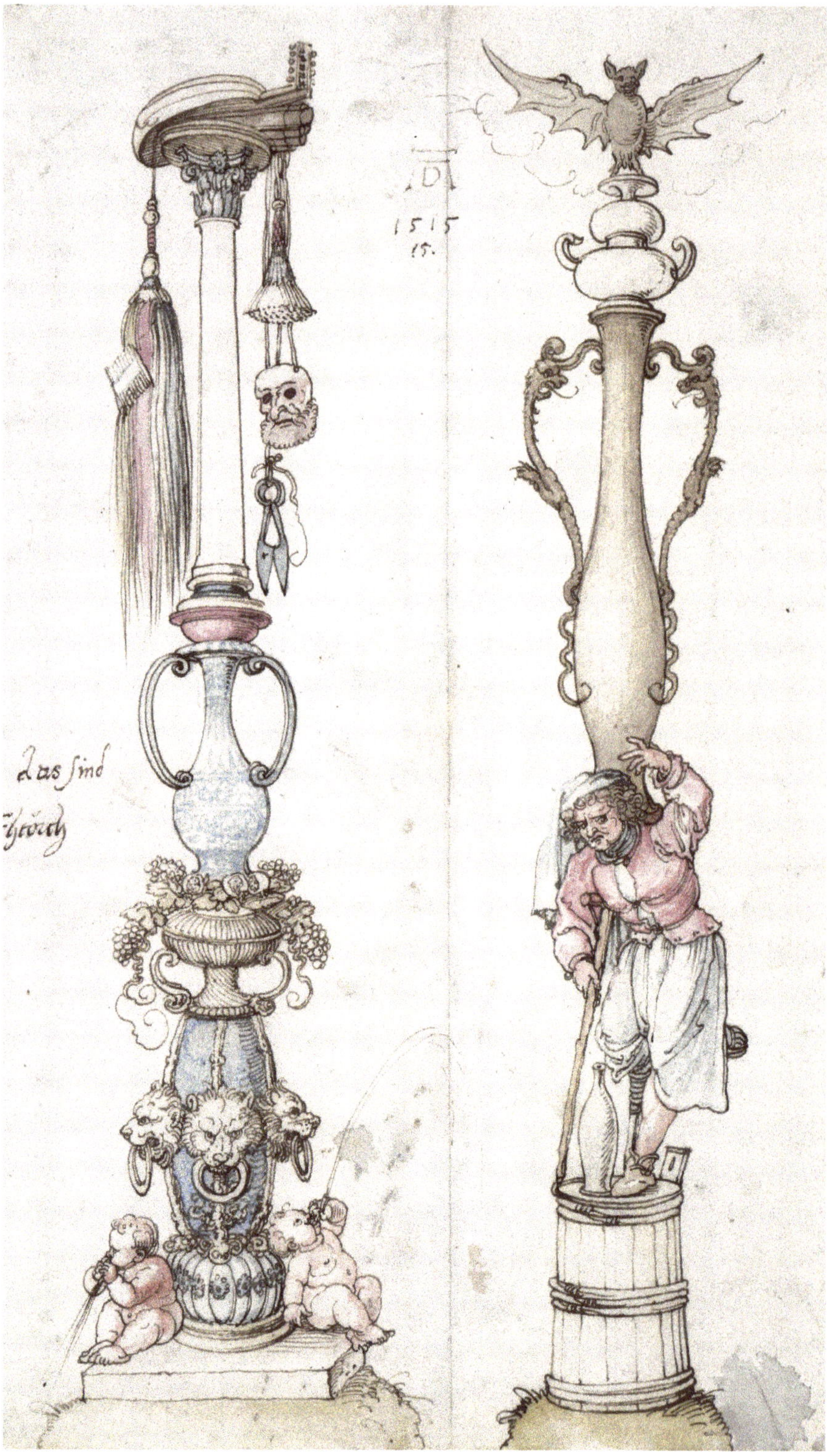

Fig. 2.15

Drawing, pen and brown ink with watercolour on paper, Albrecht Durer, 1515–18. British Museum, SL.5218.82. ©Trustees of the British Museum.

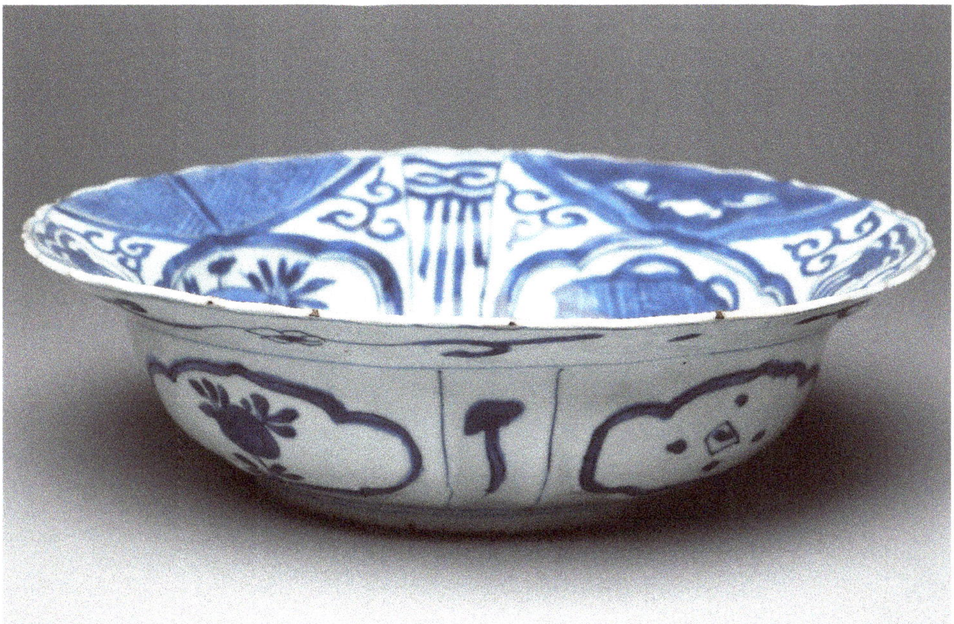

Fig. 2.16

Bowl with underglaze blue decoration in *Kraak* style, Ming dynasty, 1600–40, Ashmolean Museum, Oxford, EA 1991.24. ©Ashmolean Museum, University of Oxford.

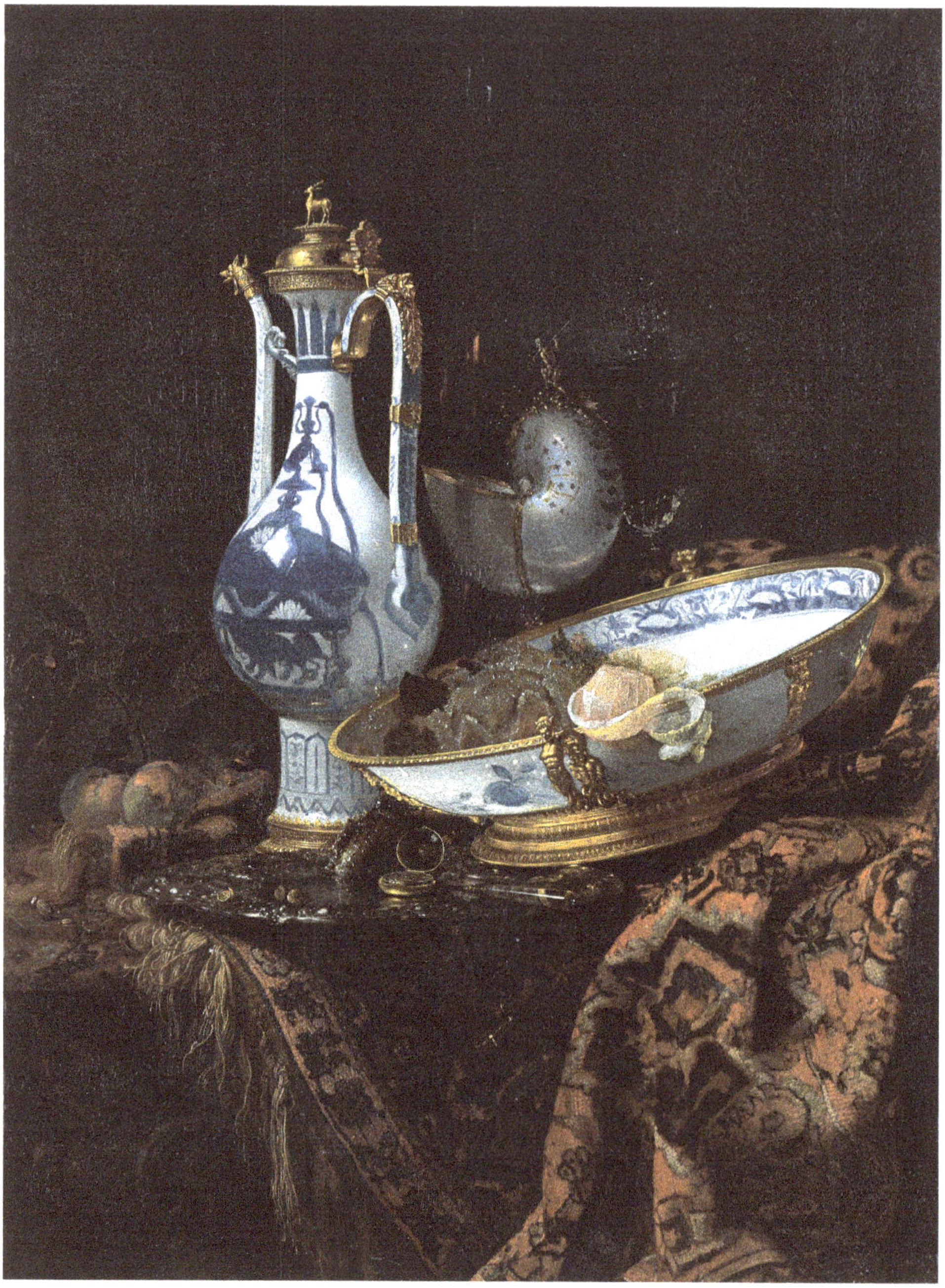

Fig. 2.17

Willem Kalf (1619–93), *Still Life with Ewer and Basin*, Fruit, *Nautilus cup and Other Objects*, c.1660, Museo Thyssen-Bornemisza, Madrid. INV. Nr. 204 (1981.77). ©Photo Scala, Florence, Museo Thyssen-Bornemisza, 2012.

This appears rather a slight reason for giving the entire group to Japan. Let us look back to history. From the Wan-li period of the Ming (1619) to the final fall of the dynasty in 1647, or from the irruption of the Tartars in 1616 down to 1662, the Khang-hi period of the Tai-thsings, we know of no porcelain having been made; but in that period, as we have seen, the industry revived. It is then that we again find a director at King-teh-chin, and seventy years later Thang-kong was reviving the bright red and devising the gold ornamentation on black which we find on the mandarin vases. Jacquemart suggests

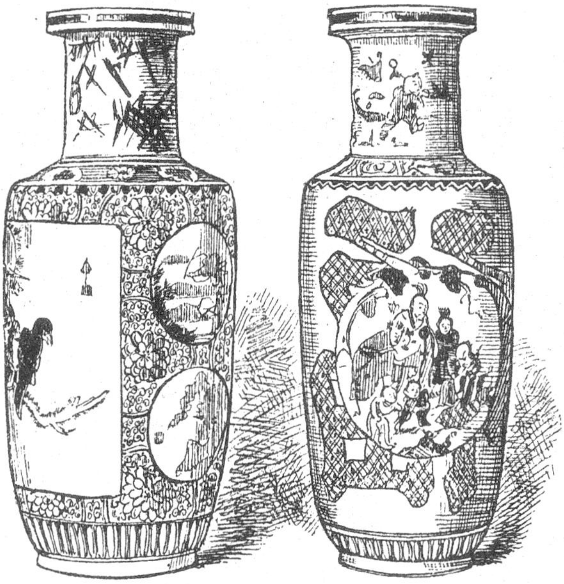

Fig. 94.—Chinese Ming Vases. White Ground. In medallions, green and brown characters and figures. Darker part red and white, with green flowers. (Geo. R. Hall Coll., Boston Museum of Fine Arts.)

"some years" after 1616 as the date when the Tartar costume was applied to vases. It is probable that it was at least from fifty to seventy years after that date, and that the best specimens belong to the Kien-long period, which began in 1736. After 1662 the imperial factory was apparently as much under the Emperor's control as it had been under the Mings; in which case he could, it is presumed, order such paintings and figures in such costumes as he pleased. We know, further, that in 1698 two foreign artists—an Italian and a Frenchman—

Fig. 3.1

Page 137 from Jennie J. Young, *The Ceramic Art: A Compendium of the History and Manufacture of Pottery and Porcelain*, 1878.

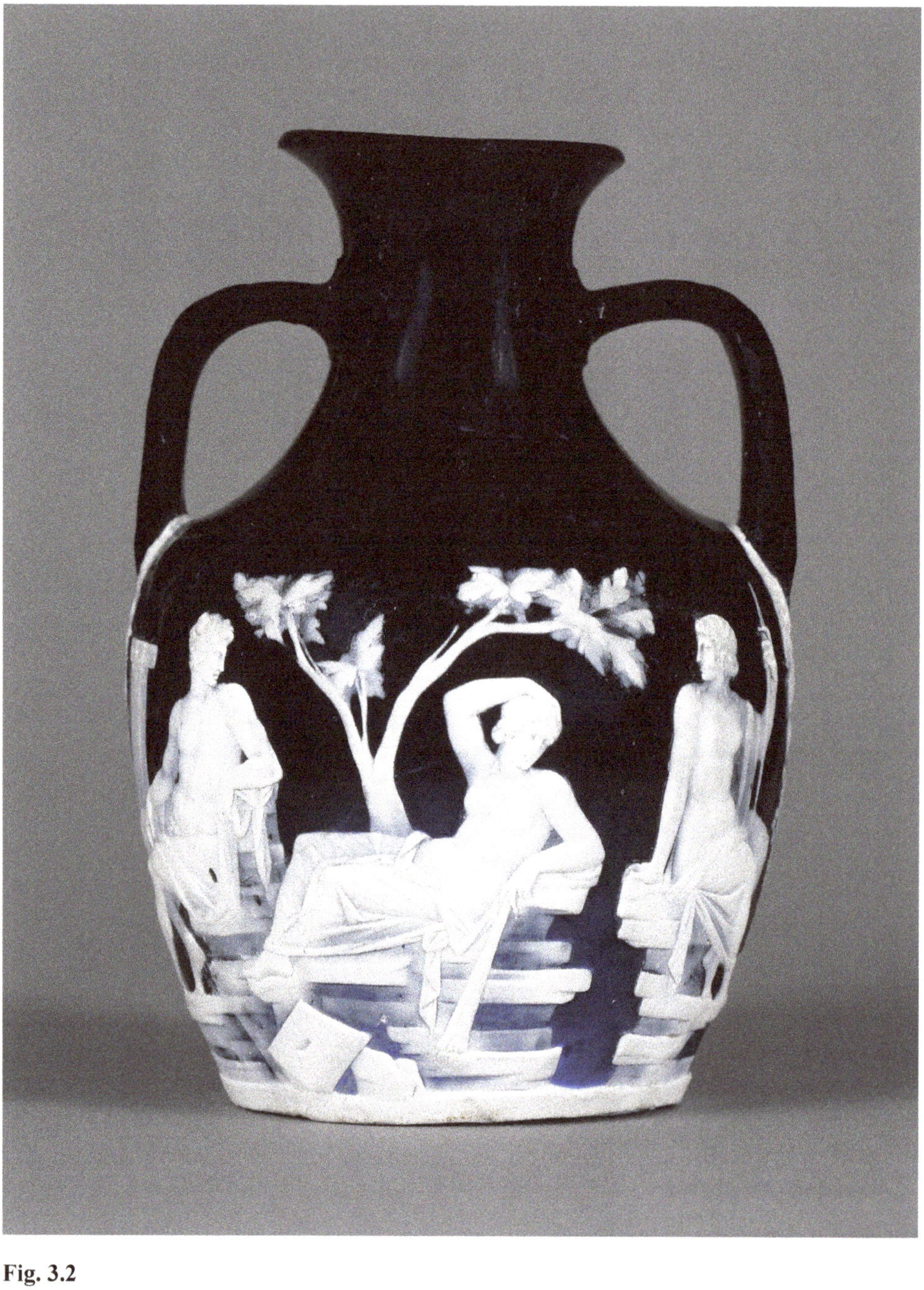

Fig. 3.2

Blue and white cameo glass amphora, Roman, c. AD 1–25, known as the Portland Vase, British Museum 1945.0927.1. ©Trustees of the British Museum.

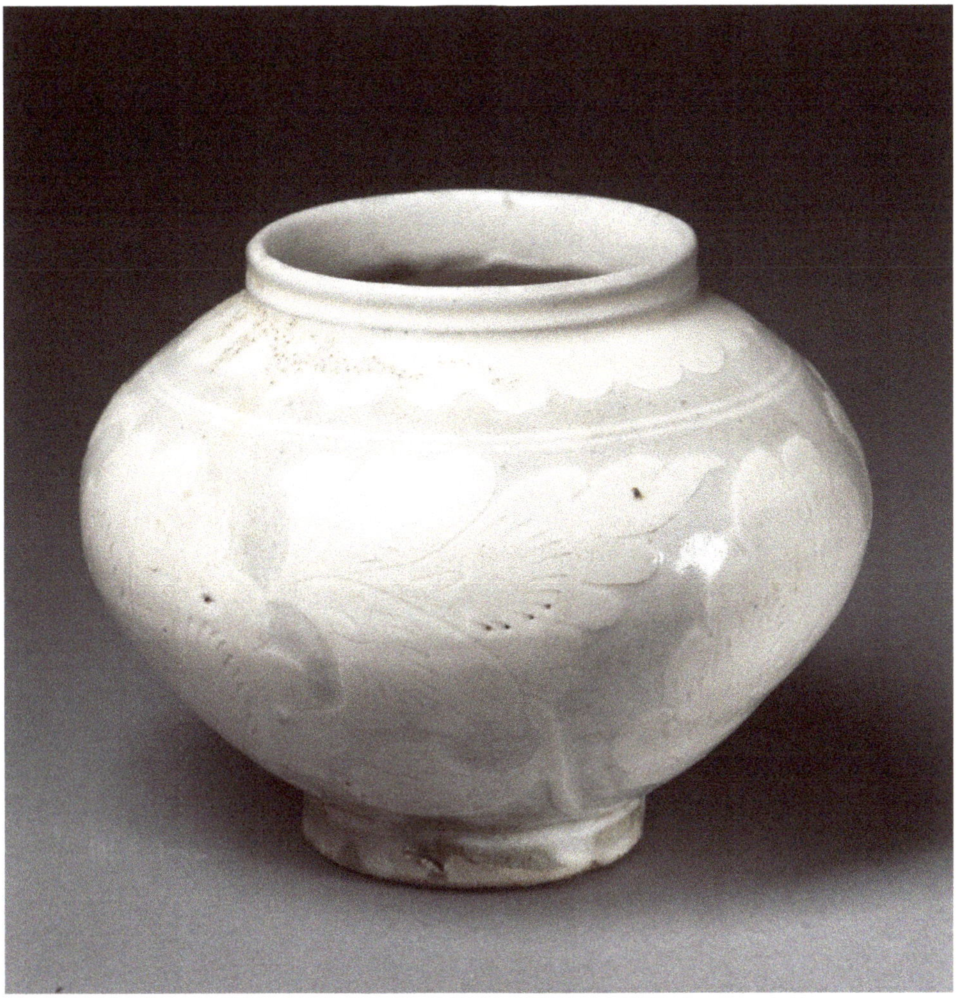

Fig. 3.3

Stoneware jar with cut slip decoration, Cizhou-type ware, Northern Song period, 1100–1200, V&A C.855–1936. ©Victoria and Albert Museum, London.

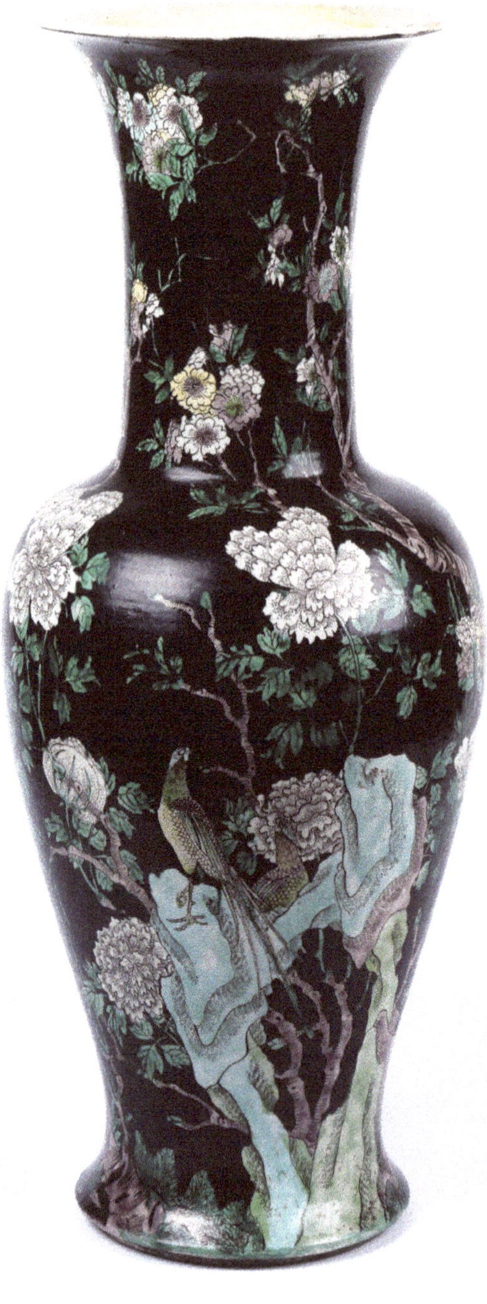

Fig. 3.4

Vase with overglaze enamel decoration in *famille noire* style, Qing dynasty, Kangxi period (1662–1722), V&A C.1315–1910. ©Victoria and Albert Museum, London.

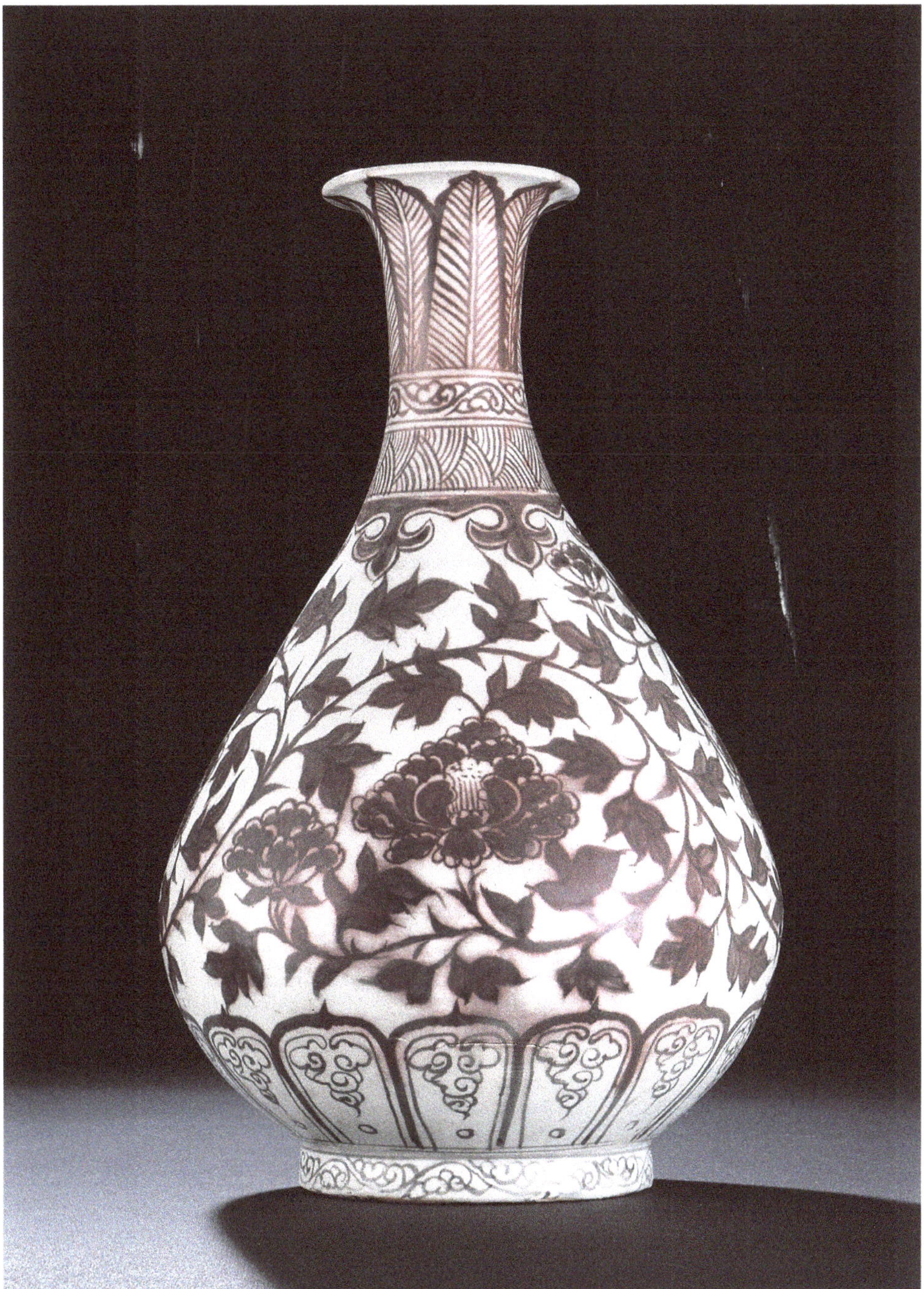

Fig. 4.1

Bottle with underglaze copper red decoration, early Ming dynasty, Hongwu period, late 14th century. Sold by Christies Hong Kong on 30 May 2006. Now in the collection of the Macao Museum. ©Christies Images Limited.

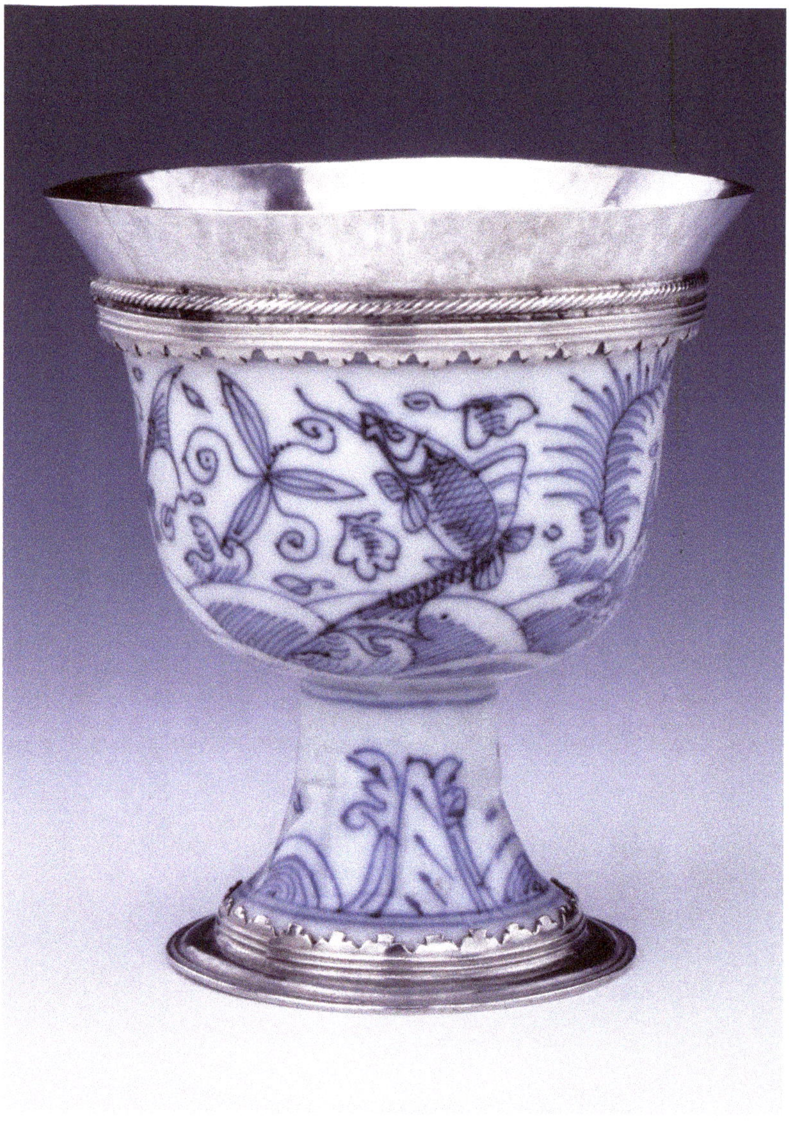

Fig. 4.2

Stem cup with underglaze blue decoration and silver mounts, Ming dynasty, c. 1600–20, known as the Leverton Harris cup, British Museum 1928.0719.1. ©Trustees of the British Museum.

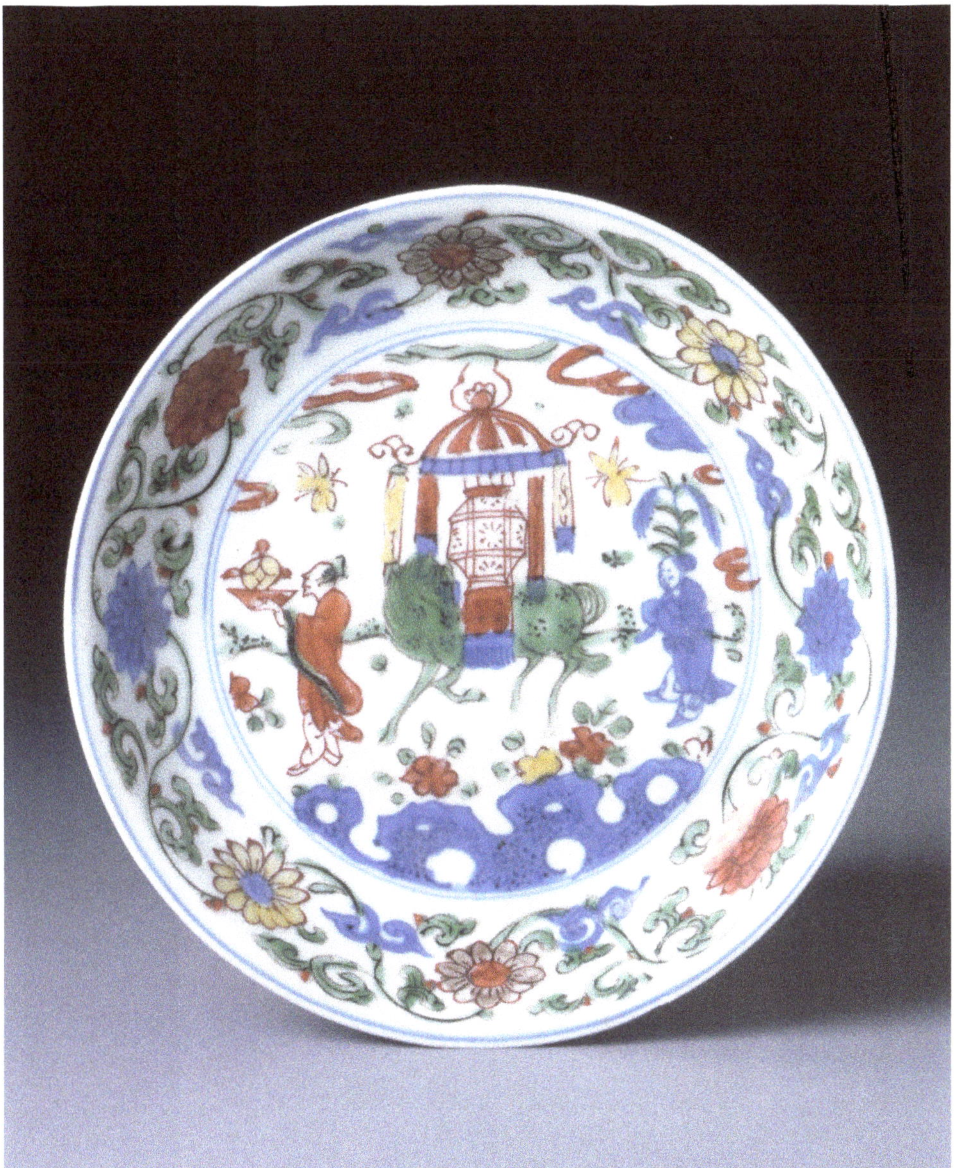

Fig. 4.3

Dish with underglaze blue and overglaze enamel decoration in *wucai* style, Ming dynasty, Wanli mark and period (1573–1620), V&A C.1037–1917. Gift of Sir Percival David. ©Victoria and Albert Museum, London.

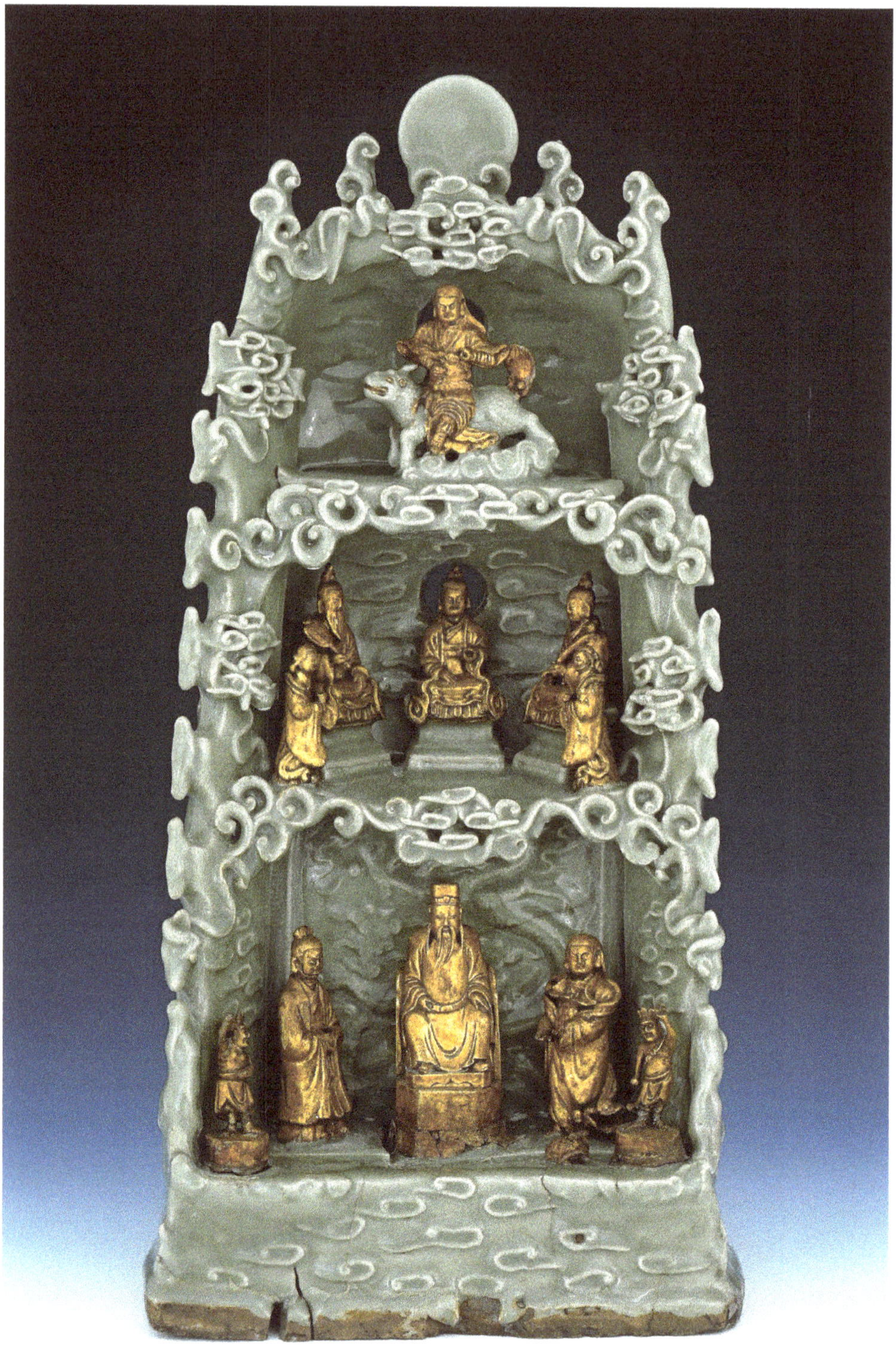

Fig. 4.4

Celadon-glazed Daoist shrine, Longquan ware, Ming dynasty, Yongle period, dated 1406, British Museum 1929.0114.1. Gift of Sir Percival David. ©Trustees of the British Museum.

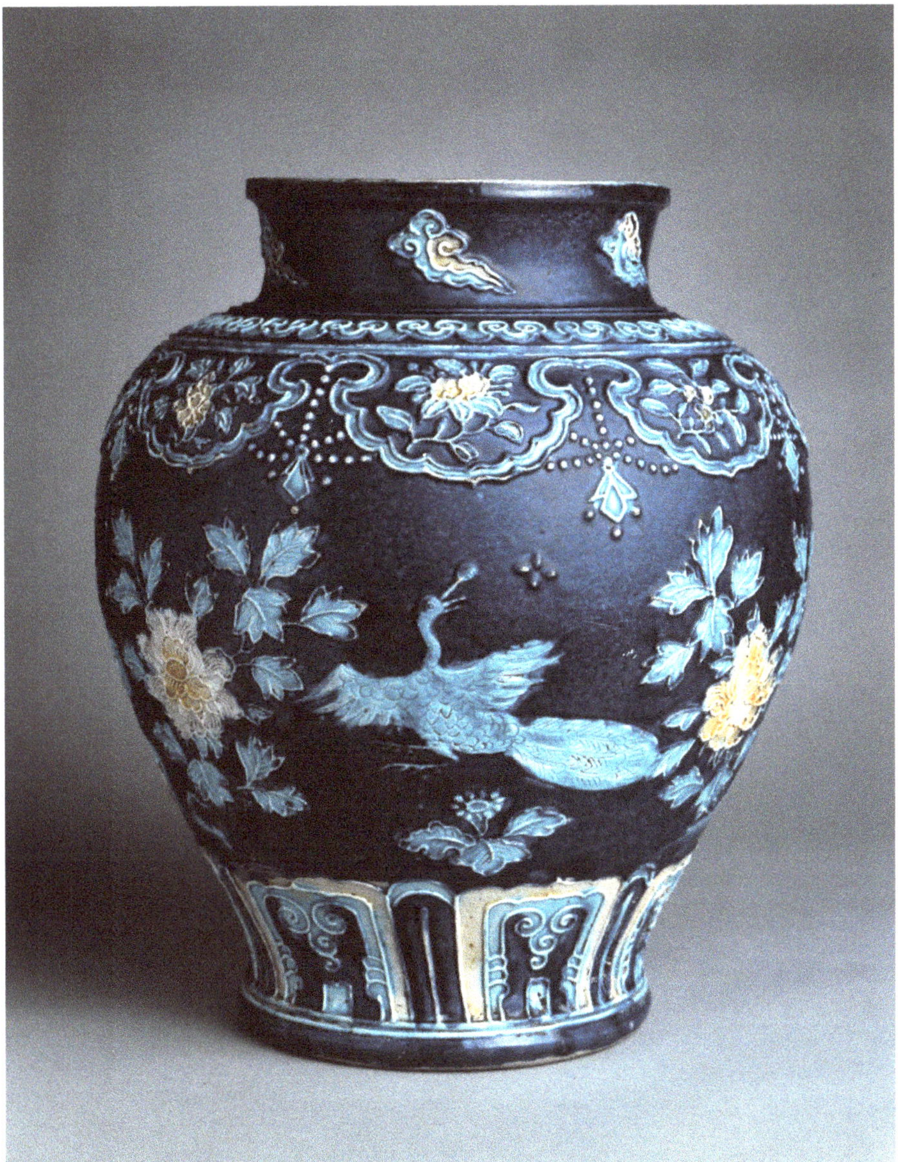

Fig. 4.5

Wine jar with on-biscuit enamel decoration in *fahua* style, Ming dynasty, Hongzhi period (1488–1505), PDF 759, British Museum. ©SOAS and the Trustees of the British Museum.

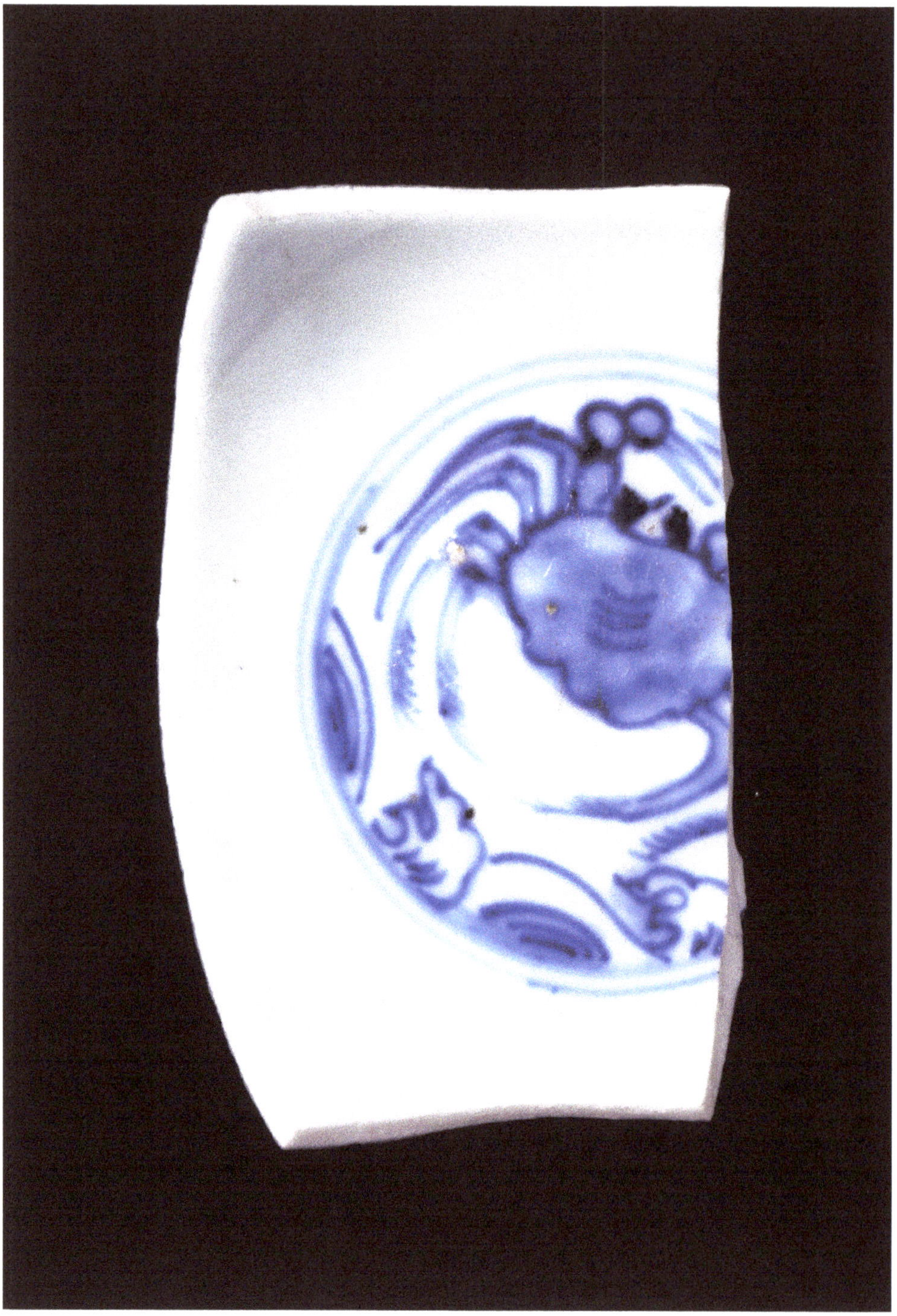

Fig. 4.6

Porcelain sherd with underglaze blue decoration, Ming dynasty, second half of 16th century, V&A C.174–1934. ©Victoria and Albert Museum, London.

3

Porcelain as Metaphor—Inventing 'the Ming Vase' (18th–20th centuries)

Introduction

In the preceding two chapters, we examined how Ming porcelain first was developed, its production and consumption in Ming-period China, and how it was appreciated in its original culture. We then considered the movement of Ming porcelain around the world during and shortly after the Ming period and how this led to forms of consumption and conceptions of Ming porcelain (and Chinese porcelain in general) different from those experienced in China. As we have seen, those cultures that did encounter and consume Ming porcelain often developed an enduring taste for it. Chinese porcelains then became part of their own material culture history, whether through the actual objects (which did not suddenly disappear after the Ming period), by means of the imitation of aspects of these objects in local products, or in the continued consumption of contemporary Chinese ceramics (usually export wares) into the subsequent Qing period. The movement of Ming porcelain studied thus far has therefore focused on its physical transfer between cultures and its appropriation by, and impact on, these cultures, as well as the impact of cultural practices on Ming porcelain itself. In this chapter, however, we will consider a different form of transfer and consumption, one which might be described as conceptual, because the physical object of Ming porcelain also inspired a linguistic invention, becoming a figure of speech in the English language. This represents an unusual and rarely explored incidence of transformation, from object to concept.

This form of transformation is not one which has previously been considered at length for any type of object, but it is one which has recently generated some comment in scholarly circles,[1] particularly those concerned with the study of Ming China. An awareness has developed that one of the most frequently stated symbols of fragility and 'preciousness' in contemporary English discourse is that of the proverbial 'Ming vase'. From something in which one would not 'grow spuds'[2] to the code name for a nuclear test,[3] references to this symbol can be found in a wide range of media, from fiction and poetry, to the popular press, commercial publications, cartoons, and theatrical scripts, as well as military jargon. The phrase 'the Ming vase' is so common now in English that its origins are generally unquestioned. What is interesting, however, is that the phrase references a specific type of object with, as we have demonstrated, its own extensive history encompassing not just Ming China but several cultures and time periods.

Generally speaking, by implication, it would seem that the phrase 'the Ming vase' literally refers to an actual, individual, Ming-period vase (see Fig. 1.4) like 'the Mona Lisa' in painting, and the usual assumption is that this vase would also be made of porcelain. As we have seen in chapter one, Ming ceramics consisted of much more than just those made of porcelain, but after the 15th century, it was certainly Ming porcelain which was the most widely traded kind of Ming ceramics. The other part of the phrase, 'vase', is also of interest. There are references in English to 'vase' as a vessel form dating back to at least the early 17th century but not in any specific material.[4] The word became more popular with the emergence of so-called 'Greek vases' on the collecting scene in the 18th century[5] and began to be associated with ceramic, particularly after the publication of William Hamilton's (1730–1803) Greek vase collection.[6] Nonetheless, throughout the 18th and first decades of the 19th centuries, the 'vase' as a form was still vaguely defined and could be either metal or ceramic in both technical literature and poetry.[7] In the catalogue of the touring exhibition of Nathan Dunn's *Ten Thousand Chinese Things* (1839), for example, the references to 'vases' range from 'superb China vase' (p. 4), to 'ancient bronze vase' (p. 40), 'sculptured marble vase' (p. 54), and 'small metallic vase' (p. 65). Porcelains are vaguely described as 'vases' or 'vessels' throughout this text with no one shape consistently referred to as one or the other.[8] By the mid-19th century, however, 'vase' came further to be specifically associated with an upright vessel form and thus was a common descriptive for a wide range of vessel-based objects, including ceramics. When the adjective 'Ming' was added to the 'vase' term, this now further defined a particular type of vase as being: a) Chinese, and b) porcelain. 'Ming' was not used to describe 'vases' in other materials. The reasons for these cultural associations will be explored in detail later in this chapter, but it is the porcelain material, and the ideas associated with it, that has engendered specific meanings for the phrase 'Ming vase': fragility, preciousness, or antique. In addition, perhaps because of its Chinese origins, 'the Ming vase' has also become a literary motif associated with exoticness and danger.

When the origins of the whole phrase are considered, therefore, a number of questions and issues arise. These reveal much about not only the appropriation of physical objects in symbolic and conceptual language but also the significance of specific objects referenced in cultures beyond that which produced them. For example, 'the Ming vase' would seem to be simply (or literally) a porcelain vase made in Ming China, that is from the 14th to the 17th centuries, but it is much more than that. Our appropriation of this physical object from China as a metaphorical symbol for several related concepts is very interesting as it is evidence of the continuing objectification of China in English cultural discourse. There is a large body of literature about this process which essentially has determined that 'China' was a locus for political and cultural aspirations as well as anxiety, and this developed as a consequence of Britain's diplomatic and economic relations with China.[9] However, there has yet to be a comprehensive study of one particular aspect of this phenomenon which, like the transformations discussed in chapter two, is associated with the impact of foreign consumption on Chinese 'things', rather than the other way around.[10] This chapter will thus explore the mechanism(s) for and history of the transformation of a foreign object into an English-language device, and consider this process as a stage in the evolution of a type of pre-modern Chinese object from physical, tangible thing to an intangible but meaningful concept.

Why Ming?

In order to examine how this particular Chinese object came to be associated with English-language symbols and concepts, we first have to ask the fundamental question, why Ming? That is, why, as one scholar of Ming material culture asked, a Ming-period vase rather than a Qing or Song one?[11] Ceramic vessels of the 'vase'-type have been made in China since the Neolithic period, and most of the Chinese vessels which were exported to, and consumed in, Europe and the Americas were of late Ming and Qing dates, that is 16th to early 20th century. Thus the actual date of manufacture of *a*, or *the*, 'Ming vase' is not a primary consideration in the phrase, because it is not one associated with connoisseurship identification, or with authenticity. Instead, 'Ming' in this context has come to mean something more than a date. It appears, in fact, that 'Ming' when associated with 'vase' is a representation of 'Chinese' above all, so in order to answer the question 'Why Ming' with respect to ceramics, we have to briefly consider the general history of the use of the word (and the concept of) 'Ming' in English-language texts.

The earliest literature about China in English pre-dates the Ming period but as a topic of English-and European-language literature, China became the subject of much wider publication during the Ming period itself. China therefore came to the consciousness of English-language readers (and others) during the 15th and 16th centuries. As is well known, earlier texts concerning China were written in the 13th century, by for example, William of Rubruck, the Flemish missionary whose work was translated into English by Richard Hakluyt, and Marco Polo (assuming he did go to China).[12] But these were not widely read until the later 15th and 16th centuries, with the advent of printing, and English translation.[13] Depending on which version of Polo's *Travels* one believes (there are, to date, 120 of them),[14] he was one of the first Europeans to actually visit China and then report on his observations, but these reports were general in nature and were perhaps created by someone else providing a fictionalized account.[15] In the 14th and 15th centuries, what Jonathan Spence has termed 'The Catholic Century', more Europeans associated with religious orders began to have direct experience of China, and reported on it at the same time, and this of course would have been during the actual Ming period.

It was perhaps because of this contemporary experience that none of these texts referred to 'the Ming dynasty'. This supports Craig Clunas' statement that distance in time and place was required for the development of 'Ming' as both a historical and chronological category. It also parallels the Chinese thinking about time periods, which are essentially named by the succeeding government or rulership. As Clunas has also noted, in China, 'Ming' thus became a subject or a category in the period of nostalgia following the demise of that dynasty.[16] In the succeeding Qing period, 'Ming' became a safe historical period, which in ceramic terms partly explains the emergence of 'Ming-style' porcelains, which often featured not just recognizably Ming designs and colours but also apocryphal Ming reign marks.[17]

Outside of China, in the later Ming period, that is the mid-16th to 17th-centuries, a few texts about China written by European visitors began to mention 'Ming' or the 'Ming period/dynasty'. One of the earliest to give a detailed account of China was printed in English in 1588: Juan González de Mendoza's *The Historie of the great and mightie kingdome of China, and the situation thereof.*[18] This book was a compilation of accounts by Spanish and Portuguese priests and was very widely read.[19] Partly inspired by Mendoza, by the 17th century there began to be specific references in English to the time or reign period of 'Ming', or 'Min' as it was often spelled. One of the earliest was in Samuel Purchas' (?1577–1626) compilation of travel works by Richard Hakluyt (see chapter two) titled *Hakluytus Posthumous* or *Purchas His Pilgrimes* (4 vols., 1625) which refers to the 'Kingdome Min'.[20] One notable slightly later example, which influenced the work of many other writers, was Martini's *De bello tartarico in Sinis historia* of 1654, which gives 'the first full account in a European language of the downfall of the Ming dynasty' and was translated into English.[21] This was based on his own direct experiences of China at the end of the Ming and was published just a decade after that dynasty's 'fall'. In the later 17th century, further histories of China began to appear in English and these also include accounts of the Ming dynasty and its decline, this being an attractive theme for such texts. One example is Elkanah Settle's *The Conquest of China* of 1669, which was inspired by Martini.[22] Also in the 17th century, China appears in a number of the traveller's accounts that were published at the time but, apart from the reference in Purchas noted above (which includes materials from the previous century), and Johann Grueber's *China and France* (1676), there appear to be very few specific references to 'Ming' China.[23]

"Chyna" and Porcelain of the Ming

However, it was in the early 17th century that more frequent references not only to China the place but also to 'china' the object made of porcelain, or 'chyna' and its related term 'purslane', began to appear not only in royal inventories, as noted in the previous chapter, but also in the popular literature, such as Shakespeare's *Measure for Measure* and Ben Jonson's *Britain's Burse*, thus contributing to the wider spread, beyond scholarly circles, of notions about China.[24] In the later 17th century, there also began to be more frequent references to porcelain and other objects as 'chyna' in fiction and literature concerned with domestic life, which associated the material with women. For example, William Wycherley's *The Country Wife* of 1675 features Lady Fidget and her collection, and Hannah Wooley's cookbook of the same year recommends the use of 'china' serving dishes.[25] There are, however, few references to 'Ming' in these texts and none which connect 'Ming' with porcelain or ceramics. For this one has to wait until the mid-19th century.

In the meantime, the Ming dynasty continued to appear in the general histories of the world which became popular in the 18th century and which acknowledged a Chinese dynastic chronology, such as that of Gibbon (1758–63);[26] it also came up as a topic in specific histories of China such as Du Halde's *History of China* of 1736.[27] Throughout the 18th century, therefore, China, more often now through ceramics or porcelain, continued to be used as subject matter in both non-fiction and fiction, and still usually in association with women. Oliver Goldsmith's *Citizen of the World* of the 1760s, for instance, mentions a woman's Chinese porcelain collection[28] and in Pope's *The Rape of the Lock* (1712) 'the narrative climax turns on a piece of porcelain'.[29] There are numerous other references to women and porcelain, and to China the place, but so far none associating 'Ming' with porcelain.

The first time this occurs is in the mid-19th century with Robert Fortune (1812–80), the British naturalist who visited China and Japan after 1842 and published his observations in 1863.[30] In this publication he states: 'Some of the foreign residents in Peking ... had, from time to time, picked up some beautiful examples of Ming porcelain.'[31] Fortune was a collector of both plants and objects, including ceramics, and these were sold by Christies in 1857, 1859 and 1860.[32] His text is essentially a continuation of the travel literature that had become so popular in the Elizabethan period[33] but this time the narrative was based on actual—often dangerous—experience of the countries concerned. Fortune is perhaps best known in popular history for his transfer of tea plants from China to India, but he made a number of other significant contributions to botanical history. Nonetheless, it is interesting that his 'collection' of ceramics should have been mentioned in one of the first comprehensive histories of ceramics in English, Joseph Marryat's *A History of Pottery and Porcelain: Medieval and Modern* of 1857. Here at last, we also have a couple of references, with respect to ceramics, to '... the great dynasty of the Ming, under which the porcelain manufacture greatly increased'.[34] There is in fact quite a long discussion of Ming ceramics in the following pages, all appearing in a chapter on the 'History of Porcelain: China'.

While Marryat's text may not have been widely read, it was certainly used as a primary reference by others whose work followed his. His inclusion of Ming ceramics confirms that this was a category of ceramics already established in 1857, at least among the ceramic literature readership (small as it might have been), and one which can be seen as part of the wider history of porcelain objects. By the 1860s, therefore, Chinese porcelain of the Ming dynasty appears in literature in two forms: as material evidence of Chinese culture of a named period (Fortune) and as part of a wider world history of ceramics (Marryat). Histories of ceramics in this period with their globalizing approach in fact parallel the interest in world history represented by the works of Gibbon and Du Halde, mentioned previously. In addition, this was also the period in which the world was on display in public exhibitions, such as that of the great Exhibition at Crystal Palace (1851),[35] demonstrating further that interest in world history much predates the current vogue today.

As 'porcelain of the Ming dynasty', by now recognized in ceramic periodization, ceramics of this type would continue to feature as a category of Chinese porcelain and of Chinese culture in texts related to connoisseurship. Possibly as a consequence of their appearance in encyclopaedic histories, the interest in and references to specifically Ming porcelain filtered down into popular literature shortly afterwards. This, in turn, is perhaps what led to this category of Chinese porcelain developing a separate and independent identity. Marryat, for example, says very little about the Chinese porcelain that was contemporary with his book. He mentions 'Ming' a number of times but 'Ts'ing' (Qing) only once. Usually, the reference to the Qing period is presented in ethnic terms instead: 'Tartar' or 'Mantchow Tartars'.[36] This would again seem to confirm Clunas' theory about distance being necessary for recognition and assimilation.

Assuming that Marryat and similar writers were used as primary sources, it is not surprising that in the connoisseurship-related essays that began to appear more often in popular publications from the 1870s, Ming porcelain came to be singled out. One of the earliest popular references to porcelain of the Ming can be found in an article on 'Curious Old China' in Charles Dickens' periodical, *All the Year Round* (vol. 14, April 1875).[37] In this, the anonymous author quite specifically stated that 'Between 1426 and 1435 was produced the finest porcelain of the Ming dynasty'.[38] This is interesting because it refers to the Xuande reign period but does not name it as such, as would have been the case in Chinese-language literature. This suggests that a source which referenced Chinese texts may have been consulted. This is possible because by that date, the *Jingdezhen taolu* of 1815 had already been translated into French and published as *Histoire et fabrication de la porcelaine chinoise*. This includes references to the Ming period in general and to the 'Siouen-te' (Xuande) period specifically.[39] This book subsequently was cited by many ceramic texts well into the 20th century. Thus the statement about Xuande-period porcelain in 'Curious Old China' is a statement of connoisseurship and as such, probably referred to blue and white porcelain. The latter was known to the general public as it was quite fashionable among artists of the Aesthetic Movement.[40] These included J. M. W. Whistler (1834–1903) and Oscar Wilde (1854–1900), who also wrote about 'blue China' and associated it with decadence. (The artists, in turn, were ridiculed for their 'passion for china'.)[41]

As will be noted in chapter four, by 1875, Chinese ceramics had been a part of English material culture for over 300 years. Consumption of it had reached a stage of overfamiliarity and thus disdain on the part of some, as it was associated with dangerous passions for things and decoration.[42] On the other hand it, and ceramics inspired by it, was commonly used in quantity as tableware and appears as such in paintings and interiors of the time.[43] Thus the notion of connoisseurship of such ceramics, as referenced in the Dickens periodical, was not novel at this time at all, especially when connoisseurship as an activity was gaining in popularity and recognition through collector's clubs and related literature. The Burlington Fine Arts Club (est. 1866), for example, staged regular exhibitions with published catalogues, and their members included the artists Whistler and Val Princep (1838–1904).[44] Art dealers were also active in this arena with a number of shops in London featuring what were still often called 'oriental ceramics'.[45] The art market was well developed and connoisseurship naturally accompanied this.

With so much exposure to Chinese porcelain, which had been deliberately collected in Britain as early as the 16th century, the fact that knowledge of the subject, at least among those who pursued the collecting of it, was becoming more specialized and widespread is not surprising. The art and interiors magazines of the time helped to promote this. Thus the earliest dedicated article on Ming porcelain in this genre of literature was published in the *Art Journal*, also in 1875. In 'Chinese Porcelain—particularly that of the Ta Ming dynasty', the author, Captain Lawrence-Archer, recounts his visits to China in the period shortly after the 'sacking' of the Summer Palace (Yuanming yuan) in 1862. But rather than giving a broad overview, he focuses on Ming porcelain. He states from the outset that before leaving for China he familiarized himself with such Chinese porcelains as were available in collections in England, and he found them wanting.

> Before leaving England, the writer had been at some pains to acquire a practical knowledge of the manufacture and ornamentation of porcelain, and, like many others, he was dissatisfied with the majority of those specimens of Chinese origin, which have been handed down as heirlooms in old families; and he felt assured that *these* could never have issued from the best manufactories in China.[46]

In this the author says much which reveals the state of the field at that time. He tells us that there are collections available with handed-down pieces, that there are enough people with knowledge of this type of object to be able to determine that such pieces are not or could not be the same as those made in China, and that his primary interest in China was its porcelain. The author then states that the porcelain of the 15th and 16th centuries had attained a form of perfection in ornamentation, crucially representing 'imperial taste', an early, if not the earliest, reference in English to what has become a trope in Chinese ceramic discourse.[47] In this case, he associated 'imperial taste' with 'true beauty of form and chaste embellishment'.[48] This is interesting because in some ways it reflects the ideals of the Arts and Crafts movement which were also current at that time and which professed to privilege form and function, but it also contrasts with that same movement's promotion of sometimes extreme ornament.[49] What Lawrence-Archer values therefore is something that normally is associated with much later Modernist taste.[50]

Apart from this, Lawrence-Archer's essay can be seen as part of the wider tradition of writing ceramic history, in particular the ceramics of China, which was current in the second half of the 19th century. He references the general porcelain history noted previously, that of Stanislas Julien of the Sévres factory (with Alphonse Salvetat and Johann Hoffman), which was published in French in 1856 and was based on a Chinese text.[51] He also considers the ceramics through the framework of the reign mark, in a period in which inscriptions were also gaining more currency in English scholarship on China.[52] The title of his essay incorporates not 'Ming' but rather 'Ta Ming' which refers to the first two characters of a Ming reign mark, so that he is thinking of this period through the porcelain, in terms of how it is named in reign marks. He also states that reign marks are how one distinguishes 'imperial taste' pieces (something which is still believed today by many) and suggests that his knowledge of these distinguishes him from the mere 'curio hunter' who is ignorant and therefore to be disdained.[53] The author is of course writing about his own collection and so is determined to promote his connoisseurship skills, but his essay is important because it is one of the first to focus exclusively on Ming porcelain, treating it as a separate category, in the wider art literature.

A Definite Article and Figure of Speech

It is perhaps these early publications about ceramics in general and then those that focused on Ming that led to a new conceptual identity for Ming porcelain, beyond a chronological category of Chinese porcelain or a form of Chinese material culture from that period: that of 'the Ming vase'. In the late 1870s, there began to be references to a more specific type of Ming porcelain, and more specific descriptions of what came to be a separately-identified type of ware with associated forms, such as 'vases'. As we have seen, the vase as a form name has a relatively long history in English, so by the later 19th century it had become a standard category of form for ceramics, one which is open and vertical. Histories of ceramics and Chinese ceramics were being written with greater frequency and often illustrations were included. In consequence, there was need for a specific vocabulary to describe and define the forms and decoration of the ceramics. This led to the development of standard names for forms such as 'coupe' or 'vases'. It is therefore in a history of ceramics published in 1878 that we see what may be the first cataloguing reference to a 'Ming vase', which assigns this English name to a type of Chinese form. In Jennie J. Young's *The Ceramic Art: A Compendium of the History and Manufacture of Pottery and Porcelain*, she lists various objects and captions a pair of illustrated pieces as 'Ming vases'[54] [Fig. 3.1]. The pieces illustrated are quite obviously not of Ming date but that demonstrates how limited connoisseurship knowledge was at the time. Histories such as this one nonetheless would have been the main sources of information on ceramics in English, so it is here that writers of fiction and journalism may have looked for names of styles or forms.

This is particularly likely in decorating literature. Chinese ceramics (mostly Qing) were widely collected and consumed in the later 19th century, as we will see; thus they were featured in interiors with some frequency. At the same time, the late 19th century saw an increasing body of literature associated with interior decoration, and thus it is not surprising that the first non-ceramic literary reference to a 'Ming vase' would be in such a publication, *The Decorator and Furnisher*, in a series of essays about 'Boston Artists' Studios'.[55] Artists like Whistler and Rossetti championed Chinese (and Japanese) porcelain in their work (particularly blue and white, which was usually purchased in Holland), so the appearance of this early reference in an article about artists' studios is fitting. In a descriptive segment, the author, Frank Robinson, says:

> You notice there is nothing in the room of a very white tone that is exposed to the light. A bust of Venus, in plaster, is in the dark corner on the piano top, side of it rests a brass tray and nearby is a Ming vase catching the light in silvery spots.[56]

The artist in question has displayed the Ming vase as an appropriately reflective prop but importantly it is not described as a Chinese vase or 'Old China', or even 'Blue China', all current at the time, but rather as a 'Ming vase', thus presenting this as a known type of object in 1885. The reader is not given an explanation of what this object is but is assumed to be familiar with it. This is confirmed by the publication of a short story titled 'The Ming Vase' in *The New York Times*, February 1888, using the definite article 'the' for the first time.[57] In this tale, which takes place in China, a young candidate for the imperial examinations travels from the countryside to the capital for the exams and is given a good luck gift by his lady love. The gift is 'the whitest, purest, most unadorned vase of porcelain he had ever seen'. [Part I] Knowing little about such things, the protagonist, Wu-tao, assumes that it is a princely object and keeps it hidden, to be looked at in secret. In spite of what is suggested by the title of the story, the location of the examination is Kaifeng, during the reign of Ming Huang, and therefore the story must take place during the Tang dynasty in the 8th century. Wu-tao stays with a patron in Kaifeng, a prominent person who examines his vase and declares:

> This vase, my son, is instinct with magic. Let none know of its existence—keep it close—at night shut all the doors, suspend within it a little paper lantern, and fix your eyes on its porcelain sides. Perhaps you will see something that will delight you; perhaps you will not be gratified at all—that depends on your own heart. [Part I]

We have here (in spite of the confused chronology) additionally an early association in English of porcelain with magic, the vase appearing to have special qualities. This is presented in language which, while intending to sound 'Chinese', reflects then current stereotypes of China and its mysteriousness. Essentially, part of China's perceived exoticness was expressed through assumed magical powers of either people or objects.[58]

In this short story therefore, the Ming vase, like the ring in the Charlemagne legend studied by Calvino or Wilkie Collins' *The Moonstone* (1868), is the true protagonist, rather than the scholar, because it is the vase that establishes the relationships between the characters.[59] The story reveals the history of the vase, but with yet another ahistorical premise: 'Later he learned that two vases had been made by a celebrated artist of the age of Confucius, one of which was destroyed, the other had disappeared.'[60] The 'Ming vase' of the title was not of the Ming period (perhaps the author meant 'Ming Huang' period) but is used as a simile for the mysteriousness and magic of China and reflects already-held beliefs among the readership of *The New York Times* in the 1880s. It is therefore perhaps because of preexisting beliefs about China, and the popularity of collecting blue and white porcelain, much of which was thought to be Ming, that 'Ming vase' came to be a kind of cultural icon and a motif in English-language literature.[61]

In 'The Ming Vase' (1888), the tone of the story intriguingly suggests a familiarity with recent works in English on Confucius. For example, James Legge had published *The Chinese Classics* in 1867, and perhaps this explains the connection with Confucius that is maintained for the vase and the young scholar's patron throughout the story. We also later learn that though initially thwarted, Wu-tao becomes a famous painter and calligrapher, with 'Prince Ming Whang' as his patron. We can conclude, therefore, that the story is about the real Tang-period painter Wu Daozi 吴道子 (Wu Daoxuan, 680–740) whose work had appeared in a British Museum catalogue of 1886.[62] This book was reviewed in the cultural literature of the time, including the *Quarterly Review*, and the story of 'Wu Tao-tsz' was noted several times in other texts, such as *The Academy and Literature*.[63] In fact, this Tang painter would come to be considered one of the most famous in English-language studies of Chinese painting, up until about the mid-20th century, perhaps because of a perceived 'mystery' surrounding his life history. In fictionalized biographies, Wu is said to have 'disappeared' into one of his mural paintings, never to be seen again....[64]

Singular Pieces

Thus our anonymous fictional story in *The New York Times* (the author is listed only as 'C de K') brings together several currents in English-language discourse about China and 'the vase'. From this period onwards, the object 'the Ming vase' becomes transformed into a sign or figure of speech and gains new meanings and associations over time, and in different genres of literature. The crucial development takes place when 'Ming vases' as a category of things gain a definite article, either 'the' or 'a', and then become a separate category which denotes a singular object, rather than a generalized category of objects, such as 'Ming porcelain'. The singular object then comes to take on other characteristics by virtue of its perceived uniqueness. A useful comparative example is perhaps that of *the* Portland vase, a Roman glass 'vase' now in the British Museum [Fig. 3.2].[65] The history of the ownership and treatment of this piece since the 18th century is well known and documented, and it has gained its identity (and notoriety) through its ownership and through industrial imitation (the Wedgwood versions, for example). As a result, the Portland Vase has been given a definite article 'the' because the 'original' is apparently unique. Its transformative trajectory, however, is quite different from that of 'the Ming vase', which was never an identifiable, singular object.[66] In contrast, this was, and is, from the outset, an invention.

For 'the Ming vase', the *New York Times* story is the first to do this but only in its title, as the story itself does not feature the term. For an example of this separate identification, and the real beginnings of the constructed sign, we must look to 20th-century literature and discourse. However, the issue of 'why Ming' still needs to be addressed as the newly invented object sign could easily have been 'the Qing vase'. Most of the Chinese porcelain consumed in Europe and America in the later 19th century was actually of Qing date, rather than Ming. However, as we have seen, connoisseurship of Ming objects was still in its infancy and the preferencing of Ming over Qing had more to do with the prevailing image of 'Ming' China, however confused it might have been. 'Ming' was more familiar than 'Qing' as a cultural signifier, probably because there was sufficient historical distance for it to be named and conceptualized. The 19th and early 20th centuries were still the Qing period, and therefore too contemporary.

Some of the answers to this remaining question of 'why Ming', with reference to ceramics at least, can be found in the discussion of Chinese objects published in 1893 by James Dyer Ball (1847–1919), *Things Chinese*.[67] Dyer Ball was a British civil servant based in Hong Kong; he had written previously a number of books on the Chinese language and an English-Chinese cookbook.[68] In his latest work, however, he chose to focus on 'things', by which he meant objects and cultural terms. The book is structured as an encyclopaedia with entries ranging from 'abacus' to 'riots' and 'zoology'. There is an entry for 'Porcelain and Pottery' and here we find a lengthy discussion of the history of ceramics in China, as well as technical information about raw materials and production techniques. Like a few others in the late 19th century, Dyer Ball states the opinion that:

> The most flourishing period of Chinese porcelain making, however, like that of most other branches of its art industry, was during the Ming dynasty, especially in the second half of the fifteenth century.[69]

He then goes on to give some interesting statistics about production during the Longqing 隆庆 (1567–72) and Wanli (1573–1619) periods which appear to have come from Chinese local gazetteers, such as the *Fuliang xianzhi*, mentioned in chapter one:

> Immense quantities of porcelain were ordered to be manufactured for imperial purposes in A.D. 1571: no less a number than 105,770 pairs of different kind of things were ordered, and in A.D. 1583 as many as 96,000 pieces, but remonstrances were made by the censors, and in some instances, at all events, the amounts were reduced in number.[70]

This information may in fact have come from Friederich Hirth ('Ancient Porcelain: A Study in Chinese Mediaeval Industry and Trade', Leipzig, 1888) or Stephen Bushell ('Chinese Porcelain before the Present Dynasty', Peking, 1886), as both are listed by Dyer Ball under 'Books recommended' and Bushell's text is his first translation of the *Tao shuo* 陶说 of 1774 which references the *Fuliang xianzhi*.[71] Interesting, and perhaps related, is the fact that on the same page as the quotation above, Dyer Ball presents information about how Ming porcelains were being used in the Ming—as serving vessels or storage jars in the markets. Thus, his earlier statement about the 'high' period of porcelain making being in the Ming period appears to have been taken indirectly from a Chinese text, such as the *Tao shuo*, where indeed Ming-period porcelain techniques, and some actual objects, were often praised (as well as denigrated by some connoisseurs—see chapter one).[72] In addition, just as in Dyer Ball's text, where the Qing dynasty (as 'Ts'ing') only appears once, in the *Tao shuo* it is referred to as 'modern ware' of the 'reigning dynasty', not as Qing or 'Ch'ing' as it was often romanised from about 1900 onwards. Thus as a category of porcelain, 'Qing' is not used in any early texts about Chinese ceramics in English (nor in Chinese) and only begins to appear in English connoisseurship texts after 1900.[73] It is possible, therefore, that at least in ceramic terms, the answer to the question 'why Ming' may lie in randomly surviving Chinese approaches to and opinions of their own ceramics which were available in English from the 1880s onward.

Thus what we have in the late 19th century is an emerging interest in Ming-period ceramics as examples of industry and culture of the Ming period (Dyer Ball), as a defined period of ceramic history (Jennie J. Young), as ceramics of a higher quality as declared by Chinese texts and exposure to Chinese connoisseurship taste in China (Lawrence-Archer), and in a few cases as separately-identified objects for admiration, particularly in the interior ('Boston Artists Studios'). In one case, we also have something called 'the Ming vase' which has been borrowed from the collecting category of 'Ming-period porcelain' to introduce a more distinctive single object. The porcelain has therefore moved from an amorphous group of objects to a singular one, but also crucially, a generic singular one, not a named piece like 'the Portland Vase' or 'the Lennard Cup'. The example of the use of the definite article with 'Ming vase', in a short piece of fiction, was also presented as being based on a Chinese story or myth so that collectively 'the Ming vase' can be seen, at least in these early cases, as reflecting a growing interest in Chinese sources for both information and inspiration, which itself was part of a wider trend towards understanding and therefore appropriating China through literature as well as objects.

Collecting in Fiction

Towards the very end of the 19th century, histories of Chinese ceramics as a single subject began to be published, demonstrating a greater interest in Chinese ceramics in general which was stimulated by collecting,[74] and more extensive publication in English of translated Chinese texts on ceramics (such as Bushell's *Oriental Ceramic Art* in 1897).[75] This would continue into the 20th century and gather pace. However, in these new, focused histories, Ming porcelain was still but part of a wider history of Chinese ceramics and not exceptionalised. In contrast, specifically-identified Ming porcelain began to appear more frequently in fiction, as the practice of collecting, considered an elite activity at the time, seems to have led to an idea of Ming porcelain (or what was thought to be Ming at that time) as well as later Chinese porcelain, as part of a smart interior. Thus it is not surprising to find references to Ming porcelain in Edith Wharton's (1862–1937) stories of the monied classes. For example, in *The Fruit of the Tree* (1907) there are several references to 'Ming' as shorthand for Ming porcelain which demonstrate its position as a symbol of class. In one scene, the character Mr. Langhope says: 'But suppose we go in before they join us? I want to show a set of Ming I picked up the other day for Bessy. I flatter myself I *do* understand Ming.'[76] We also find out later that another character, Dick (Richard Westmore) 'had always wanted a set of Ming for the drawing room mantelpiece'.[77] In both these quotations we can see references to the role of Ming porcelain in the upper class household and lifestyle, as significantly expensive, socially acceptable objects to own and have on display. They are also in consequence something it is important to be seen to know about—to 'understand' Ming. Furthermore, the reference to the mantelpiece shows that the fashion for such displays which began in 17th-century England was still current in American upper-class households of the early 20th century[78] and that such porcelains were assumed to be (or hoped to be by their owners) Ming, when in fact most of the examples used in such a way were primarily of the Kangxi period (1662–1722) and therefore Qing.

Interestingly, in these contexts, Ming is seen as better than Qing, even though it was Qing pieces which were achieving the highest prices at auction. In 1905, for example, a 'ginger jar' (a form known as a *guan* jar in Chinese) which belonged to Louis Huth (1821–1905) was sold for £6,000; it had been purchased in the 1860s for £25.[79] In contrast, seemingly authentically-Ming porcelains were not commercially in demand.[80] In spite of this, by 1907, 'Ming' had become shorthand for suitable porcelains in certain social circles, suggesting, perhaps, an association of Ming with the antique. Wharton, of course, was also known for her work on interior decoration, particularly *The Decoration of Houses*, which was published in 1897. She does not mention Ming at all in this work but does discuss, briefly, what in fact are Qing porcelains (but not identified as such) such as the 'peach-bloom' type (p. 187) and specifies how wide a mantelpiece should be to hold a display of porcelain.[81]

The same year in which Wharton published *The Fruit of the Tree*, *The Atlantic Monthly* published an article on 'An Art Museum for the People' in which the description of things that might be seen in such a museum included 'a blue Ming vase'. The article by Frank Jewett Mather is about the Boston Museum of Fine Arts, but its inclusion of a 'Ming vase' as a standard type of object to be seen in such a museum demonstrates that this type of object, now separated from the mass of Ming porcelain or even Chinese porcelain, was already familiar to the museum visitor.[82] However, museums, as this article interestingly argues, which should be for the general public, were for various reasons still the preserve of the upper classes at that time,[83] and thus the mention of the Ming vase in that context served to emphasize the current elitist perception of such an object. It was something not everyone could own and it was special enough for display in a museum. We can see this perception of Ming porcelain reinforced frequently in the English-language fiction of that time, for example in Samuel Merwin's *The Charmed Life of Miss Austin* (1914). In this, a character who had been a missionary in China states: '... I love the wonderful old porcelain of China. I've seen a moment when I would have sold my very soul for a Ming vase.'[84] Yet again it is presented as an aspirational object and one to which many different but related conceptions have been attached. Within a few years, for example, this newly invented object, 'the Ming vase' or 'a Ming vase', will have assumed further associations with delicacy, preciousness, high value and mysterious power, in addition to its pre-existing identity of an object requiring and/or representing advanced knowledge or connoisseurship. How did this one invented object come to represent so many different qualities? This becomes less puzzling if one considers that, like so much of what is perceived as 'Chinese' in western culture, 'the Ming vase' was an invention of the late 19th century which, over time, gained more and more identities, much as a snowball will increase in size as it rolls.

Pricelessness, Preciousness and the Purity of Craft

One of the first of these new qualities associated with 'Ming vases' in the early 20th century was a notion of pricelessness, and by extension, preciousness. The 'Ming vase' becomes priceless when ideas of value, in the monetary sense, become linked with it. We can see this quite clearly in the work of Henry Adams, particularly *The Education of Henry Adams: An Autobiography* of 1907.[85] In this, he very disparagingly (and facetiously) states that porcelain was the frivolous lens through which Chinese events had been perceived: '... the fall of China was chiefly studied in Paris and London as a calamity to Chinese porcelain. The value of a Ming vase was more serious than universal war.'[86] The fact that Chinese porcelain was represented here by 'a Ming vase' confirms the established nature of the simile, so much so that it could be used with irony.[87] One of the first times that such a vessel is described specifically as priceless was in 1919 in the collected volume, *The Best Short Stories of 1919 and the Yearbook of the American Short Story*, edited by J. Edward O'Brien. In one story, a shipping office in Hong Kong is described as '... invariably bare, save for a priceless Ming vase and an ornament ...'.[88] The corollary of 'pricelessness', 'preciousness', appears in print somewhat later, but once it enters the public discourse of valuable things, it becomes almost interchangeable with the quality of pricelessness.[89] The precious qualities of Ming vases were most likely an extension of the same quality as associated with porcelain in general, and this is something seen quite frequently in fiction of the later 19th century. In Henry James' novel, *The Portrait of a Lady* (1880–81, as a serial), a porcelain cup is specifically described as 'that precious object'.[90] The description of a Ming vase as priceless and/or precious ushers in an identity for the invented object which encompasses ideas about both porcelain and Chinese things, and it is culturally maintained thereafter. The association with preciousness is still in use today and has given rise to both a standard description of a Ming vase ('precious Ming vase') and to many comparisons with such a priceless and precious thing ('precious/priceless as a Ming vase'). This invented object has become a benchmark for defining the qualities of real things. Generally speaking, the notion of pricelessness is also constructed, for nothing is truly 'priceless', but as a description it elevates an object to another level where it becomes a simile, and no longer a tactile three-dimensional thing.

This is not to say that once 'a' or 'the' Ming vase was described as priceless, or associated with 'preciousness' that it was only conceived of in that way. In fact, the idea of an objectified Ming vase could still be used as an example for other arguments about things and the nature of things, such as that of the handmade v. machine-made which first emerged in the second half of the 19th century. In an essay published by the Society for the Advancement of Education, for example, the author compares a Ming vase to mass-produced pottery: 'The difference between a beautiful piece of hand-made furniture and a machine product in wood, between a Ming vase and modern pottery made by the thousand ....'[91] The author here promotes a theory of beauty which relies on the evidence of individuality that can be seen in 'true craftsmanship'. The irony, of course, is that any truly Ming vase of the porcelain type would have been essentially mass-produced in a large workshop at Jingdezhen, the Chinese industrial porcelain city. But it was widely believed at that time (and still is by some) that Chinese ceramics of the 'early' periods, interpreted in the early 20th century to mean pre-Qing, were made by individual potters who would therefore be defined as 'craftsmen' in European definitions of the time.

Building on the ideals of the Arts and Crafts movement of the second half of the 19th century and on the development of studio pottery as a reaction against factory ceramics in England (such as Wedgwood or Spode), a number of critics and commentators promoted the idea of 'early' Chinese ceramics as 'craft'. This can be seen in the work of Roger Fry (1866–1934) and Herbert Read (1893–1968).[92] In *Art and Industry*, Read, in reference to the two most popular types of objectified ceramics, compared a Song Chinese *meiping* with a Greek vase:

> The Greek vase is based on exact measurements, and its proportions are regular. ... The Chinese vase does not obey any such exact rules ... the Greek vase has been trimmed to a perfectly smooth and precise outline, symmetrical about its axis. Every trace of the potter's hand has been carefully removed. The Chinese vase, on the other hand, still shows traces of the ridges left by the potter's fingers, and the glaze has been allowed to run irregularly down the surface, and finish in an uneven surf above the foot.

> ... I do not think that there is any doubt that the average sensitive person, the 'man of taste', would find the Chinese vase superior as a work of art, and that, I believe, is because its form has an appeal which cannot be analysed, which is not intellectual, but intuitive or unconscious.[93]

It is interesting that 'the' or 'a' Ming vase was also associated with this way of thinking because its appearance alone would be contrary to the ideals of the hand-made, anti-intellectual 'craft' ceramic. When associated with Chinese ceramics, for example, this was usually taken to refer to less polished-looking stoneware vessels made in China, such as the one rhapsodized about by Read. [Fig. 3.3] That Ming porcelain has been included in this category demonstrates how well entrenched the notion or concept of 'the Ming vase' had become in object-related discourse of the first quarter of the 20th century, and of course, therefore, how flexible object categories can be.

Ming Vase Mysteries

Where the appropriation of 'the Ming vase' would seem to be most indicative of a phrase permanently entering the English lexicon is in its use in the detective and mystery fiction genre that became so popular around 1920, both in book form and shorter mysteries published in popular magazines. There had of course been a long history of crime fiction before this date, but it was the rise of what is known as the 'hard-boiled' genre[94] that coincided with or even promoted the idea of 'the Ming vase' as mysterious, desirable, exotic and precious in popular discourse. In its earliest incarnation in such fiction, 'the' Ming vase appears as a symbol of sophisticated living, mirroring the references to Ming vases in earlier domestic stories such as those by Edith Wharton. One of the earliest such references in English crime fiction is in the book *Suspense* by Isabel Ostrander, in which a rich but gauche character's living room is described thus:

> The room presented an odd mixture of real artistic treasures, and the basest of imitations; rare tapestries hung upon the walls between wretched copies of masterpieces, a hideous terra cotta statuette overshadowing a Ming vase. ...[95]

This assessment of the objects in the room was made by a secretary to a mysterious protagonist and demonstrates that the possession of a Ming vase equated to knowledge of connoisseurship—it was a thing to be seen to be familiar with, its value and importance recognized. Here it is also contrasted with fakes and less valuable things, thus confirming its exceptional status. Its presence in such a description can be clearly associated with the earlier literature of decorating the interior discussed above and suggests one source for the popularity of the Ming vase trope in later crime fiction. Interestingly, the rest of this novel also features all the standard tropes that would come to be associated with this form of crime fiction: the Egyptian pharaoh, scarred faces, treasure and exotic foreign antagonists. Ostrander thus anticipated by a few years the characteristic work of the likes of Agatha Christie and Ellery Queen.[96]

Another example from this period presents the Ming vase as an emblem of both pricelessness and connoisseurship, and consequently a collectible item. In *The Strand Magazine*, which was published monthly from 1891 to 1950 and is famous for being the first to publish the Sherlock Holmes stories, a short story by Kathlyn Rhodes called 'The Ming Vase' was published in 1921. Here a singular Ming vase is the focus of a story about the shenanigans of the antiques trade. In the story, the vase is presented as the one potentially valuable piece in a character's household goods:

> And there, in the place of honour on the top of the bookshelf, was the Ming Vase, her sole possession of any value, a relic from the days when her father's father had been a physician in China.
>
> He had had many valuable possessions, handed down in turn to her father; but during the Boxer rising of 1900 the second Dr. Lucas had been forced to fly, with all his household, leaving their goods behind; and this vase was the only relic he had been able to save from the disaster.
>
> Julie herself did not know the exact value of the vase, nor its history. There had been a sort of legend in the family that it was of great antiquity and value, and it was generally supposed to have formed part of the booty looted from the summer palace of some emperor of a bygone dynasty; but Dr. Lucas himself did not know its story and it had come to be known, laughingly, in the family as the "Ming Vase".[97]

This description of the vase's history references well-known events and presents an actual China provenance for the piece. It is proudly described as possible loot from the Summer Palace (as was customary), and in the subsequent physical description of the vase (which was clearly Qing, not Ming) references are further made to earlier notions of idealized craftsmanship:

> Taking it down from the shelf, she turned it tenderly about in her hands, noting with a pang at her heart each well-remembered figure, each delicate, distinctive colour—blue, green, a faint delicious pink. The porcelain itself was so fine, the shape so symmetrical while at the same time so definitely Asiatic; and the whole vase so evidently the work of a craftsman who had gloried in his task.[98]

The protagonist of this story, Julie, sells the family heirloom to fund a holiday but is duped by a fraudulent expert. The deception is revealed when a prominent gentleman collector of Chinese porcelain recognizes it for what it is—genuinely Ming.[99] Collections of Chinese ceramics were frequently associated with upper-class gentlemen. For example, in another monthly magazine of the time, *Munsey's*, the connoisseurship of a Ming vase is declared to be an essential part of a man's education: 'He set his will on mastering one or two sports as rapidly as possible. He didn't care a straw for them as recreations; but they were all part of one's education, like concertos, free verse, and the ability to recognize a genuine Ming vase.'[100]

Thus, with the Ming vase now firmly established as an accessory in the upper class (or aspirationally upper class) lifestyle, and an expensive object associated with crime, we need to consider how and why this singular object of admiration came to be additionally possessed of mysterious qualities. We have seen how, in a few cases, this had already happened before the 1920s but these examples were not representative of a general way of thinking about 'the' Ming vase at the time, because 'Ming vases' were not the focus of the story. In the 1920s, however, the Ming vase began to play a more frequent starring role in mysteries, both long form and short stories, and an examination of these reveals that much of the 'mystery' associated with Ming vases related not to the objects themselves but rather to their 'exotic' Chinese origins, thus reflecting the still current belief in the mysterious Chinaman trope which would develop even further in 20th century fiction and film.[101] As 'the' Ming vase had come to be seen as a singular object, and one which had previously been desired by collectors, the object itself, whether real or imagined, now became powerful, something which is seen not just with Ming vases but other singular objects like the Maltese falcon in Dashiell Hammett's eponymous tale of 1930, discussed below.

One source which can be seen to have popularized the two early conceptions of Ming vases or 'the Ming vase' in crime fiction is the work of Horace Annesley Vachell (1861–1955) who invented the character Joe Quinney, a 'crafty English art dealer' and detective. In the first book to introduce the character Quinney, *Quinney's Adventures* of 1924, there is a chapter titled 'The Ming Vase' in which a 'rare Ming Vase' was put up for auction, during which it was fought over by two elderly, competitive collectors. The victor takes vicious pride in his purchase, lording it over the loser, only to discover it lying smashed on the carpet shortly afterwards. What follows is a mystery tale which centres on an investigation into the alleged crime, which is solved by Quinney. The chapter is additionally a commentary about collectors and iconic objects, and several of the other stories in the book also focus on objects, such as 'The Paul Delamerie Cup' and 'The Jade Bouddha'.[102] Vachell's Quinney character first appeared in a play of 1915 titled *Quinney's* in which 'the theme was the antique-lover's obsession with his possessions'.[103] The crime that Quinney is first charged with solving is fraud, thus bringing into the present discussion of the invention of a new object, the Ming vase, the issue of authenticity and why this should be associated with such an invented object. Determining authenticity is one function of connoisseurship but there is an irony in associating this concept with an invented, that is, not real, object. The fact that the invented object is presented in literature as real means that it has to operate in the world of objects, particularly art objects, where authenticity and other qualities are privileged. Whether real or imagined, this is the milieu in which 'the Ming vase' is usually positioned.

While throughout the 1920s, the Ming vase appears as a motif in a number of publications, it is not until the 1930s that it, along with other singular objects, becomes the antagonist of a crime story. Beginning with one of the most popular such stories of the century, we can see this trope emerging as a strong story line in the first Sam Spade novel, *The Maltese Falcon*.[104] In this novel, considered a classic of the 'hard-boiled' genre, private detective Spade gets entangled with a smuggling ring associated with a precious object in the shape of a falcon which was said to have been given by Malta as tribute to Charles V in the 16th century. Spade grapples with the usual characters that will become standard in this type of literature: a *femme fatale* who is also needy, an Egyptian/Middle Eastern intermediary and a singular object which functions as a plot device in the story, which revolves around it. The object, through its foreign origins, its exceptionally high value and its criminal movements, has a power which is almost apotropaic in its effects.

In these object-centred stories, additionally there is usually some association with royalty or the Church which gives an added identification with treasure to the objects, and the meanings attached to that concept.[105] A story first published in England which declares in its American title that an object with ecclesiastical associations is the focus of a mystery was Margery Allingham's *The Gyrth Chalice Mystery: An Albert Campion Detective Story* (*Look to the Lady*, in England) of 1931. A down and out aristocrat is the original owner of the eponymous object, which appears to have been lost, and the story centres around the search for it and its recovery, a classic example of what is known in film studies as a 'MacGuffin': 'an object or device which precipitates the central action and is assumed to be the characters' goal, yet which turns out only to distract from the detective's true goal'.[106]

The way in which the Ming vase comes to join the roster of mysterious and powerful objects in English fiction is perhaps best demonstrated by the Rex Dark novel, *The Ming Vase Mystery* (1936). The book jacket summary describes the plot as follows:

> The famous Mr. Jim Max, commonly known as J. M., is a very successful criminal who has taken to crime for the fun of the thing. In Turkestan he has come across and appropriated the famous Ming Vase, a very valuable specimen of ancient Chinese pottery. The Vase was quite valuable in itself, but it had immense value from the fact that it had been made the receptacle for a collection of letters and documents intended to be used for purposes of blackmail. There are many people interested in getting possession of the Vase; including two Chinese Tongs, a syndicate of Franco-American crooks and Lord Bergson, the Foreign Secretary of England. None of them are at all afflicted with scruples and their efforts to get possession of the Vase make an amazing, an amusing, and a highly-satisfactory book of thrilling adventure.[107]

The 'vase' in question is therefore a vessel for important documents but also an object of desire in itself. The novel's setting is dominated by foreign criminals, Chinese, English and 'Franco-American', all of whom are after the exceptional vase for different reasons and the vase, like the criminals, represents a cultural stereotype. Throughout the story, for example, there are references and language that give a sense of the general stereotype of Chinese people at the time, who are either 'Asiatic', 'Chinamen' or 'Chinks'.[108] The vase itself is said 'to hold a curse, as the yellow dogs say' (p. 31) and is so desirable as to be dangerous, a quality that will continue to be associated with the Ming vase motif throughout the 20th century.[109]

Unusually for such an early version of this kind of literature, we are also given a detailed description of the vase in question, which is illustrated along with 'hoodlums' in the book:

> And it was the vase more than the sight of the silent, impressive figures that caused Lord Bergson to pause. The thing was a sheer miracle of beauty. Looking at it, one became aware of the true meaning of inspired craftsmanship, and one understood something of the fanaticism of the collector.
>
> It stood about two feet high, resting on a square of black velvet. The groundwork was of a cloudy, delicate orange, running here to faint pink, there to the soft yellow of a tea rose. Superimposed upon this was a bas-relief design of dragons, their under-sides of forget-me-not blue merging into the cornflower blue of their backs, each scale of which was moulded with the genius of infinite patience. The eyes of the dragons were rubies; their teeth shone with the phosphorescent, cloudy blue of cleverly cut diamonds. (p. 140)
>
> The shape of the whole was perfect in its classical symmetry. It was as though all the art in the world had been brought to the production of this breath-taking piece of beauty.

> 'The piece here exhibited is of such value that one of you might be tempted to act rashly. That will mean death. I should be fully in sympathy with any one of you who might be carried away by the sight of the exhibit …' (p. 141)

Needless to say, this is clearly an imagined description based on several types of vessels combined in one; in no way does it relate to any actual porcelains of the Ming period. However, that is not important because, as we have seen, 'the Ming vase' is an invented concept as well as an invented object so that it can take on or be associated with any characteristics as required.

By the time of this novel, certain acquired characteristics of Ming vases were becoming standard, such as preciousness, rarity and high value, all of which were presented in Rex Dark's tale. The key features described here also include the dragon designs, shorthand for 'Oriental', and the 'classical' shape, a description and perception of Chinese porcelain that was formed in the early 20th century with the common interpretation of 'early Chinese ceramics' as representing a higher cultural achievement than later wares.[110] One can see or read about similar characteristics in the 'Wan Li' vase that was a key plot device in the story 'The Broken Vase', by Rex Stout (1941), whose most famous character is Nero Wolfe. In this novel, the vase in question is described as having: 'The pure black glaze. The delicate decorations in white enamel at the bottom. The golden yellow *dragons* and flowers in the middle, interspersed with the feathery green twigs and leaves. The odd, even unique, shape.'[111] What is described, of course, yet again does not relate to any actual Ming-period ceramics; however, it does resemble closely a Qing ceramic type known as *famille noire.* [Fig. 3.4] This type of ceramic, a porcelain usually from Jingdezhen, was made primarily in the 19th century (though the date of manufacture is debated[112]) and developed from a style of black-ground porcelain of the Kangxi period. Among the most passionate collectors of *famille noire* were Americans, including J. P. Morgan and the Walters, father and son[113] (see chapter four). Some of these vessels had apocryphal Ming reign marks, including those of the Wanli period, so it is possible that an example could have been considered 'Ming' (and some no doubt were). However, it is more likely that 'Ming' was simply an important classifier to attach to a 'vase' such as the one which was the focus of the Rex Stout mystery because this had already become shorthand for 'fine Chinese porcelain'.

What is interesting in this particular example in Stout's tale is the fact that a Ming reign period ('Wan Li') has been specified. Usually only the descriptor 'Ming' is used in crime fiction, so Stout's choice suggests some familiarity on his part with connoisseurship categories. This is further reinforced by the description of a collector's room in the book: 'Fox, glancing around, saw a Lang Yao sang-de-boeuf perched on a cabinet in a corner, and a large deep peach bloom on a table against the wall.'[114] By mentioning by name two types of Qing porcelain that were popular with American collectors in the late 19th and early 20th centuries, the author situates the scene, and the character concerned, within a collecting and connoisseurship milieu, one which we saw was established early in the 20th century with works by Edith Wharton, for example. The collector in the novel, Mr Pomfret, then goes on to say: 'It's a Hsuan Te. … There's no finer peach bloom than that anywhere.'[115] Once again, a Ming reign period has been specifically named, giving the impression of deep knowledge of important things, but it is not a period in which peach bloom wares were made, so Ming and Qing (their actual period of production) also have been conflated.

Children's Literature and Comedy

By the 1940s, 'Ming' porcelain had been associated with sophisticated collecting in several different types of literature, and it is the collecting and connoisseurship theme that links the literary (and other media) references, including those in mystery/detective fiction. That the 'Ming vase' as work of art had become a firmly-established literary motif by the 1940s is demonstrated clearly by its use in children's detective fiction, such as that of *Nancy Drew*. In the 26th book by the author pen-named Caroline Keene (but actually written by a syndicate, with members still disputing authorship[116]) the teenage sleuth Nancy endeavours to find the 'Clue of the Leaning Chimney'.[117] In spite of its title, the subject of this novel is actually the theft of a 'Ming vase' and the characters include wise old Chinese art dealers as well as unassuming (that is, not connoisseurs) collectors. What is striking in this story is the amount of information provided about porcelain production—one character is a potter—and the history of Chinese porcelain, including reign marks. This type of information is typical of children's literature, which had a didactic as well as entertainment function. Also typically, much of the historical information is incorrect, with, for example, the date of 'a rare Ming piece' given as 'over two thousand years old'. (p. 12) Nonetheless, there is a fairly constant suggestion throughout the book that China made the finest porcelain (e.g. p. 17), thus reinforcing the biases promoted by decorators and collectors throughout the preceding thirty years. The descriptive terms for the missing vase and other pieces mentioned in the book are fairly consistent: 'rare', 'exquisite', 'ancient', etc.

This story is a little unusual in one respect, however, because it includes inscriptions on 'Ming vases'. This becomes part of the story line as Nancy, typically, gains expertise in these marks which helps to solve the mystery. On the missing vase and related pieces were Chinese characters described as 'markings' or 'symbols'. As translated by the character Mr Soong, the venerable Chinese dealer, these are both studio and hall names, which would in fact have appeared on some porcelains of Ming date (though most appear on Qing pieces). (p. 34) He tells Nancy of their significance: 'Such symbols have been used for centuries by the Chinese to designate an article as authentic and of fine workmanship. ... They go back centuries to the great Sung, Ming and Ch'in dynasties.' (p. 34) He further says, of the 'marks' on the vases that Nancy has copied out and shown to him: 'These particular sets of markings are very old and famous. ... They are from the Ming dynasty and are well known to all experts on porcelains.' (p. 34) Having learned this, Nancy is now able to recognize similar 'markings' and identify 'Ming' pots, such as the one owned by a friend's mother: 'It was a lovely shade of brown, showing a peach tree at the edge of a sparkling blue lake. An ancient Chinese, attired in a richly brocaded robe, sat under the tree beside a deer.' (p. 39) Despite this description being a conflation of several different types of actual Chinese porcelains (none of the Ming period), Nancy then examines the marks on the bottom and confidently declares: 'It's a Ming vase.' (p. 39) Nancy is performing connoisseurship in this scene, thus firmly reinforcing the role of 'Ming vases' within this theme in popular culture of the time.

Throughout the subsequent 1950s, 'the Ming vase' or 'a Ming vase' would continue to be a symbol of connoisseurship or fine living. A new take on this can be seen in the increasing numbers of references to the destruction through breaking, smashing or dropping of a 'Ming vase' in all kinds of literature, and even earlier, in films, such as 'Jiggs and Maggie in Court of 1948'.[118] In this film, the character Maggie is shown admiring a 'Ming vase' in a department store. After being made fun of by a salesperson (who thinks Maggie looks like a character from a comic strip), Maggie breaks the vase in anger, and then proceeds to a bakery where she starts a pie throwing fight. In this film, the 'Ming vase' acts as a measure of her extreme anger and it sets up the comic plot which follows. In texts of the 1950s, which range widely from the *Journal of Philosophy* where in a discussion of the notion of partial responsibility, a 'cripple' is said to be less accountable for 'knocking over the Ming vase than a physically well man'[119] to *A Layman's Guide to Psychiatry and Psychoanalysis*—('Next time he feels destructive, he may stop to think as follows: "Will smashing this fifteenth-century Ming vase relieve more tension than the resulting spanking will create?"'[120]), the destruction of a Ming vase comes to symbolize bad or inappropriate behaviour. That a nominally Chinese object should perform this function indicates that it had become a widely familiar example of a rare, valuable and fragile object. The 1950s reader could be suitably shocked by the destruction of such a thing so that in turn, it became instructive.

In fiction, however, such destructive behaviour is often interpreted as comic, with a notable early example featuring in P. G. Wodehouse's *The Luck of the Bodkins* of 1935: 'He had not seen anything like it since the day, years ago, when his uncle Percy, who collected old china, had come into the drawing-room and found him balancing a Ming vase on his chin ...'[121] The object in question is a collected one, thus referencing the well-established association with connoisseurship, but it is also one which is too valuable or fragile to handle carelessly, such that doing so in an extreme way comes to take on a comic significance. One can see echoes of this interpretation of 'the Ming vase' in comedy today, such as in an episode of *The Simpsons*, for example, where the scary clown Krusty puts a 'Ming vase' on a ladder so that when Bart opens a door next to it, it falls and smashes.[122] Thus it is ultimately through comedy that the notion of a 'Ming vase' as the definitive breakable thing is popularized. It is still current today as a stereotype or cliché.

That is not to say that from the 1950s earlier conceptions of 'the Ming vase' were abandoned but rather that the motif came to take on even more meanings. The idea of the Ming vase as mysterious or as treasure worth finding if lost became more widespread, even appearing in comic strips such as Disney's Mickey Mouse who starred in 'The Secret of the Ming Vase', a 3D comic book published by Walt Disney in 1954 and distributed with Cheerios cereal.[123] In television, another children's favourite of the time, *Rin Tin Tin*, became embroiled in an adventure called 'The Ming Vase' which was first broadcast in 1959.[124] The 1950s saw more and more instances of the creative use of 'a' Ming vase as a simile: 'precious as a Ming vase' which appropriates one of the earlier qualities associated with the fictional vessel that had first appeared in print in *The Cornhill Magazine* in 1934.[125] One form of this simile which did not catch on however, was its use to describe a woman's figure, presumably curvy not dumpy, which appears in the lyrics for Oscar Hammerstein's 1959 *Flower Drum Song: A Musical Play*: 'She's got skin like white jade, and she's built like a Ming vase.'[126] The characters in this musical, which was released as a film in 1961, are all Chinese, as it was based on the novel by C. Y. Lee so the comparison may have seemed apposite. This was not an isolated case of comparing a living thing to a 'Ming vase', however. Even *Field and Stream Magazine* described an African pompano (fish) as being 'rare as a Ming vase', which further suggests that the simile had become a common figure of speech by then.[127]

But none of these developments can explain what is perhaps the strangest reference to a Ming vase in existence, and one which thankfully did not catch on. In 1968–69, the US government ran a series of nuclear tests in the deserts of Nevada, at the infamous Area 51, and each was given a code name.[128] On 20 November 1968 a 20-kiloton bomb was released as part of Operation Minute Gun. The report released by the Defense Atomic Support Agency (1968) features an illustration of a Chinese *meiping* vase with what appears to be floral decoration on a dark ground. The title of the test is given in English and in Chinese characters as: 'Ming Vase, 明朝花瓶' which is how 'Ming vase' would be translated in modern Chinese.[129] None of the other test code names in the series relate to Chinese objects but a number of other objects or types of things are used as names: purse, coffer, tinderbox, thistle, etc.[130] In fact, 'Ming vase' appears to have been the second name chosen for the test originally called 'double barrel'.[131] The names for nuclear tests appear to have been chosen somewhat randomly; if any rules existed, they are not likely to have been published. In any case, that a Chinese object should be chosen is surprising, but if there were to be one, it is not surprising that it was the 'Ming vase'. While the phrase is a construction and not a reference to an actual Chinese object, it was both a meaningful and familiar figure of speech by the 1960s, and a fairly commonly used reference to China. In fact, by 1968, it had become a widespread literary and colloquial stereotype for something rare, precious, priceless, elegant or sophisticated. Thus the most surprising thing about the use of this symbol as a name for a nuclear test is the inexplicable attempt at authenticity represented by the translation of the name into correct modern Chinese. This does not appear to have been done for other test names related to China such as 'Dragon mist' of 1967, so one wonders why it was considered necessary or desirable.[132] Who would have been the audience for the paperwork associated with this test? Nevertheless, while this does appear to be an isolated use of the Ming vase concept, it is further proof of how well-established the motif was in English-language discourse by that date. Subsequently a few more new applications for the concept of 'the Ming vase' do appear, including a reference to a human sensibility which is at once brittle, old-fashioned and delicate: '(It is) remarkable that MPs should have nothing better to do than get agitated about records which were never intended for their Ming vase sensibilities.'[133] But such a comparison is still based on the best-established and most frequent meaning of the motif—its 'delicacy' or 'fragility'.

In Popular Visual Culture

After the 1950s, an additional application for the 'Ming vase' motif was based on its meanings in literary and popular discourse but translated into visual culture. In the pre-1950s period, images of what were defined as Ming vases could be seen in illustrations of comics or fiction, such as the Rex Dark novel mentioned previously. However, one of the most popular forms of visual representation of what is read as 'the Ming vase', frequently reproduced today because of the popularity of the writer and illustrator, can be seen on the cover of Hergé's *The Blue Lotus*, which was first published in French in 1934 in the magazine *Le Petit Vingtième* in Brussels. The cover illustration for the first black-and-white edition shows Tin Tin and his companion Snowy the dog, inside what appears to be a blue and white porcelain jar. The colour edition of 1946 confirms this but the jar also features other colours. In the main story, which takes place in Shanghai, porcelain jars appear frequently in room settings, and Snowy jumps into one when they encounter what they think is 'The Madman of Shanghai'.[134] Towards the end of the story, Tin Tin himself also hides in a large blue and white jar.[135] While not described as such, the use of a single jar on the cover of the story, with blue and white 'oriental'-style decoration, suggests that it would have been perceived as the then most well-known type of Chinese ceramic—a 'Ming' vase.

Visual representations of 'Ming vases' could also be seen in films as scene props and in interior design and art magazines of the period, particularly those with Orientalist settings such as *The Shanghai Gesture* of 1941,[136] but it was not until after the 1950s that 'the Ming vase' became a singular visual motif in much the way that it had in earlier literature. The use of the motif in this way was predicated on an understanding of its meaning beyond visual imagery as it also became shorthand for 'oriental porcelain'. As noted in chapter two, Ming porcelain, particularly blue and white, has appeared in paintings continuously since the 15th century, for example in paintings by Mantegna, Whistler and Matisse,[137] and its use as a motif (or prop) in popular visual culture continued in the 20th century. However, in more recent years, 'the Ming vase' has come to be an art and design subject in itself, as can be seen in the computer that was made in the shape of a 'Ming vase'[138] or the French advertisement for Artengo tennis shoes which featured dozens of pairs falling out of a crate filled with a giant blue and white porcelain vase.[139] The advertisement is named 'Ming vase' and presents a number of cultural references, including 'Ming' porcelain, even though the giant blue and white vase in the film is contemporary. As a design motif, the Ming vase is also used in fashion, as can be seen on what is now an infamous dress by the designer Roberto Cavalli and worn by Victoria Beckham in 2007.[140] In this dress, which was named 'The Ming vase', the wearer became a Ming vase with the blue and white dress creating an extreme hourglass shape that was distinctly 'vase-like'. The designs used on the dress were clearly taken from a wide range of Chinese blue and white vessels (including some of the Yuan period), but the primary dragon design which snaked around the wearer's body as well as the dress' blue and white palette declared its 'Ming vase' identity boldly and clearly.

The use of 'the Ming vase' in design has in many ways popularized the concept more widely than ever before, to such an extent that it can be seen as a concept to be subverted, not just in comedy but also in art, particularly conceptual art of the last fifteen years. Moreover, this referencing of 'the Ming vase' is being carried out by Chinese conceptual artists such as Xue Lei and Ai Weiwei, thus bringing the transformation of the original object into a concept full circle. Xue Lei, for example, has used the instantly recognizable style of Ming blue and white to subvert notions of materiality by creating blue and white porcelain crushed tin cans ('Tea' 2007, Galerie Martina Detterer, Frankfurt). 'The Ming vase' is also now so far from its origins as 'Chinese porcelain of the Ming dynasty' that it can be referenced as a style or even a colour, as the selection from the US DIY chain Ace Hardware demonstrates. Thanks to their extensive offerings, you can now paint your home in the colour 'Ming vase'. [141]

With the development of these new treatments of the Ming vase as visual and design motifs has come new applications for the concept that are in some ways unexpected but also demonstrative of its flexibility, now that the distance from its original meaning is so great. The most extreme recent example of this has to be the invention of the Ming vase weapon in the video game series *Worms*, an unconscious reflection of the actual nuclear bomb discussed earlier. According to its designers, the explosive Ming vase weapon is one of the most popular among gamers as it breaks into lethal sherds that can further become multiple weapons.[142] It is described as 'priceless', it is powerful and it is a bomb (something that can explode or shatter), thus bringing together both the standard and some of the more unusual meanings and characteristics associated with 'the Ming vase' today.

In the 21st century, 'the Ming vase' has therefore become both a literary and visual cliché, as well as a popular figure of speech which still retains distant echoes of its origins in real Chinese objects of the 14th to 17th centuries, but derives its meaning from an invented symbolic version of the originals. Nonetheless, the mythical 'Ming vase' existed and exists alongside actual vases which have been handed down from the Ming period, and these too have had an impact on the cultures of both China and foreign consumer nations. This impact is manifested in a similar reinvention of the original things through the mechanism of collecting, a process that will be examined in the next chapter.

4

Ming Porcelain in the Art World (19th–21st centuries)

Introduction

In the previous chapters, we have seen how the identity of Ming porcelain evolved; from contemporary manufactured products in Ming-dynasty China to imported luxury foreign goods in countries around the world, and ultimately to a complete rejection of the physical form of Ming ceramics in the invention of the English-language phrase 'the Ming vase'. Within this last conception, 'Ming porcelain' as a general category came to further represent in the literature examined evidence of connoisseurship knowledge and good taste in fine objects but not, interestingly, works of art. There is, therefore, one final conception of 'Ming porcelain' and form of consumption outside China which needs to be explored: its transformation into a category of art and the consequent interpretations.

In this chapter we will examine the development of a final identity for Ming porcelain which coincides with the development of the category of 'Chinese art' outside China.[1] The role of porcelain in this category today is greater than what might have been supposed by pre-20th century Chinese connoisseurs, and its prominence in most displays of 'Chinese art' would also surprise them. For it is a rare collection indeed which does not include at least some Ming ceramics or porcelains, yet porcelains do not have a place in the traditional Chinese hierarchy of the arts. The mechanism for the elevation of Ming porcelain from manufactured product to work of art is therefore multivalent. It includes collectors as the human agents for this transformation, and display and publications as the media. It also requires the development of a commercial art market for Chinese art, something which occurred at the same time as Ming porcelain began to be considered a significant category of expensive, non-functional object (discussed in chapter three).

In order to pick apart these circumstances and trace their development, we will have to examine the development of significant interpretations as well. For convenience, therefore, this conceptual transformation of Ming porcelain will be presented as a chronological and temporal process. We will also be required to limit the scope of this discussion to the English-speaking world, namely Britain and the USA, as a complete history of the invention of 'Chinese art' outside China, and the position of Ming porcelain within this, would make this book unreasonably large.[2] However, it is hoped that others will take up the challenge as the story of how an object becomes a work of art is one that has resonance for other fields of art history and related disciplines concerned with objects. Here the story of one particular example of Ming porcelain will serve to illustrate this trajectory.

Searching for China in Macao

In 2006, Christies Hong Kong sold what was then one of the most expensive examples of a Chinese ceramic in its history (in fact a record for a Ming ceramic): an early Ming porcelain 'vase' (actually a *yuhuchun ping*) with underglaze copper red decoration [Fig. 4.1].[3] This 'vase' was considered 'important' because it was an example of Hongwu-period copper red ware, which is quite rare among surviving Chinese porcelains. What was even more extraordinary is that the piece was bought by an American collector (Steve Wynn of Wynn Casino fame) and then presented to Macao as a gift.[4] This vase is now displayed in the Macao Museum in its own case in the upper galleries, where it commands attention as a singled-out 'work of art'. At the time this piece was made, in spite of what the auction catalogue text might say, this was not an exceptional object because it had been made at Jingdezhen, possibly in the imperial workshops, as one of many such vessels for use at court (then located in Nanjing). It would not have been considered a work of art at the time, nor would it be until at least the 20th century. Surviving Ming texts associated with connoisseurship do not usually mention 'Hongwu' ceramics.[5] Moreover, this piece was made before the introduction of reign marks so it did not even have that purported seal of official approval.

So how did this piece of factory-made luxury tableware come to be considered (for a time at least)[6] the most expensive piece of Chinese ceramics in the world? The transformation in the reception of this object is dramatic and seemingly instantaneous, yet it represents the culmination of a process that began as soon as Chinese porcelains arrived in Europe and were singled out by being given metal mounts and put on display in 'cabinets', as we have seen in chapter two. Steve Wynn's purchase, and the subsequent re-evaluation of the piece concerned, parallels that process in that it was not until it was put up for sale that its value and 'uniqueness' was actually recognised. As was widely reported, even in the Chinese press,[7] the vase had been used as a lamp by previous owners who were unaware of its significance. Thus, as news media presented it, the vase went in an instant from being worthless to being valued at US$10,000,000 because any object is only worth what someone will pay for it.[8]

But how did the auction house persuade buyers (and the ultimate buyer) that this vase was so valuable? The catalogue text is very helpful in this respect. Firstly, the piece was placed in 'The Imperial Sale', a name which instantly conferred a certain (unproven for the most part) identity for the objects within it. Then the vase was described as 'magnificent', which is actually a category word used by the auction houses to designate very expensive objects. It was then the subject of a long scholarly essay which positioned it among a very few surviving examples of Hongwu underglaze copper red wares, leaving no doubt about its importance in the pantheon of 'Chinese art'.[9] That the vase was then purchased by a collector with his own museum, who then gave it to a small public museum in Macao, was, at first glance, somewhat surprising. The collector stated that his reason for doing this was that he wanted the people of Macao to be able to enjoy it and to make it a gift to the PRC.[10]

Of course it is significant that Wynn had recently opened a casino in Macao, and this gift would bring not just publicity but good favour for the business now that Macao is part of China once again. Somewhat incredibly, Wynn also promoted a highly fictitious story about the vase which demonstrates how little he actually knew about the piece and the China from which it came. He said:

> For this particular piece, there is a letter from the artist begging the Emperor not to get the copper glazing. I acquired it on June second. I saw the information on it, and I said to myself, 'What a great piece of Chinese history. What a wonderful gift it would be to the People's Republic if this piece could stay in Macao.'[11]

As we know from chapter one, there was never such a letter because there were no individual artists associated with such products. But the story does remind us that the object in question was being positioned as an exceptional 'work of art', which usually would then be associated with an individual artist, as with European or Chinese paintings, for example. These are then seen to be unique and the product of genius. This categorisation of the 'vase' is interesting because, as we have seen, very few pre-20th century Chinese ceramics were signed by, or made by, what might be considered individual artists, so authorship is not an attribute associated with them. However, this kind of re-conception of Chinese porcelain parallels that which occurred in the English language in the 19th and 20th centuries. It is as much a conceptual transformation as that which was made from type of object to literary theme/motif/plot device. In chapter three, for example, we saw how an object or category of object can be transformed metaphorically, without reference to its physicality. 'The Ming vase' was no longer a physical object but a figure of speech with several meanings in the English language, and a phrase that is still current today.

But, as this chapter will demonstrate, at the same time as this conceptual transformation of Ming porcelain was being effected, the physical examples of Ming porcelain which still existed in collections were also being transformed and given a new identity as objects of a particular type: works of art. This occurred both in China and outside it, but in different time periods and through slightly different methods. Nonetheless, today, worldwide, Ming porcelains are collected, studied and sold as 'art' objects. As such, they (and Chinese ceramics in general) play a key role in exhibitions of 'Chinese art', such as the recent exhibition of Ming 'imperial' art in the USA,[12] in which an entire section was devoted to Ming ceramics. Furthermore, in almost every auction of 'fine Chinese art', Ming porcelains are a standard offering. As we have seen with the vase in Macao, in museums and galleries in China and Taiwan, as well as across Europe and America, Ming porcelains are now displayed as individual works of art. There was even in London for much of the 20th century a museum devoted to the display of Chinese ceramics, and Ming porcelains made up a considerable proportion of its holdings.[13]

Texts and Categorisation

The transformation of Ming porcelains into works of art paralleled another development that was noted in the previous chapter, when a growing awareness developed in the 19th century of Chinese ceramics as a separate category of Chinese object, one that could be collected, displayed and written about. The reasons for this were economic and political but also cultural as Britain in particular was a location where ceramics were readily appreciated for daily use, display and collecting.[14] In consequence, much of the early literature in English about Chinese ceramics was written in England, and, as we have seen, much of this made reference to the Ming period and even included translations of purported Ming texts. The deference to the authority of Chinese texts in this period is notable, and the British military presence in China during the later 19th century meant that a number of these texts were available for study and perusal as well as collecting. It can be argued that the British affinity for ceramics influenced the selection of texts for scrutiny as the most widely available translated texts in the late 19th century were those concerned with ceramics.

One of the first of these was the previously mentioned translation into English by Dr Stephen Bushell of the *Tao shuo* in 1899.[15] This book was originally written in 1774 by Zhu Yan (1713–80)[16] and was a monograph on porcelain and its industry at Jingdezhen. Bushell had been present in China for some time as medical doctor to the British legation[17] and was also a buying agent for the Victoria and Albert Museum. He was, therefore, very important in the development of Chinese ceramics as works of art through the mechanism of the museum and the art catalogue. For example, Bushell's translation of the *Tao shuo* was used as primary source material, along with his own translation of the later ceramic text, the *Jingdezhen taolu*, for a catalogue of the Walters Collection in Baltimore, *Oriental Ceramic Art*.[18] It was therefore presented as a textual authority and affirmation of the collected objects presented in the book. This was considered quite important, as Walters himself had noted the dearth of texts in English on Chinese ceramics.[19] In the Introduction, Bushell says, for example:

> The Chinese themselves maintain a profound interest in the subject (of Chinese ceramics), especially from an antiquarian point of view, and the literature which relates to it is very extensive, ranging as it does over many centuries. The best special work is the *T'ao Shuo*, "A Description of Chinese Pottery", in six books, published in the year 1774, by Chu Yen. The learned author quotes many of the older writers, and describes all the varieties of the potter's skill that became celebrated before the close of the *Ming* dynasty in 1643. I translated this work into English, at the request of the late Mr. W. T. Walters, some years ago so that I now have it before me for reference .... The author of the *T'ao Shuo* is not so satisfactory a guide to the porcelain of the reigning dynasty .... For this we must to turn to the *Ching-Te-Chen T'ao Lu*, the well known memoirs on the productions of Ching-Te-Chen, published in 1815 ...[20]

Partly as a result of the authority conferred by the Chinese texts Bushell translated, this catalogue of the Walters Collection would prove itself to be very influential and was quoted or referenced in many subsequent texts about Chinese ceramics.[21] Another Bushell translation was equally if not more influential, at least for a time. This was his translation of the *Lidai ming ci tupu* 历代名瓷图谱 (Illustrated Description of the Celebrated Porcelain of Different Dynasties)[22] which was believed to be the catalogue of ceramics owned by the 16th-century collector Xiang Yuanbian 项元汴 (1525–90).[23] The translation of this catalogue into English by Bushell was published posthumously in 1908. It was subsequently referenced in almost every English book on Chinese ceramics until the 1930s, when Sir Percival

David (1892–1964) published a definitive bibliographic study proving that it was a fake.[24] Until that time, however, this text was seen and used as a guide for 20th-century collectors in the English-speaking world. The translation, when it first appeared, was an immediate hit. *The Burlington Magazine* in a review of 1909 stated:

> Among serious students of … Chinese art, Dr. Bushell occupied a prominent place, and the famous native work on early Chinese porcelain, which now appears in an English dress, is a not unfitting conclusion to his labours. He himself relied largely for his conclusions upon this delightful sixteenth-century Chinese catalogue, and in presenting it thus to the public he has done his brother collectors an inestimable service.
>
> [The book's] authenticity … has never been called in question. The writer, Hsi'ang Yuan-P'ien, is celebrated as an artist and collector by many contemporary and later records … [25]

Interestingly, while the reviewer of Bushell's translation acknowledges that there are different opinions about the value of this book for collectors (and thus perhaps its authenticity), he goes on to state that because it was owned by Bushell, the text cannot be questioned.[26] This confirms Bushell's role in not just bringing Chinese texts on ceramics (and other materials) to the English-reading public but also his significance in the development of Chinese ceramics as a category of 'art'. Bushell also helped to create the illusion that Xiang was in fact famous for collecting porcelain whereas in Chinese history, he is much better known and celebrated as a paintings collector.[27]

Ming as a Category of Porcelain Collecting

As Chinese ceramics came to become more and more prominent as a category of art, advanced by literature and public exhibitions such as that of the Burlington Fine Arts Club's (see chapter three) 1910 showing *Early Chinese Pottery and Porcelain* which included Ming in this category,[28] Ming began to be singled out for both praise and opprobrium. Dealers such as Gorer and Sons held specialist sales of Ming ceramics which included the more familiar Kangxi (or 'Kang He' as they spelled it) porcelains which were still popular at that time.[29] And Robert Lockhart Hobson (1873–1941) would devote a whole volume of his groundbreaking (1915; and still in print) *Chinese Pottery and Porcelain* to Ming and Qing wares. In the introduction to volume II, Hobson states that Jingdezhen '… may be said to have become the ceramic metropolis of the empire, all the other potteries sinking to provincial status …' thus launching the overwhelming bias towards Jingdezhen products which still exists today in the historiography of Chinese ceramics outside China.[30] He then goes on to provide a very detailed discussion of production at Jingdezhen in the Ming, using Bushell's translation of the *Jingdezhen taolu* as his source. What follows uses a traditional Chinese dynastic chronology for Ming porcelain which concentrates on 'imperial' pieces from Jingdezhen, a framework which is still the standard today.

Hobson in so many ways was a driving force in the exceptionalisation and professionalisation of Chinese ceramics in the English-speaking world, especially as a frequent publisher of texts about the subject, many of which were illustrated exclusively with singular objects from private and public collections (he was a keeper at the British Museum). The use of singular examples in this way further promoted the identity of Chinese ceramic objects as works of art. What Hobson published after all were art catalogues based on a definition of 'art' (in which objects classified as 'fine art' could be enjoyed for themselves, set apart from the functional crafts) which can be traced to at least the 18th century.[31] This was reinforced by the display of individual ceramics in public collections such as the British Museum, the V&A and the Metropolitan Museum of Art in New York City. At this last museum, they were actively acquiring Chinese porcelains in the first quarter of the 20th century; when they published their acquisitions, they referenced Hobson's 1915 book as the authority. Their *Bulletin* of 1919, for example, stated that: 'We have lately had the good fortune to acquire in Holland some pieces of a group of Ming porcelain which Hobson in Chinese Pottery and Porcelain describes on page 70, vol. II, but which was not represented until now in the Museum.'[32] As early as 1916, this museum mounted a display titled *Early Chinese Pottery and Porcelain* with an accompanying catalogue that itself heavily borrowed from an earlier catalogue of East Asian ceramics presented by the Japan Society in New York in 1914 (for which Hobson consulted).[33] In the 1916 catalogue, the Metropolitan very skilfully associated Chinese ceramics with Chinese sculpture, itself an emerging category of 'art' which was invented by collectors and museums[34] whose frame of reference was the European definition of 'fine arts' which included sculpture but not of course, ceramics.[35] The 1916 catalogue reprinted a text about Song ceramics by Rose Sickler Williams, who had written *Keramic Wares of the Sung Dynasty* previously for the Japan Society catalogue of the exhibition of the same name.[36] Thus, much as we have seen in fiction, very early in the 20th century, individual periods of Chinese ceramics, such as 'Sung' or 'Ming' were being singled out in the art literature, in a fashion which imitates the designation of 'schools' in painting studies. It is these sub-categories which would help to give Chinese ceramics prominence as works of art; they could now be fitted into the traditional rubric of art history which dominated the discourse of art in the 20th century.

Ming Ceramics on Display

Public display of Chinese ceramics as 'works of art' was perhaps even more important than literature in promoting and defining these objects as 'art'. One of the earliest specialist displays of Chinese ceramics in the 20th century surprisingly was not at a museum in a large metropolis like London but rather the Birmingham Museum and Art Gallery (England) in 1904.[37] This city museum was the recipient of a loan of ceramics from the collection of George Veitch. Already in 1904 these ceramics were described in very apologetic terms as being 'not of the fashionable decorative type now in vogue',[38] which meant they were not covered with painted decoration but were instead primarily monochromes. This display was titled *The Veitch Collection of Chinese Porcelain*, and surviving images suggest that the individual ceramics were presented on custom Chinese stands, which would have been traditional in China, where the collection was formed.[39] Such stands were used consistently in displays of Chinese ceramics outside China until the mid-20th century when they fell out of favour. They are therefore rarely seen today, even though in the past they were seen as an integral part of any ceramic put on display.[40] For example, a Chinese ceramic acquired by the Boston Museum of Fine Arts around 1916 is shown with its stand in the announcement of its acquisition.[41] This piece is also of Qing date and is of the type that was most popular at that time—highly decorated and colourful.[42] Hobson's book is of course referenced in the announcement of the acquisition and the mark on its base, purporting to be that of the Xuande period, is declared to be archaistic as the vase is seen to be of Qing date, an indication that connoisseurship of Chinese ceramics was already in some areas (but not universally) quite well developed by this early date. What is also interesting for our purposes is that this piece was presented in print as a singular work of art: 'A Chinese Porcelain Vase', using a term that would be more and more popular as the century developed—'vase'—in reference to Chinese ceramics.

In the case of the Veitch pieces, they were displayed and published as a named collection, that is, one associated with the collector. This is further evidence that Chinese ceramics, particularly porcelain, were moving into the realm of 'art', a fact reinforced by the number of named collections of Chinese ceramics that were brought to the attention of the art collecting community through such journals as *The Connoisseur* or *The Burlington Magazine*. In the latter alone, there were articles about the Davies Collection (1913), the Richard Bennett Collection (1911) and The Ross Gift (Boston, Museum of Fine Arts, 1907) within a five-year period. Most of the Chinese ceramics published in the first decades of the 20th century, and indeed those in the Veitch display, appear to have been of Qing date (but many were thought to be earlier). For Ming ceramics, we have Hobson to thank again for the singling out of this category as worthy of collecting and therefore study. We have seen in a previous chapter how and when the notion of 'Ming' as a category of Chinese history came to prominence in English-language discourse, so that by the time Hobson published a monograph devoted to ceramic products of the Ming period, it was a name that was already familiar, and 'the Ming vase' was gaining currency as a simile in popular language. As further evidence for these developments, in 1918 *The Burlington Magazine* published an article on 'A Rare Ming Vase', thus putting together for an art history readership the words that would come to represent a simile for 'fragility' and 'rarity'. In the *Burlington* essay, the focus was a 'vase' of what is known as *fahua* 法华 or 'decoration with boundaries' type which was indeed made initially in the Ming dynasty, although the piece illustrated would today be recognised as Qing.[43]

Throughout the 1920s, Hobson was actively acquiring and displaying Ming porcelains (among other things) for the British Museum. One piece, which is given an article of its own in the *British Museum Quarterly*, was known as 'the Leverton Harris cup' [Fig. 4.2], thus naming the piece after its owner in a similar manner in which the Lennard cup was, where individual Chinese ceramics are singularised by giving the objects names which are possessive.[44] In the article announcing the acquisition of the Leverton Harris cup, Hobson notes the perceived difficulties of finding dated Ming wares, suggesting that the category of 'Ming' in ceramics was by then so well established as to produce connoisseurship anxiety:

> The difficulty of dating the finer types of Ming porcelain is proverbial. The clumsier kinds made for the export trade tell their own tale and nobody thinks to gainsay them. But the choicer wares made for the home market or for Imperial use, which are not a whit less fine in technique than those made two to three centuries later, are the cause of constant controversy.
>
> ... one might well despair of identifying the genuine fifteenth-century porcelain, and the sceptic who will accept nothing as belonging to this period would be almost impossible to confute were it not for a few priceless specimens which have indisputable pedigrees or, what is quite as good, metal mounts made in Europe at an early date.[45]

The Leverton Harris cup is one such example, which has silver gilt mounts dated to 1530, according to Hobson, and the porcelain was dated to the early Ming. However, today it is recognised that the porcelain is much later (but still Ming) and therefore so must be the mounts.[46] Nonetheless, in 1928 the presentation of this piece as a dated benchmark object gives yet more evidence that a specific connoisseurship of 'Ming porcelain' was being developed, principally by Hobson and his peers/collector friends, who were all represented in his *Wares of the Ming* book.[47] That knowledge of Chinese culture informed this connoisseurship is evidenced by the second acquisition for the British Museum presented by Hobson in 1928—that of what he called a 'Ming ritual bowl', which was in reality a mid-16th century cup in the form of an ancient bronze *jue*. This piece, which 'is surely an Imperial piece', came in at the same time as several pieces gifted from yet another named collection, the Bloxam Collection. This collection, which was formed by the Rev. J. F. Bloxam (d. 1928) and had been exhibited in the Victoria and Albert Museum from 1915,[48] did indeed contain some very interesting pieces, even by today's standards.[49]

Apart from gifts or bequests from collectors, Hobson also acquired pieces in China, which was still possible in 1930.[50] In 'Peking Notes', the text of a lecture Hobson gave to the Oriental Ceramic Society (OCS) in two parts in January and February of 1930, he recounts a visit to 'Peking' undertaken with Oscar Raphael (1874–1941) in which they visited museums and bought pieces to bring back to England.[51] Apart from these discussions of ceramics, this lecture text is also a useful historical account of what was happening in Chinese museums and archaeology at the time. Hobson and Raphael visited the museum in the Forbidden City which was at that time called the 'National Historical Museum' (p. 34) and the Institute of History and Philology where the material excavated in Anyang in 1921 by Andersson and others was exhibited (p. 34).[52] But for our purposes, what was even more interesting is Hobson's account of the exceptional quality of the Ming porcelains on display in the National Museum (later to be the Palace Museum). His astonishment suggests that there was a widespread belief, in the English-speaking world at least, that Ming porcelain could not be as high quality as Qing. He describes what he saw in China thus:

> The Ming porcelain is of great interest to the student and will lead to much discussion.
>
> ... The high finish and neat decoration of these porcelains is astonishing; and doubtless the sceptic will refuse to believe that they can be other than Yung Cheng reproductions.
>
> ... one conclusion seems certain, namely that the Ming porcelains made in the fifteenth century for palace use were objects of great delicacy and refinement, and in no way inferior in technique to the best productions of the Yung Cheng and Ch'ien Lung kilns. (p. 36)

Hobson then goes on to discuss several such pieces that he brought back from China for the British Museum, demonstrating the relative ease at that time of such transactions. In this he reveals how few 'imperial' Ming porcelains had been seen in England at that time because he states that two of them, while of a style known from Qing porcelains, were in fact Ming because he could now say that similar examples were in the palace collections. (p. 37) Interestingly, he also uses highly technical language at times which is consistent with a paper aimed at a very specialised audience, which the OCS represented. Hobson uses the Chinese term *nien hao* (*nian hao*) instead of 'reign mark' in his text, for example. (p. 37)

The display of Ming porcelain in the new Chinese national museum, while sometimes intermittent due to China's political circumstances, at the same time was a significant factor in firmly establishing Chinese ceramics as a prominent category of 'Chinese art' for foreign audiences. The foreign specialists who looked to Chinese literature for legitimacy in collecting could also now follow the lead of China in confirming that within the source culture, ceramics were part of the national art collection.[53] The display of ceramics in this new national museum was made possible by a donation from the soon to be prominent collector of Chinese ceramics, Sir Percival David, who joined the OCS in 1930 and also had been acquiring quite a few Ming porcelains up to this time. While there are no personal archives to confirm this, David was a fairly public-minded collector, so from an early date he donated Chinese ceramics to museums, such as the V&A and the British Museum. A number of his donations from before 1930 were actually Ming ceramics, such as the *wucai* enamelled dish he gave to the V&A in 1918[54] [Fig. 4.3] and a Longquan celadon Daoist shrine, dated by inscription to 1406, to the British Museum in 1929.[55] [Fig. 4.4] This latter piece is exceptionally rare and is thus considered very important, even today. The date, 1406, firmly situates it in the Yongle reign period, but the inscription, as with other temple ceramics, also precludes it from being 'imperial'. David eventually donated quite a few objects to both the British Museum and the V&A but many pieces he acquired for his own collection, which is now displayed in the British Museum after being in an eponymous museum for 55 years (see note 13 for discussion).

That David and Hobson were actively acquiring (and then promoting) Ming (and other) ceramics reflects the political situation in China which, for a time, clearly facilitated foreign purchases of Chinese objects. From 1927 to 1937, there was essentially a civil war in China, and of course in the West there was the Great Depression, which also affected the Chinese economy, itself in the throes of its own depression.[56] Little of this is apparent in the contemporaneous English-language art literature, which instead glories in the opening of the Palace Museum. For example, an interesting report on 'Peking as a Museum City', by the collector Alfred Salmony (whose jade collection would later enter the Art Institute of Chicago), was published by *Parnassus* (College Art Association) in 1931. In this report, there is almost no mention of the recent and current troubles in China; instead, Salmony applauds the opening and existence of the Palace Museum, while also criticising its contents, apart from the ceramics.

> The capital of the Chinese Empire has been changed, but Peking remains the center of art and civilization. While in the rest of China museums are still in an embryonic state, in Peking they are a logical conclusion of the great past which there alone is marvelously alive. In no other

> place in the world do such tremendous structural complexes in the heart of a city clamor for preservation as museums. What else can be made of the walled Forbidden City, that incomparable group of palaces? These sites of the recent history of China are best preserved as museums. Every hall, every pavilion speaks of historic fate and is bound up with historic events and personalities.
>
> The public has been admitted almost everywhere. Signs in front of the entrance of the historic structures direct the visitor. Inside they are all a bit dusty. Many works of art stand about, most of them decorative objects dating from the last dynasty. There is little or nothing of real value, but enough to demonstrate to the average dull globe-trotter and to the thoughtful Chinese the vanity of earthly greatness.[57]

Later in the same article, Salmony praises the ceramic displays, especially the Ming porcelain, and confirms the importance of viewing them in the Chinese national museums: 'The Ming porcelain seems even more splendid than the Sung ceramics. ... It can be asserted without exaggeration that the history of Chinese pottery, at least of the Sung-Ming periods can be written only after acquaintance with this Central Section of the Palace Museum.'[58]

Porcelain and the Idea of 'Ming'

In spite of Salmony's praise, as we have seen with Hobson's comments about the Ming porcelains he saw in Peking, the tone of the literature about Ming porcelains at this time suggests that knowledge of Ming ware was not that well developed. This might be related to a perceived lack of encounters with authentic pieces outside China, and a perception that in consequence, Ming porcelains had been somewhat disparaged.[59] This notion is summarised in an article titled 'In Defence of the Ming', which was published in 1930, also in the journal *Parnassus*. In this, Horace Jayne, the Curator of Oriental art at the Pennsylvania Museum, Philadelphia, queried what he considered to be a curious state of affairs, such that: 'There is in truth a great deal of absurdity in the lack of regard in which Ming works of all sorts are held.'[60] His explanation for the disparagement of Ming art is not what might be expected, and it summarises, if accurate, the state of the field of collecting at that time:

> In the history of appreciation of Chinese art by western people there have been two main centres of interest, and two schools of connoisseurs, as it were, have come to be recognized. There is very little sympathy between the exponents of these two schools, for those of the older, which might be called the school of porcelain collectors have their attention only focussed upon the late porcelains, lacquers, jade carvings and in general are blind to the beauties of early bronzes, sculpture and pottery, while those who collect or are interested in the artistic products of the earlier times cast scornful glances at the accomplished products of the Ch'ing dynasty and dismiss these as fussy, or overwrought or soulless.
>
> ... What we wish here to point out ... is that between the early and the late there is a lacuna of appreciation, that on the whole the arts of the Ming dynasty—too late for the joy of one school, too early to please the other—are largely overlooked by both, in a manner quite unworthy of western connoisseurs.[61]

He states that the reason for an apparent backlash against Ming art in general, including porcelain, is that its time period falls between the areas of interest of connoisseurs of the time. It is entirely possible that that was the case because very little had yet been written about 'Ming art', and 'Ming' ceramics confusingly were classified as 'early' by some exhibitors in the early 20th century.[62] However, as we have seen, among specialist collectors (including the professionals in the museums), there was a growing interest in Ming porcelain as a category in its own right, a fact Jayne mentions:

> There are, of course, exceptions: the porcelain collector prizes his Wan Li and Ch'eng Te ware infinitely, but is not tempted to look beyond these technical masterpieces and see greatness in the less accomplished but equally beautiful minor wares.[63]

In one sense he is correct because the focus in the early specialised studies of 'Ming' porcelain was on what were considered to be palace or 'imperial' wares, which were considered interesting because of their technical mastery and in their membership of the separate category of 'imperial' porcelains; the latter also included Qing porcelain not made for export. Even in the wider literature of connoisseurship, such as *The Burlington Magazine* (which at the time still featured two more words in its title: *for Connoisseurs*), there were notices about Ming porcelain which focused on, for example, the Wanli period, as Jayne noted above, including 'Altar Vessels of the Wan Li Period'[64] that discussed an 'altar set' which incidentally appears to have been purchased by the British Museum as it was published a year later in the *British Museum Quarterly*.[65]

Finally, the author of 'In Defense of the Ming' presciently (if somewhat inaccurately) noted:

> The Ming, after all, were no barbarians. They established the first native dynasty and were able to hold China unified for two hundred years or more in a manner hardly ever achieved since the early years of T'ang. It is inconceivable that in this period and with these leaders there should have been nothing save a few delicate porcelains and numerous roof tiles produced. The time will come … when a great quantity of things now called anything but Ming will unhesitatingly be called Ming, moreover with pride and satisfaction.[66]

In fact, Ming porcelain or 'Ming' as a category of Chinese porcelain only became increasingly more familiar in the years after that article was published. Just how insignificant it still was for non-specialist consumers, that is, those not specializing in Chinese ceramics, in the early 1930s is demonstrated by its presence in the glamorous *Art Treasures Exhibition* hosted by Christies in 1932 and organised by the British Antique Dealers Association.[67] In this exhibition, the majority of the Chinese ceramics were 'Ch'ing' because clearly this is what the market still wanted at that time. Viewed from the more specialist OCS perspective, however, collectors like David were hesitantly adding Ming porcelains to their collections and commenting upon them in the OCS *Transactions*. For example, in volume 9 of the *Transactions* there is a long discussion of 'specimens' presented to members by Percival David, Neill Malcolm (1870–1953), George Eumorfopoulos (1863–1939) and others, with David himself commenting on a Xuande bowl he brought along. In the commentary he compares the pieces with related ones of Yongzheng 雍正 (1723–35) date, as was customary in this period when apparently many were sceptical of early Ming attributions. (See discussion below for details) He also noted that a similar example in Peking is dated 'Hsuan Te' and concludes that on balance the examples he brought must be of Ming not Qing date, thus invoking the Chinese authority in his determination.[68]

It was the commercial members of the OCS, however, who perhaps did the most to popularise Ming porcelains in the 1930s, through their own exhibitions and accompanying catalogues. In 1932, the dealers Sparks presented a sale featuring 'a Ming vase' with a five-coloured design of dragons, and this was published in *The Burlington Magazine* in that year.[69] Here we see again the intersection of the development of the fictional 'Ming vase' that was discussed in the previous chapter and the connoisseurship definition of 'a Ming vase', thus demonstrating that the two conceptions had begun to move in different directions, even though the first was derived from the aura of the second. More than Sparks,[70] however, the Bluett brothers were responsible for the promotion of connoisseurship and the sale of much Ming porcelain in the first half of the 1930s. They were members of the OCS and more actively involved in its activities than Sparks for many years. They also published in the *Transactions* as well as bringing out numerous (sale) exhibition catalogues. In 1933, they presented an exhibition, *Ming and Ch'ing Porcelains*,[71] which has an interesting and informatively focused title; their previous exhibitions in the 1920s which featured Ming porcelain were called *Exhibition of Old Chinese Pottery and Porcelain from the Han to the Ming Period* (1924) and *A Collection of Old Chinese Monochrome Porcelain* (1925).

In 1935–36, Edgar Bluett published an essay in the *Transactions of the Oriental Ceramic Society* (*TOCS*) which was specifically designed to improve the connoisseurship of Ming porcelain (and promote his own business in that area of course) titled 'The Nien Hao and Period Identification'.[72] It was all about reign marks and focused on Ming examples. This paper also discussed a number of 'authenticated' pieces from the David and other collections, including the former Bloxam collection, mentioned earlier, which had been given to the British Museum and the V&A by bequest in 1928, after the owner's death.[73] Many of the pieces discussed by Bluett had been on view in the V&A since 1915, and the Bloxam collection was thought to be composed of mostly 'Ming' pieces (though many were later attributed to the Qing). What is interesting is that in a 1928 article about the collection in *Old Furniture* Hobson stated that 'All Ming collectors know the Bloxam collection', which suggested that there were already collectors who specialised in Ming by that date, though they would have been fairly few and far between. He then went on to state:

> The popularity of Ming porcelain is no fleeting craze. It rests on secure foundations, so secure indeed that it has been able to survive a wholly unwarranted boom, the collapse of which would infallibly have ruined a reputation less sound. Ming has always been a name to conjure within the trade, and the fact that not very long ago its true meaning was imperfectly understood only enhanced its mystic potency .... Ming porcelain is [now] so much in demand that it is fast becoming a rich man's quarry.[74]

The Problem of 'Early Ming'

Among Chinese ceramics specialists, therefore, by the 1930s, 'Ming' was an established category of Chinese ceramic collecting and knowledge of it was fairly well developed for its time. But in the wider field of 'Chinese art' it was seen to be problematic. Even within the Chinese ceramics field, certain aspects of Ming porcelain were the cause of anxiety, particularly pieces purporting to be early Ming. In a review of Hobson's 1934 catalogue of the David collection, W. W. Winkworth summed up the issue, which stemmed from, ironically, increasing knowledge of the subject, as follows:

> There is another problem which to the average man is very puzzling in Chinese ceramics. It is the fact that Chinese potters, and those of the early eighteenth century in particular, made copies of all the early wares, not only of the Sung dynasty, but also of the early Ming as well. Naturally, where it is a case of designs either incised or stamped or in blue and white under the glaze, or in enamels, stylistic differences between early and late work are easy to detect. Not only has excavation helped, but the markets of Europe have lately been so flooded with specimens likely to attract collectors of Sung and Ming wares that careful sorting, on a scale never before possible, has inevitably revealed the existence of well-defined and easily identifiable groups. Mr Hobson and Sir Percival David have also had the advantage of full access to the Palace Collections in Pekin, where especially of the wares of the Hsuan-te period and other early Ming reigns, large portions of services are still preserved intact, including, in some cases, obvious replacements in later porcelain.[75]

According to Winkworth, who was a specialist in this area, there were several key problems—greater recognition that later copies of earlier wares were being made in the 18th century in China, and greater exposure to such wares because of changes in the market for Chinese ceramics, which Hobson had also mentioned when he described actual Ming porcelain as 'a rich man's quarry'. Winkworth also admits that having more examples to look at is an advantage, however, particularly for typologies and categorisation. He of course acknowledges the authority of what is now called 'the Palace Collection', but uses the language of western ceramics to describe what can be seen there in terms of 'services'. His reference to excavation is also important because it is this last source of 'evidence' for connoisseurship which would signal a new approach to Chinese ceramic studies outside China, and which would inform the literature of Chinese ceramics in English thereafter.[76]

In terms of scholarship, there was increasing interest in Jingdezhen as a locational source for authenticating 'early Ming' wares, a category which could stretch to as late as the Hongzhi period (1488–1505) in those days (now it is considered to be 'middle Ming'). Within the small world of Chinese ceramics, it was an essay (and later book) by OCS member A. D. Brankston which signalled the beginning of this new approach to authentication. In 'An Excursion to Ching-te-chen and Chi-an-fu in Kiangsi',[77] Brankston presented the information he gained on a site visit to two ceramic production areas, with the section on Jingdezhen giving detailed information about kiln sites, production methods (with photographs of contemporary methods) and the current archaeology in that area. This paper and the visit it described led to Brankston's book on the specialised subject of *Early Ming*

Wares of Chingtechen, which was first published in 1938 and which covers the periods up to Hongzhi.

Brankston (1910–41) was a civil engineer and Assistant Keeper in the Department of Oriental Antiquities at the British Museum. As he died very young, this was his main publication on Chinese ceramics and it is dedicated to Percival David. Before his death, Brankston was recognised as an accomplished young scholar in the field. The focus of the book on Jingdezhen is authentication through a combination of archaeology and technology, two of the key tenets of Chinese ceramic connoisseurship and scholarship today. At the time Brankston's book was published, however, his work was viewed as pioneering. One review states that the book 'can be recommended to collectors and others seeking first hand information on a difficult subject'.[78] It would have been viewed as a difficult subject at the time because, as we have seen, there was still much scepticism about the 'early' Ming wares, which were not seen in great quantities outside of China. Brankston, however, provided a book 'full of enlightening information' about 'the wares made in the imperial kilns, comparing them very usefully with later copies' as the traditional method would have it.[79]

Brankston's book was published after Chinese art in general had gained much public recognition in Britain and the wider English-language press because of a major exhibition of Chinese art held at the Royal Academy in London from November 1935 to March 1936, demonstrating yet again the importance of display in the development of art history, including that of Chinese ceramics.[80] This exhibition had been organised by members of the OCS, including Percival David, who had been its director, and it featured loans from the Chinese government for the first time in any western exhibition of 'Chinese art'. The exhibition was widely publicised and was accompanied by lectures and catalogues so that it can be seen to have formalised a particular definition of 'Chinese art' which included, of course, many ceramics, as would be expected for an OCS-organized event. Within this, Ming ceramics were presented as a category, thus confirming their position in the historiography of the development of Chinese ceramics in general that had appeared in the English-language survey literature since the later 19th century. The comments about the ceramics in this exhibition did not focus on the Ming wares, however, but references to some examples were made, as well as to the apparent discrepancy between 'the British and official Chinese dating of certain examples of porcelain attributed by the latter to the early Ming period'.[81] This statement about dating is one that would be mirrored in comments about other Chinese art works and is still sometimes noted today in scholarship about Chinese art. At the time of the International Exhibition, it indicated what can be seen as a negative consequence of exposure to Chinese objects in China—an undermining of Western knowledge about Chinese art. It also suggests, paradoxically, that the earlier faith in Chinese authoritative knowledge of Chinese objects was beginning to waver as a result of direct contact, that is, contact beyond books. Chinese archaeology (much of it not performed by Chinese archaeologists, it has to be said) seemed to provide a more objective approach to authentication which could justify differences of opinion (which still exist today).

Interestingly, in David's own survey article about the International Exhibition, he presented one approach to the ambiguity about Chinese authority, by invoking the notion of

'Chinese taste' which of course could only be defined by a foreigner. He did this without mentioning Ming porcelain at all, but rather Song and Qing ceramics:

> The Exhibition ... lays particular stress on two varieties of pottery and porcelain which are at once less familiar to us and more peculiarly Chinese in taste—the Sung wares, of which a remarkable range is shown, and at the other end of the chronological scale the delicate *famille rose* porcelains of the *Ku Yueh* type. Both truly reflect the spirit and ideals of their age, the former in their dignity and austerity, the latter in their elegance and almost sophisticated refinement.[82]

Of course both types of ceramics also reflect David's own taste, as they are in his collection, and the exhibition included many other examples from his collection. But it is noteworthy that in the wider collecting world, at least, Ming porcelain had yet to stir the imagination or to be considered reflective of China—unlike in the world of fiction at that time. That is not to say that Ming porcelains were not being sold or collected, and in fact, as we have seen, there were collections formed before 1930 that were considered to be focused on Ming, but this was by the very few specialists or experts in Chinese ceramics. Around the time of the International Exhibition, in fact, an older collection formed by Charles Russell (1866–1960) was sold at auction[83] and a number of Ming and earlier pieces from this collection entered both museums and what might be seen as the second generation collections of Chinese ceramics being formed by the likes of David and his peers.[84] One of these was Reginald Palmer, of Huntley and Palmer biscuits fame, who purchased through Bluetts a Ming *guan* jar with underglaze blue and overglaze enamel decoration of fish, and a Jiajing reign mark, from the Russell collection. Palmer paid Bluetts £70 for the jar, which was not a very high price at the time, but this jar sold in 2009 for £1.1 million. This gives a further indication of how the esteem for Ming porcelain has increased since the first half of the 20th century.[85]

As a later Ming object, the 'Palmer jar', as it is now known (having become a named piece), was a fairly safe purchase in 1935 as it was the 15th-century examples which were considered controversial. David himself also purchased quite a few objects from the Russell sale, including examples of later Ming wares[86] as well as what would become one of the signature 'David vases' of the Yuan dynasty.[87] However, David owned some Ming porcelains before this date, as can be seen in the catalogue of the David collection written by Hobson and published in 1934 and the pieces he gave to the V&A and the British Museum, mentioned earlier.[88] The presence in the 1934 catalogue of the selected ceramics would give them a certain cachet for many years, but for our purposes what is important is that this catalogue played a significant role in the development of the story of 'Chinese taste' and 'imperial' Chinese ceramics, as its introductory essay positioned David as a collector who did (and could) emulate 'the' Chinese imperial collection of ceramics, having what was later described as 'Chinese taste' in such wares[89] (see Fig. 1.1).

At the time of the International Exhibition, there was further specific activity related to Ming ceramics which suggests that the category first promoted by Hobson on a wider scale in 1923 was finally established in the global commercial art world if not that of most museums. In 1935, for example, a German catalogue of Ming porcelains in Swedish collections was published, and Swedish collectors would prove to be avid consumers of Chinese ceramics in general in the first half of the 20th century.[90] In the USA, a sale exhibition *Rare Sung and Ming Porcelains* was presented by the American Art Association in 1936 in New York.[91] Generally speaking, in light of what was happening in the world after the 1935–36 exhibition, it is a little surprising that there is in fact not just interest in the specialist subject of Ming porcelain in the late 1930s and 1940s but indeed such a quantity of art-related literature at that time. There was also the beginnings of literature in other scholarly fields which referred or related to Ming porcelain. This suggests that in spite of just some interest among specialist collectors, as a type of Chinese ceramic, Ming porcelain was also established in general object discourse by then. For example, in an archaeological report published in 1941, sherds of late Ming porcelains found at a site in Northern California were discussed with reference to possible evidence for the presence of Spanish ships in that area in the 16th century. The archaeologists described them as 'blue chinaware' which was identified by a curator at the Metropolitan Museum of Art as being Chinese and of the Wanli period.[92] The report also reveals the comparative paucity of knowledge about late Ming porcelain at that time, at least in the USA among archaeologists, as one sherd was considered problematic because its decoration was very different from the other sherds (now known to be of *kinrande* type—see chapter two); it was thought to be 18th century by the porcelain specialist consulted. However, the authors of the report note: 'It must be remembered that our porcelain constitutes ordinary household utility ware … which is poorly represented in the present day collections of Ming porcelain. Our pieces are not works of art or collector's items as such, hence the rarity of strictly comparable check items.'[93] It is interesting that even for marine archaeologists in California, there was an apparent distinction between different qualities of Ming porcelain which nonetheless made their work somewhat more difficult.[94]

Fakes, Loot and Later Copies

Knowledge of 'Ming' ceramics was still deemed to be somewhat limited by a lack of authentic pieces outside China. This is evidenced by the collecting and promotion of often blatant fakes, one of which was published in the *Transactions of the Oriental Ceramic Society* for 1945–46.[95] This blue and white vase, previously owned by the venerable Eumorfopoulos, was said to have been looted from the tomb of Xuande (which in fact has never been opened). The way in which this acquisition is described is notable for its excited tone:

> In the early days of 1938 bandits broke into the tomb of the Emperor Hsuan Te … and looted considerable gold treasure. As is often the case, the thieves fell out over the spoils and apparently part of it was melted down. Some pieces, however, got into the hands of dealers and found their way to Japan and no doubt also to America.
>
> Our late President, Mr Eumorfopoulos, was fortunate in obtaining just before the war some of the finest of the gold treasure …. Amongst the Imperial treasure in Hsuan Te's tomb was a pair of very large blue and white vases. (p. 17)

One of these vases was briefly discussed in the *Transactions* by a member of the OCS Council, Mr. Kiddell, using language that was typical for the period in which 'looted' was considered an attribute. The whereabouts of this vase (and its pair) were noted subsequently[96] as being in what is now the Nelson-Atkins Museum of Art in Kansas City, and the story of their origins was questioned by the then curator (and later Director) of the Nelson Gallery (its former name) Laurence Sickman (1907–88), who nonetheless agreed with their date. The original story surrounding it thus suggests a fanciful dealer's tale.

A less breathless and better informed essay on 'Pre-Ming and Early Fifteenth Century Chinese Blue and White Porcelains' was also published in the same volume with data based on the collections in what was then called the Batavia Museum. In this the author, Peter Bodde attempted to position 'ordinary' early Ming porcelain, which conveniently can be seen not in China but in Southeast Asia, within the history of porcelain production at Jingdezhen. He examined their 'stylistic features' (a common methodology at this time) which correlate with possible imperial productions of the 14th and 15th centuries, though at the time of his writing, Hongwu and Yongle examples were either non-existent or very rare.[97]

Bodde's essay was a prelude to a significant event in the establishment of Ming porcelain as a category of art in its own right, outside of China. This was the OCS exhibition of 1946, *Ming Blue-and-White Porcelain*, which featured members' pieces; during its run from October to December of 1946 it was apparently attended by over 500 members of the public.[98] This was to be the first of a series of exhibitions mounted by the OCS (which continue today), and its catalogue was published in the *Transactions* for that year (vol. 22). Bodde himself was on the committee of the exhibition, along with Basil Gray (1904–88), who succeeded Hobson at the British Museum; W. B. Honey (1889–1956) of the V&A; A. L. Hetherington (1881–1960), a founder of the OCS; and the collector Alfred Clark (1873–1950). In their introductory essay, the committee gives an interesting short historiography of the appreciation of Ming blue and white which summarises the state of the field at that date:

> Western appreciation and understanding of these wares has shown three distinct phases. In the nineteenth century the reign-names of Ming emperors customarily inscribed on all sorts of blue-and-white were accepted by collectors uncritically, with the result that much K'ang Hsi and later porcelain was regarded as Ming, and the word became a popular designation for Chinese blue-and-white in general. It was eventually recognized that such wholesale attributions must be wrong, and a phase of scepticism followed in which none but the roughest wares were thought of as possibly Ming. This phase lasted until well into the present century, when it was observed that certain of the wares, including some of the finest, stood out as distinct, having after all on various grounds good claim to be thought early. It was realized at the same time that some of the Ming reign-marks could be 'of the period'. A phase of cautious acceptance thus continues today. It is, for example, now admitted that a piece with the classical Ming reign-mark of the fifteenth-century emperor Hsuan Te may actually date from his reign; or may be a sixteenth-century copy dating from the reign of Chia Ching or another later Ming emperor; or may date from the K'ang Hsi revival in the late seventeenth century or from one of the archaizing later Ch'ing reigns; not to mention the possibility that it could be a clever modern Chinese or Japanese forgery. These waves of imitation and emulation thus bring an exciting element of uncertainty into the collecting of Ming blue-and-white, over and above the satisfaction its beauty may give.[99]

Thus in connoisseurship terms, by 1946, much was known about the vagaries of reign marks and the stylistic fashions for what is today known as 'archaism' or *fang gu* in Chinese ceramics (see chapter one). However, because of a prevailing belief that if something was not seen in the west, it did not exist, there was still much scepticism about 'early' 'imperial' Ming porcelain. It is further interesting that, in the view of the OCS, in the past 'Ming' was a popular designation for Chinese blue and white in general, which brings us back to the question of why Ming was associated with this one type of Chinese ceramics, even though most of it was actually Qing. In the pre-1940s period, it would perhaps have been partly because of the interest in reign marks, which often had 'Ming' in their list of characters. It was the reign mark, after all, which enabled the allocation of a ceramic to the most valued category of Chinese ceramics—'imperial' porcelain—and which provided a seemingly objective measure of the porcelain's authenticity.

Later, greater knowledge about reign marks would lead to more scepticism as demonstrated by the OCS where a number of the exhibits in their display of 1946 were dated to the early Ming and the essay text (written by Honey) contains much detail (thought accurate at the time) about 15th-century blue and white and later copies in the Ming period. This was noted in subsequent reviews of this exhibition, such as the short series of articles by Gerald Reitlinger (1900–78, with Martin Button) in *The Burlington Magazine* (1948), who nonetheless thought that the OCS could have been more discerning. In the first essay, 'Early Ming Blue and White: I', the authors note that the OCS exhibition had 'a splendid array of fifteenth-century pieces' (p. 11) and that the introductory essay to the catalogue used the phrase 'cautious acceptance' about these pieces; nonetheless, 'the attributions in the catalogue were not cautious but categorical' and that a similar situation was visible in the British Museum displays of such material. (p. 11) He then goes on to explain the situation thus:

> It is well known that the reign-marks of the fifteenth-century emperors, Yung-Lo, Hsuan-Te and Ch'eng-Hua were copied on all sorts of porcelain made between the sixteenth and twentieth centuries. Rather more than thirty years ago, a few pieces, so marked, were tentatively singled out as genuine but most of them have already been discarded. Recent writers have established in their place a horde of newly discovered or newly imported specimens, thereby changing the whole history of painted porcelain.[100]

Reitlinger then further explains that where once a Xuande mark was seen as conferring unquestioning authenticity, if examined in light of how short the reign period was and the disproportionately high number of so-marked pieces in English collections, there should have been more scepticism. (p. 11) Recently, according to him, once scepticism set in, however, apparent evidence of authentic 15th-century marks of the period was dismissed, such as that provided by the 1935 exhibition and the Chinese loan pieces within. He notes that the Chinese government catalogue featured fifty-four pieces dated to the fifteenth century but the writers of the English catalogue disagreed (as we noted earlier). This confirms the apparent reversal of the earlier faith put into Chinese texts and Chinese opinions about ceramics, which were now considered suspect and biased. This is evident in Reitlinger's quoting of Honey's criticism of Brankston: 'Brankston's writing is not free from *ipse dixit* in the manner of the old Chinese textbooks on pottery and he seems at times to have been deceived.'[101]

Reitlinger then reveals his own scepticism about the current state of connoisseurship of early Ming porcelain by giving a lengthy criticism of Brankston's work and methods, followed by comments on Bluett's essay on reign marks discussed previously. He then concludes with a consideration of why Chinese texts should be treated with caution, echoing Percival David's comments about Xiang Yuanbian's album. For the connoisseur in the 1940s, therefore, the attribution of early Ming porcelain was *the* porcelain problem of the period. Connoisseurship had become more problematic in spite of the advantages of excavations, Chinese displays and published scholarship.[102]

Much activity in the art world in general had been interrupted by the War, of course, but in spite of this, the OCS exhibition of 1946 was not an isolated one. In fact it signalled the beginning of major interest in Ming ceramics outside China. In 1947, for example, the Fogg Art Museum at Harvard University mounted *The Use of Blue on Chinese Porcelain of the Ming Dynasty 1368–1644*, which was accompanied by a short catalogue.[103] The OCS then mounted a subsequent exhibition, *Monochrome Porcelains of the Ming and Manchu Dynasties*, in 1948 (using a somewhat eccentric method of periodisation), which was followed by an exhibition at the Philadelphia Museum, *Blue-Decorated Porcelain of the Ming Dynasty*.[104] The catalogue for this exhibition states predictably that there are 'problems' with 15th century blue and white which the exhibition was designed to grapple with. Ending with 'a note of warning', the author of the catalogue essay states:

> This exhibition and catalogue are not intended to provide a final solution of all the problems concerning Ming blue-and-white. For the moment we can only make conjectures, and until confirmed by excavation or new discoveries, every theory is fraught with argument.[105]

This problem clearly was viewed as ongoing and in need of a solution, here said to be waiting in future excavations. But herein lies one of the problems of the problem, so to speak. Excavations were beginning to take place at kiln sites in China (having begun with Japanese excavators in the 1930s), but very little of this information was reaching the English-reading world, not least because of the turbulent political situation in China. But this faith in archaeology represents a wider change in attitude towards the connoisseurship of Chinese things, especially porcelain, from the veritable worship of ancient connoisseurship texts to a developing faith in physical sciences and material evidence. Incidentally, the acknowledgements for the Philadelphia catalogue represent a rare statement about the mechanics and scope of Chinese porcelain exhibition planning at that time. They state that the show was inspired by a gift of early Ming blue and white in 1944 (the Jenks collection), conversations between the 'experts' Jean-Pierre Dubosc (1903–88, collector and specialist) and John Alexander Pope (1906–82, Freer Gallery, Washington D. C.) and was informed by a study of the OCS exhibition of 1946.[106]

The Rise of Porcelain in 'Ming Art'

The interest in Ming porcelain demonstrated in the later 1940s probably contributed to the developing prominence of Ming ceramics in exhibitions of 'Ming art' and 'Chinese art' in general which began to appear more frequently in the 1950s, in both Britain and the US. One of the first of these, which concentrated on paintings, was *Great Painters of the Ming and Ch'ing Dynasties*. Held at a commercial gallery in New York, it is seen as a benchmark in the development of interest and scholarship on Ming paintings outside China.[107] In Britain, the first exhibition of Ming art, which represents British approaches to the subject, was the British Museum's *Chinese Art of the Ming Period* of 1950. This contained paintings, ceramics and a few lacquers yet 'provides a comprehensive survey of the aesthetic ideals of the Ming period in all its aspects', according to a short review of the time.[108] This was followed by an exhibition in Detroit in 1952 titled *Arts of the Ming Dynasty*, which similarly emphasised paintings and ceramics. The prominence of ceramics in these allegedly 'comprehensive' exhibitions is of course related to the fact that ceramics were abundant in collections, both public and private, and thus their significance in 'Chinese' or 'Ming' art was not questioned at the time (and still is not in many cases).

In the early 1950s, the more prominent presence of Chinese ceramics in the art world was reinforced by the opening of Percival David's museum at the University of London.[109] The Percival David Foundation of Chinese Art, which, in spite of its name, only contained Chinese ceramics, opened to the public in 1952 and mounted its first display shortly thereafter.[110] Included in the displays were a number of Ming ceramics that David had acquired before the museum opened. As we have seen, at the beginning of the decade, Ming porcelain specifically and in fact Ming arts in general, became more popular subjects for exhibitions and books. Crucially, this soon would include dedicated auction sales with Sotheby's perhaps pioneering the field with its sale in March 1953 of 'Important Ming Porcelain (a portion of the well-known collection of Mr and Mrs Alfred Clark)'.[111] Mrs Clark (Ivy, d.1976) began to sell off parts of this collection, which had been formed by her husband and then herself after he died in 1950. In this first sale were a wide range of Ming porcelains, but mostly of the 16th century, and in the advertisements for the sale, only 16th-century polychrome wares were illustrated, suggesting that these were more likely to attract buyers at the time.[112] Another Sothebys sale the same month focused on 'Fine Coloured Ming Porcelain', suggesting that there was enough material to divide up into several sales, and therefore enough potential buyers for a specialist area of Chinese ceramics. Some Clark material appeared in the OCS exhibition *Polychrome Porcelain of the Ming*, in which an interesting comment was made about the success of the show: 'The Ming exhibition was popular, partly because, to the uninitiated, Ming is a synonym for Chinese porcelain ....'[113] At the same time, a new commercial sub-category of Ming porcelain was presented in a sale exhibition *Imperial Porcelains of the Ming Dynasty (1368–1644 A.D.)* in New York in 1951.[114] As we have seen, 'imperial' Ming was an early designation for some of the porcelain pertaining to that period, but it had yet to become a named category of Ming in public exhibitions.

Shortly after the Sothebys sales in 1953, the British Museum acquired further items from the Brankston collection which had been given to museum by the collector's father and sister over several years.[115] In a notice about the gift, the keeper at that time, Soame Jenyns (1904–76), noted that thirteen of the pieces acquired by the Museum had been published in Brankston's book of 1938 'which revolutionized our arrangement of the early blue-and-white wares of the Ming dynasty'. (p. 55) Brankston had thus become a historical collector and expert in that subject area. Jenyns illustrated several of these pieces in his own book *Ming Pottery and Porcelain* of 1953, which was the first specialist book on Ming ceramics since Hobson's of 1923. In this book, Jenyns presented a state of the field essay in the introduction, confirming what were considered then the problems and controversies, including, still, that of 'early' blue and white. He says:

> Today one of the pressing problems of Ming ceramics is to link the imperial wares of the fifteenth and sixteenth centuries with their more humble provincial counterparts.
>
> The field of Ming ceramics is far more controversial than that of the Ch'ing. Many attributions must remain a matter of personal conjecture until time and usage have sanctified or rejected them.
>
> ... The difficulties that attend the study of Chinese texts on ceramics ...[116] And the interpretation of ambiguous Chinese texts, together with the traditional but often highly inaccurate lore of the Chinese dealer, is flimsy material with which to build .... But the outline of the picture of the blue and white porcelain of the fifteenth century is now fairly clear, although it has still to be filled in and substantiated in details. The identification of fifteenth-century enamelled pieces still presents a problem.[117]

Jenyns also demonised 'the Chinese dealer', thus confirming the tenaciousness of certain stereotypes about China.

In an essay of 1955, Sherman Lee (1918–2008), who would become one of the most prominent museum specialists (and museum directors) in Chinese art of the mid-20th century, stated that the interest in early Ming blue and white, which in his view, had recently developed (but in London was earlier, as noted above) was related to 'the relatively new-found enthusiasm for the paintings of the Ming and Ch'ing dynasties and indeed the two go together'.[118] His reasoning for this is somewhat flawed from today's perspective (but very much representative of its time and place) but he says that this is because those paintings were by 'classic masters' (e.g. scholar-painters or 'literati') and that the porcelains, therefore, are 'classic for Chinese taste'.[119]

> In both, the sympathetic and sensitive student finds a refinement and purity not devoid of strength and capable of both intellectual and emotional satisfaction. Certainly these blue-and-white porcelains, products of the Imperial kilns at Ching-te Chen in Kiansi province, should not be confused with recent 'Chinese-style' wares made for ordinary use. Aesthetic judgment begins in discrimination. (p. 29)

The fact that a painting specialist should present such reasoning confirms that the interest in Ming porcelains in the 1950s was driven by traditional connoisseurs and that this now included museum specialists outside of England, such as Lee himself and his peers. The Freer Gallery in Washington, for example, published its own small catalogue, *Ming Porcelains in the Freer Gallery*, in 1953.[120] As is true of most categories of art, with Ming porcelain too the interest began as a reaction against earlier 'taste' that was defined by the very colourful and decorative wares of the Qing which had been so widely collected outside China up to that date. That this coincided with a wider interest in Ming China among scholars in other disciplines meant that Ming ceramics were given a wider profile as a result.

Perhaps the best example of this is the fact that in 1957 there was yet another exhibition, *Arts of the Ming Dynasty*, which prominently featured ceramics.[121] That the exhibition was organised by the OCS of course meant that ceramics would automatically be given some prominence (in fact the greatest number of exhibits), even though the organizing committee stated that the exhibition was 'an attempt … to present an all-round view of the culture of this great dynasty'.[122] In spite of this, the framework for the interpretation of 'Ming art' in this exhibition was still porcelain:

> … the difficulty of presenting the art of the Ming dynasty as an organic whole is seen to be formidable. The importance of an exhibition of this kind is that we can see the paintings, porcelain, lacquer, metal work and carvings side by side and study the influence of one art on another. We can see resemblances between the shapes of porcelain and metal vessels, and in their decoration, between lacquer and cloisonné and in other fields. What is more difficult is to see the connections between the major art of painting and the minor arts. Apart from the obvious resemblance between paintings and textiles … the closest connection here, although tenuous enough, is between painting and porcelain …. (p. 3)

Interestingly, in the exhibition catalogue, the OCS reveals a further bias in its discussion of Ming ceramics which are, to some extent, compared unfavourably with those of the earlier Tang and Song periods, thus suggesting that 'taste' in Ming porcelain was still in the process of being cultivated:

> Although to the Chinese, painting and calligraphy are the major arts, to most Western connoisseurs porcelain and pottery are still held in the highest esteem. Perhaps the greatest interest today lies in pots which depend for their beauty on their shape and the colour and texture of their glazes. Even a simple carved or moulded decoration may be regarded as an intrusion by the purist. This kind of porcelain reached its greatest heights during the late T'ang and Sung periods, when shapes unsurpassed in the whole realm of ceramic art were achieved. (p. 5)

The Mongols are then blamed for bringing in decoration and colour but Ming monochromes could be seen 'to represent the more simple tastes of the Ming period'. (p. 6) Nonetheless, Ming blue and white and polychromes 'are undoubtedly the glory of Ming ceramics', but clearly not of Chinese ceramics, which are still viewed through the Modernist lens, which favours 'simplicity' and monochromes. (p. 6) This was an ambitious exhibition for the OCS, involving as it did the Arts Council and loans from institutions around the world, and was given quite favourable reviews in the press.[123] The essays in the catalogue were also quite detailed, containing recent research. In the ceramics section, for example, there are references to two foreign 'collections' containing Ming ceramics which had recently been published by the OCS and others, those of the Ardebil Shrine in Iran and the Ottoman palace in Istanbul.[124] The former collection as a whole would be the subject of an extensive study by Pope and published in 1956.[125] The Istanbul collection was first published by Ernst Zimmerman in 1930 in his *Altchinesische Porzellane im Alten Serai*: *Meisterwerke der Turkischen Museen II*. Today these are still considered among the most important historical 'collections' of Chinese ceramics.

Perhaps the most high profile display of Ming porcelain after the 1950s was that presented as part of the major loan exhibition from museums in Taiwan which took place in the US from 1961 to 1962, *Chinese Art Treasures*.[126] In this exhibition, which was seen as a smaller follow up to the International Exhibition of 1935 in London, ceramics again featured prominently, with 85 of the 253 exhibits being ceramic. However, this time the number of ceramics was matched by those of paintings, perhaps in deference to American taste in Chinese art at that time which favoured paintings over ceramics to some extent.[127] There were a number of significant and previously unseen examples presented, and this exhibition is therefore seen as a landmark in the study of Chinese painting in the US. *Chinese Art Treasures* was widely publicised and once again demonstrated the perceived significance of Ming porcelain in a survey history of Chinese art (if not in connoisseurship). For example, the catalogue essay states: 'As works of art, Ming porcelains are distinguished by a sense of purity and perfection; minor flaws and accidental markings that were allowed or even cultivated in Sung pottery could no longer be tolerated in the chaste, white vessels of the Ming.'[128] Thus, in many ways, the descriptions of Ming porcelain of the 1950s and 60s are contradictory, suggesting that Ming porcelain was popular as a Chinese art category precisely because it could be seen as more perfect than Song ceramics (in contrast to the earlier 20th-century view which was predicated on negative perceptions of Qing porcelain) and less decorative than Qing, or not as 'simple' and admirably rustic as Song but still preferable to Qing.[129] In fact, according to the introduction to Jenyns' 1953 book, it had lately been 'a fashionable pursuit to "spot" the Ming pieces in cabinets mainly devoted to the wares of K'ang Hsi (1662–1722)'.[130] The Chinese Art Treasures exhibition had originally been planned for 1937, immediately after the London show, but the war intervened and it was not until 1953 that negotiations resumed.[131] Its selection therefore represents taste of the later period (1950s) rather than of 1937, when it might have been more similar to that of the London exhibition.

In spite of the presence of Ming porcelain in such a high profile show, there were fewer specialist exhibitions and specialist sales in Britain and America in the 1960s as compared to the 1950s. Nonetheless, it continued to appear in a few single-period exhibitions such as The Art Institute of Chicago's *Ming-Ch'ing Dynasties, a.d. 1368–1644, a.d. 1644–1912*.[132] Such chronologically-themed exhibitions were quite popular in the 1950s and 1960s.[133] But, in spite of the relative dearth of displays, according to one source, the 1960s was a high period for the commercial market in Ming porcelains, probably as a result of its greater profile in the preceding decade:

> Early Ming was one of the most exciting sections of the art market in the 1960s. ... Richness and colour play very little part in determining the prices in this market which is dominated by blue and white. On the other hand there is nothing very wild about early Ming, nothing *outré* to titivate the intellectual *avant garde* like Kava bowls and wooden idols from the Pacific Islands. Early Ming is learned and analytical in its appeal, certainly not rarer than European ceramics of the same age and very much more repetitious. Yet the eight most expensive ceramic objects, sold in the 1960s, were all of them early Ming porcelain.
>
> In the course of the 1960s Chinese porcelain of the 14th, 15th and early 16th centuries was capable of multiplying its paper-money value ten times over, but in reality the movements,

> recorded in this list, are much smaller than those of the previous decade. In 1950 early Ming porcelain had scarcely advanced since the 1930s, when collectors first began to compete seriously for it. £150 in 1950 could have bought practically anything, whereas late Ming porcelain had sometimes fetched very much more. No one could have predicted in 1950 that early Ming blue and white would approach the £3,000 mark in a matter of seven years, still less that it would reach £25,000 in fifteen years. The speed with which the normal pace of the art market was overtaken remains even now partially a mystery ... A Ch'eng Hua mark on a blue and white piece, which can be trusted as an authentic 15th century original, has turned out to be rarer than was supposed, and this at least was the prettiest example of its kind.[134]

This same source, the art dealer Gerald Reitlinger, was sceptical about the high numbers of supposedly early Ming pieces available in the market[135] but was certain at the time of his writing (1970) that in the 1960s the most expensive wares were the small later 15th-century *doucai* pieces of the Chenghua period,[136] in contrast to 'the massive *fa-hua* jars in relief on background colour and only slightly later in date, [which] are a declining market. Their apogee was in the 1920s before *early Ming had been discovered* [emphasis added], but they were no novelty. They are in decidedly late 19th century taste and had some influence on ceramics of that period.'[137] *Fahua* wares were in fact a Ming type in origin and style but those that were exported were mostly of later date, and therefore the actual Ming-period examples were not well known and the style was disparagingly considered 'Qing' in the west.[138] [Fig. 4.5] As such, it was associated with an older form of taste in Chinese ceramics which contrasted unfavourably with taste in 'earlier' ceramics, a taste that, as noted earlier, was arguably established with encounters with Song (or thought to be Song) ceramics in the early 20th century. Reitlinger's statement, 'before the early Ming had been discovered', is also interesting because it confirms that ceramic categories, just like those of other 'works of art', are constructed and have a history themselves. As we have seen, there was a time before even 'Ming' existed outside China.

In spite of all the contradictory and sometimes forced representations of Ming porcelain, the 1960s would prove to be a defining period for Ming porcelain scholarship, primarily because of archaeology in China. For example, one of the major finds of early Ming porcelain was discovered during the dredging of the Yudai river in Nanjing, which ran along the remains of the early Ming palace and revealed many sherds of Hongwu and early 15th-century porcelain.[139] This was reported in the Chinese archaeology press which had begun in the 1950s[140] and was then being consulted by foreign specialists who could read Chinese such as Margaret Medley (1918–2000) at the University of London (SOAS). Medley would go on to a prominent career in Chinese ceramic studies while working as the curator of the Percival David Foundation until 1984. Trained as a sinologist, she made much use of Chinese texts, both ancient and modern, in her work, and cast an often sceptical eye over their translation and interpretation by earlier scholars.[141]

There were a few specialist exhibitions of Ming porcelain in the 1960s, including a large one at the Museum of Far Eastern Antiquities in Stockholm (MFEA), and importantly, two at the new National Palace Museum in Taiwan, in 1963 and 1964, with English-language catalogues. The catalogues represented a major work in six volumes, arranged by reign period, and came to be considered important literature in the history of Ming ceramics.[142] With the opening of the 'second' Palace Museum in Taiwan in the 1960s, there came to be another layer of difficulty in the identification and scholarship of Ming porcelain, and Chinese art in general. The 'original' palace collection, as gathered in the first Palace Museum, had been divided, and much of the best material in terms of objects went to Taiwan. Scholarship on Chinese court objects then developed along parallel lines, and both museums subsequently added to their collections such that what can be seen on view today may not necessarily have been acquired by the Chinese court. Nonetheless, the National Palace Museum (Taipei) has consistently mounted more high profile exhibitions on Ming porcelain than the Palace Museum (Beijing) and has consequently had a greater influence in the field.

Interestingly, by 1970, the China Institute in America felt that it was already time to stage a retrospective of Ming porcelain, *Ming Porcelains: A Retrospective*, perhaps signalling (or hoping to signal) that interest had reached a peak.[143] In the preface to the catalogue, the author and curator of the exhibition stated: 'An attempt has been made to illustrate the broad scope of Ming wares, from superb pieces of what is considered "Imperial" quality to relatively crude export ceramics.'[144] And that, in spite of the exhibition's title, seems to be the purpose of the exhibition—to present a small survey. The use of the word 'retrospective' clearly therefore was not intended to be used in the sense of a body of work, as for that of a painter or period, but rather to suggest comprehensiveness. Nevertheless, it is significant that by 1970, such a comprehensive (but actually rather small) show was deemed appropriate; this suggests that the subject of Ming porcelain was sufficiently well established so as to have its own history.

This perception of the field of Ming porcelain was confirmed by a much more authoritative work, *The History of the History of Ming Porcelain*, which was designed as a historiography and which by its existence confirmed the necessity of such a study in 1971, when it was published.[145] In the lecture (and text thereof), the author John Pope, whom we have encountered before, gave a comprehensive and newly constructed history of Ming porcelain outside of China, primarily in Europe. He began with the porcelains from the wreck of the ship *Santa Catarina* which arrived in Amsterdam in 1604 and then proceeded to review the textual sources in European languages, which have also been discussed in this chapter. While much of this history and bibliography is well known, the value in Pope's own text lies in his commentary and accompanying topical details, some of which are colourfully described. The 19th century, for example, was 'the Dark Ages in the history of the history of Ming porcelain' (p. 7) but also, the 1935–36 exhibition at Burlington House 'provided for most of us the first view we had ever had of pieces that really belonged to the Imperial Palace Collection in Peking' (p. 8). While he is also critical of some of the assumptions made about Ming porcelain, his outlook on the subject was positive:

> It may well be that no product, either industrial or artistic, or both, ever combined greater beauty and utility or exercised wider influence over such a large part of the world as did Ming porcelain. No wonder some of us find it an absorbing subject of study. (p. 14)

It is thus, in his opinion, the global impact of Ming porcelain which has made it a separate area of ceramic studies, a notion which anticipated by some thirty years the interest in Ming porcelain by scholars of world history whose now numerous studies of Jingdezhen as a source for a global commodity have also elevated ceramics beyond their relatively lowly place in the history of art. Beyond 'world history', however, it is ceramic archaeology in China, and the exhibitions of finds from the Ming imperial kilns (dating from the mid-1980s onward), which have finally answered the questions surrounding Ming porcelain production (if not consumption), such as the suspicion about 'early' attributions, and which have secured it within the now archaeologically-focused history of Chinese 'art' within and outside China. The Wynn vase in Macao, which opened this chapter, can be, and was, authenticated by comparison with excavated Hongwu porcelain. Today, in fact, in an interesting approach to display, exhibitions of reconstructed excavated Ming porcelains are very popular[146] and can be seen to represent yet another conception of Ming porcelain: as fragments of China's past.[147] Unlike the other identities established for Ming porcelain, however, this latest one has been entirely Chinese-driven and Ming porcelain has been most prominent in this because the Ming levels at Jingdezhen have been the most extensively excavated (and published). Thus the sherd can now stand for the whole piece and, inevitably, has become a commodity in the art world. [Fig. 4.6]

Conclusion

With the metonymic display of Ming porcelain through broken sherds, once again the original object has been superseded in the process of transformation. In this case, the transformation was effected in two stages: initially, and physically, through the discarding of flawed whole objects on a sherd heap at the time of manufacture and then later, conceptually, from objects of daily use in the Ming period to examples of Ming trash in the present day, which nonetheless are used as a tool for connoisseurship. In China, and the rest of the world, the dating of many whole pieces is today confirmed by comparison with excavated sherds, which are both items for display and for scholarship. What this new and still evolving identity for Ming porcelain suggests is that we need to look not only at the 'social life' of things but also, in parallel, at what might be called their 'conceptual life'. As this book has demonstrated, a single Ming bowl can be a simple, anonymous eating bowl in Ming China, then become an expensive silver-gilt mounted drinking cup in England, and then acquire a name and a definite article (*the* Lennard Cup). The same object can then be interpreted as a model for the consumption of foreign luxury goods in sixteenth-century England and then it can return to the physical and become a museum piece after being purchased by yet another named collector (e.g. Percival David). Yet similarly, the category of porcelain in which this bowl is placed, 'Chinese porcelain', can be reduced in popular discourse to an association with one period in Chinese history, the Ming; and then with connoisseurship activity in Anglo-American society, it can be transformed into a literary motif and figure of speech representing numerous qualities: erudition, elite status, wealth, rarity, fragility and mystery, among others. In this process, consumers as agents have transformed a simple object from the early modern period in China into a global symbol and cultural icon of the present day, demonstrating the complex and mutually transformative relationship between people and the things they encounter.

Appendix

Text of Shao Bao's *Guan tao shuo* (from the online *Wenyuange* edition of the *Siku quanshu*)
Rongchuntang qianji 榮春堂前集, *juan* 9, 13–14

觀陶說

邵子觀于景德之陶歷群工所咸造焉客或嘆曰吁陶之為器其難矣哉方其取土於山猶夫石也碓而粉之澄之以水濾之以渠浥之以甓和之以漿始可以揉而規之又必削其未整焉因以壞者什一磨其未澤焉壞者什二潤之以膏飾之以采内諸火而出焉壞者什五其幸不壞者璺隙疵玷又什之三葢自始規而至成器以獻于尚膳其不得與焉者多矣然取土而舁者若干人碓者若干人澄者濾者浥者和而揉者削者磨者潤且飾者納諸火者各若干人凡越工者十而后器斯得其成也其獻之上不過備一御耳為之如是其難而用之不以為異是可嘆也邵子曰是誠難矣雖然吾猶以為易也夫取土而制其質澄濾浥和而後就規刮磨潤飾而後就火苟不壞者皆成器矣器而獻之不過三月則離山野而薦諸郊廟陳諸宮寢祭祀享燕實與有用

14

焉斯亦異矣視其為之之難亦何負哉乃若君子之修身以待用者材以為土學以為碓戒以為澄省以為濾從義以為浥力行以為和循禮以為規研精以為刮師友以為磨出詞以為潤表儀以為采自試而徵之以去其疵隙玷璺近者十年遠者三四十年曾不得望君門而效用焉甚或終其身於山野其視夫陶也又何如邪竇方陶於人才知其難焉故陶吾猶以為易也客起而謝曰吾聞萬室不足於一陶今乃知其難若是雖然器猶末也請著以為說俾用才者知焉

Notes

Introduction

1. For a good overview of the state of the field of Ming ceramics in Chinese, see Wang Guangyao 王光尧, *Mingdai guanting taoci shi* 明代官廷陶瓷史 (History of Ming Imperial Ceramics), Beijing, 2010; in English, see Jessica Harrison-Hall, *Ming Ceramics in the British Museum*, London, 2001.
2. Among the major publications on these subjects are Fung Ping Shan Museum, *Jingdezhen chutu taoci* 景德镇出土陶瓷 (Ceramic Finds from Jingdezhen Kilns), Hong Kong, 1992 and Zhejiang sheng wenwu ju 浙江省文物局, *Zhongguo Longquan qingci* 中国龙泉青瓷 (Longquan Celadon of China), Zhejiang, 1998.
3. The most recent and comprehensive example of this is Robert Finlay, *The Pilgrim Art: Cultures of Porcelain in World History*, Berkeley, 2010; for the Ming period, see also Stacey Pierson, 'The Movement of Chinese Ceramics: Appropriation in Global History', *Journal of World History* 23, no. 1 (2012): 9–39.
4. Arjun Appadurai, ed., *The Social Life of Things: Commodities in Cultural Perspective*, Cambridge, 1986.
5. James Clifford, ed., *The Predicament of Culture: Twentieth-Century Ethnography, Literature and Art*, Cambridge, MA, 1988; Nicholas Mirzoeff, ed., *An Introduction to Visual Culture*, London, 1999.
6. Jean Baudrillard, *The System of Objects*, trans. James Benedict, London, 2006, pp. 80, 88.
7. For discussions of transculturation with reference to objects, see for example: Nicholas Mirzoeff, 'Transculture: from Kongo to Congo', in *An Introduction to Visual Culture*, London, 1999, chap. 4, pp. 129–161 and Elizabeth Hutchinson, *The Indian Craze: Primitivism, Modernism and Transculturation in American Art, 1890–1915*, Durham, 2009. The original concept was developed in Fernando Ortiz, *Cuban Counterpoint: Tobacco and Sugar*, trans. Harriet de Onís, New York, c.1947 (and multiple reprints).
8. Most recently in Rose Kerr and Luisa E. Mengoni, with Ming Wilson, *Chinese Export Ceramics*, London, 2011 and William R. Sargent, *Treasures of Chinese Export Ceramics from the Peabody Essex Museum*, New Haven, 2012.
9. Howard S. Becker, *Art Worlds*, Berkeley, 1982.

Chapter 1 Porcelain in Ming China (14th–17th centuries)

1. In China, the framework for the study of ceramics is primarily archaeology. Categorically, ceramics are usually defined as 'craft' (*shouyi* 手艺 or *gongyi* 工艺) or 'antiques' (*guwu* 古物 or *guwan* 古玩). However, with the recent spectacular sales of Ming and Qing ceramics at auction, their status as collected items is changing, and sometimes now they are described as 'works of art' (*yishu zuopin* 艺术作品) in consequence.
2. See Craig Clunas, *Art in China*, Oxford University Press, 2009, pp. 175–191.

3. Rose Kerr, ed., *Ceramic Technology*, vol. 5, part 12, of *Science and Civilisation in China*, Cambridge, 2004, p. 184; Fung Ping Shan Museum 1992, pp. 11–12.
4. Kerr ed. 2004, pp. 214–216.
5. Kerr ed. 2004, pp. 560–562.
6. A good overview in English of Jingdezhen as a place and as a location for ceramic manufacture and production, from a historian's perspective, is given in Anne Gerritsen, 'Ceramics for Local and Global Markets: Jingdezhen's Agora of Technologies', in Dagmar Schafer, ed., *Cultures of Knowledge: Technology in Chinese History*, Leiden, 2012, pp. 161–184.
7. With reference to porcelain, specific textual sources surviving from the Ming period are not numerous, but plenty of data concerning production, manufacture and distribution can be found in a fairly wide range of documents and texts. Edicts concerning official porcelains can be found in the various editions of the *Ming shilu* 明实录 (Veritable Records of the Ming Dynasty) and the *Ming shi* 明史 (History of the Ming; compiled in the Qing period); and concerning taxation, ceremonial requirements, etc., in the *Da Ming huidian* 大明会典. Information about raw materials, colours, etc., can be found in the *Jiangxi tongzhi* 江西通志 (Jiangxi gazetteer), which was begun in the Jiajing period (1522–66). The earliest surviving edition is from 1525. Much useful data concerning Jingdezhen production during the 16th century can be found in the Jiangxi provincial gazetteer, *Jiangxi sheng da zhi* 江西省大志, which was compiled in 1556 and reprinted with additional material in 1597. As noted by Rose Kerr (2004) in her much needed English-language survey of the primary literature of ceramics in Chinese, the most useful section of the second edition of this text is the chapter called *Tao shu* (book of ceramics–*juan* 7). Margaret Medley completed an extensive study of this section which was published in part in Rosemary Scott, ed., *The Porcelains of Jingdezhen*, London, 1993, pp. 69–82. As she notes, some of the information from the Ming period comes from unusual sources, such as the *Shuibu beikao* 水部备考 (handbook produced for the Board of Public Works for the Water Transport and Canals department), Wanli edition. Anecdotal descriptions of Jingdezhen porcelain and production can be found in more personalised Ming-period writings such as Wang Shimao's 王世懋 16th-century *Minbushu* 闽部疏 (Memorials about Fujian Province) or the classic connoisseurship text, the *Gegu yaolun* 格古要论 (1388, and later editions). A comprehensive selection of historical texts on Chinese ceramics is provided in Xiong Liao 熊寥 and Xiong Wei 熊微, comps., *Zhongguo taoci guji jicheng* 中国陶瓷古籍集成 (Annotated Collection of Historical Documents on Ancient Chinese Ceramics), Shanghai, 2006.
8. See Michael Dillon, 'Jingdezhen as a Ming Industrial Center', *Ming Studies* 6 (Spring 1978), pp. 37–44 and for a European perspective, Maxine Berg, 'Asian Luxuries and the Making of the European Consumer Revolution', in Maxine Berg and Elizabeth Egar, eds., *Luxury in the Eighteenth Century: Debates, Desires and Delectable Goods*, Basingstoke, 2003, pp. 228–244.
9. Rosemary Scott and Rose Kerr, *Ceramic Evolution in the Middle Ming Period: Hongzhi to Wanli*, London/Singapore, 1994, p. 8; *Jiangxi sheng da zhi* 江西省大志 (1597 edn.), chap. 7, pp. 33a–44b. For more figures tabulated in English, see Kerr ed. 2004, p. 199.
10. For general introductions to these wares in English, see: Kerr and Mengoni 2011, chap. 7; Rose Kerr, John Ayers and Ho Chuimei, *Blanc de Chine: Porcelain from Dehua*, Richmond, 2002; Rita C. Tan et al., *Zhangzhou Ware Found in the Philippines: "Swatow" Export Ceramics from Fujian 16th–17th century*, Manila, 2007. In Chinese see: Fujian sheng bowuguan 福建省博物馆, *Zhangzhou yao* 漳州窑, Fuzhou, 1997; Wang Wenjing 王文径, *Zhangpu yao* 漳浦窑 (Zhangpu Kilns), Zhongguo Fujian gu taoci biaoben daxi 中国福建古陶瓷标本大系, Fuzhou, 2004; Chen Jianzhong 陈建中 and Chen Lifang 陈丽芳, *Dehua yao* 德化窑 (Dehua Kilns), 3 vols., Zhongguo Fujian gu taoci biaoben daxi 中国福建古陶瓷标本大系, Fuzhou, 2005; Fujian sheng bowuguan, ed., *Dehua yao* 德化窑, Beijing, 1990.

11. Michael Dillon, 'Transport and Marketing in the Development of the Jingdezhen Porcelain Industry during the Ming and Qing Dynasties', *Journal of the Economic and Social History of the Orient* 35, no. 3 (1992), p. 278; Liang Miaotai 梁淼泰, *Ming Qing Jingdezhen chengshi jingji yanjiu* 明清景德镇城市经济研究, Nanchang, 1991. Recent global studies in English include Finlay 2010.
12. Dillon 1978, pp. 37–44.
13. Dillon 1992, p. 278.
14. Dillon 1992, p. 279; Kerr ed. 2004, p. 240.
15. Dillon 1992, p. 279; Kerr ed. 2004, p. 185.
16. Dillon 1992, pp. 279–280; Christine Moll-Murata, 'Chinese Guilds from the Seventeenth to the Twentieth Centuries', in Jan Lucassen et al., ed., *The Return of the Guilds*, Cambridge, 2008a, pp. 213–248. One must bear in mind that there has been some debate about the definition of 'guilds' as applied to pre-20th century China. See for example: Lu Zuoxie 吕作燮, 'Ming Qing shiqide huiguan bing fei gongshangye de hanghui' 明清时期的会馆并非工商业的行会 (Ming-Qing Guilds and Non-commercial, Non-industrialized Professional Associations), *Zhongguo shi yanjiu* 3, 1982, p. 66.
17. Anne Gerritsen, 'Fragments of a Global Past: Ceramics Manufacture in Song-Yuan-Ming Jingdezhen', *Journal of the Economic and Social History of the Orient* 52 (2009), p. 138.
18. Wang Zongmu 王宗沐, *Jiangxi sheng da zhi*, preface dated 1597, reprinted in the *Zhongguo fangzhi congshu*, Taiwan, 1989, no. 779; also the focus of a paper by Margaret Medley, 'Organisation and Production at Jingdezhen in the Sixteenth Century', in Rosemary E. Scott, ed., *The Porcelains of Jingdezhen*, London, 1993, pp. 69–82.
19. Translated in Gerritsen 2009, p. 140.
20. Timothy Brook, *Confusions of Pleasure: Commerce and Culture in Ming China*, Berkeley, 1998, p. 118.
21. Gerritsen 2009, pp. 117–152.
22. Gerritsen 2009, p. 145.
23. The inventory of goods belonging to Yan Song 严嵩 (1480–1565). Timothy Brook, *The Troubled Empire: China in the Yuan and Ming Dynasties*, Cambridge, MA, 2010, pp. 187–88; Craig Clunas, 'The Cost of Ceramics and the Cost of Collecting Ceramics in the Ming Period', *Oriental Ceramic Society of Hong Kong Bulletin*, no. 8, 1986–88, p. 48.
24. Clunas 1986–88, p. 48.
25. Benjamin I. Schwartz, 'Some Stereotypes in the Periodization of Chinese History', in *China and Other Matters*, Cambridge, MA, 1996, pp. 18–43.
26. Kerr ed. 2004, p. 188. For the Chinese perspective and definition of 'imperial', which views this as production in a separate kiln system, see Wang Guangyao, *Zhongguo gudai guanyao zhidu* 中国古代官窑制度 (China's Ancient Official Kiln System), Zijin shuxi 6, Beijing, 2004.
27. Instead, from the Zhengde reign period, references to the 'imperial vessels factory' (*yuqi chang* 御器厂) appear, which refer to the location rather than the consumer. Kerr ed. 2004, p. 188 and fn. 283, citing the *Jiangxi sheng da zhi* 江西省大志 and the *Jingdezhen taolu* 景德镇陶录.
28. For example, in Shen Defu's 沈德符 *Wanli ye huo bian* 万历野获编 (Random Gleanings of the Wanli Period, 1606) as noted in Craig Clunas, *Superfluous Things: Material Culture and Social Status in Early Modern China*, Cambridge, 1991; Honolulu, 2004, p. 104: 'Thus the prices of Yongle carved red lacquer, Xuande bronzes and Chenghua porcelain vie with those of antiques.'
29. See 'Inscriptions on Ming Lacquer', in Peter Lam, ed., *Layered Beauty: The Baoyizhai Collection of Chinese Lacquer*, Hong Kong, 2010, pp. 191–200. Lacquer examples from both the early and later Ming periods were recently published in Li He and Michael Knight, *Power and Glory: Court Arts of China's Ming Dynasty*, San Francisco, 2004, nos. 50, 53, 54. A famous cloisonné example with a Xuande reign mark can be seen in the British Museum collection, 1957.0501.1.

30. Perhaps through the system of *guanda minshao* 官搭民烧 'official partnership with private kilns', which is discussed below. Medley 1993, p. 80; Kerr ed. 2004, p. 200; Dagmar Schafer, 'Inscribing the Artifact and Inspiring Trust: The Changing Role of Markings in the Ming Era', *East Asian Science, Technology and Society: An International Journal* 5 (2011), p. 260.
31. For a discussion of the latter, see Anthony J. Barbieri-Low, *Artisans in Early Imperial China*, Seattle/London, 2007, pp. 7–9; Schafer 2011a.
32. For example in the *Jiangxi sheng da zhi, juan* 7, pp. 4a–b (Zhongguo fangzhi congshu, Taipei, 1998 edn.). Kerr ed. 2004, pp. 235–236.
33. See Tsai Meifen, 'The Role of the Government in the Development of Ceramics in the Sung Dynasty', in *China at the Inception of the Second Millennium: Art and Culture of the Sung Dynasty, 960–1279* 千禧年宋代文物大展, Taipei, 2000, pp. 321–337; English language supplement, pp. 86–93, esp. 322–323/90–91 for Ru and Guan wares.
34. Scott and Kerr 1994, p. 8.
35. As recorded in the *Fuliang xianzhi* 浮梁县志 (1682 edn.), *juan* 4, p. 46b. See Kerr ed. 2004 on *guanda minshao*, p. 200; Medley 1993, p. 73.
36. Craig Clunas, *Empire of Great Brightness: Visual and Material Cultures of Ming China, 1368–1644*, London, 2007a, p. 21; for reign marks as a visual representation of Ming time, p. 24.
37. Christine Lau, 'Ceremonial Monochrome Wares of the Ming Dynasty', in Rosemary Scott, ed., *The Porcelains of Jingdezhen*, London, 1993, p. 90, 99, citing the *Ming shilu*, vol. 80, p. 4193 (Taipei, 1962) and Li Dongyang 李东阳 et al., *Da Ming huidian* 大明会典 (Collected Statues of the Ming), 5 vols., 1587; reprinted, Taipei, 1963, *juan* 201, p. 2715.
38. Kerr ed. 2004, pp. 202–206. Official consumption in general was also regulated in that lower ranked officials were not allowed silver tableware and were confined to porcelain or lacquered wood examples. As noted in the *Ming shi* (comp. Zhang Tingyu 张廷玉, 1739; Beijing: Zhonghua shuju, 1974), p. 1072, cited in Craig Clunas, 'The Art of Social Climbing in Sixteenth-Century China', *The Burlington Magazine* 133, no. 1059 (June 1991), p. 371.
39. Margaret Medley, 'Imperial Patronage and Early Ming Porcelain', *TOCS* 55 (1990–91), pp. 31–32.
40. Translated by Medley in Medley 1990–91, p. 37. Li Dongyang et al. 1963, chap 194, p. 2632.
41. Kerr ed. 2004, p. 190, with Ming examples cited in the *Jiangxi sheng da zhi*, 1597 edn.
42. There are examples of these in many European and American museums. See for example the export watercolours depicting porcelain production in the Winterthur collection, c. 1820, watercolour on paper, 2003.47.14.1–10. Recently published in Ronald W. Fuchs II with David S. Howard, *Made in China: Export Porcelain from the Leo and Doris Hodroff Collection at Winterthur*, Delaware, 2005, figs. 1–10. Another set of 24 can be seen in the Victoria & Albert Museum, London: E.-59-1910. These are dated 1770–1790. A set in the National Palace Museum, Taipei, attributed to three painters, was published in National Palace Museum, *Emperor Ch'ien-lung's Grand Cultural Enterprise; Qianlong huangdi de wenhua daye* 乾隆皇帝的文化大业, Taipei, 2002, no. V-I.
43. By Song Yingxing 宋应星 (b. 1587); for an English translation, see E-Tu Zen Sun and Shiou-Chuan Sun, trans., *T'ien-kung k'ai-wu by Sung Ying-hsing. Chinese Technology in the Seventeenth Century*, Philadelphia/London, 1966. This book was recently the subject of a dedicated study in English by Dagmar Schafer: *The Crafting of the 10,000 Things: Knowledge and Technology in Seventeenth-Century China*, Chicago, 2011.
44. Sun and Sun trans. 1966, pp. 135–158. It should be noted that two editions of the *Tiangong kaiwu* [henceforth *TGKW*] appeared before 1644 but no new ones were printed in the Qing period. Various sections were preserved in the *Gujin tushu jicheng* 古今图书集成 and two other compendia of the 18th and 19th centuries. A Ming copy was reprinted in Japan in the 18th century, and only later were two Ming copies discovered in the Bibliothèque Nationale in Paris. The first Chinese reprint of the original

1637 edition, based on the Japanese version and the texts of the 18th century, was published in 1929 (the Tao edition). It is from this edition that the illustrations have been taken, so they are of Qing date, not Ming. Sun and Sun trans., pp. ix–x. A number of studies have been published recently which focus on the illustrations to the *Tiangong kaiwu*, including Peter J. Golas, '"Like Obtaining a Great Treasure": The Illustrations in Song Yingxing's *The Exploitation of the Works of Nature*', in Francesca Bray et al., ed., *Graphics and Text in the Production of Technical Knowledge in China: The Warp and the Weft*, Leiden/Boston, 2007, who presents a complete chronology of them on pp. 594–597. With reference to porcelain in the *TGKW*, Schafer (2011b) notes that in both images and text 'the work process is somewhat vaguely explained' (p. 149) and in (2005) that the *TGKW* should perhaps be seen as a metaphysical statement as much as a technical treatise because Song could not claim any experience with crafts or technology (p. 54). The problems with recreating some of the technologies and techniques described in the *TGKW* were also explored by various authors in Yabuuchi Kiyoshi 藪内清, ed., *Tenkō kaibutsu no kenkyū* 天工開物の研究 (Studies on the *Tiangong kaiwu*), Tokyo, 1953. On ceramics, pp. 123–136.

45. In present-day Chinese texts on ceramic history, the fact of their production circumstances is not what classifies or qualifies the objects in connoisseurship. In these texts, ceramics are treated as a separate, fully formed tradition with the criteria for connoisseurship traditionally focused on formal characteristics—forms, decoration, techniques of both, etc. In general texts on the history of Chinese art in Chinese, ceramics appear as part of the object chronology, as they do in histories of Chinese art in Western languages, with perhaps less emphasis on ceramics than is usual in these latter types of art histories.
46. Stacey Pierson, '"The Sung Standard": Chinese Ceramics and British Studio Pottery in the 20 Century', in Stacey Pierson, ed., *Song Ceramics: Art History, Archaeology and Technology*, Colloquies on Art and Archaeology, no. 22, London, 2004, p. 82.
47. Shafer 2011a, p. 251. As Shafer suggests, the reign mark 'effectively displayed the dynasty's power and each ruler's proprietary right to porcelain.'
48. Kerr ed. 2004, p. 209, citing the *Ming Shizong shilu* 明世宗实录 (Veritable Records of the Shizong [Jiajing] Reign), *juan* 240, p. 5; Taipei reprint, 1962–67.
49. The fact that these 'potters' were not associated with the imperial factory may be why their names have been passed down to us. Most of the information about Ming porcelain production is focused on the imperial factory as this was activity that was deliberately recorded for regulation and taxation. Unlike painters in court workshops, the makers of standardized items would not have been identified. The popular notion of Ming 'imperial' ceramics as works of art or the products of independent craftsmen is therefore even less applicable to the Ming period.
50. Li Rihua, *Weishuixuan riji*, ed. and annot. Tu Youxiang 屠友祥, Song Ming Qing xiaopin wenji jizhu 2, Shanghai, 1996 [henceforth *WSXRJ*]. For a discussion in English of this text, see Craig Clunas, 'The Art Market in Seventeenth Century China: The Evidence of the Li Rihua Diary', *History of Art and History of Ideas* 1 (2003), pp. 201–223.
51. 十九精于陶事，所作永窑宣窑成窑，皆逼真。人亦文雅好吟，喜绘画。*WSXRJ* 1996, p. 92. English translation from Brook 2010, p. 207.
52. *WSXRJ*, 1996, p. 92 where Shen Biehe is written 沈别驾. English translation from Brook 2010, p. 207.
53. Brook 2010, p. 207.
54. Brook 2010, p. 207. *WSXRJ*, 1996, p. 92.
55. Excavated in 1973 at Duobaogong and now in the Jiangxi Provincial Museum. Published in Zhang Bai 张柏, ed., *Zhongguo chutu ciqi quanji* 中国出土瓷器全集 (Complete collection of ceramic art unearthed in China), 16 vols., Beijing, 2008, vol. 14, no. 220. The text on the tablet consists of 359 characters and is written in concentric circles with two large characters in the centre: 墓誌 'tomb tablet'.

56. The essay is part of the longer text *Rong chun tang ji* 容春堂集 (Collection of the Hall Where Spring Appears). For the English translation and information about Shao, see Stephen Little, 'Shao Bao on Porcelain: A Ming Scholar-Official's View of Jingdezhen', paper presented at the conference 'Asian Ceramics: Effect of Religion and Ritual'; held at the Field Museum, Chicago, IL, 24–26 May 1996; available online through *ACRO: Asian Ceramics Research*; http://acrochicago.homestead.com/Little.html (accessed 4 August 2012). Edition consulted by Little: Shao Bao, *Rong chun tang ji*, 1518 edn., *juan* 9, 13a–14a, 'Essay on Ceramics', reprinted, Shanghai, 1991. Shao Bao does not appear in L. Carrington Goodrich and Chaoying Fang, eds., *Dictionary of Ming Biography*, 2 vols., New York/London, 1976.
57. Little 1996 translation.
58. Little 1996. The original text is reprinted in the Appendix.
59. Little 1996.
60. Ouyang Shibin 欧阳世彬, 'A Study of Ceramics Made at Ching-te-chen Commercial Kilns during the 15th Century', *Meishushi yanjiu jikan* 美术史研究集刊 7 (July 1999), pp. 58–87.
61. Christine Moll-Murata, 'Guilds and Apprenticeship in China and Europe: The Ceramics Industries of Jingdezhen and Delft', paper presented to the S.R. Epstein Memorial Conference: "Technology and Human Capital Formation in the East and West", 18–21 June 2008, http://www2.lse.ac.uk/economicHistory/Conferences/Epstein%20Memorial%20Conference/PAPER-MollMurata.pdf, p. 4, referencing Kerr ed. 2004, p. 209 (accessed 4 August 2012) and generally on Chinese guilds, Moll-Murata 2008a, pp. 213–248. On taxation, see Ray Huang, *Taxation and Governmental Finance in Sixteenth-Century Ming China*, Cambridge, 1974, pp. 32–38. A comprehensive overview of the porcelain industry at Jingdezhen, up to the present day, is given in Jingdezhen shi difangzhi bangongshi 景德镇市地方志办公室, ed., *Zhongguo cidu Jingdezhenshi ciyezhi, Shizhi er juan* 中国瓷都·景德镇市：瓷业志：市志2卷 (Monograph on the Porcelain Industry of China's Porcelain City Jingdezhen), 2 vols., Beijing, 2004.
62. Moll-Murata 2008b, p. 3; Kerr ed. 2004, p. 209.
63. Moll-Murata 2008b, p. 4.
64. The *Jingdezhen taolu* 景德镇陶录 (1815), originally by Lan Pu 蓝浦, has been the source for much information about Jingdezhen and its ceramic production. Parts of it were translated by Stephen W. Bushell; and a full English translation was published by Geoffrey Sayer, *Ching-te-chen T'ao-lu*, or *The Potteries of China*, London, 1951. It has recently been the subject of a chapter of a Ph.D. thesis by Ellen Huang, 'China's China: Jingdezhen Porcelain and the Production of Art in the Nineteenth Century', University of California at San Diego, 2008.
65. Ellen Johnston Laing, 'Chou Tan-Ch'uan is Chou Shih Ch'en. A Report on a Ming Dynasty Potter, Painter and Entrepreneur', *Oriental Art* 21, no. 3 (1975), p. 224, fn 2. Edition consulted: *Meishu congshu* II, 8, Taipei, 1963, pp. 208–209.
66. Laing 1975, p. 224, fn. 3.
67. See http://www.npm.gov.tw/exh95/lateming/works/work_06_en.html (accessed 4 August 2012).
68. See http://www.npm.gov.tw/exh95/lateming/index.html for catalogue information on this piece (accessed 4 August 2012).
69. See Clunas, 'Gifts and Giving in Chinese Art', *TOCS* 62 (1997–98), pp. 1–18.
70. The earliest porcelains decorated with underglaze cobalt blue, and therefore 'blue and white', were made at kilns in Henan province during the Tang dynasty. The style was then next produced on a much larger scale in south east China, at Jingdezhen, during the Yuan period. For a broad history of blue and white in China, see Stacey Pierson, *Chinese Ceramics: A Design History*, 2009, London, p. 34.
71. As suggested in the popular book by John Carswell, *Blue and White: Chinese Porcelain Around the World*, Chicago, 2000.

72. See for example, Fung Ping Shan Museum 1992.
73. For example, Shen Defu in the *Wanli ye huo bian* (1591), as noted in Clunas 1986–88, pp. 50–51. In a recent auction, a single Chenghua *doucai* stem cup sold for 23,060,000 HKD. Christies Hong Kong, 1 June 2011, lot no. 3582.
74. Lau 1993, p. 94.
75. For detailed information (and glaze recipes) about monochrome glaze production in China, see Nigel Wood, *Chinese Glazes: Their Origins, Chemistry and Recreation*, London, 1999.
76. Department of Archaeology, Beijing University et al., *Guantai Cizhou yaozhi* 观台磁州窑址 (The Cizhou Kiln Site at Guantai), Beijing, 1997.
77. Fung Ping Shan Museum 1992, figs. 177, 178.
78. The earliest polychrome examples with underglaze blue are those from the Xuande period and these appear to have been a special commission for a Tibetan temple. The most famous surviving example belongs to the Sa'gya Temple in Sa'gya county, Tibet. Published in Beijing Cultural Relics Publishing House, *Gems of China's Cultural Relics; Zhongguo wenwu jinghua* 中国文物精华, Beijing, 1993, no. 34. Related sherds were also excavated at Jingdezhen in 1988. See Hong Kong Urban Council, *Imperial Porcelain of the Yongle and Xuande Periods Excavated from the Site of the Ming Imperial Factory at Jingdezhen*, Hong Kong, 1989, no. 89.
79. Pierson 2009, p. 14.
80. Francesca Bray, 'Technics and Civilization in Late Imperial China: An Essay in the Cultural History of Technology', *Osiris*, 2nd Series 13, *Beyond Joseph Needham: Science, Technology, and Medicine in East and Southeast Asia* (1998), pp. 11–33.
81. This is because copper is a volatile pigment and sensitive to both glaze chemistry (and consistency) and firing atmosphere. Wood 1999, pp. 168–169.
82. Rosemary Scott, 'Southern Chinese Provincial Kilns: Their Importance and Possible Influence on South East Asian Ceramics', in Rosemary Scott and John Guy, eds., *South East Asia and China: Art, Interaction and Commerce*, Colloquies on Art and Archaeology in Asia, no. 17, London, 1995, p. 194.
83. The sources of cobalt used in Chinese ceramics from the Tang through the Qing period have been subject to numerous and still inconclusive studies. In summary (from Kerr ed. 2004, pp. 658–692), in the Ming period, two types were used, one with a significant iron component and the other with manganese. It is the high iron cobalt which is traditionally said to have been sourced outside of China, particularly near Kashan in Persia. Persian cobalt-decorated ceramics have been analysed, and one type made there does feature high iron cobalt. The other does not. This would mean that Jingdezhen potters would have had to know that this was a source, specify which Kashan cobalt they wanted, and assume that miners in Kashan could tell the difference. In Ming texts, cobalt is sometimes referred to as *huiqing* 回青 or Mohammedan blue, and this is thought to be confirmation that it was imported. However, this could be a reference to Yunnan, which was also a source for cobalt, or even to Central Asia. In other texts, the description *sumali* 苏麻离 is used, possibly referring to Qamsar. Other sources for high manganese cobalt used in the Ming include Zhejiang and Jiangxi. Ming 'imperial' porcelains are sometimes authenticated by the supposed source of the cobalt used, as there appear to have been patterns in the use of the two different types of cobalt. For example, in the Hongwu period, high manganese cobalt was used, whereas in the Xuande period, a mixture of both cobalts is apparent. See R. Wen et al., 'The Chemical Composition of Blue Pigment on Chinese Blue-and-White Porcelain of the Yuan and Ming Dynasties (AD 1271–1644)', *Archeometry* 49, no. 1 (2007), pp. 101–115. The assumption that 'imported' cobalt was superior does not seem to be borne out in the usually very high quality Xuande court wares. Thus with reference to Ming blue and white, the interest in the source of cobalt used for decoration is slightly out of proportion to its applications and significance. For information about the mixing of cobalts and refining methods in the later Ming period, see Scott and Kerr 1994, p. 9; Wang Qingzheng 汪庆正, ed., *Qinghua youli hong* 青花釉里红 (Underglaze Blue and Red), Shanghai, 1987, p. 12.

84. A pictorial reading of such framing devices in late Ming and Qing ceramics is presented in Jonathan Hay, *Sensuous Surfaces: The Decorative Object in Early Modern China*, London, 2010.
85. Li Rihua referred to the Yuan painter Huang Gongwang by his sobriquet—the 'silly Daoist' 大痴, not as 'the painter'. See *WSXRJ*, p. 86.
86. The Ming 'literati' responsible for such texts of course had different responses to ceramics and other objects, but one text was cited more often than others and thus was somewhat influential in its opinions. In the early Ming (1388 and later) text by Cao Zhao 曹昭, the *Gegu yaolun* 格古要论, Song stonewares (not defined broadly as such) are described much more favourably than those of the Yuan period, even if they are a continuation of Song production at the same site. One of the earliest surviving editions of this text is in the collection of the Percival David Foundation [henceforth, PDF] library at SOAS. The version published between 1388 and 1397 (the Shu Ming edition) was translated and published in English by Percival David, trans. and ed., *Chinese Connoisseurship: The Ko Ku Yao Lun, the Essential Criteria of Antiquities*, New York/Washington, 1971, where Song ceramics are discussed on pp. 139–143.
87. This practice is normally associated with Qing porcelain, but it started in the Ming period.
88. Hay 2010, p. 10.
89. The introduction to a recently published series of conference papers on the subject of archaism in Chinese culture provides a useful summary of the current thinking on this aspect of Chinese cultural studies. See Wu Hung, ed., *Reinventing the Past: Archaism and Antiquarianism in Chinese Art and Visual Culture,* Chicago, 2010.
90. Tsui Museum of Art, *A Legacy of Chenghua: Imperial Porcelain of the Chenghua Reign Excavated from Zhushan, Jingdezhen*; *Chengyao yizhen: Jingdezhen Zhushan chutu Chenghua guanyao ciqi* 成窑遗珎：景德镇珠山出土成化官窑瓷器, Hong Kong, 1993, pp. 110–111. This is the earliest excavated example of such a practice. The use of such apocryphal reign marks further complicates the interpretation of the function and meaning of reign marks in general.
91. Hay 2010, pp. 157–161.
92. The *Ming shi* is quite specific when certain ancient bronze shapes ordered by the court in porcelain are named, such as the *jue* 爵 and the *dou* 豆. See Lau 1993, p. 86 citing the *Ming shi*, *juan* 47, p. 540.
93. Maggie C. K. Wan, 'Motifs with an Intention: Reading the Eight Trigrams on Official Porcelain of the Jiajing period (1522–1566)', *Artibus Asiae* LXIII, no. 2 (2003), pp. 191–221.
94. Wan 2003, p. 192.
95. Harrison-Hall 2001, p. 239, fig. 9:52.
96. John D. Langlois, Jr., 'The Hung-wu Reign, 1368–1398', in Frederick W. Mote and Denis Twitchett, eds., *The Cambridge History of China*, vol. 7, *The Ming Dynasty, 1368–1644, Part I*, Cambridge, 1988, p. 109.
97. Harrison-Hall 2001, p. 239, fig. 9:52.
98. Stacey Pierson, 'On Location: Situating Chinese Ceramics', *TOCS* 73 (2010), p. 97.
99. Maxwell K. Hearn, *Splendors of Imperial China: Treasures from the National Palace Museum, Taipei*, New York, 1996, pp. 94–95.
100. See note 90.
101. It has been suggested that this piece is a random survivor from the actual Xuande period, but it is very unlikely that such a piece would have survived the succeeding three reign periods after that of Xuande and before Chenghua, only to be dumped in a Chenghua-period sherd heap.
102. James Watt and Denise Patry Leidy, *Defining Yongle: Imperial Art in Early Fifteenth Century China*, New York, 2005, p. 17. The broader history of the interaction between Tibet and China during the Ming period is explored in Weirong Shen, '"Accommodating Barbarians from Afar": Political and Cultural Interactions between Ming China and Tibet', *Ming Studies* 56 (Fall 2007), pp. 37–93.

103. Archaeological evidence from the imperial kilns at Jingdezhen suggests that the references in some Ming texts to the popularity of cricket games at the Xuande court may in fact have been true. See for example Liu Xinyuan, 'Amusing the Emperor: the Discovery of Xuande Period Cricket Jars from the Ming Imperial Kilns', *Orientations* 26, no. 8 (1995), pp. 62–77.
104. Sunchuan Clarence Eng, 'The Use of Ceramic in Chinese Late Imperial Architecture', Ph.D. thesis, SOAS, University of London, 2008, pp. 125–127, 422–423.
105. Peter Lam, ed., *A Legacy of the Ming: Ceramic Finds from the Site of the Ming Palace at Nanjing; Zhu Ming yicui: Nanjing Ming Gugong chutu taoci* 朱明遗萃：南京明故宫出土陶瓷, 香港中文大学文物馆, Hong Kong, 1996.
106. Chang Foundation Museum 鴻禧美術館基金會, *Xuande Imperial Porcelain Excavated at Jingdezhen; Jingdezhen chutu Ming Xuande guanyao ciqi* 景德鎮出土明宣德官窯瓷器, Taipei, 1998, figs. 18–21, p. 122.
107. For example, the jars with the inscription *Neifu gong yong* 内府供用, one of which can be seen in the Percival David Collection, British Museum, PDF 518.
108. Hay 2010, p. 21.
109. Ming Wilson, *Rare Marks on Chinese Ceramics*, London, 1998, p. 22.
110. Wilson 1998, p. 22.
111. Craig Clunas, 'The Other Ming Tombs: Kings and Their Burials in Ming China', *Transactions of the Oriental Ceramic Society* [henceforth, *TOCS*] 70 (2007), pp. 9–10 and *Screen of Kings: Art, Power and Imperial Clan in Ming China*, forthcoming.
112. Harrison-Hall 2001, p. 274; on *meiping* in Ming burials, see also Kong Fanshi 孔繁峙, 'Shi tan Ming mu suizang meiping de shiyong zhidu' 试谈明墓随葬梅瓶的使用制度 (The use of *meiping* jar grave goods in Ming tombs), *Wenwu* 12 (1985), pp. 90–91. The Wanli emperor's tomb, Dingling, is the only one to have been excavated to date.
113. From the tomb of King Zhuang of Liang, 9th son of the Hongxi emperor, d. 1441. See Hubei sheng wenwu kaogu yanjiusuo 湖北省文物考古研究所 et al., 'Hubei Zhongxiang Mingdai Liangzhuangwang mu fajue jianbao' 湖北钟祥明代梁庄王墓发掘简报 (A Brief Report on the Discovery of the Ming-dynasty Tomb of King Zhuang of Liang at Zhongxiang, Hubei), *Wenwu* 5 (2003), pp. 4–23. This piece was recently published in Yang Xiaoneng, 'Ming Art and Culture from an Archaeological Perspective—Part 1: Royal and Elite Tombs', *Orientations* 37, no. 5 (June 2006), fig. 8. The object is in the Hubei Provincial Institute of Cultural Heritage and Archaeology.
114. The tomb of Prince Zhoujing, Henan—see Zhang Bai ed. 2008, vol. 12, no. 235.
115. Zhang Bai ed. 2008, vol. 14, no. 213.
116. Like other tomb goods, the difference in quality and presentation of the ceramics found in elite tombs also reflects social hierarchies and the status of the occupants. The tomb of King Zhuang is one of the most lavishly furnished of all the princely tombs. Yang 2006, p. 45.
117. Zhang Bai ed., 2008, vol. 13, no. 114.
118. A recently published example can be seen in Zhao Yueting 赵月汀, ed., *Huangdi de ciqi: Jingdezhen chutu "Ming san dai" guanyao ciqi zhenpin huicui* 皇帝的瓷器：景德镇出土"明三代"官窑瓷器珍品荟萃 上：永乐卷 (The Emperor's Porcelain: A Collection of Porcelain Treasures from Three Ming Reign-periods Excavated at the Imperial Kilns at Jingdezhen), 2 vols., Shanghai, 2010, vol. 1 (Yongle 永乐), no. 63.
119. Clunas 2007, Harrison-Hall 2001, p. 46.
120. For example, ancestral ceremonies and burial objects as well as ownership of burial land were subjected to often strict rules and requirements in the Ming period, overseen by the Ministry of Rites or *Libu* 礼部. See Charles Hucker, 'Governmental Organization of the Ming Dynasty', *Harvard Journal of Asiatic Studies* 21 (Dec. 1958): 1–66; see pp. 33–35 on the Ministry of Rites.

121. Zhang Bai ed. 2008, vol. 1, no. 167.
122. Zhang Bai ed. 2008, vol. 1, no. 165.
123. Zhang Bai ed. 2008, vol. 1, no. 160.
124. Zhang Bai ed. 2008, vol. 1, no. 151.
125. Zhang Bai ed. 2008, vol. 1, nos. 187, 186.
126. Harrison-Hall 2001, p. 47.
127. See Fung Ping Shan Museum 1992.
128. Zhang Bai ed. 2008, vol. 13, no. 115; Hubei sheng wenwu kaogu yanjiusuo 湖北省文物考古研究所 et al., 'Wuchang Longquanshan Mingdai Chuzhaowang mu fajue jianbao' 武昌龙泉山明代楚昭王墓发掘简报 (A Brief Report on the Discovery of the Ming-dynasty Tomb of King Zhao of Chu at Longquanshan in Wuchang), *Wenwu* 2 (2003), pp. 4–18.
129. Eg. Lau 1993, p. 86.
130. Hsieh Ming-liang 谢明良, 'Some Issues Related to Chinese Ceramics of the Fifteenth Century', *Meishushi yanjiu jikan* 美术史研究集刊7 (July 1999), p. 44.
131. This is the tomb of the young girl identified as being of the Hešeri 赫舍里 clan, which has been widely publicized in Chinese. See for example Beijing wenwu yanjiusuo 北京文物研究所, *Beijing kaogu sishi nian* 北京考古四十年 (Forty Years of Beijing Archaeology), Beijing, 1990, p. 209. For the ceramics from the tomb, see Zhang Bai ed. 2008, vol. 1, nos. 176, 177. The tomb was recently the subject of a short film on CCTV, http://www.cctv.com/program/civilization/20090710/103722.shtml (accessed 4 August 2012).
132. Zhang Bai ed. 2008, vol. 1, no. 176.
133. Zhang Bai ed. 2008, vol. 1, nos. 177, 180.
134. Zhang Bai ed. 2008, vol. 15, no. 219. In this tomb, the Daoist figures indicate the religious nature or character of the burial, a notable feature of both elite and non-elite burials in the Ming dynasty. Harrison-Hall 2001, p. 46.
135. Zhang Bai ed. 2008, vol. 15, no. 220.
136. The figurines were part of a set of tomb sculptures; the tomb is located in Nancheng county, Jiangxi province. They were recently published in English in Yang Xiaoneng 2006, p. 46, fig. 12.
137. Hsieh Ming-liang 1999, p. 40.
138. Zhang Bai ed. 2008, vol. 14, no. 190–191.
139. Shelagh Vainker, *Chinese Pottery and Porcelain*, London, 1991, p. 170. For an extensive history of the subject, see Joshua Chun-chong Yiu, 'The Display of Fragrant Offerings: Altar Sets in China', DPhil thesis, University of Oxford, 2006. Altar sets in general, consisting of either three or five pieces, began to appear in the Northern Song period, probably introduced by Buddhist temples. These can be seen in Song and Yuan woodblock-printed books. Machida International Print Museum, *Exhibition of Ancient Chinese Woodblock Prints: Third Section of an Exhibition of 2000 Years of Chinese Printing*, Tokyo, 1988, as cited in Robert Mowry, ed., *Hare's Fur, Tortoiseshell and Partridge Feathers: Chinese Brown- and Black-Glazed Ceramics, 400–1400*, Cambridge, MA, 1996, p. 264, note 9.
140. Zhang Bai ed. 2008, vol. 7, no. 192.
141. He does not appear in the *Dictionary of Ming Biography*, for example.
142. For two published examples from the Qing period, see Wilson 1998, no. 10 and no. 52.
143. This is also the case in the tombs of non-imperial consorts, such as Lady Tsai whose tomb of 1464 was mentioned above with reference to the pre-Chenghua *doucai* bowl.
144. Zhang Bai ed. 2008, vol. 13, no. 116.
145. Zhang Bai ed. 2008, vol. 13, nos. 117, 118, 122.
146. Hsieh Ming-liang 1999, pp. 41–43.

147. Examples of these were made in celadon stoneware and *qingbai* porcelain up to the end of the Song period.
148. The hoard found at the village Hejiacun is the largest Tang hoard found to date. Examples of gold, silver and objects of other materials recovered from the hoard were recently published in English in Carol Michaelson, *Gilded Dragons: Buried Treasures from China's Golden Ages*, London, 1999; Qi Dongfang, 'The Burial Location and Dating of the Hejia Village Treasures', *Orientations* 34, no. 2 (2003), pp. 20–24; and in James C. Y. Watt, ed., *China: Dawn of a Golden Age, 200–750 AD*, New York, 2004.
149. This hoard contained mainly ceramics from Southeast China, *qingbai* and Longquan wares. See Asahi Shimbun, ed., *Newly Discovered Southern Song Ceramics: A Thirteenth Century 'Time Capsule'; Fūin sareta Nansō tōji ten* 封印された南宋陶磁展, Tokyo, 1998.
150. This site was discovered during roadworks in the area. Some of the many ceramics discovered here were published in English in James C. Y. Watt, ed., *The World of Khubilai Khan: Chinese Art in the Yuan Dynasty*, New York, 2010, and in Chinese in Chen Yongzhi 陈永志, ed., *Nei Menggu Jininglu gucheng yizhi chutu ciqi* 内蒙古集宁路古城遗址出土瓷器 (Porcelain Unearthed from Jininglu Ancient City Site in Inner Mongolia), Beijing, 2004.
151. Eg. Zhang Bai ed. 2008, vol. 12, nos. 239, 238, 237, 236.
152. Zhang Bai ed. 2008, vol. 13, no. 123.
153. The main inscription is dated 1555. The text is a communication with the spirit world and includes biographical details of the deceased, an epitaph, a eulogy and a record of re-internment. The name of the deceased was Pan Zhaosheng, literary name Xianwen. He died in AD 1545 and was re-interred in 1555. His sons commissioned the epitaph tablet from Jingdezhen to record this event. PDF B633, in the British Museum. On Ming ceramic epitaph tablets, see Harrison-Hall 2001, p. 43.
154. For example, the piece in the British Museum collection, 1975.1028.23, a blue and white jar with an inscription dated 1549 which declares a wish for a son as the reason for a temple donation.
155. Both of these are in the Percival David Collection, on display in the British Museum: PDF 237 and PDF B613, B614.
156. See note 139.
157. PDF 680. The inscription visible in fig. 1.13 has been translated as: The faithful disciple Chen Biao, of the Chen family in Liren village in the Fouxian district of Raozhou prefecture in the province of Jiangxi, rejoices to send a set of three vessels, an incense burner and [two] vases, as an offering to the Guanwang Temple of Shuntian Prefecture in Beijing, in prayer for the support and protection of the whole family, that they may have peace and prosperity, and that their business affairs may flourish. Made on an auspicious day [the twentieth] in the fifth month [which corresponds to June] of the ninth year of the Hongzhi period [AD 1496] by the disciple Chen Cun'er.
158. Anthony du Boulay, 'Oriental Ceramics in National Trust Houses and Their Importance in Producing Documentary Evidence', *Oriental Art* XLVII, no. 2 (2001), pp. 21–24.
159. British Museum collection, OA F326+, published in Harrison-Hall 2001, p. 312, fig. 11:99. The painting is in the National Palace Museum, Taipei.
160. PDF A815. Published in Wilson 1998, no. 40.
161. Wilson 1998, p. 100.
162. Clunas 1986–88, p. 48; Clunas 1991/2004, p. 132, Goodrich and Fang 1976, p. 828.
163. See Hay 2010, pp. 344–349.
164. On Ji Cheng and the significance of his text, see Klass Ruitenbeek, *Carpentry and Building in Late Imperial China: A Study of the Fifteenth-Century Carpenter's Manual, Lu Ban Jing*, Brill, 1996, pp. 30–31; Vera Schwarcz, *Place and Memory in the Singing Crane Garden*, Philadelphia, 2008, pp. 23–24; and Jack Goody, *The Culture of Flowers*, Cambridge, 1993, p. 352. The original text has been

translated into English by Alison Hardie: Ji Cheng, *The Craft of Gardens*, trans. Alison Hardie, New Haven, 1989. The term 'systematic' is taken from *xitong de* 系统的, as translated by Craig Clunas, *Fruitful Sites: Garden Culture in Ming Dynasty China*, London, 1996, p. 138. However, this text concentrates on rocks and pavilions (see Clunas 1996, pp. 174–176 for discussion); there is more about flowers specifically in other late Ming texts with a wider subject matter, such as the *Treatise on Superfluous Things* (*Zhangwu zhi jiaozhu* 长物志校注, Nanjing, 1984, p. 41), by Wen Zhenheng 文震亨 (1585–1645). See Clunas 1996, p. 167 and Clunas 1991/2004 for a book-length study of this work.

165. Hay 2010, p. 344.
166. Clunas 1991/2004.
167. Discussed in Patricia Sieber, 'Seeing the World through *Xianqing ouji* (1671): Performance, Visuality and Narratives of Modernity', *Modern Chinese Literature and Culture* 12, no. 2 (2000), pp. 1–43; and briefly in Hay 2010.
168. H. L. Li, trans., *Chinese Flower Arrangement*, Philadelphia, 1956, p. 101–103. Note that the most valuable ceramics are Song stonewares.
169. Clunas 1986–88, p. 49; Clunas 1991/2004, pp. 82–89; and Frank Trentmann, ed., *The Oxford Handbook of the History of Consumption*, Oxford, 2012, p. 58.
170. Duncan Campbell, 'Yuan Hongdao's "A History of the Vase"', *New Zealand Journal of Asian Studies* 5, no. 2 (Dec. 2003), pp. 77–93. Edition cited: Qian Bocheng 钱伯城, ed., *Yuan Hongdao ji jianjiao* 袁宏道集笺校 [The Complete Works of Yuan Hongdao: Annotated and Collated], 3 vols. (Shanghai: Guji chubanshe, 1981), vol. 2.
171. Campbell 2003, p. 78.
172. Campbell 2003, p. 84.
173. See David, trans. and ed. 1971, pp. 139–143.
174. Clunas 1986–88, p. 49, citing Wen Zhenheng, *Zhangwu zhi jiaozhu*, Nanjing 1984, pp. 317–318.
175. Clunas 1986–88, p. 51; Shen Defu, vol. 2, p. 613.
176. Clunas 1986–88, p. 51; Shen Defu, vol. 2, p. 613.
177. See, for example Clunas 1991/2004.
178. Clunas 1986–88, p. 50.
179. Clunas 1986–88, p. 51, citing Jiang Shaoshu 姜绍书 (fl. c.1640–80), *Yunshizhai bitan* 韵石斋笔谈 [Jottings from the Yunshi Studio] (Shanghai, 1935–37), *juan* 1, p. 8.
180. Brook 1998, p. 760, citing *Dijing jingwu lüe* 帝京景物略 [Sights of the Imperial Capital] (1635; reprinted, Beijing: Beijing chubanshe, 1980).
181. Brook 1998, pp. 225–226.
182. Laing 1975, p. 224—her trans., citing Jiang Shaoshu, *Yunshizhai bitan*, chap. 1, *Meishu congshu*, vol. II/10, pp. 185–186.

Chapter 2 Ming Porcelain in the World (16th–17th centuries)

1. Brook 2010, pp. 219–220.
2. Berg 2003.
3. Stacey Pierson, *Collectors, Collections and Museums: The Field of Chinese Ceramics in Britain, 1560–1960*, Oxford, 2007.
4. Kerr ed. 2004, pp. 716–717, citing Yu Changsen, *Yuandai haiwai maoyi* 元代海外贸易 (Overseas Trade in the Yuan Dynasty) (Xi'an: Xibei daxue chubanshe, 1994), pp. 90–98, 106–116.
5. Brook 2010, p. 219; Francois Gipouloux, *The Asian Mediterranean: Port Cities and Trading Networks in China, Japan and Southeast Asia, 13th to 21st Century*, Cheltenham, UK/Northampton, MA, 2011, pp. 84–86.

6. Brook 2010, p. 219.
7. Kerr ed. 2004, p. 717, quoting the *Ming shi*, comp. Zhang Tingyu 张廷玉 et al., 6 vols. (1739; reprinted, Taipei: Guofang yanjiuyuan, 1962), chap. 324, pp. 3, 13, 16.
8. Kerr ed. 2004, p. 717.
9. Brook 2010, p. 222.
10. Kerr ed. 2004, p. 717.
11. Roxanna Brown, *Ming Gap and Shipwreck Ceramics in Southeast Asia: Towards a Chronology of Thai Trade Ware*, Bangkok, 2009. For a general history of Vietnamese ceramics, see John Stevenson and John Guy, *Vietnamese Ceramics: A Separate Tradition*, Chicago, 1997; John A. Stevenson and Donald Wood, *Dragons and Lotus Blossoms: Vietnamese Ceramics from the Birmingham Museum of Art*, Seattle, 2011.
12. William S. Atwell, 'Time, Money and the Weather: Ming China and the "Great Depression" of the Mid-Fifteenth Century', *Journal of Asian Studies* 61, no. 1 (Feb. 2002), p. 88.
13. Shelagh Vainker, *Chinese Silk: A Cultural History*, London, 2004, p. 169; Gang Deng, *Maritime Sector, Institutions and Sea Power of Premodern China*, Westport/London, 1999.
14. Andrew Watsky, 'Locating "China" in the Arts of Sixteenth-Century Japan', *Art History* 29, no. 4 (Dec. 2006), pp. 600–624. Han mirrors have been excavated in Japan. See for example, Walter Edwards, 'Mirrors on Ancient Yamato: The Kurozuka Kofun Discovery and the Question of Yamatai', *Monumenta Nipponica*, 54, no. 1 (Spring 1999), pp. 75–110. For a survey of Chinese ceramics found in Japan, see *Nihon shutsudo no Chûgoku tôji* 日本出土の中国陶磁 (Chinese Ceramics Excavated in Japan), catalogue of an exhibition held at Tokyo National Museum, Tokyo, 1975, and Hasebe Gakuji 長谷部楽爾 and Imai Atsushi 今井敦, *Nihon shutsudo no Chûgoku tôji* 日本出土の中国陶磁 (Chinese Ceramics Excavated in Japan), vol. 12 of *Chûgoku tôji* 中国の陶磁 (Chinese Ceramics), Tokyo, 1997.
15. Watsky 2006, p. 616.
16. Watsky 2006, p. 616.
17. Nicole Coolidge Rousmaniere, 'Dining on China in Japan: Shifting Taste for Chinese Ceramics in 15th-to 17th-century Japan', in Stacey Pierson, ed., *Transfer: The Influence of China on World Ceramics*, Colloquies on Art and Archaeology in Asia, no. 24, London, 2009, p. 52.
18. Richard Wilson, 'Notes on Chinese Ceramics Excavated in Japan', in Judith G. Smith, ed., *Tradition and Transformation: Studies in Chinese Art in Honor of Chu-tsing Li*, Seattle/Kansas, 2005, p. 482.
19. Rousmaniere 2009, p. 52.
20. Rousmaniere 2009, p. 53.
21. R. Wilson 2005, p. 481; Hasebe and Imai 1997, no. 69.
22. R. Wilson 2005, pp. 483, 485; Hasebe and Imai 1997, no. 89; Barbara Seycock, 'Trade Ceramics from Selected Sites in Western Japan', *Indo-Pacific Prehistory Association Bulletin* 26 (2006), pp. 131–139.
23. Gipouloux 2011, chap. 6.
24. Rousmaniere 2009, p. 49; Tsuji Nobuo in Nicole Coolidge Rousmaniere, ed., *Kazari: Decoration and Display in Japan, 15th–19th Centuries*, London/New York, 2002.
25. Rousmaniere 2009 notes that specific decorative rules were imposed and sumptuary laws were issued with increasing regularity in the early 17th century, p. 27.
26. Morgan Pitelka, *Handmade Culture: Raku Potters, Patrons and Tea Practitioners in Japan*, Honolulu, 2005, p. 40.
27. Rousmaniere 2009, p. 51.
28. Rousmaniere 2009, p. 51.
29. Oliver Impey, 'Chinese Porcelain Exported to Japan', *Oriental Art* XLV, no. 1 (Spring 1999), p. 18.
30. R. Wilson 2005, p. 487.
31. Hasebe and Imai 1997, nos. 83, 84.

32. Song tea bowls were brought to Japan by Buddhist monks, and these are said to have inspired the production of Raku ware locally. Pitelka (2005) argues that this narrative is, however, overly simplistic, p. 3. Specially commissioned *qingbai* porcelain sutra covers, a form not in use in China, were also made for temples in Japan. Impey 1999, p. 16; Hasebe and Imai 1997, no. 24. Evidence from tags found in the Sinan shipwreck suggest that the shipment was bound for a Japanese temple, the Tōfuku-ji; see Munhwa Kongbu Munhwajae Kwalliguk 文化公報部文化財管理局, ed., *Sinan Haejŏ Yumul* 新安海底遺物 (Objects from the Sinan Shipwreck), Seoul, 1985.
33. Kerr and Mengoni 2011, p. 130; Julia Curtis, *Trade Taste and Transformation: Jingdezhen Porcelain for Japan, 1620–1645*, New York, 2006.
34. Curtis 2006, fig. 9, pp. 41–42. Acc. No. B69P98L.
35. Seizo Hayashiya, 'Chinese Ceramics in Japanese Collections', in Seizo Hayashiya and Henry Trubner, *Chinese Ceramics from Japanese Collections, T'ang through Ming Dynasties*, New York, 1977, p. 18.
36. Seizo Hayashiya states that in the 1630s, over 50,000 pieces were brought to Japan by a single merchant in Sakai; see Hayashiya and Trubner 1977, p. 18.
37. Olah Csaba, 'Troubles during Trading between Japan and China in the Ming Period', in Angela Schottenhammer, ed., *The East Asia Mediterranean: Maritime Crossroads of Culture, Commerce and Human Migration*, Weisbaden, 2008, pp. 317–318.
38. Kenneth R. Robinson, 'From Raiders to Traders: Border Security and Border Control in Early Choson, 1392–1450', *Korean Studies* 16 (1992), p. 96; Philip de Heer, 'Three Embassies to Seoul: Sino-Korean Relations in the Fifteenth Century', in Leonard Blussé et al., eds., *Conflict and Accommodation in Early Modern East Asia*, Leiden/New York, 1993, pp. 240–258.
39. Heekyung Lee, 'The Introduction of Blue-and-White Wares from Ming China to Choson Korea', *Oriental Art* 45, no. 2 (1999), p. 26 and 'Institutions and Vessels in East Asia: Exploring a New Approach for the Study of Medieval and Early Modern Wares, Applied to the Origin of Early Ming Imperial Underglaze Blue Ceramics and Their Introduction into Korea', Ph.D. dissertation, SOAS, University of London, 2003.
40. H. Lee 1999, p. 31, referencing the *Choson Wangjo Sillok* 朝鮮王朝實錄 (Annals of the Choson Dynasty), *Yijo Sillok* 李朝實錄, vol. 7: *Sejong Sillok* 世宗實錄, *kwon* 41, p. 605; *Yijo Sillok*, vol. 8: *Sejong Sillok*, *kwon* 49, pp. 35–36; Jay Levenson, ed., *Circa 1492: Art in the Age of Exploration*, New Haven, 1991, p. 426 where it is also stated that these included vessels with dragon and cloud designs.
41. Yong-i Yun and Regina Krahl, *Korean Art from the Gompertz and Other Collections in the Fitzwilliam Museum: A Complete* Catalogue, Cambridge, 2006, p. 7.
42. Yun and Krahl 2006, p. 7.
43. Yun and Krahl 2006, p. 7.
44. Donald N. Clark, 'Sino-Korean Tributary Relations Under the Ming', in Denis Twitchett and Frederick W. Mote, *The Cambridge History of China*, vol. 8, *The Ming Dynasty, Part 2*, Cambridge, 1998, pp. 279–281.
45. Kerr ed. 2004, pp. 537, 719.
46. Kerr ed. 2004, pp. 719–720.
47. Chinese blue and white porcelain was first exported to the Near East in the 9th century. John Carswell, *Blue and White: Chinese Porcelain Around the World*, Art Media Resources, 2000; Finlay 2010, chap. 5.
48. Ayse Erdočdu, 'Chinese Porcelains', *Arts of Asia* 31, no. 6 (Nov.–Dec. 2001), pp. 88–89: Regina Krahl, with J. Ayers and N. Erbahar, *Chinese Ceramics in the Topkapi Saray Museum, Istanbul*, 3 vols., London, 1986; Takatoshi Misugi, *Chinese Porcelain Collections in the Near East: Topkapi and Ardebil*, Hong Kong University Press, 1981 (English edition).
49. In the Ottoman Topkapi Saray collection is an album painted in Tabriz (Iran) c. 1470–80 which demonstrates that Chinese porcelain, of either Yuan or early Ming date, was considered a valuable category of object as it is depicted being transported on carts during what has been interpreted as a wedding

procession; see Levenson ed. 1991, p. 206, no. 100. These blue and white wares may have been part of the bride's dowry and thus were considered important objects with an exchange value as established by the local nuptial system. There are also miniature paintings which depict blue and white wares on display in niches in palace locations, as well as literary references from the early Safavid period which suggest that porcelains were displayed in palace buildings specifically dedicated to the material, such as the *chinikhaneh* or 'China house'. The *chinikhaneh* or 'China house' in its best known form from the 17th century, was a type of architectural space which consisted of multiple shelves and niches installed on walls in which were placed ceramics for display, thus making the ceramics part of the architecture of the room. For a recent discussion, see Kishwar Rizvi, 'Sites of Pilgrimage and Objects of Devotion', in Sheila Canby, ed., *Shah 'Abbas: The Remaking of Iran*, London, 2009, p. 104.

50. J. A. Pope, *Chinese Porcelains from the Ardebil Shrine*, Washington, D.C., 1956; Misugi 1981; and more recently, Canby 2009.
51. Rizvi 2009, p. 102.
52. See L. Golombek and D. Wilber, *The Timurid Architecture of Iran and Turan*, Princeton, 1988, p. 177.
53. Rizvi 2009, p. 103. Interestingly, the niches are shaped for vertical forms such as bottles or jars but almost none of these survive. This was noted by Regina Krahl, 'Chinese Ceramics in Early Safavid Iran', in Sheila Canby and Jon Thompson, eds., *Hunt for Paradise: Court Arts of Safavid Iran, 1501–76*, Milan, 2003, p. 258, but has not been discussed elsewhere. It is surprising if one considers that most of the surviving ceramics from the Ardebil Shrine are large dishes.
54. Rizvi 2009, p. 121.
55. Kishwar Rizvi, 'The Imperial Setting: Shah 'Abbas I at the shrine of Shaykh Safi al-din Ishaq', in Sheila Canby, ed., *Safavid Art and Architecture*, London, 2002, p. 14.
56. A *waqf* was a form of a charitable donation with a long history in the Islamic world. Shrines all over Iran received valuable gifts which would bestow spiritual benefit on the person buried there, but farms, etc. were also given as *waqf* to help support the institutions. 'Abbas's gift was also to demonstrate the dynastic and purely Iranian nature of his Islamic belief—sufi rather than sunni, as with the other more orthodox shrines; the gifts were part of this as representations of earlier historical periods presented in an up-to-date space. Canby 2009, p. 14.
57. Rizvi 2009, p. 104.
58. Canby 2009, p. 22.
59. A thorough attempt to trace their history and provenance has been made by Pedro Carvalho, 'Porcelains for the Shah: Ardabil and the Chinese Ceramics Trade in the Persian Gulf', *TOCS* 66, pp. 47–56, following on from Pope 1956.
60. Which has recently been added along with its main site to the UNESCO World Heritage List.
61. For a complete list of the remaining ceramics see Pope 1956.
62. These have been the subject of a book-length study: Yolande Crowe, *Persia and China: Safavid Blue and White Ceramics in the Victoria and Albert Museum, 1501–1738*, London, 2002, and several are published in Canby 2009. Some have white decoration on a blue ground, which is a style known from 14th-century China, while others have more conventional blue decoration on a white ground, classic 'blue and white', often with Chinese design elements such as waves or dragons.
63. See Lisa Golombek, Robert B. Mason and Gauvin A. Bailey, *Tamerlane's Tableware: A New Approach to the Chinoiserie Ceramics of Fifteenth- and Sixteenth-Century Iran*, Islamic Art and Architecture, no. 6, Costa Mesa/Toronto, 1996 for a comprehensive discussion and typology of these.
64. This discussion is based on work previously published in Pierson 2010 and Pierson 2012.
65. For a summary of these approaches, see C. Gosden and Y. Marshall, 'The Cultural Biography of Objects', *World Archaeology* 31, no. 2 (Oct. 1999), pp. 169–178.
66. Peter Burke, *Cultural Hybridity*, Cambridge, 2009.

67. This is the implication in studies of 'Chinese influence' on foreign ceramics. See for example, Carswell 1985/2000, Finlay 2010, and general texts like Twitchett and Mote 1998.
68. Qarachaghay was governor of Ardebil from 1617 to 1619 and a number of Chinese porcelains with his inscription are in the Ardebil Shrine collection. It has been suggested that he gave the porcelains to the Shrine directly, to complement the gift from the Shah. Canby 2009, p. 142. They are further discussed in Pierson 2012.
69. Gadi Algazi, Valentin Groebner, and Bernhard Jussen, *Negotiating the Gift: Pre-Modern Figurations of Exchange*, Gottingen, 2003, pp. 9, 10, 13.
70. Anna Jackson and Amin Jaffer, eds., *Encounters: The Meeting of Asia and Europe, 1500–1800*, London, 2004, p. 66, no. 5.16
71. Ibn Battuta, *The Travels of Ibn Battuta, A.D. 1325–1354*, trans. H. A. R. Gibb, 3 vols, Cambridge, 1958–71; Ellen Smart, 'Fourteenth Century Chinese Porcelain from a Tughlaq Palace in Delhi', *TOCS* 41 (1975–77), pp. 199–230.
72. Jackson and Jaffer 2004, p. 63.
73. Jackson and Jaffer 2004, p. 63 and the *Baburnama* (Memoirs of Babur, 1453–1530). An edition in English, *Baburnama: Memoirs of Babur, Prince and Emperor*, was published by the Modern Library in 2002, where a *chinikhaneh* is mentioned on p. 59 and vessels of porcelain on pages 292 and 373.
74. Jackson and Jaffer 2004, p. 64, no. 5.15.
75. Evelyn Welch, 'Public Magnificence and Private Display: Giovanni Pontano's *De splendore* (1498) and the Domestic Arts', *Journal of Design History* 15, no. 4 (2002), pp. 211–221.
76. Jackson and Jaffer 2004, p. 67, no. 5.18.
77. Misugi 1981, p. 23, vol. 2.
78. Misugi 1981, p. 23, vol. 2; David J. Roxburgh, ed., *Turks: A Journey of a Thousand Years, 600–1600*, London, 2005, p. 447.
79. See Joyce Hedda Matthews, 'Toward an *Isolario* of the Ottoman Inheritance Inventory with Special Reference to Manisa (ca. 1600–1700)', in Donald Quataert, ed., *Consumption Studies and the History of the Ottoman Empire, 1550–1922: An Introduction*, Albany, NY, 2000, p. 58.
80. Erdočdu 2001, pp. 88–89.
81. Erdočdu 2001, pp. 88–89.
82. Roxburgh ed. 2005, p. 465.
83. Lynda Carroll, 'Could've Been a Contender: The Making and Breaking of "China" in the Ottoman Empire', *International Journal of Historical Archaeology* 3, no. 3 (Sept. 1999), p. 177.
84. Erdočdu 2001, p. 88.
85. TKS 15/4386, 15/2663.
86. See David M. Robinson, 'The Ming Court and the Legacy of the Yuan Mongols', in David M. Robinson, ed., *Culture, Courtiers and Competition: The Ming Court (1368–1644)*, Cambridge, MA, 2008, pp. 401–410.
87. Erdočdu 2001, p. 89.
88. Roxburgh ed. 2005, p. 466.
89. TKS 15/2944.
90. Roxburgh ed. 2005, p. 465.
91. Roxburgh ed. 2005, p. 465.
92. E.g. TKS 15/2761. Roxburgh ed. 2005, no. 350.
93. There are examples of Isnik wares with foreign metal mounts in European collections, however.
94. Jay Levenson, ed., *Encompassing the Globe: Portugal and the World in the 16th and 17th Centuries*, Washington, D.C., 2007, p. 110. On artificialia: 'The *Kunstkammer* included not only natural objects that revealed God's ingenuity but also human handiwork that showed the artist's ability to compete

with the divine by combining imagination with technical skill. In addition to ethnographic works from distant cultures, this category extended to marvellous artworks wherever they may have originated, including beautifully constructed scientific instruments utilized to understand and master the phenomena of the world.' p. 128.

95. TKS 15/2771.
96. Roxburgh ed. 2005, p. 464; TKS 15/1853.
97. As confirmed by an inscription on a bowl in the Museo degli Argenti, Palazzo Pitti, Florence. Rosamund E. Mack, *Bazaar to Piazza: Islamic Trade and Italian Art, 1300–1600*, Berkeley, 2002, p. 206, note 57.
98. Erik Ringmar, 'Audience for a Giraffe: European Expansionism and the Quest for the Exotic', *Journal of World History* 17, no. 4 (Dec. 2006), p. 381.
99. Ringmar 2006, p. 382.
100. Suzanne B. Butters, 'The Uses and Abuses of Gifts in the World of Ferdinando de' Medici (1549–1609)', *I Tatti Studies: Essays in the Renaissance* 11 (2007), pp. 243–354.
101. David Whitehouse, 'Chinese Porcelain in Medieval Europe', *Medieval Archaeology* 16 (1972), p. 75, citing an 18th century source cited by Arthur Lane, *Italian Porcelain* (London: Faber and Faber, 1954). According to Stefano Carboni, 'the earliest evidence of Chinese porcelain belonging to Venetians is found in the estate inventory of Jacobello del Fiore, who died in Venice in 1439, which lists … a bowl of porcelain.' *Venice and the Islamic World, 828–1797*, New Haven, 2007, p. 265.
102. Karl-Heinz Spiess, 'Asian Objects and Western European Court Culture' in Michael North, ed., *Artistic and Cultural Exchanges Between Europe and Asia, 1400–1900*, Farnham/Burlington, 2010, p. 26.
103. Iside Carbone, 'The Enchantment of Chinese Porcelain in Italy: Artistic Fruition, Technological Creativity and Intercultural Discourse', in Stacey Pierson, ed., *Transfer: The Influence of China on World Ceramics*, Colloquies on Art and Archaeology in Asia, no. 24, London, 2009, p. 81.
104. Eva Strober, 'The Earliest Documented Ming Porcelain in Europe: A Gift of Chinese Porcelain from Ferdinando De' Medici (1549–1609) to the Dresden Court', first published in the handbook for the International Ceramic Fair and Symposium, London, 2004, p. 27; www.haughton.com/articles/archive/2005/9, subsequently published in Gugong bowuyuan, ed., 2007 *nian guoji Zisha yantaohui lunwenji* 2007 年国际紫砂研讨会论文集 (Proceedings of the 2007 International Symposium on Zisha Wares), Beijing, 2009; Spiess 2010, p. 26.
105. Mack 2002, p. 110.
106. Ibid.
107. Mack 2002, p. 110; Kerr ed. 2004, pp. 747–748.
108. Kerr ed. 2004, pp. 748–749. This flask is now in the Musée National de Céramique, Sévres, France.
109. Strober 2004, p. 27.
110. Strober 2004, p. 28; Maureen Cassidy-Geiger, *Fragile Diplomacy: Meissen Porcelain for the European Court, ca. 1710–63*, New Haven, 2007, p. 5.
111. Strober 2004, p. 5.
112. Butters 2007, p. 278, described here as a shrimp. Dresden inv. No. P.O. 3479.
113. Strober 2004, p. 31.
114. From G. Pontano, *I libri delle virtu sociali* (Rome: Bulzoni, 1999) (*De splendore* 1498), cited in Welch 2002, p. 2.
115. Strober 2004, fig. 8 and Cassidy-Geiger 2007, p. 5. For a similar example in the Topkapi collection, see Krahl with Ayers and Erbahar, 1986, vol. II, no. 1881–91, pp. 676–678.
116. James Boyajian, *Portuguese Trade in Asia Under the Habsburgs, 1580–1640*, Baltimore, 2007.
117. They were used as tablewares, items for display, diplomatic gifts and collectibles. There are few literary references to such uses but there is an interesting comparison of the shell of the very rare 'turban snail' (a truly exotic, luxury object) to the lustre of Chinese porcelain, which dates from the 16th or

17th century. See Antje Scherner and Dirk Syndham, eds., *Princely Splendour: The Dresden Court, 1580–1620*, Milan, 2005, p. 83.

118. Whitehouse 1972, p. 71; Jackson and Jaffer 2004, p. 47, fig. 4.3. The bowl is also recorded in a 15th-century inventory.
119. See Oriental Ceramic Society, *Chinese Export Art in Schloss Ambras: A Lecture Given by Sir Harry Garner on the Occasion of the Second Presentation of the Hills Gold Medal*; 5 June 1975; London, 1975.
120. See note 94.
121. See V&A catalogue information reference for M.16–1970; published in Jackson and Jaffer 2004, p. 47, fig. 4.4. The pair to this piece was sold in 1970 by Sotheby's.
122. Stacey Pierson, *The Percival David Foundation of Chinese Art: A Guide to the Collection,* London, 2002, p. 71.
123. Gillian Wilson, *Mounted Oriental Porcelain in the J. Paul Getty Museum*, Los Angeles, 2000, p. 12; Mimi Hellman, 'The Nature of Artifice: French Porcelain Flowers and the Rhetoric of the Garnish', in Alden Cavanaugh and Michael E. Yonan, eds., *The Cultural Aesthetics of Eighteenth-Century Porcelain*, Farnham, 2010, pp. 40–41; Kerr and Mengoni 2011, p. 87.
124. See catalogue information for c.222–1931 and Maria Antonia Pinto de Matos, 'The Portuguese Trade', *Oriental Art* XLV, no. 1 (1999), p. 25.
125. Reino Liefkes and Hilary Young, *Masterpieces of World Ceramics*, London, 2009, pp. 68–69.
126. Pinto de Matos 1999, p. 25.
127. Appadurai ed. 1986.
128. Clifford ed. 1988.
129. Metropolitan Museum of Art, acc. no. 61.196.
130. The problem of the art historical category 'Islamic' is discussed in Sheila S. Blair and Jonathan M. Bloom, 'The Mirage of Islamic Art: Reflections on the Study of an Unwieldy Field', *Art Bulletin* 85, no. 1 (March 2003), pp. 152–184.
131. Some of this tableware arrived in Europe from the Near East, as the finds (primarily cups for coffee drinking) from Buda and Eger castles in Hungary demonstrate. A probate inventory of 1587 records examples of Chinese porcelain used in Hungary by the sultan's court and archaeological finds confirm use by private individuals. Ibolya Gerelyes, 'Types of Oriental Pottery in Archaeological Finds From the 16th and 17th Centuries in Hungary', *Acta Orientalia Academiae Scientiarum Hung.* 61, no. 1–2 (2008), pp. 66, 70. Gerelyes notes that these Chinese porcelains 'arrived on Hungarian soil as part of the material culture of the Turks.'
132. Most of the literature concerned with Chinese 'armorial porcelain' focuses on the Qing period examples that were part of a widespread consumer pattern in the 18th century.
133. Levenson ed. 2007, figs. C20, C15.
134. Walters Museum website: http://art.thewalters.org/viewwoa.aspx?id=411, object no. 9.1616 (accessed 4 August 2012).
135. Jorge Alvares (d. 1521) was the first Portuguese to visit China, in 1513. See Pinto de Matos 2002, p. 37; A. J. R. Russell-Wood, *The Portuguese Empire, 1415–1808: A World on the Move*, Baltimore, 1998, p. 3; Levenson ed. 2007, p. 277.
136. As translated and illustrated in Gerald Davison, *The New and Revised Handbook of Marks on Chinese Ceramics*, Somerset, 2010, p. 143, no. 1895.
137. Levenson ed. 2007, C15.
138. For its use by Michelangelo, see for example: Charles Burroughs, 'Michelangelo at the Campidoglio: Artistic Identity, Patronage and Manufacture', *Artibus et Historiae* 14, no. 28 (1993), pp. 85–111.
139. BM 1925.0512.1. Published in Harrison-Hall 2001, p. 313, fig. 11:103. *Kraak* is a style of blue and white porcelain that was developed in the 16th century and was made primarily at Jingdezhen. Its

design is characterized by radiating panels of decoration around the sides of vessels, primarily bowls and dishes. The name it is known by now was given to it in the mid-17th century, and of course it was not known as such in China. As this type of porcelain is blue and white and highly decorated, the usual assumption is that it was primarily made for export. Most of the extant examples have indeed come from overseas locations, whether shipwrecks or collections, but that is not to say that it was not consumed in China. Several examples have been found in Chinese tombs, including some in the later Ming imperial tombs. See Jiangxi Province Team of Cultural Heritage, 'Jiangxi Nancheng Ming Yi Xuanwang Zhu Yiyin fufu hezangmu' 江西南城明益宣王朱翊鈏夫妇合葬墓 (The Joint Tomb of Zhu Yiyin, the Ming Prince Xuan of Yi, and his Wives at Nancheng, Jiangxi), *Wenwu* 8 (1982): 16–32; Yao Chengqing 姚澄清, Sun Jingmin 孙敬民 and Yao Lianhong 姚连红, 'Shitan Guangchang jinian mu chutude qinghua cipan' 试谈广昌纪年墓出土的青花瓷盘 (A Brief Discussion on the Blue and White Porcelain Plates Unearthed From Datable Tombs in Guangchang), *Jiangxi wenwu* 2 (1990): 92–95, 134. These finds and others have been discussed by Li Baoping in '*Kraak* Porcelain from Chinese Tombs and Jingdezhen Kilns: Discoveries and Associated Issues', a paper prepared for the conference 'Cultures of Ceramics in Global History: 1300–1800', held at the University of Warwick, 22 April 2010. Like other blue and white wares, *kraak* was made in a range of qualities; what distinguishes it as a group or collective style type is simply the placement of the decoration in radiating panels around the sides.

140. Harrison-Hall 2001, p. 313.
141. BM 1957.1216.19. Harrison-Hall 2001, p. 300, fig. 11:63.
142. The Willem Claesz Heda (1594–c.1681) painting is in the Hamburger Kunsthalle. Information from Jessica Harrison-Hall, posted on the British Museum web page for this object: http://www.britishmuseum.org/research/search_the_collection_database/search_object_details.aspx?objectid=255538&partid=1&searchText=hydra+latin&fromADBC=ad&toADBC=ad&numpages=10&orig=/research/search_the_collection_database.aspx&currentPage=2 (accessed 4 August 2012).
143. V&A 2904–1876.
144. Julie Emerson, Jennifer Chen and Mimi Gardner Gates, *Porcelain Stories: From China to Europe*, Seattle, 2000, p. 252; Levenson ed. 2007, C17, 18; Maria Antonia Pinto de Matos, 'Chinese Porcelain in Portuguese Written Sources', *Oriental Art* XLVIII, no. 3 (2002), p. 39.
145. Pinto de Matos 2002, pp. 36–37.
146. Pinto de Matos 2002, p. 37.
147. Pinto de Matos 2002, p. 37.
148. Emerson, Chen and Gates 2000, p. 252; Levenson ed. 2007, C17, 18.
149. Gipouloux 2011, pp. 123–125; Donna Pierce and Ronald Otsuka, eds., *Asia and Spanish America: Trans-Pacific Artistic and Cultural Exchange, 1500–1850; Papers from the 2006 Mayer Center Symposium at the Denver Art Museum*, Denver, 2009.
150. Emerson, Chen and Gates 2000, p. 135.
151. Maura Rinaldi, *Kraak Porcelain: A Moment in the History of Trade*, London, 1989, pp. 63–64; Daisy Lion-Goldschmidt, 'Ming Porcelains in the Santos Palace Collection, Lisbon', *TOCS* 49 (1986), pp. 79–93.
152. S. A. M. Adshead, *Material Culture in Europe and China, 1400–1800*, Basingstoke, 1997, p. 130; Linda Shulsky, 'Chinese Porcelain in Spanish Colonial Sites in the Southern Part of North America and the Caribbean', *TOCS* 63 (1998–99), p. 86; Linda Shulsky, 'Phillip II of Spain as Porcelain Collector', *Oriental Art* XLIV, no. 2 (1998), pp. 51–54.
153. Jaume Coll Conesa, 'Documented Influence of China on Maiolica in Spain and New Finds of Chinese Ceramics with Dates to the 16th Century', in Stacey Pierson ed., *Transfer: The Influence of China on World Ceramics*, Colloquies on Art and Archaeology in Asia, no. 24, London, 2009, p. 123.
154. Conesa 2009, p. 134, quoting J. P. Desroches, 'Las porcelanas', in *El San Diego, un tesoro bajo el Mar*, Madrid, 1995, pp. 310–369.

155. Pinto de Matos 1999, pp. 28–29; along with a charger in the Peabody Essex Museum (PEM-AE 85571) and at least 11 other pieces identified in Sargent 2012, p. 66.
156. George Kuwayama, *Chinese Ceramics in Colonial Mexico*, Los Angeles, 1997, p. 28, no. 1. However, one scholar believes that, because of the buildings represented in part of the design, this piece and the 4 others like it which are known may have a history associated with Mexico (Sargent 2012, p. 49); Macao has also been suggested (Lion-Goldschmidt 1978, p. 154).
157. Maria Antonia Pinto de Matos, ed., *Chinese Export Porcelain: From the Museum of Anastacio Goncalves, Lisbon*, London, 1996, p. 138, no. 63.
158. The traditional date for the founding of the Society of Jesus (Jesuits) is 1540.
159. Pinto de Matos ed. 1996, p. 138.
160. Harrison-Hall 2001, p. 379, fig. 12:73.
161. Dana Leibsohn and Carolyn Dean, 'Hybridity and its Discontents: Considering Visual Culture in Colonial Spanish America', *Colonial Latin American Review* 12, no. 1 (June 2003), p. 6.
162. The term was coined by the Cuban anthropologist Fernando Ortiz in 1940 and refers to the creation of new cultures through encounters with others. An example related to objects in Africa is discussed in Nicholas Mirzoeff, 'Transculture: from Kongo to Congo', in *An Introduction to Visual Culture*, London, 1999, chap. 4.
163. Dennis O. Flynn and Arturo Giraldez, 'Born with a Silver Spoon: The Origins of World Trade in 1571', *Journal of World History* 6, no. 2 (Fall 1995), pp. 201–221; Katharine Bjork, 'The Link that Kept the Philippines Spanish: Mexican Merchant Interests and the Manila Trade, 1571–1815', *Journal of World History* 9, no. 1 (Spring 1998), pp. 25–50; William S. Atwell, 'International Bullion Flows and the Chinese Economy circa 1530–1650', *Past and Present* 95, no. 1 (1982), pp. 68–90.
164. Flynn and Giraldez 1995, p. 203.
165. Etsuko Miyata Rodriguez, 'Early Manila Galleon Trade: Merchants' Networks and Markets in 16th and 17th Century Mexico', in Donna Pierce and Ronald Otsuka eds., *Asia and Spanish America: Trans-Pacific Artistic and Cultural Exchange, 1500–1850; Papers from the 2006 Mayer Center Symposium at the Denver Art Museum*, Denver, 2009, p. 42.
166. Rodriguez 2009 and Shulsky 1998–99, p. 84.
167. Museo Franz Mayer and Museum of Fine Arts, Houston, *The Grandeur of Viceregal Mexico: Treasures from the Museo Franz Mayer*, Houston, 2002, p. 32.
168. Robin Farwell Gavin, Donna Pierce and Alfonzo Pleguezuelo, *Ceramica y Cultura: The Story of Spanish and Mexican Mayolica*, Albuquerque, 2003.
169. Jean McClure Mudge, *Chinese Export Porcelain in North America*, New York, 1986, pp. 43–44; Natale Zappia, 'Porcelain and Cocoa: the Pacific Rim and the Early Modern World Economy', University of California, Santa Cruz, Center for World History, http://www2.ucsc.edu/cwh/porcelainpaper.htm. This is the same word for 'pebbles' in modern Spanish. Museo Franz Mayer and Museum of Fine Arts, Houston 2002, p. 18.
170. E.g. T. Volker, *Porcelain and the Dutch East India Company, as Recorded in the Dagh-Registers of Batavia Castle, Those of Hirado and Deshima, and Other Contemporary Papers, 1602–1682*, Leiden, 1954 and Christiaan J. A. Jorg, *Porcelain and the Dutch China Trade, 1729–94*, trans. Patricia Wardle, The Hague, 1982.
171. Chuimei Ho, 'The Ceramic Trade in Asia, 1602–82', in A. J. H. Latham and Heita Kawakatsu, eds., *Japanese Industrialization and the Asian Economy*, London/New York, 1994, p. 36.
172. The standard reference on this is Simon Schama, *The Embarrassment of Riches: An Interpretation of Dutch Culture in the Golden Age*, Berkeley/London, 1988.
173. Jorg 1982.
174. Levenson 1991, p. 117.

175. Jane Campbell Hutchison, *Albrecht Durer: A Guide to Research*, New York/London, 2000, pp. 123–124. Rembrandt is also known to have been a collector as his Chinese porcelains were sold off in 1660, and thus the porcelains would have been of Ming date, at the latest.
176. Mentioned in Michael Sullivan, *The Meeting of Eastern and Western Art*, Berkeley/London, 1989, p. 91.
177. Fitzwilliam Museum, Cambridge, attributed to Bernart van Orley, c. 1492–1542, and mentioned in A. I. Spriggs, 'Oriental Porcelain in Western Painting', *TOCS* 36 (1967), p. 74.
178. Spriggs 1967 and Timothy Brook, *Vermeer's Hat: The Seventeenth Century and the Dawn of the Global World*, London/New York, 2008, p. 76.
179. Brook 2008, pp. 62–63.
180. Rinaldi 1989, p. 45.
181. Volker 1954.
182. C. van der Pijl-Ketel, '*Kraak* Type Porcelain and Other Ceramic Wares Recovered from the Dutch East Indiaman the "*Witte Leeuw*", Sunk in 1613', *TOCS* 67 (2004), p. 91, note 3.
183. Brook 2008, p. 59.
184. Claire Le Corbeiller and Alice Cooney Frelinghuysen, *Chinese Export Porcelain*, special issue of *Metropolitan Museum of Art Bulletin* 60, no. 3 (Winter 2003), p. 8.
185. Le Corbellier and Frelinghuysen 2003, p. 8 and Volker 1954, p. 148.
186. Rinaldi 1989, pp. 118–119.
187. Le Corbellier and Frelinghuysen 2003, p. 11; a practice which was seen frequently in domestic Chinese ceramics, such as those made in Near Eastern glass forms, mentioned in chapter one. These were foreign forms for Chinese consumption, rather than foreign forms for foreign consumption, as with the *klapmuts*.
188. Le Corbellier and Frelinghuysen 2003, p. 11 and Volker 1954, p. 142.
189. AK-RBK 14774. Jorg, for example, believes that this shape is actually just a development of an earlier Chinese shape. Christiaan J. A. Jorg, *Chinese Ceramics in the Collection of the Rijksmuseum, Amsterdam: The Ming and Qing Dynasties*, Amsterdam, 1997, p. 60.
190. For example, inv. No. AK–RAK 1991–21 in the Rijksmuseum. See Jorg 1997, p. 64.
191. Jorg 1997, p. 273.
192. Norman Bryson, *Looking at the Overlooked: Four Essays on Still Life Painting*, London, 2004, p. 99, quoting Schama 1988.
193. Bryson 2004, p. 104.
194. Bryson 2004, p. 124.
195. This painting is illustrated in Sam Segal and William B. Jordan, *A Prosperous Past: The Sumptuous Still Life in the Netherlands, 1600–1700*, The Hague, 1988, fig. 7.1, p. 124. It is said to be in a private collection and formerly of the Lorenzelli Gallery, Bergamo (Italy).
196. The 'magic fountain' motif is so called because it is apparently derived from European prints of the 16th century and it consists of a fountain with either a horse or an elephant in front of it. Both can be seen on an example in the Percival David Collection, PDF 689, in the British Museum.
197. BM 1963.0520.7, Harrison-Hall 2001, pp. 384–385, fig. 12:79.
198. Ibid.
199. Ina Baghdiantz McCabe, *Orientalism in Early Modern France: Eurasian Trade, Exoticism and the Ancien Régime*. Oxford/New York, 2008, pp. 80–81; Barry Shifman and Guy Walton, eds., *Gifts to the Tsars, 1500–1700: Treasures from the Kremlin*. New York, 2001, p. 36.
200. Anthony Farrington, *Trading Places: The East India Company and Asia, 1600–1834*, London, 2002.
201. Pierson 2007, p. 28.
202. Pierson 2007, pp. 19–20.
203. Pierson 2007, p. 20.
204. V&A 7915–1862.

205. Le Corbellier and Frelinghuysen 2003, fig. 2.
206. Pierson 2007, pp. 22–23.
207. The *Madre de Dios*, 1592, according to James McDermott, *Martin Frobisher, Elizabethan Privateer*, New Haven/London, 2001, p. 398.
208. Pierson 2007, p. 24.
209. Japan Society, New York, *The Burghley Porcelains: An Exhibition from The Burghley House Collection and Based on the 1688 Inventory and 1690 Devonshire Schedule*, New York, 1980.
210. Richard Grassby, *The Business Community of Seventeenth-Century England*, Cambridge, 2002, p. 340.
211. Pierson 2007, p. 29.
212. Susan Bracken, '"Chyna" in England Before 1614', *Oriental Art* XLVII, no. 2 (2001), p. 9.
213. Arthur MacGregor, ed., *Tradescant's Rarities: Essays on the Foundation of the Ashmolean Museum, 1683, with a Catalogue of the Surviving Early Collections*, Oxford, 1983. The earliest royal porcelain rooms or 'cabinets' were built in Holland around 1645. This is said to have established a fashion for such rooms within European courts, and through their relations with other courts, in England in the late 17th century. See Tessa Murdock, 'Les cabinets de porcelain', in Georges Brunel, ed., *Pagodes et dragons: exotisme et fantasie dans l'Europe rococo 1720–1770*, Paris, 2007, pp. 42–49; John Ayers, Oliver R. Impey and J.V.G. Mallet, *Porcelain for Palaces: The Fashion for Japan in Europe, 1650–1750*, London, 1990; Michael E. Yonan, 'Igneous Architecture: Porcelain, Natural Philosophy, and the Rococo *cabinet chinois*', in Alden Cavanaugh and Michael E. Yonan, eds., *The Cultural Aesthetics of Eighteenth-Century Porcelain*, Farnham, 2010, pp. 65–85.
214. Pierson 2007, pp. 30–31; see Arthur MacGregor, *The Late King's Goods: Collections, Possessions and Patronage of Charles I in the Light of the Commonwealth Sale Inventories*, London, 1989, p. 59.

Chapter 3 Porcelain as Metaphor—Inventing 'the Ming Vase' (18th–20th centuries)

1. Porcelain in general as a metaphor for various human qualities, such as desire and the body, is discussed in Cavanaugh and Yonan, eds. 2010, pp. 1–3.
2. Cynthia Payne, *The Independent*, 2 May 1987, cited in Carmen Rosa Caldas-Coulthard, 'Reporting Speech in Narrative Discourse: Stylistic and Ideological Implications', *Ilha do desterro: A Journal of English Language, Literatures in English and Cultural Studies* 27 (1992), p. 72; http://www.periodicos.ufsc.br/index.php/desterro/article/viewFile/8759/8119.
3. Defense Atomic Support Agency, 'Operation Minute Gun. Shot Ming Vase', Interim Summary Report, Nevada Test Site, 1969. Defense Technical Information Center document POR 6337. http://www.dtic.mil/dtic/tr/fulltext/u2/a286666.pdf (accessed 28 August 2012).
4. Cited in a letter of 1629, extracted in Adolf Michaelis, *Ancient Marbles in Great Britain*, Cambridge, 1882, p. 205.
5. Vinnie Norskov, *Greek Vases in New Contexts: The Collecting and Trading of Greek Vases—An Aspect of the Modern Reception of Antiquity*, Aarhus, 2002, introduction.
6. Michael Vickers, 'Value and Simplicity: Eighteenth-Century Taste and the Study of Greek Vases', *Past and Present* 116 (Aug. 1987), pp. 98–137.
7. For example, in Emerson and Pope there are references to both porcelain and silver vases. Ralph Waldo Emerson, *Poems*, Boston, 1847, 'Woodworks II', p. 79; Henry W. Boynton, ed., *The Complete Poetical Works of Alexander Pope*, Cambridge edition, Boston/New York, 1903, 'The Rape of the Lock', p. 90, line 122.
8. *Ten Thousand Things* was an exhibition of objects collected by the American merchant Nathan Dunn (1782–1844); it was first displayed in Philadelphia in 1839 and then in London in 1942. William B. Langdon, *Wan-t'ang jen-wu = "Ten thousand Chinese things" : a descriptive catalogue of the Chinese*

collection in Philadelphia, with miscellaneous remarks upon the manners, customs, trade, and government of the Celestial Empire, Philadelphia, 1839; William B. Langdon, *Wan tang ren wu, Ten Thousand Things relating to China and the Chinese, an Epitome of the genius, government, history, literature, agriculture, arts, trade, manners, customs, and social life of the people of the Celestial Empire, together with a synopsis of the Chinese Collection*, London, 1842; John Haddad, 'The Romantic Collector in China: Nathan Dunn's Ten Thousand Chinese Things', *Journal of American Culture* 21, no. 1 (Spring 1998), pp. 7–26; Elizabeth Hope Chang, *Britain's Chinese Eye: Literature, Empire and Aesthetics in Nineteenth-Century Britain*, Stanford, 2010; Catharine Pagani, 'Chinese Material Culture and British Perceptions of China in the Mid-nineteenth Century', in T. J. Barringer and Tom Flynn, eds., *Colonialism and the Object: Empire, Material Culture and the Museum*, London, 1998, pp. 28–40; Helen Saxbee, 'An Orient Exhibited: The Exhibition of the Chinese Collection in England in the 1840s', Ph.D. dissertation, Royal College of Art, 1990.

9. For example: Jackson and Jaffer 2004; David Porter, *Ideographia: The Chinese Cypher in Early Modern Europe*, Stanford, 2002; E. H. Chang 2010.
10. See for example, Berg 2003, pp. 228–244, Robert Batchelor, 'On the Movement of Porcelains: Rethinking the Birth of Consumer Society as Interactions of Exchange Networks, 1600–1750', in John Brewer and Frank Trentmann, eds., *Consuming Cultures, Global Perspectives: Historical Trajectories, Transnational Exchanges*, Oxford, 2006, pp. 95–121, and E. H. Chang 2010.
11. Clunas 2007, pp. 224–225.
12. Frances Wood, *Did Marco Polo Go To China?* Boulder, CO, 1998. Of course many did (and still do) believe that he went to China so his text is relevant for the present discussion.
13. Jonathan D. Spence, *The Chan's Great Continent: China in Western Minds*, New York, 1999, introduction, pp. xii–xiii.
14. Peter Jackson, 'Marco Polo and His "Travels"', *Bulletin of the School of Oriental and African Studies* 61, no. 1 (1998), p. 84 and generally for a measured bibliographic history of the Travels.
15. P. Jackson 1998, p. 86.
16. Clunas 2007, p. 211.
17. See chapter one, note 90.
18. Porter 2002, pp. 35–39.
19. Porter 2002, p. 35.
20. Samuel Purchas, *Hakluytus Posthumus* or *Purchas His Pilgrimes*, 4 vols., London, 1625, vol. III, p. 96.
21. Chen Shouyi, 'John Webb: A Forgotten Page in the Early History of Sinology in Europe', in Adrian Hsia, ed., *The Vision of China in English Literature of the Seventeenth and Eighteenth Centuries*, Hong Kong, 1998, p. 94; David E. Mungello, *Curious Land: Jesuit Accommodation and the Origins of Sinology*, Honolulu, 1989, p. 110.
22. Chen Shouyi 1998, p. 111.
23. Some of this travel literature is discussed in John Barnard, ed., *The Cambridge History of the Book in Britain, vol. 4, 1557–1695*, Cambridge, 2002, p. 273.
24. Pierson 2007, p. 27.
25. Porter 2002, p. 137; Pierson 2007, pp. 33–34.
26. For example, p. 66 of *The History of the Decline and Fall of the Roman Empire*, vol. II, 2008 edition (Cosimo, Inc.), which says: 'The Illustrious Hongvou, founder of the dynasty of *Ming*…'.
27. The full title of the first English translation is: *The General History of China. Containing a Geographical, Historical, Chronological, Political and Physical Description of the Empire of China, Chinese-Tartary, Corea and Thibet*, London, 1736.
28. Porter 2002, p. 138.
29. Porter 2002, p. 184; see note 7 for full Pope citation.

30. Fa-ti Fan, *British Naturalists in Qing China: Science, Empire and Cultural Encounter*, Cambridge, MA, 2004.
31. Robert Fortune, *Yedo and Peking: A Narrative of a Journey to the Capitals of Japan and China*, London, 1863, p. 364.
32. See Joseph Marryat, *A History of Pottery and Porcelain: Medieval and Modern*, London, 1857, p. 240.
33. Steve Clark, ed., *Travel Writing and Empire: Postcolonial Theory in Transit*, London, 1999.
34. Marryat 1857, p. 202.
35. Jeffrey A. Auerbach, *The Great Exhibition of 1851: A Nation on Display*, New Haven, 1999.
36. Marryat 1957, p. 264.
37. Launched in 1859. Claire Tomalin, *Charles Dickens: A Life*, London, 2011, p. 304.
38. 'Curious Old China', in Charles Dickens, ed., *All the Year Round*, vol. 14, part III, p. 66.
39. Stanislas Julien, trans. and Alphonse Salvetat, annot. with Johann Joseph Hoffman, *Histoire et fabrication de la porcelaine chinoise*, Paris, 1856 ([Whitefish, MT], 2009), p. 95. On the *Jingdezhen taolu*, see Peter Lam, 'Chinese Making China: Technical Illustration in the *Jingdezhen taolu* (1815)', in Stacey Pierson and Ming Wilson, eds., *The Art of the Book in China*, Colloquies on Art and Archaeology in Asia, no. 23, London, 2006, pp. 117–137; E. Huang 2008.
40. Pierson 2007, p. 68; Stephen Calloway, *The Cult of Beauty: The Aesthetic Movement, 1860–1900*, London, 2011.
41. Pierson 2007, pp. 65–66.
42. Pierson 2007, pp. 65–66.
43. Pierson 2007, pp. 66–68.
44. Pierson 2007, p. 70.
45. Such as Murray Marks and the Duveens. See Pierson 2007, p. 66 and pp. 80–81.
46. Captain J. H. Lawrence-Archer, 'Chinese Porcelain—particularly that of the Ta Ming dynasty', *Art Journal*, New Series, XIV (1875), p. 251.
47. Pierson 2007, p. 61.
48. Lawrence-Archer 1875, p. 251.
49. On the ideals of the Arts and Crafts Movement, see Wendy Kaplan, ed., *The Arts and Crafts Movement in Europe and America: Design for the Modern World, 1880–1920*, New York/London, 2004.
50. See for example, Judith Green, 'Ancient China/Modern Art', in Christiaan J. A. Jorg, ed., *The History of Collecting Oriental Ceramics in East and West: Proceedings of the Symposium in the Groninger Museum, 13 and 14 November 2003*, Amsterdam, 2005, pp. 87–99.
51. Julien, Salvetat, and Hoffman 1856/2009.
52. The first book dedicated to marks was published in 1863 [Chaffer's *Marks and Monograms on Pottery and Porcelain*] and this included a section on 'Oriental porcelain—Chinese' which references Julien's translation of the *Jingdezhen taolu*. Subsequently, no respectable collector's library was complete without a dictionary of 'marks' on ceramics.
53. Lawrence-Archer 1875, p. 251.
54. Jennie J. Young, *The Ceramic Art: A Compendium of the History and Manufacture of Pottery and Porcelain*, New York, 1878, p. 138.
55. Frank T. Robinson, 'Boston Artists' Studios. No. III', *The Decorator and Furnisher* 6, no. 1 (Apr. 1885), pp. 17–19.
56. Robinson 1885, p. 19.
57. C de K (full name not given), 'The Ming Vase', *The New York Times*, 19 February 1888.
58. Hope Chang 2010, pp. 14–15.
59. Italo Calvino, 'Quickness', in *Six Memos for the Next Millennium*, Cambridge, MA, 1988, p. 32; Wilkie Collins, *The Moonstone*, Leipzig, 1868.

60. C de K 1888, Part II.
61. The term 'cultural icon' is used here in reference to Tomaselli and Scott's *Cultural Icons*, as 'constructed icons' which are usually associated with the 20th-century practice of manufacturing signs (in semiotic terms) to sell a product or idea (Keyan G. Tomaselli and David Scott, *Cultural Icons*, Walnut Creek, CA, 2009, p. 18). Certainly 'the Ming vase' is a sign that resembles (its) object, whether that object is 'a thing in the real world, an idea or another sign'. (Ibid) The 'vases' have an imitative quality, but one that can be deceitful, as we have seen with the myth of the singular, 'precious', Ming vase. Clearly the manufacturing of object-related icons was happening in the 19th century as well.
62. William Anderson, *Descriptive and Historical Catalogue of a Collection of Japanese and Chinese Paintings in the British Museum*, London, 1886.
63. *The Academy and Literature* 30 (1886), pp. 399–400.
64. See for example, the Swedish 'classic': Sven Lindqvist, *Myten om Wu Tao-tzu* (*The Myth of Wu Tao-tzu*), [Stockholm] 1967.
65. BM 1945.0927.1.
66. There are numerous histories of the Portland Vase and its reconstruction. See for example, Susan Walker, *The Portland Vase*, London, 2004; Milo Keynes, 'The Portland Vase: Sir William Hamilton, Josiah Wedgwood and the Darwins', *Notes and Records of the Royal Society, London* 52, no. 2, 1998, pp. 237–259.
67. James Dyer Ball, *Things Chinese: Being Notes on Various Subjects Connected with China*. London, 1892.
68. For example: *Cantonese Made Easy* (1888); *The English-Chinese Cookery Book: Containing 200 Receipts in English and Chinese* (1890).
69. Dyer Ball 1892, p. 366.
70. Dyer Ball 1892, p. 367.
71. On the *Tao shuo* and its relationship to both earlier and later texts on ceramics in China, see E. Huang 2008.
72. In Qing texts in general, not just ceramic-related ones, the Ming period is often negatively assessed, reflecting a traditional approach to historiography in China which disparages a dynasty that fell. On Ming and Qing official historiography in China, see Achim Mittag, 'Chinese Official Historical Writing under the Ming and Qing', in José Rabasa et al., eds., *The Oxford History of Historical Writing, vol. 3, 1400–1800*, Oxford/New York, 2012, pp. 30–32.
73. In fact, the first English-language book-length study dedicated to Qing porcelain was not published until 1951—Soame Jenyns, *Later Chinese Porcelain: The Ch'ing Dynasty, 1644–1912* (London: Faber and Faber, 1951). However volume II of R. L. Hobson's *Chinese Pottery and Porcelain* of 1915 includes a section on Ch'ing porcelain.
74. See Pierson 2007, pp. 75–80.
75. S. W. Bushell, *Oriental Ceramic Art*, New York, 1897. This is partly based on Bushell's translation of the *Tao shuo* and other Chinese texts. See chapter four for discussion.
76. Edith Wharton, *The Fruit of the Tree*, New York, 1907, book I, pp. 218–219.
77. Wharton 1907, p. 288.
78. Pierson 2007, pp. 35–37.
79. Linda Merrill, *The Peacock Room: A Cultural Biography*, Washington, D. C., 1998, p. 270.
80. See Gerald Reitlinger, *The Economics of Taste, vol. II: The Rise and Fall of the Objets d'Art Market since 1750*, London, 1964, p. 313 onward for prices.
81. Edith Wharton and Ogden Codman, *The Decoration of Houses*, New York, 1897, p. 78. I am grateful to Patricia Pierson for bringing this work to my attention.
82. Frank Jewett Mather, 'An Art Museum for the People', *The Atlantic Monthly* 100 (Dec. 1907), p. 734.

83. Gail Anderson, ed., *Reinventing the Museum: Historical and Contemporary Perspectives on the Paradigm Shift*, Walnut Creek, CA, 2004, p. 213; Robert E. Weir, *Class in America: H to P*, Westport, 2007, p. 554.
84. Samuel Merwin, *The Charmed Life of Miss Austin*, New York, 1914, p. 192.
85. Henry Adams, *The Education of Henry Adams: An Autobiography*, Washington, 1907; Boston and New York, 1918.
86. Adams 1907/1918, p. 391, said as a criticism of both inflated values for art and frivolousness with regard to world events.
87. Adams may also have been a collector of Ming porcelain as he stated in a letter to a friend: 'I buy only Ming porcelain'. To John Hay, Paris, 7 November 1900. Ernest Samuel, ed., *Henry Adams, Selected Letters*, Cambridge, MA, 1992, p. 395.
88. 'An Instrument of the Gods', by Lincoln Colcord, p. 87. The story also features a number of common Chinese stereotypes of the time. Boston, 1919.
89. The first printed reference to the preciousness of a Ming vase appears in a short poetic musing on the coming dawn by P. W. Yuille in 'The Lift of the Morning', *The Cornhill Magazine* 149 (1934), pp. 86–87. In this, the author states that the dawn silence 'is as precious as a Ming vase', thus providing the first use of this form of simile as well, p. 86.
90. Henry James, *The Portrait of a Lady*. Harvard Classics Shelf of Fiction, vol. 11, New York, 1917/2000, chap. 49, p. 7.
91. Peter Sandiford, 'Craftsmanship and Education', *School and Society*, eds. James McKeen Cattell et al., 8, no. 186 (1918), p. 69.
92. Herbert Edward Read, *Art and Industry: The Principles of Industrial Design*, London, 1934, pp. 21–23; Roger Eliot Fry, 'The Artist's Vision', in *Vision and Design*, London, 1920, cited in Pierson 2007, p. 114 [Fry] and Pierson 2004, p. 85.
93. Read 1934, pp. 21–23.
94. C D Malmgren, 'Anatomy of Murder: Mystery, Detective and Crime Fiction', *The Journal of Popular Culture* 30, no. 4 (Spring 1997), pp. 115–135.
95. Isabel Ostrander, *Suspense*, New York, 1918, p. 86.
96. A good historical overview, with critical essays on topics related to motifs in detective fiction is provided in Charles J. Rzepka and Lee Horsely, *A Companion to Crime Fiction*, Chichester/Malden, MA, 2010.
97. Kathlyn Rhodes, 'The Ming Vase', *The Strand Magazine* 61 (1921), p. 140.
98. Rhodes 1921, p. 141.
99. Rhodes 1921, p. 145.
100. John D. Swain, 'Logan Berry, From Oregon', *Munsey's Magazine* 75, no. 2 (1922), p. 376.
101. For a recent discussion, see Yunte Huang, *Charlie Chan: The Untold Story of the Venerable Detective and His Rendezvous with American History*, New York, 2010.
102. Horace Annesley Vachell, *Quinney's Adventures*, London, 1924.
103. Deborah Cohen, *Household Gods: The British and Their Possessions*, New Haven, 2006, p. 160.
104. Dashiell Hammett. *The Maltese Falcon*. New York, 1930.
105. The literature of the treasure motif, and its corollary the treasure hunt, is extensive but lacking a monograph on the subject. For selected treatments, see for example: Joseph Kestner, *Masculinities in British Adventure Fiction, 1880–1915*, Farnham/Burlington, 2010; Laurence Kitzan, *Victorian Writers and the Image of Empire: The Rose-Colored Vision*, Westport, 2001.
106. Mitzi M. Brunsdale, *Icons of Mystery and Crime Detection: From Sleuths to Superheroes*, Santa Barbara, 2010, p. 650.
107. Rex Dark, *The Ming Vase Mystery*, London, 1936, frontispiece summary.
108. Dark 1936, e.g. pp. 10, 75.

109. Ironically, an actual Ming vase did become dangerously valuable recently, with the record-breaking sale of an early 15th-century vessel in Hong in 2011. Sotheby's Hong Kong, 'The Meiyintang Collection, part II', October 2011. The sale price was £14 million, thus generating a lot of Ming-vase related headlines.
110. This process mirrors that of the interpretation and reception of 'Gandharan sculpture', as discussed by Stanley Abe in 'Inside the Wonder House: Buddhist Art and the West', in Donald Lopez, ed., *Curators of the Buddha: The Study of Buddhism under Colonialism*, Chicago, 1995, pp. 63–106.
111. Rex Stout, *The Broken Vase*, New York, 1941; Boston, 1988, pp. 144–145.
112. Linda Rosenfeld Pomper, Jeffrey P. Stamen, and Norman R. Weiss, 'Research on the Question of Dating Chinese Famille Noire Porcelain', in Blythe McCarthy, ed., *Scientific Research on Historic Asian Ceramics: Proceedings of the Fourth Forbes Symposium at the Freer Gallery of Art*, Washington D. C., 2009, pp. 104–112.
113. James J. Lally, 'Collecting Chinese Ceramics in America: Morgan and Freer', *TOCS* 73 (2010), pp. 25–37.
114. Stout 1941/1988, p. 44.
115. Stout 1941/1988, p. 44.
116. Kent Baxter, 'Nancy Drew and Her Sister Sleuths: Essays on the Fiction of Girl Detectives (review)', *The Lion and the Unicorn* 33, no. 3 (Sept. 2009), pp. 418–422.
117. Carolyn Keene, *The Clue of the Leaning Chimney* (Nancy Drew book 26), New York, 1949.
118. 'Jiggs and Maggie in Court', William Beaudine, director, released in USA 12 December 1948.
119. Michael Scriven, 'The Present Status of Determinism in Physics', *The Journal of Philosophy* 54, no. 23 (1957), p. 739.
120. Eric Berne, *A Layman's Guide to Psychiatry and Psychoanalysis*, New York, 1957, p. 60.
121. P. G. Wodehouse, *The Luck of the Bodkins*, London, 1956, p. 12.
122. *The Simpsons,* season 5, episode 1F11, 'Ming vase on a ladder' sketch, written by John Swartzwelder.
123. These are still available for sale and are referenced in the main guide to American comics, Robert M. Overstreet, *The Overstreet Comic Book Price Guide*, New York, 1993 edition consulted.
124. *The Adventures of Rin Tin Tin,* series 5, episode 23, first broadcast 23 March 1959. Screen Gems, USA.
125. Yuille 1934.
126. Joseph Fields, Oscar Hammerstein and C. Y. Lee, *Flower Drum Song: A Musical Play*, Farrar, Straus & Cudahy, 1959, p. 20.
127. A. J. McClane, 'From Aawa to Zooplankton', *Field and Stream* 70, no. 7 (1965), p. 128.
128. See Wayne D. LeBaron, *America's Nuclear Legacy*, Commack, NY, 1998, for information about the Nevada tests which began in 1951.
129. Defense Atomic Support Agency, 'Operation Minute Gun. Shot Ming Vase. Interim Summary Report', Nevada Test Site, November 1969, Defense Technical Information Center document POR 6337; accession number ADA286666, 1968; http://www.dtic.mil/dtic/tr/fulltext/u2/a286666.pdf (accessed 28 August 2012).
130. U. S. Department of Energy, Nevada Operations Office, 'United States Nuclear Tests: July 1945 through September 1992', DOE/NV--209-REV 15, December 2000; http://www.nv.doe.gov/library/publications/historical/DOENV_209_REV15.pdf (accessed 4 November 2010).
131. Defense Nuclear Agency, 'Operation Minute Gun Shot Hudson Seal Summary Report', ADA286667, May 1969, p. 11. http://www.dtic.mil/cgi-bin/GetTRDoc?Location=U2&doc=GetTRDoc.pdf&AD=ADA286667 (accessed 28 August 2012).
132. Defense Nuclear Agency 1969, p. 14 of the pdf file, p. 10 of the original report.
133. BBC bans sex pistols god save the queen, 13 May 1977. http://www.history.com/this-day-in-history/the-bbc-bans-the-sex-pistols-quotgod-save-the-queenquot (accessed 4 November 2010).
134. Hergé, *The Blue Lotus*. English edition, London, 1983, p. 16. The title is also given in Chinese: 藍蓮花. The Tin Tin reference was first noted by Jessica Harrison-Hall.

135. Hergé 1983, p. 55.
136. Homay King, *Lost in Translation: Orientalism, Cinema and the Enigmatic Signifier*, Durham, 2010, pp. 44–74.
137. Mantegna's *Adoration of the Magi* (1495–1505); Whistler's *Purple and Rose*: *The Lange Lijzen of the Six Marks* (1864); and Matisse's *Les Pensées de Pascal* (1924).
138. See 'I'm a Ming Vase but also a PC', http://www.youtube.com/watch?v=gkvtmiRWypE (accessed 2 August 2012).
139. See http://adsoftheworld.com/media/print/artengo_tennis_shoes_ming_vase (accessed 19 June 2010).
140. Widely reported, see, for example: http://www.look.co.uk/pictures/victoria-beckhams-dramatic-style-transformation/victoria-beckham-wearing-a-red-roberto-cavalli-dress-2005#./victoria-beckham-wearing-roberto-cavalli-to-elton-johns-annual-party-20?&_suid=134564350483909738591063552051, image 86 (accessed 22 August 2012).
141. See http://digi.color-swatches.com/ace/colors-for-your-life/ming-vase/b44-7/swatch.html (accessed 28 August 2012).
142. The 'Priceless Ming Vase' weapon appears in Worms World Party of 2001. http://www.worms2.com/main.html?page=good&area=weap,weapons guide, F10–F12 (accessed 22 August 2012).

Chapter 4 Ming Porcelain in the Art World (19th–21st centuries)

1. See Clunas 2009, introduction, p. 9.
2. There is a significant body of literature on Ming ceramics in non-English language sources. For the most part, these treat the subject as a natural category of Chinese ceramics, as the concept and phrase 'the Ming vase' is primarily confined to the culture of English-speaking societies. For bibliographies of literature on Ming ceramics in Chinese, Japanese and other languages, see for example Wang Guangyao 2010; Kerr ed. 2004; Hasebe Gakuji, *Chūgokū no tōji* 中国の陶磁 (Chinese Ceramics), 12 vols., Tokyo, 1995–99, vols. 8–10 on Ming and related ceramics.
3. 'A Magnificent Early Ming Underglaze Copper-red Vase, *yuhuchunping*', Fine Chinese Ceramics and Works of Art, 30 May 2006. This was widely reported. See for example the Bloomberg report: Le-Min Lim, 'Las Vegas Developer Wynn Pays Record HK$78.5 Mln for Ming Vase', *Bloomberg,* 30 May 2006: http://www.bloomberg.com/apps/news?pid=newsarchive&sid=alq0LeAjK1_M (accessed 3 August 2012).
4. 'Steve Wynn Officially Donates Ming Vase to Macau,' http://www.a2zmacau.com/2129/steve-wynn-officially-donates-ming-vase-to-macau/ (accessed 3 August 2012).
5. Hongwu is only mentioned in Cao Zhao's preface [Tianshun (1457–64) edn.]. The date the book was written was the 21st year of the Hongwu reign period; David 1971, p. 3. In later texts, as noted in chapter one, it is usually Ming porcelains of the 15th century onward that are mentioned, such as those of the Yongle, Xuande and Chenghua periods.
6. At the time of writing, another Chinese 'vase', this time of Qing date, sold for £531,000,000. Bainbridges auctioneers, Pinner, near London, 11 November 2010. This is currently the world record for any Chinese 'work of art'. See for example Murray Wardrop, 'Chinese Vase Sells for World Record-Breaking £53.1 Million at Auction', *The Telegraph*, 11 November 2010: http://www.telegraph.co.uk/culture/art/artsales/8127919/Chinese-vase-sells-for-world-record-breaking-53.1-million-at-auction.html (accessed 3 August 2012). To date, the piece has not been paid for, however.
7. 'Wynn Pays Record Price for Chinese Ming Vase', *China Daily*, 31 May 2006: http://www.chinadaily.com.cn/china/2006-05/31/content_604893.htm (accessed 3 August 2012).
8. However, it had been sold by the 'unaware' collectors in 1984, then was in two private collections before being sold in 2006.

9. A hardcopy catalogue was published for this lot and its text can be found online: http://www.christies.com/LotFinder/lot_details.aspx?from=salesummary&intObjectID=4721902&sid=883af8b8-866b-4ff9-af7b-2672b4e3b09d.
10. Interview: Artworks Magazine, 15 May 2008. http://artworksmagazine.com/2008/05/steve-wynn/ (accessed 23 August 2012).
11. Interview: http://artworksmagazine.com/2008/05/steve-wynn/.
12. Li and Knight 2008.
13. The Percival David Foundation of Art, formerly at SOAS, University of London. The main collection is now displayed in the Sir Joseph Hotung Ceramic Study Centre Gallery in the British Museum. Jessica Harrison-Hall and Regina Krahl, *Chinese Ceramics: Highlights of the Sir Percival David Collection*, London, 2009. For a history of the museum, see Stacey Pierson, 'Private Collecting, Teaching and Institutionalisation: The Percival David Foundation and the Field of Chinese Art in Britain, 1920–1964', Ph.D. dissertation, University of Sussex, 2004a.
14. Pierson 2007.
15. It was published in its complete form in 1910: *Description of Chinese Pottery and Porcelain: Being a Translation of the T'ao shuo, with notes*, Oxford, 1910.
16. For a recent reprint, see Zhu Yan 朱琰, *Tao shuo* 陶说. *Xuxiu siku quanshu* 续修四库全书, vol. 1111. Shanghai: Shanghai guji chubanshe, 1995–99.
17. Judith Green, 'Britain's Chinese Collections: Private Collecting and the Invention of Chinese Art, 1842–1943', Ph.D. dissertation, University of Sussex, 2003; Nick Pearce, 'Collecting, Connoisseurship and Commerce: An Examination of the Life and Career of Stephen Wooton Bushell (1844–1908)', *TOCS* 70 (2007), pp. 17–25.
18. The history of the Walters family and their collections is presented in William R. Johnston, *William and Henry Walters: The Reticent Collectors*, Baltimore, 1999. A more recent study of Henry Walters examines his relationship with Bernard Berenson: Stanley Mazaroff, *Henry Walters and Bernard Berenson: Collector and Connoisseur*, Baltimore, 2010.
19. See Bushell 1897/1981, preface, p. iii.
20. Bushell 1897/1981, introduction, p. 2.
21. For example in Hobson 1915, which itself would prove to be an enduring reference on the subject.
22. Stephen Bushell, *Chinese Porcelain: Sixteenth-Century Coloured Illustrations with Chinese MS Text, Translated and Annotated by S. W. Bushell*, Oxford, 1908.
23. On Xiang, see Clunas 1991/2004, p. 124; Goodrich and Fang 1976, vol. 1, pp. 539–544.
24. Percival David, 'Hsiang and His Album', *TOCS* 11 (1933–34), pp. 22–47.
25. 'A Porcelain Collector of the Ming Dynasty', *The Burlington Magazine for Connoisseurs* 14, no. 71 (Feb. 1909), p. 290.
26. 'A Porcelain Collector of the Ming Dynasty' 1909, p. 291.
27. Clunas 1991/2004, p.124 and David 1933–34.
28. Burlington Fine Arts Club, *Exhibition of Early Chinese Pottery and Porcelain 1910*, London, 1911.
29. Edgar Gorer, *Catalogue of Rare Specimens of Ming and early Kang-he Porcelain*. Exhibited at the Galleries of S. Gorer and Son, London, 1907.
30. Hobson 1915, vol. II, p. xvii.
31. Larry Shiner, *The Invention of Art: A Cultural History*, Chicago, 2001, p. 5.
32. S. C. Bosch Reitz, 'Two Different Kinds of Ming Porcelain', *The Metropolitan Museum of Art Bulletin* 14, no. 11 (Nov. 1919), p. 236.
33. Japan Society, *Chinese, Corean and Japanese Potteries: Descriptive Catalogue of Loan Exhibition of Selected Examples*; all exhibited under the auspices of the Japan Society at the galleries of M. Knoedler & Co; Chinese and Corean authenticated by R. L. Hobson; Japanese by Edward S. Morse, New York, 1914.

34. Stanley Abe, 'Collecting Chinese Sculpture: Paris, New York, Boston', in Alan Chong and Noriko Murai, eds., *Journeys East: Isabella Stewart Gardner and Asia*, Boston, 2009, pp. 432–442.
35. Shiner 2001, p. 5.
36. Rose Sickler Williams was the wife of Edward Thomas Williams (1854–1944), who had gone to China in 1887 and then served in a number of official posts there. Later he was Professor of Oriental Languages at University of California Berkeley. See 'Edward Thomas Williams, Oriential [*sic*] Languages and Literature: Berkeley', *University of California: In Memorium, 1943–1945*: http://texts.cdlib.org/view?docId=hb696nb2rz&doc.view=frames&chunk.id=div00035&toc.depth=1&toc.id= (accessed 3 August 2012).
37. 'Notes on the Veitch Collection of Chinese Porcelain in the Birmingham Art Gallery', *The Burlington Magazine for Connoisseurs* 4, no. 12 (Mar. 1904), pp. 232–241.
38. 'Notes on the Veitch Collection' 1904, p. 232.
39. 'Notes on the Veitch Collection' 1904, pp. 232–241. For an art historical discussion of Chinese stands, see Jan Stuart, 'Practices of Display: The Significance of Stands for Chinese Art Objects', in Jerome Silbergeld et al., eds., *Bridges to Heaven: Essays on East Asian Art in Honor of Professor Wen Fong*, vol. 2, part 6, Princeton, 2011, pp. 693–712.
40. Visual evidence for this can be seen in the well-known Chinese court paintings of the Yongzheng period, the versions of 'the Scroll of Antiquities' or *Gu wan tu* 古玩图. One version is in the Percival David Collection. See Shane McCausland, 'The Emperor's Old Toys: Rethinking the Yongzheng (1723–35) Scroll of Antiquities in the Percival David Foundation', *TOCS* 66 (2000–01), pp. 65–75.
41. F. S. K., 'A Chinese Porcelain Vase', *Museum of Fine Arts Bulletin* 14, no. 82 (Apr. 1916), p. 17.
42. Ironically now once again seeing a resurgence in popularity with Chinese collectors, about 100 years later.
43. 'A Rare Ming Vase', *The Burlington Magazine for Connoisseurs* 33, no. 189 (Dec. 1918), p. 194. *Fahua* wares are discussed later in this chapter.
44. As noted in chapter two, this practice, with different implications, was also employed in Japan.
45. R. L. Hobson, 'The Leverton Harris Cup', *The British Museum Quarterly* 3, no. 2 (Sept. 1928), p. 33.
46. See Harrison-Hall 2001, p. 279, fig. 11:7.
47. There is also evidence of concern about 'early Ming' attributions, an issue which will be discussed later in this chapter.
48. Harrison-Hall 2001, p. 586.
49. For example, the Hongwu-period copper red-decorated cup stand, BM 1928.0718.2.
50. R. L. Hobson, 'Peking Notes', *TOCS* 8 (1928–30), p. 36.
51. Very little is known about Raphael, apart from his collecting activities. A brief history of these can be found in Harrison-Hall 2001, p. 593.
52. The Palace Museum had recently opened in 1925 and was preceded by displays in the Institute for Exhibiting Antiquities which were first opened to the public in 1914. This history, and its consequences for the conceptualisation of the former imperial 'collections', was recently considered by Wang Cheng-hua, 'The Qing Imperial Collection, Circa 1905–25: National Humiliation, Heritage Preservation, and Exhibition Culture', in Wu Hung, ed., *Reinventing the Past: Archaism and Antiquarianism in Chinese Art and Visual Culture*, Chicago, 2010, pp. 320–341. See also Sarah E. Fraser, 'Antiquarianism or Primitivism?: The Edge of History in the Modern Chinese Imagination', pp. 342–367 in the same volume.
53. For a discussion of the transition of the objects from imperial household goods to objects in the national art collection, see Wang Cheng-hua 2010.
54. C.1037–1917. Published in Pierson 2009, p. 36.
55. BM OA 1929.1–14.1. Published in Harrison-Hall 2001, pp. 499–500, fig. 16:95.
56. Shigeru Akita and Nicholas J. White, *The International Order of Asia in the 1930s and 1950s*, Farnham, 2010, p. 208.

57. Alfred Salmony and D. E. Berenberg, 'Peking as a Museum City', *Parnassus* 3, no. 1 (Jan. 1931), p. 35.
58. Salmony and Berenberg 1931, p. 37. This was the section which Percival David paid to refurbish, as noted in the same article and in Pierson 2004a.
59. With the opening of the Palace Museum came an officially-sanctioned display and a perception that there was an authentic knowledge of Ming porcelains that could not be replicated outside China, especially with a lack of precisely dated examples.
60. Horace H. F. Jayne, 'In Defense of the Ming', *Parnassus* 2, no. 2 (Feb. 1930), pp. 18–19.
61. Jayne 1930, p. 19.
62. Eg. Burlington Fine Arts Club, *Exhibition of Early Chinese Pottery and Porcelain*, London, 1910 (illustrated catalogue published in 1911).
63. Jayne 1930, p. 19.
64. W. P. Y., 'Altar Vessels of the Wan Li Period' 55, no. 320 (Nov. 1929), pp. 252–253; WPY must have been W. Perceval Yetts.
65. R. L. Hobson, 'A Ming Porcelain Altar Set', *The British Museum Quarterly* 5, no. 3 (Dec. 1930), pp. 81–83.
66. Jayne 1930, p. 19. Interestingly, unlike Salmony a year later, who bemoans the availability of authentic objects for sale in China, Horace Jayne notes that because of 'political upheavals in China', supplies of objects for sale are limited and that 'in China certain restrictions are actually being enforced, that stone sculpture, for instance, is absolutely prohibited to be exported and that at last the Chinese are inclined to preserve their antiquities' (see p. 17).
67. A review of this exhibition appeared in *The Burlington Magazine*; see Tancred Borenius et al., 'Art Treasures Exhibition', *The Burlington Magazine for Connoisseurs* 61, no. 355 (Oct. 1932), p. 178.
68. Percival David, 'Description of Specimens Exhibited', *TOCS* 9 (1930–31), pp. 12–13.
69. 'Chinese Ceramics at Messrs. Sparks', *The Burlington Magazine for Connoisseurs* 61, no. 356 (Nov. 1932), p. 232.
70. Sparks is the subject of a current dissertation at the School of Oriental and African Studies, University of London, where the firm's archives are located.
71. For the catalogue, see Edgar E. Bluett, *Ming and Ch'ing Porcelains: A Short Treatise Concerning Some Dated Specimens Together With Some Account of Their Distinguishing Features*, London, 1933.
72. Edgar Bluett, 'The Nien Hao and Period Identification', *TOCS* 13 (1935–36), pp. 51–63.
73. Pierson 2007, p. 147. In this period (as now), named collectors and collections were considered essential 'data' for connoisseurship writing about collected objects in general, not just Chinese ceramics.
74. R. L. Hobson, 'Ming Porcelain and Some Others from the Bloxam Collection', *Old Furniture* 5, no. 16 (1928), p. 3.
75. W. W. Winkworth, 'The David Collection Catalogue', *The Burlington Magazine for Connoisseurs* 65, no. 381 (Dec. 1934), pp. 264–270.
76. And, it can be argued, the literature in Chinese. Most of the Chinese texts specifically about Ming ceramics published in the 20th century have been archaeological reports or museum catalogues referencing archaeological material. The most prominent example of this is the literature of Ming imperial ceramics from Jingdezhen, which is extensive. See the final section of this chapter for a discussion of the role of archaeology in the interpretation and presentation of Ming porcelain in China.
77. A. D. Brankston, 'An Excursion to Ching-te-chen and Chi-an-fu in Kiangsi', *TOCS* 16 (1938–39), pp. 19–32.
78. B.R., review of *Early Ming Wares of Chingtechen*, by A. D. Brankston, *The Burlington Magazine* 75, no. 437 (Aug. 1939), p. 88.
79. B. R. 1939, p. 88.
80. Royal Academy of Arts, London, *Exhibition of Chinese Art—Catalogue and Illustrated Supplement* London, 1935. For a brief discussion, see Pierson 2007, pp. 154–160.
81. Bernard Rackham, review, *The Burlington Magazine* 70, no. 407 (Feb. 1937), p. 95.

82. Percival David, 'The Exhibition of Chinese Art. A Preliminary Survey', *The Burlington Magazine* 67, no. 393 (Dec. 1935), p. 246.
83. Sotheby and Co., 'Catalogue of the Well-Known Collection of Rare Early Chinese Blue and White Porcelain of the Sung, Yuan and Ming Dynasties and Some Choice Examples of Enamelled Porcelain of the Ch'ing Dynasty, the Property of Charles E. Russell, Esq.', 6 June 1935.
84. Pierson 2007, pp. 159–160.
85. http://www.bonhams.com/auctions/16789/lot/54/ (accessed 29 August 2012).
86. A well-published example is the blue and white Jiajing mark and period ewer, PDF B617. For an obituary of Russell, see Soame Jenyns, 'Charles Ernest Russell', *TOCS* 32, 1959–60, p. ix.
87. PDF B614. See Pierson 2004a, p. 142; Pierson 2007, p. 147.
88. R. L. Hobson, *A Catalogue of Pottery and Porcelain in the Collection of Sir Percival David, Bt., FSA*, London, 1934; PDF 688, 600, A644—ex Russell, 662, B658, etc.
89. Hobson 1934, pp. xi–xii; Pierson 2007, p. 152; and Lady David, 'Introduction', in R. Scott, *The Percival David Foundation of Chinese Art: A Guide to the Collection* (London, 1989), pp. 9–26.
90. Leopold Reidemeister and J Hellner, *Ming-Porzellane in Schwedischen Sammlungen*, Berlin, 1935.
91. From what is considered an important collection today: American Art Association, 'Rare Sung and Ming Porcelains and Pottery, Ch'ing Decorated Porcelains, Including Ku-yueh Hsuan and Other Imperial Wares: Collection of Mrs. S. K. De Forest', New York, 11 January 1936, Sale 4219.The American Art Association was an auction house founded in 1884 in New York. It was widely admired at the time and is credited with creating/inventing the modern auction style and enhancing the reputation of auctioneers. Its archives are located in the Frick Art Reference Library, New York City.
92. Robert Fleming Heizer et al., 'Archaeological Evidence of Sebastian Rodriquez Cermeño's California Visit in 1595', *California Historical Society Quarterly* 20, no. 4 (Dec. 1941), p. 321.
93. Heizer 1941, pp. 326–327, fn. 17.
94. This report would go on to become a seminal reference in the history of Chinese export porcelain, and the sherds discussed in it would be used to date related finds in several surface and shipwreck sites around the world. Clarence Shangraw and Edward P. von der Porten, *The Drake and Cermeño Expeditions' Chinese Porcelains at Drakes Bay, California, 1579 and 1595*, Santa Rosa, CA, 1981. A new book on the subject by Von der Porten is apparently in press.
95. A. J. B. Kiddell, 'Note on a Blue and White Vase from the Tomb of the Emperor Hsuan Te', *TOCS* 21 (1945–46), p. 17.
96. A. J. B. Kiddell, 'Further Note on a Pair of Blue-and-White Vases from the Tomb of the Emperor Hsuan Te', *TOCS* 22 (1946–47), p. 39.
97. Peter Bodde, 'Pre-Ming and Early Fifteenth Century Chinese Blue and White Porcelains', *TOCS* 21 (1945–46), pp. 16–17.
98. Oriental Ceramic Society, 'Transactions for the Year 1946–47', *TOCS* 22 (1946–47), preliminary pages, p. 7.
99. Oriental Ceramic Society, 'Catalogue of the Exhibition of Ming Blue-and-White Porcelain', *TOCS* 22 (1946–47), pp. 40–41.
100. Gerald Reitlinger and Martin Button, 'Early Ming Blue and White: I', *The Burlington Magazine* 90, no. 538 (Jan. 1948), p. 11.
101. Reitlinger and Button 1948, p. 11, quoting Honey in *The Ceramic Art of China*, London, 1944, p. 111 and fn.
102. It should be noted that Reitlinger was a dealer and thus had an interest in improving the commercial prospects for 'early Ming' porcelain.
103. Fogg Art Museum, *The Use of Blue on Chinese Porcelain of the Ming Dynasty, 1368–1644*, Cambridge, MA, 1947.

104. The catalogue was published in the museum's *Bulletin*, Jean Gordon Lee, 'An Exhibition of Ming Blue-and-White', *Philadelphia Museum of Art Bulletin* XLIV, no. 223 (Autumn 1949), pp. 1–72.
105. J. G. Lee 1949, p. 5.
106. J. G. Lee 1949, p. 6.
107. Jean-Pierre Dubosc, *A Loan Exhibition: Great Chinese Painters of the Ming and Ch'ing Dynasties, XV to XVIII Centuries, for the Benefit of The Asia Institute: March 11 to April 2, 1949*, New York, 1949; Ellen J. Laing, 'The State of Ming Painting Studies', *Ming Studies* 4 (Spring 1977), pp. 9–16 (18).
108. A. Bulling, 'Chinese Art of the Ming Period, A.D. 1368–1644', short notice in *The Burlington Magazine* 92, no. 570 (Sept. 1950), p. 271.
109. Pierson 2004a, chap. 4.
110. See Pierson 2004a, pp. 215–233 for a discussion of the museum's early activities.
111. Sotheby's London, 'Important Ming Porcelain', 24 March 1953.
112. Eg. in *The Burlington Magazine* 95, no. 600 (Mar. 1953), p. v.
113. Oriental Ceramics Society, 'Transactions for the Year 1950–51', *TOCS* 26 (1950–51), preliminary pages, p. 9.
114. Mathias Komor, *Imperial Porcelains of the Ming Dynasty (1368–1644 A.D.)*, New York, 1951.
115. See Soame Jenyns, 'The A. D. Brankston Collection of Chinese Porcelain', *The British Museum Quarterly* 19, no. 3 (Sept. 1954), pp. 54–57.
116. Soame Jenyns, *Ming Pottery and Porcelain*, 2nd edn., London, 1953/1988, p. 2.
117. Jenyns 1953/1988, p. 4.
118. Sherman Lee, 'Early Ming Blue and White Porcelains', *Bulletin of the Cleveland Museum of Art* 42, no. 2, part 1 (Feb. 1955), p. 28.
119. Lee 1955, p. 29.
120. Freer Gallery of Art, *Ming Porcelains in the Freer Gallery of Art*, Washington, D.C., 1953.
121. The Arts Council of Great Britain and The Oriental Ceramic Society, *Catalogue of an Exhibition of the Arts of the Ming Dynasty, November 15th to December 14th, 1957*, London, 1957.
122. Sir Harry Garner, 'The Arts of the Ming Dynasty: Introduction', *TOCS* 30 (1955–57), preliminary pages, p. 1.
123. E.g. Desmond Gure, 'The Arts of the Ming Dynasty', *Artibus Asiae* 20, no. 4 (1957), pp. 309–320.
124. For example, John A. Pope, 'Some Blue-and-White in Istanbul', *TOCS* 26 (1950–51), pp. 37–50.
125. Pope 1956.
126. *Chinese Art Treasures: A Selected Group of Objects from the Chinese National Palace Museum and the Chinese National Central Museum, Taichung, Taiwan. / Exhibited in the United States by the Government of the Republic of China at the National Gallery of Art, Washington [and others] 1961–1962*, Geneva, 1961. At the same time, the National Palace Museum in Taipei published a catalogue, *Underglaze Red Ware of the Ming Dynasty; Ming youli hongci* 明釉里红瓷 (Hong Kong, 1963), a very specialized topic in Ming ceramics, demonstrating the disparity in the appreciation and specialist knowledge of Ming ceramics among readers and collectors in greater China and those of the rest of the world.
127. Warren Cohen, *East Asian Art and American Culture: A Study in International Relations*, New York, 1992.
128. *Chinese Art Treasures* 1961, p. 25.
129. The fact that the conception of Song ceramics as rustic and therefore hand-crafted is still current at that time is also interesting. As noted in chapter two, this was a notion that had currency in both early modern Japan and 20th century Britain, which itself was influenced by Japanese ideals of the so-called *Mingei* (民芸 'folk craft') movement, through the agency of Bernard Leach. See, for example, Yuko Kikuchi, 'A Japanese William Morris: Yanagi Soetsu and *Mingei* Theory', *Journal of William Morris Studies* 12, no. 2 (Spring), pp. 39–45.

130. W. B. Honey, introduction to Jenyns 1953/1988, p. xi.
131. H. C. Tseng, 'Chinese Art Treasures', *Bulletin of the Museum of Fine Arts, Boston* 59, no. 317 (1961), p. 64.
132. Art Institute of Chicago, *Ming-Ch'ing Dynasties, a.d. 1368–1644, a.d. 1644–1912*, Chicago, 1964.
133. On single-period Chinese art exhibitions in the 1950s and 1960s as a trend, see Pierson 2004a, p. 231.
134. Gerald Reitlinger, *The Economics of Taste, vol. III: The Art Market in the 1960s*, London, 1970, p. 436.
135. Reitlinger 1970, p. 436.
136. Reitlinger 1970, p. 442.
137. Reitlinger 1970, p. 442.
138. *Fahua* ware is normally a stoneware with dark blue, or sometimes turquoise, ground colours and slip lines containing yellow and green low-fired lead glazes. These were first made at kilns in north China during the Yuan period, and the tradition is associated with architectural and temple ceramic production. Some examples were also made in porcelain at Jingdezhen during the 16th century.
139. See Lam ed. 1996.
140. Enzheng Tong, 'Thirty Years of Chinese Archaeology (1949–1979)', in Philip L. Kohl and Clare P. Fawcett, eds., *Nationalism, Politics, and the Practice of Archaeology*, Cambridge, 1995, pp. 177–197.
141. For example, Margaret Medley, 'Ching-te Chen and the Problem of the 'Imperial Kilns', *Bulletin of the School of Oriental and African Studies* 29, no. 2 (1966), pp. 326–338.
142. National Palace Museum, *Blue and White Ware of the Ming Dynasty*, compiled by the joint board of the National Palace Museum and the National Central Museum, 6 vols., Hong Kong, 1963 (also published in Chinese, along with a series of other books on Chinese ceramics in the 1960s).
143. For the catalogue, see Suzanne G. Valenstein, *Ming Porcelains: A Retrospective*, New York, 1970. The exhibition ran from October 1970 to January 1971.
144. Valenstein 1970, preface, p. 7.
145. John Alexander Pope, *The History of the History of Ming Porcelain*, London, 1972. This is the published version of what was presented as an OCS lecture in June 1971.
146. The most recent was in China; see Zhao 2010.
147. As described by Gerritsen 2009.

Bibliography

'A Porcelain Collector of the Ming Dynasty'. 1909. *The Burlington Magazine for Connoisseurs*. Review, 14, no. 71 (Feb.): 290.

'A Rare Ming Vase'. 1918. *The Burlington Magazine for Connoisseurs* 33, no. 189 (Dec.): 194.

Abe, S. 2009. 'Collecting Chinese Sculpture: Paris, New York, Boston.' In *Journeys East: Isabella Stewart Gardner and Asia*, eds. Alan Chong and Noriko Murai. 432–442. Boston: Periscope.

———. 1995. 'Inside the Wonder House: Buddhist Art and the West'. In *Curators of the Buddha: the Study of Buddhism under Colonialism*, ed. Donald Lopez. 63–106. Chicago: University of Chicago Press.

Adams, H. 1918. *The Education of Henry Adams: An Autobiography*. Washington: Adams, 1907; Boston and New York: Houghton Mifflin.

Adshead, S. A. M. 1997. *Material Culture in Europe and China, 1400–1800*. Basingstoke: Palgrave.

Akita, Shigeru and White, N. J. 2010. *The International Order of Asia in the 1930s and 1950s*. Farnham: Ashgate.

Algazi, G., Groebner, V. and Jussen, B., eds. 2003. *Negotiating the Gift: Pre-Modern Figurations of Exchange*. Gottingen: Vandenhoeck and Ruprecht.

American Art Association. 1936. 'Rare Sung and Ming Porcelains and Pottery, Ch'ing Decorated Porcelains, Including Ku-yueh Hsuan and Other Imperial Wares: Collection of Mrs. S. K. De Forest'. New York, 11 January. Sale 4219.

Anderson, G., ed. 2004. *Reinventing the Museum: Historical and Contemporary Perspectives on the Paradigm Shift*. Walnut Creek, CA: AltaMira Press.

Anderson, W. 1886. *Descriptive and Historical Catalogue of a Collection of Japanese and Chinese Paintings in the British Museum*. London: Longmens and Co.

Appadurai, A., ed. 1986. *The Social Life of Things: Commodities in Cultural Perspective*. Cambridge: Cambridge University Press.

Art Institute of Chicago. 1964. *Ming-Ch'ing Dynasties, a.d. 1368–1644, a.d. 1644–1912*. Chicago: Art Institute of Chicago.

The Arts Council of Great Britain and The Oriental Ceramic Society. 1957. *Catalogue of an Exhibition of the Arts of the Ming Dynasty, November 15th to December 14th, 1957*. London: Arts Council of Great Britain.

Asahi Shimbun, ed. 1998. *Newly Discovered Southern Song Ceramics: A Thirteenth Century 'Time Capsule'; Fūin sareta Nansō tōji ten* 封印された南宋陶磁展. Tokyo: Asahi Shimbun.

Atwell, W. S. 2002. 'Time, Money and the Weather: Ming China and the "Great Depression" of the Mid-Fifteenth Century'. *Journal of Asian Studies* 61, no. 1 (Feb.): 83–113.

———. 1982. 'International Bullion Flows and the Chinese Economy circa 1530–1650', *Past and Present* 95, no. 1: 68–90.

Auerbach, J. A. 1999. *The Great Exhibition of 1851: A Nation on Display*. New Haven: Yale University Press.

Ayers, J., Impey, O. R. and Mallet, J. V. G. 1990. *Porcelain for Palaces: The Fashion for Japan in Europe, 1650–1750*. London: Oriental Ceramic Society.

Baburnama: Memoirs of Babur, Prince and Emperor, trans., ed., and annot. Wheeler M. Thackston. 2002. New York: Modern Library.

Ball, J. D. 1892. *Things Chinese: Being Notes on Various Subjects Connected with China.* London: S. Low, Marston.

Barbieri-Low, A. J. 2007. *Artisans in Early Imperial China*. Seattle/London: University of Washington Press.

Barnard, J., ed. 2002. *The Cambridge History of the Book in Britain, vol. 4, 1557–1695*. Cambridge: Cambridge University Press.

Batchelor, R. 2006. 'On the Movement of Porcelains: Rethinking the Birth of Consumer Society as Interactions of Exchange Networks, 1600–1750'. In *Consuming Cultures, Global Perspectives: Historical Trajectories, Transnational Exchanges*, eds. John Brewer and Frank Trentmann. 95–121. Oxford: Berg.

Baudrillard, J. 2006. *The System of Objects*, trans. James Benedict. London: Verso.

Baxter, K. 2009. 'Nancy Drew and Her Sister Sleuths: Essays on the Fiction of Girl Detectives (review)'. *The Lion and the Unicorn* 33, no. 3 (Sept.): 418–422.

Becker, H. S. 1982. *Art Worlds*. Berkeley: University of California Press.

Beijing Cultural Relics Publishing House. 1993. *Gems of China's Cultural Relics; Zhongguo wenwu jinghua* 中国文物精华. Beijing: Cultural Relics Publishing House.

Beijing wenwu yanjiusuo 北京文物研究所. 1990. *Beijing kaogu sishi nian* 北京考古四十年 (Forty Years of Beijing Archaeology). Beijing: Yanshan chubanshe.

Berg, M. 2003. 'Asian Luxuries and the Making of the European Consumer Revolution'. In *Luxury in the Eighteenth Century: Debates, Desires and Delectable Goods*, eds. Maxine Berg and Elizabeth Eger. 228–244. Basingstoke: Palgrave Macmillan.

Berne, Eric. 1957. *A Layman's Guide to Psychiatry and Psychoanalysis*. 2nd edn. New York: Simon and Schuster.

Bjork, K. 1998. 'The Link that Kept the Philippines Spanish: Mexican Merchant Interests and the Manila Trade, 1571–1815'. *Journal of World History* 9, no. 1 (Spring): 25–50.

Blair, S. S. and Bloom, J. M. 2003. 'The Mirage of Islamic Art: Reflections on the Study of an Unwieldy Field'. *Art Bulletin* 85, no. 1 (Mar.): 152–184.

Bluett, E. E. 1935–36. 'The Nien Hao and Period Identification', *TOCS* 13: 51–63.

———. 1933. *Ming and Ch'ing Porcelains: A Short Treatise Concerning Some Dated Specimens Together with Some Account of Their Distinguishing Features*. London: The Chiswick Press.

Bodde, P. 1945–46. 'Pre-Ming and Early Fifteenth Century Chinese Blue and White Porcelains', *TOCS* 21: 9–16.

Borenius T. et al. 1932. 'Art Treasures Exhibition', *The Burlington Magazine for Connoisseurs* 61, no. 355 (Oct.): 164–167, 170–173, 176–179, 182–183.

Bosch Reitz, S. C. 1919. 'Two Different Kinds of Ming Porcelain'. *The Metropolitan Museum of Art Bulletin* 14, no. 11 (Nov.): 236–238.

Boyajian, J. C. 2007. *Portuguese Trade in Asia under the Habsburgs, 1580–1640*. Baltimore: Johns Hopkins University Press.

Boynton, H. W., ed. 1903. *The Complete Poetical Works of Alexander Pope.* Cambridge edition. Boston/New York: Houghton, Mifflin and Co.

B. R., 1939. Review of *Early Ming Wares of Chingtechen*, by A. D. Brankston, *The Burlington Magazine* 75, no. 437 (Aug.): 88.

Bracken, S. 2001. '"Chyna" in England Before 1614'. *Oriental Art* XLVII, no. 2: 8–10.

Brankston, A. D. 1938–39. 'An Excursion to Ching-te-chen and Chi-an-fu in Kiangsi', *TOCS* 16: 19–32.

———. 1938. *Early Ming Wares of Chingtechen.* Peking: H. Vetch.

Bray, F. 1998. 'Technics and Civilization in Late Imperial China: An Essay in the Cultural History of Technology'. *Osiris*, 2nd Series, 13 (*Beyond Joseph Needham: Science, Technology, and Medicine in East and Southeast Asia*): 11–33.

Brook, T. 2010. *The Troubled Empire: China in the Yuan and Ming Dynasties*. Cambridge, MA: Harvard University Press.

———. 2008. *Vermeer's Hat: The Seventeenth Century and the Dawn of the Global World*. London/New York: Bloomsbury Press.

———. 1998. *Confusions of Pleasure: Commerce and Culture in Ming China*. Berkeley: University of California Press.

Brown, R. 2009. *Ming Gap and Shipwreck Ceramics in Southeast Asia: Towards a Chronology of Thai Trade Ware*. Bangkok: River Books.

Brunsdale, M. M. 2010. *Icons of Mystery and Crime Detection: From Sleuths to Superheroes*. Santa Barbara: ABC-CLIO.

Bryson, N. 2004. *Looking at the Overlooked: Four Essays on Still Life Painting*. London: Reaktion Books.

Bulling, A. 1950. 'Chinese Art of the Ming Period, A.D. 1368–1644'. Short notice in *The Burlington Magazine* 92, no. 570 (Sept.): 271.

Burke, P. 2009. *Cultural Hybridity*. Cambridge: Polity Press.

Burlington Fine Arts Club. 1911. *Exhibition of Early Chinese Pottery and Porcelain 1910*. London: Burlington Fine Arts Club.

The Burlington Magazine for Connoisseurs. 1909. Review, 'A Porcelain Collector of the Ming Dynasty'. 14, no. 71 (Feb.): 290.

———. 1918. 'A Rare Ming Vase'. 33, no. 189 (Dec.): 194.

———. 1904. 'Notes on the Veitch Collection of Chinese Porcelain in the Birmingham Art Gallery'. 4, no. 12 (Mar.): 232–241.

Burroughs, C. 1993. 'Michelangelo at the Campidoglio: Artistic Identity, Patronage and Manufacture'. *Artibus et Historiae* 14, no. 28: 85–111.

Bushell, S. W. 1910. *Description of Chinese Pottery and Porcelain: Being a Translation of the T'ao shuo, with notes*. Oxford: Clarendon Press.

———. 1908. *Chinese Porcelain: Sixteenth-Century Coloured Illustrations with Chinese MS Text, Translated and Annotated by S. W. Bushell*. Oxford: Clarendon Press.

———. 1897/1981. *Oriental Ceramic Art*. New York: D. Appleton; London: Frederick Muller.

———. 1886. *Chinese Pottery Before the Present Dynasty*. Peking: Pei-Tang Press.

Butters, S. B. 2007. 'The Uses and Abuses of Gifts in the World of Ferdinando de' Medici (1549–1609)'. *I Tatti Studies: Essays in the Renaissance* 11: 243–354.

C de K (full name not given). 1888. 'The Ming Vase'. *The New York Times*, 19 February.

Caldas-Coulthard, C. R. 1992. 'Reporting Speech in Narrative Discourse: Stylistic and Ideological Implications'. *Ilha do desterro: A Journal of English Language, Literatures in English and Cultural Studies* 27 (1992): 67–82; http://www.periodicos.ufsc.br/index.php/desterro/article/viewFile/8759/8119.

Calloway, S. 2011. *The Cult of Beauty: The Aesthetic Movement, 1860–1900*. London: V&A Publications.

Calvino, I. 1988. 'Quickness'. In *Six Memos for the Next Millennium*. Cambridge, MA: Harvard University Press.

Campbell, D. 2003. 'Yuan Hongdao's "A History of the Vase"', *New Zealand Journal of Asian Studies* 5, no. 2 (Dec.): 77–93.

Canby, S., ed. 2009. *Shah 'Abbas: The Remaking of Iran*. London: British Museum Press.

———. 2002. *Safavid Art and Architecture*. London: British Museum Press.

Carbone, I. 2009. 'The Enchantment of Chinese Porcelain in Italy: Artistic Fruition, Technological Creativity and Intercultural Discourse'. In *Transfer: The Influence of China on World Ceramics*, ed. Stacey Pierson. 79–91. Colloquies on Art and Archaeology in Asia, no. 24. London: SOAS.

Carboni, S. 2007. *Venice and the Islamic World, 828–1797*. New Haven: Yale University Press.

Carroll, L. 1999. 'Could've Been a Contender: The Making and Breaking of "China" in the Ottoman Empire'. *International Journal of Historical Archaeology* 3, no. 3 (Sept. 1999): 177–190.

Carswell, J. 2000. *Blue and White: Chinese Porcelain around the World*. Chicago: Art Media Resources; London: British Museum.

———. 1985. *Blue and White: Chinese Porcelain and Its Impact on the Western World*. Chicago: The Gallery.

Carvalho, P. 2002. 'Porcelains for the Shah: Ardabil and the Chinese Ceramics Trade in the Persian Gulf'. *TOCS* 66: 47–56.

Cassidy-Geiger, M. *Fragile Diplomacy: Meissen Porcelain for the European Court, ca. 1710–63*. New Haven: Yale University Press.

Cavanaugh, A. and Yonan, M. E. eds. 2010. *The Cultural Aesthetics of Eighteenth-Century Porcelain*. Farnham: Ashgate.

Chang, E. H. 2010. *Britain's Chinese Eye: Literature, Empire and Aesthetics in Nineteenth-Century Britain*. Stanford: Stanford University Press.

Chang Foundation Museum 鴻禧美術館基金會. 1998. *Xuande Imperial Porcelain Excavated at Jingdezhen*; *Jingdezhen chutu Ming Xuande guanyao ciqi* 景德鎮出土明宣德官窯瓷器. Taipei: Hongxi bowuguan.

Chen Jianzhong 陈建中 and Chen Lifang 陈丽芳. 2005. *Dehua yao* 德化窑 (Dehua Kilns). 3 vols. Zhongguo Fujian gu taoci biaoben daxi 中国福建古陶瓷标本大系. Fuzhou: Fujian Meishu chubanshe.

Chen, Shouyi. 1998. 'John Webb: A Forgotten Page in the Early History of Sinology in Europe'. In *The Vision of China in English Literature of the Seventeenth and Eighteenth Centuries*, ed. Adrian Hsia. 87–116. Hong Kong: Chinese University Press.

Chen Yongzhi 陈永志, ed. 2004. *Nei Menggu Jininglu gucheng yizhi chutu ciqi* 内蒙古集宁路古城遗址出土瓷器 (Porcelain Unearthed from Jininglu Ancient City Site in Inner Mongolia), Beijing: Wenwu chubanshe.

Chinese Art Treasures: A Selected Group of Objects from the Chinese National Palace Museum and the Chinese National Central Museum, Taichung, Taiwan. / Exhibited in the United States by the Government of the Republic of China at the National Gallery of Art, Washington [and others] 1961–1962. 1961. Geneva: Skira.

'Chinese Ceramics at Messrs. Sparks', *The Burlington Magazine for Connoisseurs* 61, no. 356 (Nov. 1932): 232.

Clark, D. N. 1998. 'Sino-Korean Tributary Relations under the Ming'. In *The Cambridge History of China*, vol. 8, *The Ming Dynasty, Part 2*, eds. Denis Twitchett and Frederick W. Mote. 272–300. Cambridge: Cambridge University Press.

Clark, S., ed. 1999. *Travel Writing and Empire: Postcolonial Theory in Transit*. London: Zed Books.

Clifford, J., ed. 1988. *The Predicament of Culture: Twentieth-Century Ethnography, Literature and Art*. Cambridge, MA: Harvard University Press.

Clunas, C. *Screen of Kings: Art, Power and Imperial Clan in Ming China*, forthcoming.

———. 2009. *Art in China*. Oxford: Oxford University Press.

———. 2007a. *Empire of Great Brightness: Visual and Material Cultures of Ming China, 1368–1644*. London: Reaktion Books.

———. 2007b. 'The Other Ming Tombs: Kings and Their Burials in Ming China'. *TOCS* 70: 9–10.

———. 2003. 'The Art Market in Seventeenth Century China: The Evidence of the Li Rihua Diary'. *History of Art and History of Ideas* 1: 201–223.

———. 1997–98. 'Gifts and Giving in Chinese Art'. *TOCS* 62: 1–18.

———. 1996. *Fruitful Sites: Garden Culture in Ming Dynasty China*. London: Reaktion Books.

———. 1991. 'The Art of Social Climbing in Sixteenth-Century China'. *The Burlington Magazine* 133, no. 1059 (Jun.): 368–375.

———. 1991/2004. *Superfluous Things: Material Culture and Social Status in Early Modern China*. Cambridge: Polity Press; Honolulu: University of Hawaii Press.

———. 1986–88. 'The Cost of Ceramics and the Cost of Collecting Ceramics in the Ming Period'. *Oriental Ceramic Society of Hong Kong Bulletin* 8: 47–53.

Cohen, D. 2006. *Household Gods: The British and Their Possessions*. New Haven: Yale University Press.

Cohen, W. 1992. *East Asian Art and American Culture: A Study in International Relations*. New York: Columbia University Press.

Colcord, L. 1919. 'An Instrument of the Gods'. In *The Best Short Stories of 1919 and the Yearbook of the American Short Story*, ed. J. Edward O'Brien. 82–108. Boston: Small, Maynard.

Coll Conesa, J. 2009. 'Documented Influence of China on Maiolica in Spain and New Finds of Chinese Ceramics with Dates to the 16th Century'. In *Transfer: The Influence of China on World Ceramics*, ed. Stacey Pierson. 123–141. Colloquies on Art and Archaeology in Asia, no. 24. London, SOAS.

Collins, W. 1868 *The Moonstone*. Leipzig: Bernhard Tauchnitz.

Crowe, Y. 2002. *Persia and China: Safavid Blue and White Ceramics in the Victoria and Albert Museum, 1501–1738*. London: V&A Publications.

Csaba, O. 2008. 'Troubles during Trading between Japan and China in the Ming Period'. In *The East Asia Mediterranean: Maritime Crossroads of Culture, Commerce and Human Migration*, ed. Angela Schottenhammer. 317–330. Wiesbaden: Harrassowitz.

'Curious Old China." In *All the Year Round*, ed. Charles Dickens, 14, part III (April).

Curtis, J. B., ed. 2006. *Trade Taste and Transformation: Jingdezhen Porcelain for Japan, 1620–1645*. New York: China Institute Gallery.

Dark, R. 1936. *The Ming Vase Mystery*. London: Wright and Brown.

David, Lady. 1989. 'Introduction'. In Rosemary Scott, *The Percival David Foundation of Chinese Art: A Guide to the Collection*. 9–26. London: SOAS.

David, P. 1935. 'The Exhibition of Chinese Art. A Preliminary Survey'. *The Burlington Magazine* 67, no. 393 (Dec): 238–251.

———. 1933–34. 'Hsiang and His Album'. *TOCS* 11: 22–47.

———. 1930–31. 'Description of Specimens Exhibited'. *TOCS* 9: 12–13.

———. trans. and ed. 1971. *Chinese Connoisseurship: The Ko Ku Yao Lun, the Essential Criteria of Antiquities*. New York/Washington: Praeger.

Davison, G. 2010. *The New and Revised Handbook of Marks on Chinese Ceramics*. Somerset: Gerald Davison, Ltd. de Heer, P. 1993. 'Three Embassies to Seoul: Sino-Korean Relations in the Fifteenth Century'. In *Conflict and Accommodation in Early Modern East Asia*, eds. Leonard Blussé et al. 240–258. Leiden/New York: Brill.

Defense Atomic Support Agency, 'Operation Minute Gun. Shot Ming Vase. Interim Summary Report', Nevada Test Site, November 1969, Defense Technical Information Center document POR 6337. http://www.dtic.mil/dtic/tr/fulltext/u2/a286666.pdf.

Deng, Gang. 1999. *Maritime Sector, Institutions and Sea Power of Premodern China*. Westport/London: Greenwood Publishing Group.

Department of Archaeology, Beijing University et al. 1997. *Guantai Cizhou yaozhi* 观台磁州窑址 (The Cizhou Kiln Site at Guantai). Beijing: Wenwu chubanshe.

Dillon, M. 1992. 'Transport and Marketing in the Development of the Jingdezhen Porcelain Industry during the Ming and Qing Dynasties'. *Journal of the Economic and Social History of the Orient* 35, no. 3: 278–290.

———. 1978. 'Jingdezhen as a Ming Industrial Center'. *Ming Studies* 6 (Spring): 37–44.

du Boulay, A. 2001. 'Oriental Ceramics in National Trust Houses and Their Importance in Producing Documentary Evidence'. *Oriental Art* XLVII, no. 2: 21–24.

Dubosc, J.-P. 1949. *A Loan Exhibition: Great Chinese Painters of the Ming and Ch'ing Dynasties, XV to XVIII Centuries, for the Benefit of The Asia Institute: March 11 to April 2, 1949*. New York: Wildenstein.

Edwards, W. 1999. 'Mirrors on Ancient Yamato: The Kurozuka Kofun Discovery and the Question of Yamatai', *Monumenta Nipponica* 54, no. 1 (Spring): 75–110.

Emerson, J., Chen, J. and Gardner Gates, M. 2000. *Porcelain Stories: From China to Europe*. Seattle: Seattle Art Museum.

Emerson, R. W. 1847. *Poems*. Boston: J. Munroe & Co.

Eng, S. C. 2008. 'The Use of Ceramic in Chinese Late Imperial Architecture'. Ph.D thesis, SOAS, University of London.

Erdočdu, A. 2001. 'Chinese Porcelains'. *Arts of Asia* 31, no. 6 (Nov.–Dec.): 88–100.

F. S. K. (full name not given). 1916. 'A Chinese Porcelain Vase'. *Museum of Fine Arts Bulletin* 14, no. 82 (Apr.): 16–17.

Fan, Fa-ti. 2004. *British Naturalists in Qing China: Science, Empire and Cultural Encounter*. Cambridge, MA: Harvard University Press.

Farrington, A. 2002. *Trading Places: The East India Company and Asia, 1600–1834*. London: British Library.

Fields, J., Hammerstein, O. and Lee, C. Y. 1959. *Flower Drum Song: A Musical Play*. New York: Farrar, Straus & Cudahy.

Finlay, R. 2010. *The Pilgrim Art: Cultures of Porcelain in World History*. Berkeley: University of California Press.

Flynn, D. O. and Giraldez, A. 1995. 'Born with a Silver Spoon: The Origins of World Trade in 1571'. *Journal of World History* 6, no. 2 (Fall): 201–221.

Fogg Art Museum. 1947. *The Use of Blue on Chinese Porcelain of the Ming Dynasty, 1368–1644*. Cambridge, MA: Harvard University.

Fortune, R. 1863. *Yedo and Peking: A Narrative of a Journey to the Capitals of Japan and China*. London: John Murray.

Fraser, S. E. 2010. 'Antiquarianism or Primitivism?: The Edge of History in the Modern Chinese Imagination'. In *Reinventing the Past: Archaism and Antiquarianism in Chinese Art and Visual Culture*, ed. Wu Hung. 342–367. Chicago: University of Chicago Press.

Freer Gallery of Art. 1953. *Ming Porcelains in the Freer Gallery of Art*. Washington, D.C.: Smithsonian Institution.

Fry, R. E. 1920. *Vision and Design*. London: Chatto and Windus.

Fuchs, R. W. with Howard, D. S. 2005. *Made in China: Export Porcelain from the Leo and Doris Hodroff Collection at Winterthur*. Delaware: The Henry Francis Du Pont Museum.

Fujian sheng bowuguan 福建省博物馆. 1997. *Zhangzhou yao* 漳州窑 (Zhangzhou Kilns). Fuzhou: Fuzhou renmin chubanshe.

———. 1990. *Dehua yao* 德化窑 (Dehua Kilns). Beijing: Wenwu chubanshe.

Fung Ping Shan Museum. 1992. *Jingdezhen chutu taoci* 景德镇出土陶瓷 (Ceramic Finds from Jingdezhen Kilns). Hong Kong: Fung Ping Shan Museum, University of Hong Kong.

Garner, H. 1955–57. 'The Arts of the Ming Dynasty: Introduction'. *TOCS* 2: 1–12.

Gavin, R. F., Pierce, D. and Pleguezuelo, A. 2003. *Ceramica y Cultura: The Story of Spanish and Mexican Mayolica*. Albuquerque: University of New Mexico Press.

Gerelyes, I. 2008. 'Types of Oriental Pottery in Archaeological Finds from the 16th and 17th Centuries in Hungary'. *Acta Orientalia Academiae Scientiarum Hung* 61, no. 1–2: 65–76.

Gerritsen, A. 2012. 'Ceramics for Local and Global Markets: Jingdezhen's Agora of Technologies'. In *Cultures of Knowledge: Technology in Chinese History*, ed. Dagmar Schafer. 161–184. Leiden: Brill.

———. 2009. 'Fragments of a Global Past: Ceramics Manufacture in Song-Yuan-Ming Jingdezhen'. *Journal of the Economic and Social History of the Orient* 52: 117–152.

Gibbon, E. 2008. *The History of the Decline and Fall of the Roman Empire, vol. II*. 1776. Reprinted, Cosimo Classics.

Gipouloux, F. 2011. *The Asian Mediterranean: Port Cities and Trading Networks in China, Japan and Southeast Asia, 13th–21st Century*. Cheltenham, UK/Northampton, MA: Edward Elgar Publishing.

Golas, P. J. 2007. '"Like Obtaining a Great Treasure": The Illustrations in Song Yingxing's *The Exploitation of the Works of Nature*'. In *Graphics and Text in the Production of Technical Knowledge in China: The Warp and the Weft*, eds. Francesca Bray et al. 569–614. Leiden/Boston: Brill.

Golombek, L. and Wilber, D. 1988. *The Timurid Architecture of Iran and Turan*. Princeton: Princeton University Press.

Golombek, L. Mason, R. and Bailey, G. 1996. *Tamerlane's Tableware: A New Approach to the Chinoiserie Ceramics of Fifteenth- and Sixteenth-Century Iran*. Islamic Art and Architecture, no. 6. Costa Mesa, CA: Mazda Publishers; Toronto: Royal Ontario Museum.

Goodrich, L. C. and Fang, C. 1976. *The Dictionary of Ming Biography*. 2 vols. New York/London: Association for Asian Studies, Cambridge University Press.

Goody, J. 1993. *The Culture of Flowers*. Cambridge: Cambridge University Press.

Gorer, E. 1907. *Catalogue of Rare Specimens of Ming and Early Kang-he Porcelain*. Exhibited at the Galleries of S. Gorer and Son. London.

Gosden, C. and Marshall, Y. 1999. 'The Cultural Biography of Objects'. *World Archaeology* 31, no. 2 (Oct.): 169–178.

Grassby, R. 2002. *The Business Community of Seventeenth-Century England*. Cambridge: Cambridge University Press.

Green, J. 2005. 'Ancient China/Modern Art'. In *The History of Collecting Oriental Ceramics in East and West: Proceedings of the Symposium in the Groninger Museum, 13 and 14 November 2003*, ed. Christiaan J. A. Jorg. 87–99. Amsterdam: Staatsdrukkerij.

———. 2003. 'Britain's Chinese Collections: Private Collecting and the Invention of Chinese Art, 1842–1943'. Ph.D. dissertation, University of Sussex.

Gure, C. 1957. 'The Arts of the Ming Dynasty'. *Artibus Asiae* 20, no. 4: 309–320.

Haddad, J. 1998. 'The Romantic Collector in China: Nathan Dunn's Ten Thousand Chinese Things'. *Journal of American Culture* 21, no. 1 (Spring): 7–26.

Hammett, D. 1930. *The Maltese Falcon*. New York: Alfred A. Knopf.

Harrison-Hall, J. 2001. *Ming Ceramics in the British Museum: Catalogue of Late Yuan and Ming Ceramics in the British Museum*. London: British Museum Press.

Harrison-Hall, J. and Krahl, R. 2009. *Chinese Ceramics: Highlights of the Sir Percival David Collection*. London: British Museum Press.

Hasebe Gakuji 長谷部楽爾. 1995–99. *Chûgoku tôji* 中国の陶磁 (Chinese Ceramics). 12 vols. Tokyo: Heibonsha.

Hasebe Gakuji 長谷部楽爾 and Imai Atsushi 今井敦. 1997. *Nihon shutsudo no Chûgoku tôji* 日本出土の中国陶磁 (Chinese Ceramics Excavated in Japan), vol. 12 of *Chûgoku tôji* 中国の陶磁 (Chinese Ceramics). Tokyo: Heibonsha.

Hay, J. 2010. *Sensuous Surfaces: The Decorative Object in Early Modern China*. London: Reaktion Books.

Hayashiya, Seizo and Trubner, H. 1977. *Chinese Ceramics from Japanese Collections, T'ang through Ming Dynasties*. New York: The Asia Society.

Hearn, M. K. 1996. *Splendors of Imperial China: Treasures from the National Palace Museum, Taipei*. New York: Metropolitan Museum of Art.

Heizer, R. F. 1941. 'Archaeological Evidence of Sebastian Rodriquez Cermeño's California Visit in 1595'. *California Historical Society Quarterly* 20, no. 4 (Dec.): 315–328. Published in 1942 as a single volume.

Hellman, M. 2010. 'The Nature of Artifice: French Porcelain Flowers and the Rhetoric of the Garnish'. In *The Cultural Aesthetics of Eighteenth-Century Porcelain*, eds. Alden Cavanaugh and Michael E. Yonan. Farnham: Ashgate.

Hergé. 1983. *The Blue Lotus*, trans. Leslie Lonsdale-Cooper and Michael Turner. London: Methuen Children's, 1983.

———. 1934–35. 'Le Lotus Bleu' (The Blue Lotus). *Le Petit Vingtième*. Brussels.

Hirth, F. 1888. *Ancient Porcelain: A Study in Chinese Mediaeval Industry and Trade*. Leipzig: G. Hirth.

Ho, Chuimei. 1994. 'The Ceramic Trade in Asia, 1602–82'. In *Japanese Industrialization and the Asian Economy*, eds. A. J. H. Latham and Heita Kawakatsu. 35–70. London/New York: Routledge.

Hobson, R. L. 1934. *A Catalogue of Pottery and Porcelain in the Collection of Sir Percival David, Bt., FSA*. London: The Stourton Press.

———. 1930. 'A Ming Porcelain Altar Set'. *The British Museum Quarterly* 5, no. 3 (Dec.): 81–83.

———. 1928–30. 'Peking Notes'. *TOCS* 8: 34–37.

———. 1928a. 'The Leverton Harris Cup'. *The British Museum Quarterly* 3, no. 2 (Sept.): 33–34.

———. 1928b. 'Ming Porcelain and Some Others from the Bloxam Collection'. *Old Furniture* 5, no. 16: 3–6.

———. 1923. *Wares of the Ming Dynasty*. New York: Scribner's.

———. 1915. *Chinese Pottery and Porcelain: An Account of the Potter's Art in China from Primitive Times to the Present Day*, 2 vols. London: Cassell.

Honey, W. B. 1944. *The Ceramic Art of China*. London: Faber and Faber.

Hong Kong Urban Council. 1989. *Imperial Porcelain of the Yongle and Xuande Periods Excavated from the Site of the Ming Imperial Factory at Jingdezhen*. Hong Kong: Hong Kong Museum of Art and Jingdezhen Museum of Ceramic History.

Hsieh Ming-liang 谢明良. 1999. 'Some Issues Related to Chinese Ceramics of the Fifteenth Century', *Meishushi yanjiu jikan* 美术史研究集刊 7 (July): 29–58.

Huang, E. 2008. 'China's China: Jingdezhen Porcelain and the Production of Art in the Nineteenth Century'. Ph.D. dissertation, University of California, San Diego.

Huang, R. 1974. *Taxation and Governmental Finance in Sixteenth-Century Ming China*. Cambridge: Cambridge University Press.

Huang, Yunte. 2010. *Charlie Chan: The Untold Story of the Venerable Detective and His Rendezvous with American History*. New York: W. W. Norton.

Hubei sheng wenwu kaogu yanjiusuo 湖北省文物考古研究所 et al. 2003a. 'Hubei Zhongxiang Mingdai Liangzhuangwang mu fajue jianbao' 湖北钟祥明代梁庄王墓发掘简报 (A Brief Report on the Discovery of the Ming-dynasty Tomb of King Zhuang of Liang at Zhongxiang, Hubei). *Wenwu* 5 (2003): 4–23.

———. 2003b. 'Wuchang Longquanshan Mingdai Chuzhaowang mu fajue jianbao' 武昌龙泉山明代楚昭王墓发掘简报 (A Brief Report on the Discovery of the Ming-dynasty Tomb of King Zhao of Chu at Longquanshan in Wuchang). *Wenwu* 2 (2003): 4–18.

Hucker, C. 1958. 'Governmental Organization of the Ming Dynasty'. *Harvard Journal of Asiatic Studies* 21 (Dec.): 1–66.

Hutchinson, E. 2009. *The Indian Craze: Primitivism, Modernism and Transculturation in American Art, 1890–1915*. Durham: Duke University Press.

Hutchison, J. C. 2000. *Albrecht Durer: A Guide to Research*. New York/London: Taylor and Francis.

Ibn Battuta. 1958–71. *The Travels of Ibn Battuta, A.D. 1325–1354*, trans. H. A. R. Gibb. 3 vols. Cambridge: University Press.

Impey, O. 1999. 'Chinese Porcelain Exported to Japan'. *Oriental Art* XLV, no. 1 (Spring): 15–21.

Jackson, A. and Jaffer, A. eds. 2004. *Encounters: The Meeting of Asia and Europe, 1500–1800*. London: V&A Publications.

Jackson, P. 1998. 'Marco Polo and His "Travels"'. *Bulletin of the School of Oriental and African Studies* 61, no. 1: 82–101.

James, H. 1917. *The Portrait of a Lady*. Harvard Classics Shelf of Fiction, vol. 11. New York: Bartleby.

Japan Society, New York. 1980. *The Burghley Porcelains: An Exhibition from The Burghley House Collection and Based on the 1688 Inventory and 1690 Devonshire Schedule*. New York: Japan Society.

———. 1914. *Chinese, Corean and Japanese Potteries: Descriptive Catalogue of Loan Exhibition of Selected Examples*. All exhibited under the auspices of the Japan Society at the galleries of M. Knoedler & Co; Chinese and Corean authenticated by R. L. Hobson; Japanese by Edward S. Morse. New York: Japan Society.

Jayne, H. H. F. 1930. 'In Defense of the Ming'. *Parnassus* 2, no. 2 (Feb.): 18–19.

Jenyns, S. 1959–60. 'Charles Ernest Russell'. *TOCS* 32: ix.

———. 1954. 'The A. D. Brankston Collection of Chinese Porcelain'. *The British Museum Quarterly* 19, no. 3 (Sept.): 54–57.

———. 1953/1988. *Ming Pottery and Porcelain*. 2nd edn. London: Faber and Faber.

Ji Cheng [计成]. 1989. *The Craft of Gardens* [*Yuan ye* 园冶], trans. Alison Hardie. New Haven: Yale University Press.

Jiangxi Province Team of Cultural Heritage. 1982. 'Jiangxi Nancheng Ming Yi Xuanwang Zhu Yiyin fufu hezangmu' 江西南城明益宣王朱翊鈏夫妇合葬墓 (The Joint Tomb of Zhu Yiyin, the Ming Prince Xuan of Yi, and his Wives at Nancheng, Jiangxi), *Wenwu* 8: 16–32.

Jingdezhen shi difangzhi bangongshi 景德镇市地方志办公室, ed. 2004. *Zhongguo cidu Jingdezhenshi ciyezhi: Shizhi er juan* 中国瓷都 ·景德镇市：瓷业志：市志2卷 (Monograph on the Porcelain Industry of China's Porcelain City Jingdezhen). 2 vols. Beijing: Fangzhi chubanshe.

Johnston, W. R. 1999. *William and Henry Walters: The Reticent Collectors*. Baltimore: Johns Hopkins University Press.

Jorg, C. J. A. 1997. *Chinese Ceramics in the Collection of the Rijksmuseum Amsterdam: The Ming and Qing Dynasties*. Amsterdam: Philip Wilson.

———. 1982. *Porcelain and the Dutch China Trade, 1729–94*, trans. Patricia Wardle. The Hague: Martinus Nijhoff.

Julien, S., trans. and Salvetat, A., annot., with Hoffman, J. 1856/2009. *Histoire et fabrication de la porcelaine chinoise: ouvrage traduit du chinoise*. Paris: Mallet-Bachelier; [Whitefish, MT:] Kessinger Publishing.

Kaplan, W., ed. 2004. *The Arts and Crafts Movement in Europe and America: Design for the Modern World, 1880–1920*. New York/London: Thames and Hudson, with the Los Angeles County Museum of Art.

Keene, C. 1949. *The Clue of the Leaning Chimney*. (Nancy Drew book 26). New York: Grosset and Dunlap.

Kerr, R. ed. 2004. *Ceramic Technology*, vol. 5, part 12, of *Science and Civilisation in China*. Cambridge: Cambridge University Press.

Kerr, R., Ayers, J. and Ho Chuimei. 2002. *Blanc de Chine: Porcelain from Dehua*. Richmond: Curzon Press.

Kerr, R. and Mengoni, L. with Wilson, M. 2011. *Chinese Export Ceramics*. London: V&A Publications.

Kestner, J. 2010. *Masculinities in British Adventure Fiction, 1880–1915*. Farnham/Burlington: Ashgate.

Keynes, M. 1998. 'The Portland Vase: Sir William Hamilton, Josiah Wedgwood and the Darwins'. *Notes and Records of the Royal Society, London* 52, no. 2: 237–259.

Kiddell, A. J. B. 1946–47. 'Further Note on a Pair of Blue-and-White Vases from the Tomb of the Emperor Hsuan Te'. *TOCS* 22: 39–40.

———. 1945–46. 'Note on a Blue and White Vase from the Tomb of the Emperor Hsuan Te'. *TOCS* 21: 17–18.

Kikuchi, Yuko. 1997. 'A Japanese William Morris: Yanagi Soetsu and *Mingei* Theory'. *Journal of William Morris Studies* 12, no. 2 (Spring): 39–45.

King, H. 2010. *Lost in Translation: Orientalism, Cinema and the Enigmatic Signifier*. Durham: Duke University Press.

Kitzan, L. 2001. *Victorian Writers and the Image of Empire: The Rose-Colored Vision*. Westport: Greenwood.

Komor, M. 1951. *Imperial Porcelains of the Ming Dynasty (1368–1644 A.D.)*. New York: Komor.

Kong Fanshi 孔繁峙. 1985. 'Shi tan Ming mu suizang meiping de shiyong zhidu' 试谈明墓随葬梅瓶的使用制度 (The use of *meiping* jar grave goods in Ming tombs). *Wenwu* 12: 90–91.

Krahl, R. 2003. 'Chinese Ceramics in Early Safavid Iran'. In *Hunt for Paradise: Court Arts of Safavid Iran, 1501–76*, eds. Sheila Canby and Jon Thompson. 257–270. Milan: Skira.

Krahl, R. with Ayers, J. and Erbahar, N. 1986. *Chinese Ceramics in the Topkapi Saray Museum, Istanbul*, 3 vols. London: Sothebys.

Kuwayama, G. 1997. *Chinese Ceramics in Colonial Mexico*. Los Angeles: Los Angeles County Museum of Art.

Laing, E. J. 1977. 'The State of Ming Painting Studies'. *Ming Studies* 4 (Spring): 9–16 (18).

———. 1975. 'Chou Tan-Ch'uan Is Chou Shih Ch'en: A Report on a Ming Dynasty Potter, Painter and Entrepreneur'. *Oriental Art* 21, no. 3: 224–228.

Lally, J. J. 2010. 'Collecting Chinese Ceramics in America: Morgan and Freer'. *TOCS* 73: 25–37.

Lam, P. 2006. 'Chinese Making China: Technical Illustration in the *Jingdezhen taolu* (1815)'. In *The Art of the Book in China*, eds. Stacey Pierson and Ming Wilson. 117–137. Colloquies on Art and Archaeology in Asia, no. 23. London: SOAS.

———, ed. 2010. *Layered Beauty: The Baoyizhai Collection of Chinese Lacquer*. Hong Kong: Art Museum, Chinese University of Hong Kong.

———, ed. 1996. *A Legacy of the Ming: Ceramic Finds from the Site of the Ming Palace at Nanjing; Zhu Ming yicui: Nanjing Ming Gugong chutu taoci* 朱明遗萃：南京明故宫出土陶瓷. Hong Kong: Art Museum, The Chinese University of Hong Kong and Nanjing Museum.

Langdon, W. B. 1842. *Wan tang ren wu, Ten Thousand Things relating to China and the Chinese, an Epitome of the genius, government, history, literature, agriculture, arts, trade, manners, customs, and social life of the people of the Celestial Empire, together with a synopsis of the Chinese Collection*. London.

———. 1839. *Wan-t'ang jen-wu = "Ten thousand Chinese things": a descriptive catalogue of the Chinese collection in Philadelphia, with miscellaneous remarks upon the manners, customs, trade, and government of the Celestial Empire*. Philadelphia: printed for the proprietor.

Langlois, John D., Jr., 'The Hung-wu Reign, 1368–1398'. In *The Cambridge History of China*, vol. 7, *The Ming Dynasty, 1368–1644, Part I*, eds. Frederick W. Mote and Denis Twitchett. 107–181. Cambridge: Cambridge University Press, 1988.

Lau, C. 1993. 'Ceremonial Monochrome Wares of the Ming Dynasty'. In *The Porcelains of Jingdezhen*, ed. Rosemary Scott. 83–100. Colloquies on Art and Archaeology in Asia, 16. London: SOAS.

Lawrence-Archer, J. H. 1875. 'Chinese Porcelain—Particularly that of the Ta Ming Dynasty'. *Art Journal*, New Series, XIV: 241–244.

Le Corbeiller, C. and Frelinghuysen, A. C. 2003. *Chinese Export Porcelain*. Special issue of *Metropolitan Museum of Art Bulletin* 6, no. 3 (Winter): 1–60.

LeBaron, W. D. 1998. *America's Nuclear Legacy*. Commack, NY: Nova Science Publishers.

Ledderose, L. 2000. *Ten Thousand Things: Module and Mass Production in Chinese Art*. Princeton: Princeton University Press.

Lee, Heekyung. 2003. 'Institutions and Vessels in East Asia: Exploring a New Approach for the Study of Medieval and Early Modern Wares, Applied to the Origin of Early Ming Imperial Underglaze Blue Ceramics and Their Introduction into Korea'. Ph.D. dissertation, SOAS, University of London.

———. 1999. 'The Introduction of Blue-and-White Wares from Ming China to Choson Korea'. *Oriental Art* 45, no. 2: 26–37.

Lee, J. G. 1949. 'An Exhibition of Ming Blue-and-White'. *Philadelphia Museum of Art Bulletin* XLIV, no. 223 (Autumn): 1–72.

Lee, S. 1955. 'Early Ming Blue and White Porcelains'. *Bulletin of the Cleveland Museum of Art* 42, no. 2 (Feb.): 27–31.

Leibsohn, D. and Dean, C. 2003. 'Hybridity and its Discontents: Considering Visual Culture in Colonial Spanish America'. *Colonial Latin American Review* 12, no. 1 (June): 5–35.

Levenson, J., ed. 2007. *Encompassing the Globe: Portugal and the World in the 16th and 17th Centuries*. Washington, D. C.: Smithsonian Books.

———. 1991. *Circa 1492: Art in the Age of Exploration*. New Haven: Yale University Press.

Li, Baoping. 2010. '*Kraak* Porcelain from Chinese Tombs and Jingdezhen Kilns: Discoveries and Associated Issues'. Paper prepared for the conference 'Cultures of Ceramics in Global History: 1300–1800'. Held at the University of Warwick, 22 April 2010.

Li Dongyang 李东阳 et al. 1587. *Da Ming huidian* 大明会典 (Collected Statutes of the Ming), 5 vols. Reprinted, Taipei: Dongnan chubanshe, 1963.

Li, He and Knight, M. et al. 2008. *Power and Glory: Court Arts of China's Ming Dynasty*. San Francisco: Asian Art Museum.

Li, H. L. 1956. *Chinese Flower Arrangement*. Philadelphia: Hedera House.

Li Rihua 李日华. 1996. *Weishuixuan riji* 味水轩日记 (Diary from the Water Tasting Studio), ed. and annot. Tu Youxiang 屠友祥. Song Ming Qing xiaopin wenji jizhu 宋明清小品文集辑注2. Shanghai: Shanghai yuandong chubanshe.

Liang Miaotai 梁淼泰. 1991. *Ming Qing Jingdezhen chengshi jingji yanjiu* 明清景德镇城市经济研究 (Studies of Jingdezhen's Urban Economy during the Ming and Qing Dynasties). Nanchang: Jiangxi renmin chubanshe.

Liefkes, R. and Young, H. 2009. *Masterpieces of World Ceramics*. London: V&A Publications.

Lindqvist, S. 1967. *Myten om Wu Tao-tzu* (The Myth of Wu Tao-tzu). [Stockholm]: Bonniers.

Lion-Goldschmidt, D. 1986. 'Ming Porcelains in the Santos Palace Collection, Lisbon'. *TOCS* 49: 79–93.

Little, S. 'Shao Bao on Porcelain: A Ming Scholar-Official's View of Jingdezhen'. Paper presented at the conference 'Asian Ceramics: Effect of Religion and Ritual'. Held at the Field Museum, Chicago, IL, 24–26 May 1996; available online through *ACRO: Asian Ceramics Research*; http://acrochicago.homestead.com/Little.html.

Liu, Xinyuan. 1995. 'Amusing the Emperor: The Discovery of Xuande Period Cricket Jars from the Ming Imperial Kilns'. *Orientations* 26, no. 8: 62–77.

Lu Zuoxie 吕作燮. 1982. 'Ming Qing shiqide huiguan bing fei gongshangye de hanghui' 明清时期的会馆并非工商业的行会 (Ming-Qing Guilds Are Non-commercial, Non-industrialized Professional Associations), *Zhongguo shi yanjiu* 3: 66–79.

MacGregor, A., ed. 1989. *The Late King's Goods: Collections, Possessions and Patronage of Charles I in the Light of the Commonwealth Sale Inventories*. London: A. McAlpine and Oxford University Press.

———. 1983. *Tradescant's Rarities: Essays on the Foundation of the Ashmolean Museum, 1683, with a Catalogue of the Surviving Early Collections*. Oxford: Oxford University Press.

Mack, R. E. 2002. *Bazaar to Piazza: Islamic Trade and Italian Art, 1300–1600*. Berkeley: University of California Press.

Malmgren, C. D. 1997. 'Anatomy of Murder: Mystery, Detective and Crime Fiction'. *The Journal of Popular Culture* 30, no. 4 (Spring): 115–135.

Marryat, J. 1857. *A History of Pottery and Porcelain: Medieval and Modern*. London: John Murray.

Mather, F. J. 1907. 'An Art Museum for the People'. *The Atlantic Monthly* 100 (Dec.): 729–740.

Matthews, J. H. 2000. 'Toward an *Isolario* of the Ottoman Inheritance Inventory with Special Reference to Manisa (ca. 1600–1700)'. In *Consumption Studies and the History of the Ottoman Empire, 1550–1922: An Introduction*, ed. Donald Quataert. 45–84. Albany: State University of New York Press.

Mazaroff, S. 2010. *Henry Walters and Bernard Berenson: Collector and Connoisseur*. Baltimore: Johns Hopkins University Press.

McCabe, I. B. 2008. *Orientalism in Early Modern France: Eurasian Trade, Exoticism and the Ancient Régime*. Oxford/New York: Berg.

McCausland, S. 2000–01. 'The Emperor's Old Toys: Rethinking the Yongzheng (1723–35) Scroll of Antiquities in the Percival David Foundation'. *TOCS* 66: 65–75.

McClane, A. J. 1965. 'From Aawa to Zooplankton'. *Field and Stream* 70, no. 7: 46–47, 126–128.

McDermott, J. 2001. *Martin Frobisher, Elizabethan Privateer*. New Haven/London: Yale University Press.

Medley, M. 1993. 'Organisation and Production at Jingdezhen in the Sixteenth Century'. In *The Porcelains of Jingdezhen*, ed. Rosemary Scott. 69–82. Colloquies on Art and Archaeology in Asia, no. 16. London: SOAS.

———. 1990–91. 'Imperial Patronage and Early Ming Porcelain'. *TOCS* 55: 29–42.

———. 1966. 'Ching-te Chen and the Problem of the "Imperial Kilns"'. *Bulletin of the School of Oriental and African Studies* 29, no. 2: 326–338.

Merrill, L. 1998. *The Peacock Room: A Cultural Biography*. Washington, D.C.: Smithsonian Institution with Yale University Press.

Merwin, S. 1914. *The Charmed Life of Miss Austin*. New York: Century Co.

Michaelis, A. 1882. *Ancient Marbles in Great Britain*. Cambridge: University Press, 1882

Michaelson, C. 1999. *Gilded Dragons: Buried Treasures from China's Golden Ages*. London: British Museum Press.

Ming shi 明史. 1974. Comp. Zhang Tingyu 张廷玉. 28 vols. 1739; Beijing: Zhonghua shuju.

Ming shilu 明实录 [Veritable Records of the Ming Dynasty]. 1962–67. 133 vols. Taibei: Zhongyang yanjiuyuan lishi yuyan yanjiusuo.

Mirzoeff, N., ed. 1999. *An Introduction to Visual Culture*. London: Routledge.

Misugi, Takatoshi. 1981. *Chinese Porcelain Collections in the Near East: Topkapi and Ardebil*. Hong Kong: Hong Kong University Press (English edition).

Mittag, A. 2012. 'Chinese Official Historical Writing under the Ming and Qing'. In *The Oxford History of Historical Writing, vol. 3, 1400–1800*, eds. José Rabasa et al. 24–42. Oxford/New York: Oxford University Press.

Moll-Murata, C. 2008a. 'Chinese Guilds from the Seventeenth to the Twentieth Centuries'. In *The Return of the Guilds*, eds. Jan Lucassen et al. 213–248. Cambridge: Cambridge University Press.

———. 2008b. 'Guilds and Apprenticeship in China and Europe: The Ceramics Industries of Jingdezhen and Delft'. Paper presented to the S.R. Epstein Memorial Conference: "Technology and Human Capital Formation in the East and West", 18–21 June 2008 http://www2.lse.ac.uk/economicHistory/Conferences/Epstein%20Memorial%20Conference/PAPER-MollMurata.pdf

Mowry, R., ed. 1996. *Hare's Fur, Tortoiseshell and Partridge Feathers: Chinese Brown-and Black-Glazed Ceramics, 400–1400*. Cambridge, MA: Harvard University Art Museums.

Mudge, J. M. 1986. *Chinese Export Porcelain in North America*. New York: Clarkson Potter.

Mungello, D. E. 1989. *Curious Land: Jesuit Accommodation and the Origins of Sinology*. Honolulu: University of Hawaii Press.

Munhwa Kongbu Munhwajae Kwalliguk 文化公報部文化財管理局, ed. 1985. *Sinan Haejŏ Yumul* 新安海底遺物 (Objects from the Sinan Shipwreck). Seoul: Haptong Ch'ulp'an Kongsa.

Murdock, T. 'Les cabinets de porcelain'. In *Pagodes et dragons: exotisme et fantasie dans l'Europe rococo 1720–1770*, ed. Georges Brunel. 42–49. Paris: Paris Museés.

Museo Franz Mayer and Museum of Fine Arts, Houston. 2002. *The Grandeur of Viceregal Mexico: Treasures from the Museo Franz Mayer.* Houston: University of Texas Press.

National Palace Museum. 2002. *Emperor Ch'ien-lung's Grand Cultural Enterprise; Qianlong huangdi de wenhua daye* 乾隆皇帝的文化大业. Taipei: National Palace Museum, Taipei.

———. 1963. *Blue and White Ware of the Ming Dynasty; Ming Qing huaci* 明青花瓷, compiled by the joint board of the National Palace Museum and the National Central Museum, 6 vols. Hong Kong: Cafa [開發] Co.

———. 1963. *Underglaze Red Ware of the Ming Dynasty; Ming youli hongci* 明釉里红瓷, compiled by the joint board of the National Palace Museum and the National Central Museum, Hong Kong: Cafa [開發] Co.

Nihon shutsudo no Chûgoku tôji 日本出土の中国陶磁 (Chinese Ceramics Excavated in Japan). 1975. Tokyo: Tokyo National Museum.

Norskov, V. 2002. *Greek Vases in New Contexts: The Collecting and Trading of Greek Vases—An Aspect of the Modern Reception of Antiquity.* Aarhus: Aarhus University Press.

'Notes on the Veitch Collection of Chinese Porcelain in the Birmingham Art Gallery'. 1904. *The Burlington Magazine for Connoisseurs* 4, no. 12 (Mar.): 232–241.

Oriental Ceramic Society. 1975. *Chinese Export Art in Schloss Ambras: A Lecture Given by Sir Harry Garner on the Occasion of the Second Presentation of the Hills Gold Medal.* 5 June 1975. London: Oriental Ceramic Society.

———. 1950–51. 'Transactions for the Year 1950–51'. *TOCS* 2: 9–10.

———. 1946–47. 'Catalogue of the Exhibition of Ming Blue-and-White Porcelain'. *TOCS* 22: 40–49.

———. 1946–47. 'Transactions for the Year 1946–47'. *TOCS* 22: 7.

Ortiz, F. c. 1947. *Cuban Counterpoint: Tobacco and Sugar*, trans. Harriet de Onís. New York: Knopf (and multiple reprints).

Ostrander, I. 1918. *Suspense.* New York: Robert McBride & Co.

Ouyang Shibin 欧阳世彬. 1999. 'A Study of Ceramics Made at Ching-te-chen Commercial Kilns during the 15th Century'. *Meishushi yanjiu jikan* 7 (July): 58–87.

Overstreet, R. M. 1993. *The Overstreet Comic Book Price Guide.* New York: Avon Books.

Pagani, C. 1998. 'Chinese Material Culture and British Perceptions of China in the Mid-nineteenth Century'. In *Colonialism and the Object: Empire, Material Culture and the Museum*, eds. T. J. Barringer and Tom Flynn. 28–40. London: Routledge.

Pearce, N. 2007. 'Collecting, Connoisseurship and Commerce: An Examination of the Life and Career of Stephen Wooton Bushell (1844–1908)'. *TOCS* 70: 17–25.

Pierce, D. and Otsuka, R. eds. 2009. *Asia and Spanish America: Trans-Pacific Artistic and Cultural Exchange, 1500–1850; Papers from the 2006 Mayer Center Symposium at the Denver Art Museum.* Denver: Denver Art Museum.

Pierson, S. 2012. 'The Movement of Chinese Ceramics: Appropriation in Global History'. *Journal of World History* 23, no. 1 (Mar.): 9–39.

———. 2010. 'On Location: Situating Chinese Ceramics'. *TOCS* 73: 91–106.

———. 2009. *Chinese Ceramics: A Design History.* London: V&A Publications.

———. 2007. *Collectors, Collections and Museums: The Field of Chinese Ceramics in Britain, 1560–1960.* Oxford: Peter Lang.

———. 2004a. 'Private Collecting, Teaching and Institutionalisation: The Percival David Foundation and the Field of Chinese Art in Britain, 1920–1964'. Ph.D. dissertation, University of Sussex.

———. 2004b. '"The Sung Standard": Chinese Ceramics and British Studio Pottery in the 20th Century'. In *Song Ceramics: Art History, Archaeology and Technology*, ed. Stacey Pierson. 81–102. Colloquies on Art and Archaeology, no. 22. London: SOAS.

———. 2002. *The Percival David Foundation of Chinese Art: A Guide to the Collection.* London: SOAS.
———, ed. 2009. *Transfer: The Influence of China on World Ceramics*. Colloquies on Art and Archaeology in Asia, no. 24. London: SOAS.
Pinto de Matos, M. A. 2002. 'Chinese Porcelain in Portuguese Written Sources'. *Oriental Art* XLVIII, no. 3: 36–40.
———. 1999. 'The Portuguese Trade'. *Oriental Art* XLV, no. 1: 22–29.
———, ed. 1996. *Chinese Export Porcelain: From the Museum of Anastacio Goncalves, Lisbon.* London: Philip Wilson.
Pitelka, M. 2005. *Handmade Culture: Raku Potters, Patrons and Tea Practitioners in Japan.* Honolulu: University of Hawaii Press.
Pomper, L. R., Stamen, J. P. and Weiss, N. R. 2009. 'Research on the Question of Dating Chinese Famille Noire Porcelain'. In *Scientific Research on Historic Asian Ceramics: Proceedings of the Fourth Forbes Symposium at the Freer Gallery of Art*, ed. Blythe McCarthy. 104–112. Washington, D. C.: Smithsonian Institution.
Pope, J. A. 1972. *The History of the History of Ming Porcelain*. London: Oriental Ceramic Society.
———. 1956. *Chinese Porcelains from the Ardebil Shrine*. Washington, D.C.: Smithsonian Institution.
———. 1950–51. 'Some Blue-and-White in Istanbul'. *TOCS* 26: 37–50.
Portal, J., ed. 2007. *The First Emperor: China's Terracotta Army*. London: British Museum Press.
Porter, D. 2002. *Ideographia: The Chinese Cypher in Early Modern Europe*. Stanford: Stanford University Press.
Purchas, S. 1625. *Hakluytus Posthumus* or *Purchas His Pilgrimes*, 4 vols. London.
Qi, Dongfang. 2003. 'The Burial Location and Dating of the Hejia Village Treasures', *Orientations* 34, no, 2 : 20–24.
Rackham, B. 1937. 'Review'. *The Burlington Magazine* 70, no. 407 (Feb.): 95.
Read, H. E. 1934. *Art and Industry: The Principles of Industrial Design*. London: Faber and Faber.
Reidemeister L. and Hellner, J. 1935. *Ming-Porzellane in Schwedischen Sammlungen*. Berlin: W. de Gruyter and Co.
Reitlinger, G. 1970. *The Economics of Taste, vol. III: The Art Market in the 1960s*. London: Barrie and Jenkins.
———. 1964. *The Economics of Taste, vol. II: The Rise and Fall of the Objets d'Art Market since 1750.* London: Barrie and Rockliff.
Reitlinger, G. and Button, M. 1948. 'Early Ming Blue and White: I'. *The Burlington Magazine* 90, no. 538 (Jan.): 10–16.
Rhodes, K. 1921. 'The Ming Vase'. *The Strand Magazine* 61: 138–145.
Rinaldi, M. 1989. *Kraak Porcelain: A Moment in the History of Trade*. London: Bamboo Publishing.
Ringmar, E. 2006. 'Audience for a Giraffe: European Expansionism and the Quest for the Exotic'. *Journal of World History* 17, no. 4 (Dec.): 375–397.
Rizvi, K. 2009. 'Sites of Pilgrimage and Objects of Devotion'. In *Shah 'Abbas: The Remaking of Iran*, ed. Sheila Canby. 98–115. London: British Museum Press.
———. 2002. 'The Imperial Setting: Shah 'Abbas I at the Shrine of Shaykh Safi al-din Ishaq'. In *Safavid Art and Architecture*, ed. Sheila Canby. 9–15. London: British Museum Press.
Robinson, D. M. 2008. 'The Ming Court and the Legacy of the Yuan Mongols'. In *Culture, Courtiers and Competition: The Ming Court (1368–1644)*, ed. David M. Robinson. 400–410. Cambridge, MA: Harvard East Asia Center.
Robinson, F. T. 1885. 'Boston Artists' Studios. No. III'. *The Decorator and Furnisher* 6, no. 1 (Apr.): 17–19.
Robinson, K. R. 1992. 'From Raiders to Traders: Border Security and Border Control in Early Choson, 1392–1450'. *Korean Studies* 16: 94–115.

Rodriguez, E. M. 2009. 'Early Manila Galleon Trade: Merchants' Networks and Markets in 16th- and 17th-Century Mexico'. In *Asia and Spanish America: Trans-Pacific Artistic and Cultural Exchange, 1500–1850; Papers from the 2006 Mayer Center Symposium at the Denver Art Museum*, eds. Donna Pierce and Ronald Otsuka. 37–57. Denver: Denver Art Museum.

Rousmaniere, N. C. 2009. 'Dining on China in Japan: Shifting Taste for Chinese Ceramics in 15th- to 17th-century Japan'. In *Transfer: The Influence of China on World Ceramics*, ed. Stacey Pierson. 47–58. Colloquies on Art and Archaeology in Asia, no. 24. London: SOAS.

Rousmaniere, N., ed. 2002. *Kazari: Decoration and Display in Japan, 15th–19th Centuries*. London: British Museum Press; New York: Japan Society.

Roxburgh, D. J., ed. 2005. *Turks: A Journey of a Thousand Years, 600–1600*. London: Royal Academy Books.

Royal Academy of Arts, London. 1935. *Exhibition of Chinese Art—Catalogue and Illustrated Supplement*. London: Royal Academy.

Ruitenbeek, K. 1996. *Carpentry and Building in Late Imperial China: A Study of the Fifteenth-Century Carpenter's Manual, Lu Ban Jing*. Leiden: Brill.

Russell-Wood, A. J. R. 1998. *The Portuguese Empire, 1415–1808: A World on the Move*. Baltimore: Johns Hopkins University Press.

Rzepka, C. J. and Horsely, L. 2010. *A Companion to Crime Fiction*. Chichester/Malden, MA: Wiley-Blackwell.

Salmony, A. and Berenberg, D. E. 1931. 'Peking as a Museum City'. *Parnassus* 3, no. 1 (Jan.): 35–37.

Salvetat, A., Julien, S. and Hoffman, J. J. 1856. *Histoire et fabrication de la porcelaine chinoise*. Paris: Mallet-Bachelier (new edition, Kessinger Publishing, 2009).

Samuel, E., ed. 1992. *Henry Adams, Selected Letters*. Cambridge, MA: Harvard University Press.

Sandiford, P. 1918. 'Craftsmanship and Education'. *School and Society* 8, no. 186: 68–70.

Sargent, W. R. 2012. *Treasures of Chinese Export Porcelain from the Peabody Essex Museum*. New Haven: Yale University Press.

Saxbee, H. 1990. 'An Orient Exhibited: The Exhibition of the Chinese Collection in England in the 1840s'. Ph.D. dissertation, Royal College of Art.

Sayer, G. R., trans. [1951]. *Ching-tê-chên t'ao-lu, or The Potteries of China*. London: Routledge and K. Paul.

Schafer, D. 2011a. 'Inscribing the Artifact and Inspiring Trust: The Changing Role of Markings in the Ming Era'. *East Asian Science, Technology and Society: An International Journal* 5: 239–265.

———. 2011b. *The Crafting of the 10,000 Things: Knowledge and Technology in Seventeenth-Century China*. Chicago: University of Chicago Press.

Schama, S. 1988. *The Embarrassment of Riches: An Interpretation of Dutch Culture in the Golden Age*. Berkeley/London: University of California Press.

Scherner, A. and Syndham, D. eds. 2005. *Princely Splendour: The Dresden Court, 1580–1620*. Milan: Mondadori Electa.

Schwarcz, V. 2008. *Place and Memory in the Singing Crane Garden*. Philadelphia: University of Pennsylvania Press.

Schwartz, B. I. 1996. *China and Other Matters*. Cambridge, MA: Harvard University Press.

Scott, R. 1995. 'Southern Chinese Provincial Kilns: Their Importance and Possible Influence on South East Asian Ceramics', In *South East Asia and China: Art, Interaction and Commerce*, eds. Rosemary Scott and John Guy. 187–204. Colloquies on Art and Archaeology in Asia, no. 17. London: SOAS.

———, ed. 1993. *The Porcelains of Jingdezhen*, Colloquies on Art and Archaeology in Asia, no. 16. London: SOAS.

Scott, R. and Kerr, R. 1994. *Ceramic Evolution in the Middle Ming Period: Hongzhi to Wanli*. London: V&A Museum, Percival David Foundation; Singapore: Sun Tree.

Scriven, M. 1957. 'The Present Status of Determinism in Physics'. *The Journal of Philosophy* 54, no. 23: 727–741.

Segal, S. and Jordan, W. J. 1988. *A Prosperous Past: The Sumptuous Still Life in the Netherlands, 1600–1700*. The Hague: SDU Publishers.

Seycock, B. 2006. 'Trade Ceramics from Selected Sites in Western Japan'. *Indo-Pacific Prehistory Association Bulletin* 26: 131–139.

Shangraw, C. and von der Porten, E. P. 1981. *The Drake and Cermeño Expeditions' Chinese Porcelains at Drakes Bay, California, 1579 and 1595*. Santa Rosa: Santa Rosa Junior College.

Shao Bao 邵宝. 1991. *Rong chun tang ji* 容春堂集 (Collection of the Hall Where Spring Appears). Shanghai: Shanghai guji chubanshe.

Shen, Weirong. 2007. 'Accommodating "Barbarians from Afar": Political and Cultural Interactions between Ming China and Tibet'. *Ming Studies* 56 (Fall): 37–93.

Shifman, B. and Walton, G., eds. 2001. *Gifts to the Tsars, 1500–1700: Treasures from the Kremlin*. New York: Harry N. Abrams.

Shiner, L. 2001. *The Invention of Art: A Cultural History*. Chicago: University of Chicago Press.

Shulsky, L. 1998–99. 'Chinese Porcelain in Spanish Colonial Sites in the Southern Part of North America and the Caribbean'. *TOCS* 63: 83–98.

———. 1998. 'Phillip II of Spain as Porcelain Collector'. *Oriental Art* XLIV, no. 2: 51–54.

Sieber, P. 2000. 'Seeing the World through *Xianqing ouji* (1671): Performance, Visuality and Narratives of Modernity'. *Modern Chinese Literature and Culture* 12, no. 2: 1–43.

Smart, E. 1975–77. 'Fourteenth Century Chinese Porcelain from a Tughlaq Palace in Delhi'. *TOCS* 41: 199–230.

Sotheby and Co., 1935. 'Catalogue of the Well-Known Collection of Rare Early Chinese Blue and White Porcelain of the Sung, Yuan and Ming Dynasties and Some Choice Examples of Enamelled Porcelain of the Ch'ing Dynasty, the Property of Charles E. Russell, Esq.' 6 June 1935.

Sotheby's, London. 1953. "Important Ming Porcelain (A Portion of the Well-known Collection of Mr and Mrs Alfred Clark)'. 24 March.

Spence, J. D. 1999. *The Chan's Great Continent: China in Western Minds*. New York: W. W. Norton and Company.

Spiess, K.-H. 2010. 'Asian Objects and Western European Court Culture'. In *Artistic and Cultural Exchanges between Europe and Asia, 1400–1900: Rethinking Markets, Workshops and Collections*, ed. Michael North. 9–28. Farnham, Surrey/Burlington, VT: Ashgate.

Spriggs, A. I. 1967. 'Oriental Porcelain in Western Painting'. *TOCS* 36: 73–88.

Stevenson, J. and Wood, D. 2011. *Dragons and Lotus Blossoms: Vietnamese Ceramics from the Birmingham Museum of Art*. Seattle: University of Washington Press.

Stevenson, J. and Guy, J. 1997. *Vietnamese Ceramics: A Separate Tradition*. Chicago: Art Media Resources with Avery Press.

Stout, R. 1941/1988. *The Broken Vase*. New York: Farrar & Rinehart; Boston: G. K Hall.

Strober, E. 2004. 'The Earliest Documented Ming Porcelain in Europe: A Gift of Chinese Porcelain from Ferdinando De' Medici (1549–1609) to the Dresden Court'. First published in the handbook for the International Ceramic Fair and Symposium. London: Haughton. 26–35; http://www.haughton.com/articles/archive/2005/9. Subsequently published in Gugong bowuyuan (Palace Museum), ed. 2009. 2007 *nian guoji zisha yantaohui lunwenji* 2007年国际紫砂研讨会论文集 (Proceedings of the 2007 International Symposium on Zisha Wares). Beijing: Palace Museum.

Stuart, J. 2011. 'Practices of Display: The Significance of Stands for Chinese Art Objects'. In *Bridges to Heaven: Essays on East Asian Art in Honor of Professor Wen Fong*, eds. Jerome Silbergeld et al. Vol. 2, part 6: 693–712. Princeton: Princeton University Press.

Sullivan, M. 1989. *The Meeting of Eastern and Western Art*. Berkeley/London: University of California Press.

Sun, E-Tu Zen and Sun Shiou-Chuan, trans. 1966. *T'ien-kung k'ai-wu; Chinese Technology in the Seventeenth Century*. Philadelphia/London: Pennsylvania State University Press.

Swain, J. D. 1922. 'Logan Berry, From Oregon: A Complete Novelette'. *Munsey's Magazine* 75, no. 2: 356–384.

Tan, R. et al. 2007. *Zhangzhou Ware Found in the Philippines: "Swatow" Export Ceramics from Fujian 16th–17th century*. Manila: Yugchengco Museum.

Thompson, J. and Canby, S., eds. 2003. *Hunt for Paradise: Court Arts of Safavid Iran, 1501–76*. Milan: Skira.

Tokyo National Museum. 1975. *Nihon shutsudo no Chûgoku tôji* 日本出土の中国陶磁 (Chinese Ceramics Excavated in Japan). Tokyo: Tokyo National Museum.

Tomalin, C. 2011. *Charles Dickens: A Life*. London: Viking.

Tomaselli, K. G. and Scott, D. 2009. *Cultural Icons*. Walnut Creek, CA: Left Coast Press.

Tong, Enzheng. 1995. 'Thirty Years of Chinese Archaeology (1949–1979)'. In *Nationalism, Politics, and the Practice of Archaeology*, eds. Philip L. Kohl and Clare P. Fawcett. 177–197. Cambridge: Cambridge University Press.

Trentmann, F., ed. 2012. *The Oxford Handbook of the History of Consumption*. Oxford: Oxford University Press.

Tsai, Meifen. 2000. 'The Role of the Government in the Development of Ceramics in the Sung Dynasty'. In *China at the Inception of the Second Millennium: Art and Culture of the Sung Dynasty, 960–1279*; *Qianxinian Songdai wenwu dazhan* 千禧年宋代文物大展. 321–327. Taipei: National Palace Museum. Also English language supplement: 86–93.

Tseng, H. C. 1961. 'Chinese Art Treasures'. *Bulletin of the Museum of Fine Arts, Boston* 59, no. 317: 64.

Tsui Museum of Art. 1993. *A Legacy of Chenghua: Imperial Porcelain of the Chenghua Reign Excavated from Zhushan, Jingdezhen*; *Chengyao yizhen: Jingdezhen Zhushan chutu Chenghua guanyao ciqi* 成窑遗珎：景德镇珠山出土成化官窑瓷器. Hong Kong: University of Hong Kong.

Twitchett, D. and Mote, F. W. eds. 1998. *The Cambridge History of China*, vol. 8, *The Ming Dynasty, Part 2*. Cambridge: Cambridge University Press.

U. S. Department of Energy, Nevada Operations Office. 'United States Nuclear Tests: July 1945 through September 1992'. DOE/NV—209-REV 15, December 2000; http://www.nv.doe.gov/library/publications/historical/DOENV_209_REV15.pdf (accessed 4 November 2010).

Vachell, H. A. 1924. *Quinney's Adventures*. London: George H. Doran Company.

Vainker, S. 2004. *Chinese Silk: A Cultural History*. London: British Museum Press.

———. 1991. *Chinese Pottery and Porcelain*. London: British Museum Press.

Valenstein, S. G. 1970. *Ming Porcelains: A Retrospective*. New York: China House Gallery, China Institute in America. van der Pijl-Ketel, C. 2004. '*Kraak* Type Porcelain and Other Ceramic Wares Recovered from the Dutch East Indiaman the "*Witte Leeuw*", Sunk in 1613'. *TOCS* 67: 91–98.

Vickers, M. 1987. 'Value and Simplicity: Eighteenth-Century Taste and the Study of Greek Vases'. *Past and Present* 116 (Aug.): 98–137.

Volker, T. 1954. *Porcelain and the Dutch East India Company, as Recorded in the Dagh-Registers of Batavia Castle, Those of Hirado and Deshima, and Other Contemporary Papers, 1602–1682*. Leiden: Brill.

W. P. Y. [probably Yetts, W. P.]. 1929. 'Altar Vessels of the Wan Li Period'. *The Burlington Magazine for Connoisseurs* 55, no. 320 (Nov.): 252–253.

Walker, S. 2004. *The Portland Vase*. London: British Museum Press.

Wan, M. C. K. 2003. 'Motifs with an Intention: Reading the Eight Trigrams on Official Porcelain of the Jiajing period (1522–1566)'. *Artibus Asiae* LXIII, no. 2: 191–221.

Wang, Cheng-hua. 2010. 'The Qing Imperial Collection, Circa 1905–25: National Humiliation, Heritage Preservation, and Exhibition Culture'. In *Reinventing the Past: Archaism and Antiquarianism in Chinese Art and Visual Culture*, ed. Wu Hung. 320–341. Chicago: University of Chicago Press.

Wang Guangyao 王光尧. 2010. *Mingdai guanting taoci shi* 明代官廷陶瓷史 (History of Ming Imperial Ceramics). Beijing: Zijincheng chubanshe.

———. 2004. *Zhongguo gudai guanyao zhidu* 中国古代官窑制度 (China's Ancient Official Kiln System). Zijin shuxi 紫禁书系, 6. Beijing: Zijincheng chubanshe.

Wang Qingzheng 汪庆正, ed. 1987. *Qinghua youli hong* 青花釉里红 (Underglaze Blue and Red). Shanghai: Shanghai bowuguan; Hong Kong: Liangmu chubanshe.

Wang Wenjing 王文径. 2004. *Zhangpu yao* 漳浦窑 (Zhangpu Kilns). Zhongguo Fujian gu taoci biaoben daxi 中国福建古陶瓷标本大系. Fuzhou: Fujian Meishu chubanshe.

Wang Zongmu 王宗沐. 1989. *Jiangxi sheng da zhi* 江西省大志 [Gazetteer of Jiangxi province]. 8 *juan* in 2 vols. Preface dated 1597. Zhongguo fangzhi congshu 中国方志丛书, no. 779. Taiwan: Chengwen chubanshe.

Watsky, A. 2006. 'Locating 'China' in the Arts of Sixteenth-Century Japan'. *Art History* 29, no. 4 (Dec.): 600–624.

Watt, J. C. Y. ed. 2010. *The World of Khubilai Khan: Chinese Art in the Yuan Dynasty*. New York: Metropolitan Museum of Art.

———. 2004. *China: Dawn of a Golden Age, 200–750 AD*. New York: Metropolitan Museum of Art.

Watt, J. C. Y. and Leidy, D. P. 2005. *Defining Yongle: Imperial Art in Early Fifteenth Century China*. New York: Metropolitan Museum of Art.

Weir, R. E. 2007. *Class in America: H to P*. Westport: Greenwood Publishing.

Welch, E. 2002. 'Public Magnificence and Private Display: Giovanni Pontano's *De splendore* (1498) and the Domestic Arts'. *Journal of Design History* 15, no. 4: 211–221.

Wen, R. et al. 2007. 'The Chemical Composition of Blue Pigment on Chinese Blue-and-White Porcelain of the Yuan and Ming Dynasties (AD 1271–1644)'. *Archeometry* 49, no. 1: 101–115.

Wharton, E. 1907. *The Fruit of the Tree*. New York: Charles Scribner's Sons.

Wharton, E. and Codman, O., Jr. 1897. *The Decoration of Houses*. New York: Charles Scribner's Sons.

Whitehouse, D. 1972. 'Chinese Porcelain in Medieval Europe'. *Medieval Archaeology* 16: 63–78.

Wilson, G. 2000. *Mounted Oriental Porcelain in the J. Paul Getty Museum*. Los Angeles: J. Paul Getty Museum.

Wilson, Ming. 1998. *Rare Marks on Chinese Ceramics*. London: SOAS and V&A Publications.

Wilson, R. 2005. 'Notes on Chinese Ceramics Excavated in Japan'. In *Tradition and Transformation: Studies in Chinese Art in Honor of Chu-tsing Li*, ed. Judith G. Smith. 472–489. Seattle/Kansas: University of Kansas and University of Washington Press.

Winkworth, W. W. 1934. 'The David Collection Catalogue'. *The Burlington Magazine for Connoisseurs* 65, no. 381 (Dec.): 264–270.

Wodehouse, P. G. 1936/1956. *The Luck of the Bodkins*. London: Heron Books; London: H. Jenkins.

Wood, F. 1998. *Did Marco Polo Go To China?* Boulder, CO: Westview Press.

Wood, N. 1999. *Chinese Glazes: Their Origins, Chemistry and Recreation*. London: A and C Black.

Wu, Hung, ed. 2010 *Reinventing the Past: Archaism and Antiquarianism in Chinese Art and Visual Culture*. Chicago: University of Chicago Press.

Xiong Liao 熊寥 and Xiong Wei 熊微, comps. 2006. *Zhongguo taoci guji jicheng* 中国陶瓷古籍集成 (Annotated Collection of Historical Documents on Ancient Chinese Ceramics). Shanghai: Shanghai wenhua chubanshe.

Yabuuchi Kiyoshi 藪内清, ed. 1953. *Tenkō kaibutsu no kenkyū* 天工開物の研究 (Studies on the *Tiangong kaiwu*). Tokyo: Kōseisha Kōseikaku.

Yang, Xiaoneng. 2006. 'Ming Art and Culture from an Archaeological Perspective—Part 1: Royal and Elite Tombs'. *Orientations* 37, no. 5 (Jun.): 40–49.

Yao Chengqing 姚澄清, Sun Jingmin 孙敬民 and Yao Lianhong 姚连红 1990. 'Shitan Guangchang jinian mu chutude qinghua cipan' 试谈广昌纪年墓出土的青花瓷盘 (A Brief Discussion on the Blue and White Porcelain Plates Unearthed from Datable Tombs in Guangchang). *Jiangxi wenwu* 2: 92–95, 134.

Yiu, J. C-C. 2006. 'The Display of Fragrant Offerings: Altar Sets in China'. Ph.D. dissertation, University of Oxford.

Yonan, M. E. 2010. 'Igneous Architecture: Porcelain, Natural Philosophy, and the Rococo *cabinet chinois*'. In *The Cultural Aesthetics of Eighteenth-Century Porcelain*, eds. Alden Cavanaugh and Michael E. Yonan. 65–85. Farnham: Ashgate.

Young, J. J. 1878. *The Ceramic Art: A Compendium of the History and Manufacture of Pottery and Porcelain*. New York: Harper and Brothers.

Yuille, P. W. 1934. 'The Lift of the Morning'. *The Cornhill Magazine* 149: 86–87.

Yun, Yong-i and Krahl, R. 2006. *Korean Art from the Gompertz and Other Collections in the Fitzwilliam Museum: A Complete Catalogue*. Cambridge: Cambridge University Press.

Zappia, N. 'Porcelain and Cocoa: The Pacific Rim and the Early Modern World Economy'. University of California, Santa Cruz, Center for World History. http://www2.ucsc.edu/cwh/porcelainpaper.htm.

Zhang Bai 张柏, ed. 2008. *Zhongguo chutu ciqi quanji* 中国出土瓷器全集 (Complete Collection of Ceramic Art Unearthed in China). 16 vols. Beijing: Kexue.

Zhao Yueting 赵月汀, ed. 2010. *Huangdi de ciqi: Jingdezhen chutu "Ming san dai" guanyao ciqi zhenpin huicui*, vol. 1, *Yongle juan* 皇帝的瓷器：景德镇出土"明三代"官窑瓷器珍品荟萃 (The Emperor's Porcelain: A Collection of Porcelain Treasures from Three Ming Reign-periods Excavated at the Imperial Kilns at Jingdezhen), 2 vols. Shanghai: Dongfang chuban zhongxin.

Zhejiang sheng wenwu ju 浙江省文物局. 1998. *Zhongguo Longquan qingci* 中国龙泉青瓷 (Longquan Celadon of China). Zhejiang: Zhejiang Sheying chubanshe.

Index

www.ingramcontent.com/pod-product-compliance
Ingram Content Group UK Ltd.
Pitfield, Milton Keynes, MK11 3LW, UK
UKHW051043120926
8556IPUK00031B/872

9 789888 139835